W9-CCH-684

TASTING ITALY

The 14th-century Ponte
delle Torri and Rocca
Albornoziana fortress,
Spoleto, Umbria

TASTING ITALY

A Culinary Journey

Foreword by Jack Bishop

Essays by Eugenia Bone and Julia della Croce

Recipes by America's Test Kitchen

AMERICA'S
TEST KITCHEN

NATIONAL
GEOGRAPHIC

WASHINGTON, D.C.

A gondolier plies his gondola on the Grand Canal past Punta della Dogana, the old customs building, now a museum.

Contents

List of Recipes

Discovering the Real Italy

....

MY FIRST LOVE IN THE KITCHEN WAS ITALIAN. I'm speaking about my maternal grandmother, Katherine Pizzarello. But I'm also thinking about the dishes of my childhood. Veal involtini filled with Parmigiano, garlic, raisins, pine nuts, and parsley. Bitter radicchio salad, sumptuous lasagna studded with tiny meatballs, and chewy pine nut macaroons. These dishes taught me to love food and shaped my earliest culinary sensibilities.

Even among those without familial roots in Italy, the cuisine holds sway. I've had amazing Italian food in a remote seaside village in the Dominican Republic as well as in global capitals from Mexico City to Stockholm. The world loves what Italy makes.

But as much as we think we know Italian food, the story is often incomplete. This became apparent to me as a twenty-year-old visiting Italy for the first time. (I loved it so much I stayed for six months!) Like many Italian Americans, I assumed my grandmother had been cooking real Italian food. However, as I traveled the country, I realized Italian food isn't a monolith; there is no national cuisine. And the food I loved as a child—rooted in southern Italy but transformed by the abundance of ingredients and newfound wealth in America—wasn't anywhere on the menu.

The real Italy is so much more multifaceted, and so much more remarkable, than the Italy that lives on in popular imagination. For the traveler to Italy, this diversity means an incredible range of experiences and tastes, from heavenly white truffles in Alba to musky blood oranges in Sicily. These locally produced ingredients—everything from farro in Umbria to fontina in Valle d'Aosta—shape the local cooking and produce the wide variety of regional cuisines explored in the pages that follow. And 21st-century transport means these artisanal ingredients are likely available at your local market.

Embarking on this project with National Geographic has been an exciting way for the test kitchen team to connect recipes with their culture and to tell the full story of Italian cuisine. The regional structure of this book reflects the reality that Italian

cooking is really a loose federation of local dishes. Look at *canederli* (bread dumplings flavored with speck, onions, and herbs) from Trentino–Alto Adige and you see plenty in common with dishes from Austria and Germany. Move 600 miles to the south and the culinary vocabulary is quite different. *Fava e scarola,* a fava bean puree with sautéed escarole that hails from Puglia, shares DNA with dishes made in Greece and the eastern Mediterranean.

Given all this, it's no surprise that we have organized the book into three chapters—northern, central, and southern Italy—that feature sections on the food and culture of each of Italy's 20 administrative regions. Within each section, we have chosen dishes that represent that region and then developed recipes that any cook—even ones without an Italian grandmother—can make at home.

The recipes have been tested, sometimes dozens of times, to work with readily available ingredients. And in the test kitchen, we're not afraid of using a modern convenience to simplify a recipe (such as a microwave to drive off excess moisture in eggplant for *pasta alla Norma*). The Why This Recipe Works text that precedes each recipe explains the traditions of the dish and how our test kitchen thinks it's best prepared by home cooks. For instance, we discovered that a pinch of baking soda helps produce soft, creamy polenta without endless stirring. Extra egg yolks make fresh pasta easy to roll out. And brining dried beans—rather than soaking in plain water—helps them cook up perfectly, with intact skins and creamy centers.

Choosing just 100 recipes to represent the breadth of Italian cooking was a challenge. Some recipes highlight famous culinary exports, such as *porchetta* or *pesto alla genovese*. But you will also discover dishes barely known outside their local region. Liguria's *farinata* is a delightful pancake made from chickpea flour that is topped with rosemary and olive oil and eaten as a snack. *Olive all'ascolana*—fried large green olives stuffed with pork—are a favorite from Le Marche, along Italy's eastern coast, and might just be the world's best finger food. My favorite pasta in the book comes from Lombardy and is made with buckwheat flour: *Pizzoccheri della Valtellina* has an earthy flavor and toothsome texture that matches perfectly with Swiss chard, potatoes, and Taleggio cheese.

Pairing all this good food with history, stories about local food producers, and amazing photography from National Geographic captures the essence of Italy. You're in for some exciting reading and eating. As my grandmother would say before her magnificent Sunday supper: *Buon appetito!*

JACK BISHOP
Chief Creative Officer, America's Test Kitchen

The Italian Way of Eating

An Extended Feast

· ·

ITALIAN FOOD ISN'T THE RESULT OF A SINGLE CULINARY STYLE. It's a mosaic of many cooking traditions that stem from each province's geography and climate, agriculture, history, and culture. • An Italian meal—with its focus on fresh and local foods, variety of courses, and selective approach to sweets—is a delicious, interesting, and healthy way to eat. It is also meaningful, as it ties diners to their place and time. Food is one of the ways Italians define themselves.

Diversity is ingrained in the history of this peninsula. More than a dozen tribes occupied Iron Age Italy when the Roman Empire expanded into their territories. While the Romans engulfed these tribal cultures and imposed political control through military rulers or in situ governors, each conquered territory was allowed to retain its own customs and cultural identity. After Rome collapsed, Italy had neither a capital nor a center; rather, it was a country of many capitals and many centers. Later, the city-state system reinforced regional differences and even encouraged them as a point of pride. This is why if you question your Milanese waiter why the *fritto misto* isn't served with lemon as they do in Urbino, he will tell you the Marchigiani don't know anything about food. Regional control in Italy was passed between competing European empires. In some parts of Italy this led to a kind of doubling down of their own milieu, as experienced in Tuscany; but in other areas, a long foreign presence led to other strong influences, such as in the Austrian flavors apparent in Friuli. Trade products also impacted the cuisines they encountered, such as cinnamon: Imported by the Venetians, it found its way into Italian medieval dishes and is still key to the Veronese dish *pastissada*, an aromatic sauce for potato gnocchi. In the modern era Italy has settled into 20 regions, each with its own inherited culinary character. But changes wrought by post-unification, world wars, and most significantly, the establishment of the European Union and spread of the global economy, mean that cooking is changing in Italy. Despite the efforts of traditional food preservation groups such as Slow Food, importation and fast-food values are taking hold.

A snack of speck, fresh Asiago, bread, and wine, staples of South Tyrol

Nonetheless, Italian food remains a marvelous mosaic, differing depending on where in Italy it is from. The notion of terroir—that flavors of foods and wine are influenced by the specificity of geography, soil, and climate—is key to appreciating Italy's culinary variety. What's more, regional traditions are reinforced by the Italian way of dining. The few particulars that define Italian dining stem from the ancient Etruscans of central Italy. First, it is rare for an Italian to have just one course, even if she is eating light. The courses, however, are small. It takes up to 30 minutes for the brain to recognize you have had one mouthful of food. Multiple small courses take longer to eat, giving your brain a chance to tell your stomach when it is full before you have overeaten. So while it may seem like Italian meals are food orgies, you may actually eat less.

The largest meal of an Italian's day is lunch. Visitors find themselves disappointed if they grab a sandwich and think they can head to the stores. Shops close from 1 p.m. to 4 p.m., leaving time for a leisurely lunch at home or in a restaurant, plus a nap (though this is changing). Lunch typically includes two courses: the *primo*, consisting of a soup, risotto, or pasta, followed by the *secondo*, a smaller portion of protein, either meat or fish, *contorni* (vegetable side dishes or salad), and then finished with fruit, and perhaps cheese. (Salad after the main course, Italians say, helps the digestion). Italian dinners tend to be lighter, a bowl of soup, a plate of vegetables, *due spagnetti* (a little bit of spaghetti) or a pizza (not slices, but typically a 10-inch pie per person). Meals are never eaten with sugary soft drinks, but served with wine, beer, or water.

Italy's health-giving traditional diet makes room for sweets on Sundays and holidays.

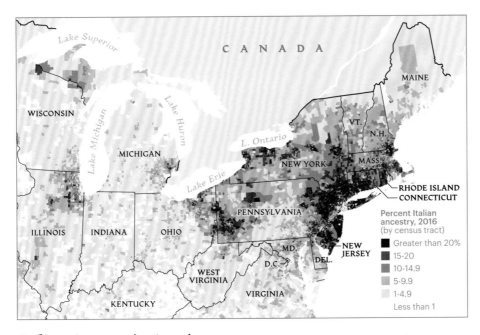

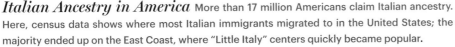

Italian Ancestry in America More than 17 million Americans claim Italian ancestry. Here, census data shows where most Italian immigrants migrated to in the United States; the majority ended up on the East Coast, where "Little Italy" centers quickly became popular.

Maybe one of the biggest misconceptions about Italian cookery is that it is a starch-based diet. While Italians do eat a lot of pasta (about four ounces per serving), the second course is usually small. In impoverished areas of the south, pasta is a staple food, much as corn polenta has been in times of poverty in the north. Seasonal vegetables and wheat predominate in the southern Italian diet, and meat, rice, and corn dominate in the richer, cooler north. In the south, olive oil is the primary cooking fat, with lard typically used for baking. Animal-based fats including butter and cream are traditional to the north, but this has changed in recent decades, and these staples are becoming more integrated: the northerners are utilizing olive oil and eating dried

real vs. fake: WHAT'S ITALY TO DO?

As you make your way through this book, you'll see that Italy's cherished products and their lavish use in cooking are what combine to make Italian food what it is: an extraordinary expression of local traditions and terroir rather than a homogeneous national cuisine. Made from raw materials that reflect a remarkable range of landscapes using time-honored methods that were developed over centuries, even millennia, these artisan foodstuffs have long been the lifeblood of regional economies and entire villages. Treasured around the world, glorious estate-bottled olive oils, traditional cheeses infused with an alpine spring meadow or the sultry ethers of a Mediterranean summer, vinegars aged in aromatic wood barrels for 25 years—these and other Italian-made products are rightfully the pride of a culture.

To celebrate and protect the sanctity of this regional artisan tradition, the Italian government passed the *Denominazione di Origine Controllata* (DOC) laws for wines in 1963, regulations modeled on the French system, establishing strict parameters for making and protecting the origin of its elite wines. For example, Champagne, a sparkling wine from a particular grape of the Champagne region produced in Champagne and only in Champagne, cannot be made in a similar style but without the grape in, say, California, and also labeled "champagne." In 1996, the *Denominazi-*

Government certifications distinguishing traditional foods appear on labels, seals, or markings etched onto the product.

one di Origine Protetta (DOP) laws were passed for many artisan foods. Foods with centuries-old pedigrees (Gorgonzola and Parmigiano Reggiano cheeses, for example) earn this designation. DOP Gorgonzola is only the Gorgonzola that originated in the village of Gorgonzola in Lombardy. DOP Parmigiano is made only in historically designated lands. They carry distinct tastes and deserve to be sought out when available.

The expanding DOC system—which includes DOCG and IGT categories for wines, and IGP, STG, and the aforementioned DOP for foods (see glossary, p. 364)—also serves to codify recipes with a cultural heritage, much like copyright protects creative works of literature or music. An example is the century-old art of STG Neapolitan pizza (now also inscribed on UNESCO's list of intangible world treasures). Born at the local level and recognized by the European Union, the classification system protects an original work and a way of life. Fewer southern Italian products carry these designations, not because they aren't up to snuff, but because their producers often lack the substantial funding and political will needed to apply collectively for these government classifications that certify conformity with strict enforcement rules. The official government seal for guarantees of authenticity is carried on packages or wine bottle labels. Look for it when you shop.

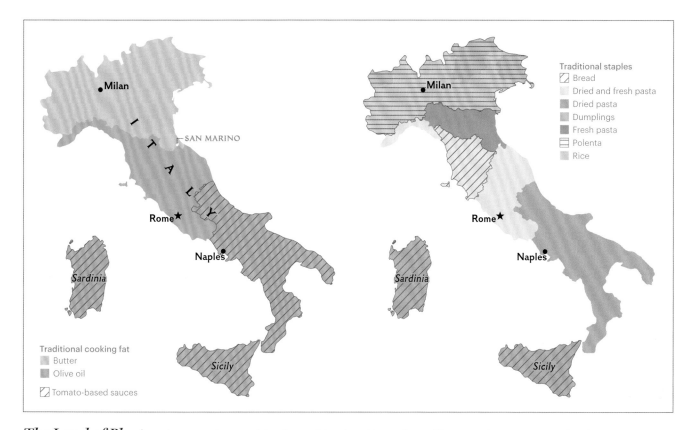

The Land of Plenty Italy's 20 regions each has its traditional cooking styles and key ingredients. Some cook with olive oil, some, butter; some use dried pasta, some, fresh; some prefer polenta, some, rice.

pasta, and southerners now and then resort to butter when baking sweets. The central areas have a bit of both; here you are as likely to find *spaghetti aglio e olio* as *tagliatelle al doppio burro* (tagliatelle with double butter).

In Italy a meal tells you where you are in the year, both in terms of seasonal foods and religious holidays—and the two are often combined. In some southern regions, for example, dishes made for St. Joseph's Day use breadcrumbs to symbolize sawdust, as he was a carpenter. In the beginning of the 16th century every third day celebrated one religious figure or another—it was so excessive the church itself tried to reduce the number of saint days, as did the government in the 1970s. St. Valentine was one who lost his national status, but celebrations tied to the calendar continue.

Sweets are also coordinated with holidays: Italians don't eat desserts after every meal, though they do like sweets with their coffee in the morning. At this time of day Italians typically eat cornetto, a brioche-like pastry, with their cappuccino, standing at a "bar." Bars in Italy are neighborhood imbibing joints, where locals get their coffee, maybe a *panino* (sandwich) snack or a gelato in the afternoon, and an *aperitivo* like prosecco before dinner. It's not unusual for a store owner, in the midst of a promising sale, to contact a local bar, and within minutes a waiter crosses the street, holding aloft a tray of *espressi* or Campari and soda.

Buona forchetta (literally "a good fork") and avere il naso ("having the nose") are Italian expressions for a gourmet.

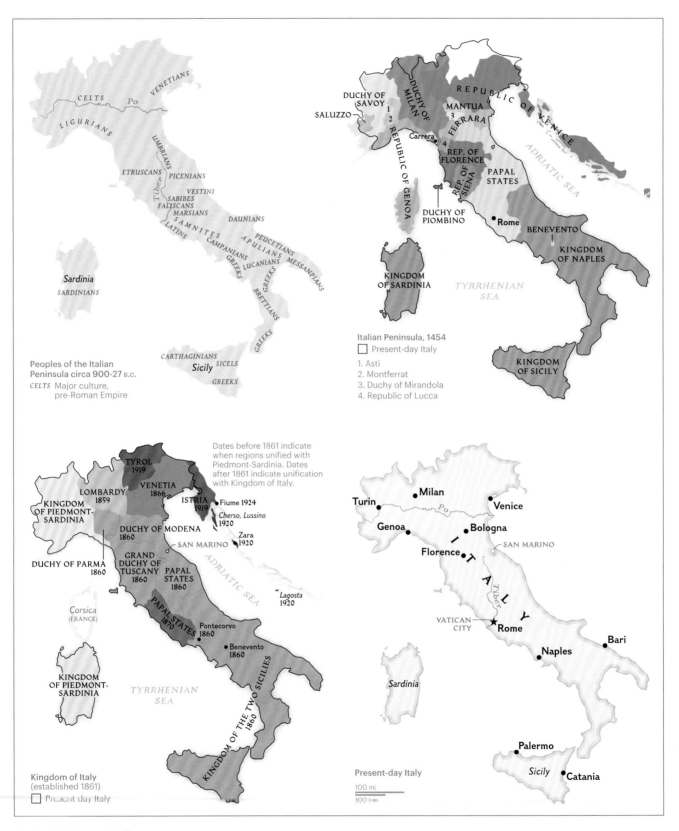

Peoples of the Italian Peninsula circa 900–27 B.C.

CELTS Major culture, pre-Roman Empire

CELTS
Po
VENETIANS
LIGURIANS
Tiber
UMBRIANS
ETRUSCANS
PICENIANS
VESTINI
SABINES
FALISCANS
MARSIANS
S A M N I T E S
LATINS
CAMPANIANS
DAUNIANS
APULIANS
PEUCETIANS
LUCANIANS
MESSANPIANS
GREEKS
GREEKS
BRETTIANS
GREEKS
Sardinia
SARDINIANS
CARTHAGINIANS
Sicily
SICELS
GREEKS

Italian Peninsula, 1454

☐ Present-day Italy

1. Asti
2. Montferrat
3. Duchy of Mirandola
4. Republic of Lucca

DUCHY OF SAVOY
SALUZZO
DUCHY OF MILAN
REPUBLIC OF VENICE
MANTUA
FERRARA
Carrera
REP. OF FLORENCE
REP. OF SIENA
PAPAL STATES
ADRIATIC SEA
REPUBLIC OF GENOA
DUCHY OF PIOMBINO
Rome
BENEVENTO
KINGDOM OF SARDINIA
TYRRHENIAN SEA
KINGDOM OF NAPLES
KINGDOM OF SICILY

Kingdom of Italy (established 1861)

☐ Present-day Italy

Dates before 1861 indicate when regions unified with Piedmont-Sardinia. Dates after 1861 indicate unification with Kingdom of Italy.

TYROL 1919
LOMBARDY 1859
VENETIA 1866
ISTRIA 1919
Fiume 1924
Cherso, Lussino 1920
KINGDOM OF PIEDMONT-SARDINIA
DUCHY OF MODENA 1860
Zara 1920
SAN MARINO
DUCHY OF PARMA 1860
GRAND DUCHY OF TUSCANY 1860
PAPAL STATES 1860
ADRIATIC SEA
Lagosta 1920
Corsica (FRANCE)
PAPAL STATES 1870
Pontecorvo 1860
Benevento 1860
KINGDOM OF PIEDMONT-SARDINIA
TYRRHENIAN SEA
KINGDOM OF THE TWO SICILIES 1860

Present-day Italy

100 mi
100 km

Turin
Milan
Venice
Genoa
Po
Bologna
Florence
SAN MARINO
I T A L Y
Tiber
VATICAN CITY
★ Rome
Bari
Naples
Sardinia
Palermo
Sicily
Catania

Italy's Many Rulers For centuries, Italy has been divided by various eras of political rule, most significantly through four time periods: pre-Roman (900 B.C.–27 B.C.), the Renaissance (ca 1454), Unification (1861), and today's unified Italy.

Dinner under the stars in the historic center of the city of Potenza, Basilicata

Italians have a genius for living, evident in their talent for bringing out the flavor of foods. Indeed, this is the one unifying concept in Italian cookery: Effort is made to preserve and intensify the natural integrity of any given food. And this is reflected in the country's agriculture and animal husbandry as well. While industrial agriculture is increasingly impacting the Italian economy, by and large the nation's mountainous geography favors sustainable, time-honored farming practices and smaller farms that are carefully tended to ensure raw materials with optimal flavor. Why does a tomato salad taste so extraordinary in Capri? Because the tomato seed has been carefully bred for decades, even centuries. Because the tomato was farmed carefully, picked ripe, and delivered to markets nearby. Because the chef who made the salad knows that for maximum flavor the tomato must never be refrigerated. That sensitivity to the products of a specific region is what ultimately defines Italian food.

The secret to Italian cooking isn't a particular recipe; it's the backstory of that recipe: the geography, the agriculture, the history, and the culture of a place and a people. That's what we have tried to illustrate in these essays. Our discussions are based on traditional cooking, and they show how every region in Italy tells a different food story. Italian food, with its myriad regional flavors, does not have a national character, but the Italian way of eating does: a reverence for local ingredients, sensitively and simply prepared, and enjoyed alongside family and friends, slowly, and with gusto.

A view of the Odle mountains from the church of Santa Maddalena in Südtirol, Trentino-Alto Adige

PART ONE

Northern Italy

From the Alps to the Apennines, the Adriatic to the Ligurian Sea, northern Italy provides a feast of well-heeled cuisines.

Europe's Culinary Gateway to Italy

IF THERE WAS BUT ONE WORD to describe the food of Italy's northern regions, it would be "rich." This territory, which tumbles from the snow-peaked Dolomites down to the vast Po River Valley, is Italy's butter belt, where dairy trumps olive oil, fresh egg pasta beats dried, and meat is supreme. Except for Liguria's Mediterranean climate, this is not the sunny, dry Italy of tourist brochures. The weather is wetter and cooler and greener than the rest of Italy—with sangfroid to match. This is ground zero for

Italian capitalism: The people are sophisticated, career-oriented, and serious. But while northern Italians may live a fast-paced, modern lifestyle, their cuisine remains rooted in the rustic flavors of the land.

The territory is a mix of mountain terrain supporting a prosperous dairy culture and plains well watered by rivers that drain from the mineral-rich mountains. These plains, dominated by the Po River, are among the most productive agricultural lands in Italy. They are also home to a robust industrial landscape. Led by Lombardy, the north has the nation's highest GDP, with Milan as its business and finance center. As they say in Italy, "For every church in Rome, there is a bank in Milan."

The north shares a certain affinity with Europe, both geographically and culturally. Its varied populations, and most especially its foods, reflect millennia of migration, assimilation, trade, and war with the continent and with the East. The Romans dominated all the tribes of Italy from the first century B.C. to the fifth century A.D., when the rule of kings and popes displaced the imperial tradition. Like the rest of Italy, the north fractured into many rival city-states. Due to the north's proximity to

Dining out in a Veronese restaurant often includes a wide selection of local wines.

competing interests in Europe, regional borders and overlords changed with bewildering frequency up until unification in the 1800s. This made for chaotic government (a problem that continues to this day) but also an enormous trove of recipes reflecting diverse local—and some far-flung—ingredients and traditions.

Mint

The area spans south from the mountainous borders of France, Switzerland, and Austria, and across from the Ligurian Sea to the Adriatic—which means no destination is more than 75 miles from a coastline. Consequently, anchovies can show up in a traditional dish from a landlocked region. It's also the most forested part of the country. And where there are trees, there are mushrooms and wild herbs and game, all of which are important players in northern cuisine. The mountain valleys produce exceptional butter, cream, and cheese, including Gorgonzola, Fontina (the original, not the Danish or Swedish copies), Taleggio, Robiola, Asiago, and countless more. Farther south, Emilia–Romagna in the Po Valley produces the superstar Parmigiano Reggiano.

But even this land of milk and honey (another product of the wildflower-filled Alpine meadows) cannot do without pork. *Che te possa morir el mascio!*—Your pig should die!—used to be the worst curse a Venetian could hurl. From the north come the most delicious hams and *salumi* in the world: Parma and San Daniele's prosciutti; speck, mortadella, *culatello,* and *coppa* are just the internationally known cured meats. There are as many particular variations as there are towns.

Home of the Polenta-Heads

The primary agricultural products are rice and maize. Lombardy and Piedmont are the rice bowl of Europe. In Italy rice is most famously consumed as risotto. Maize is used predomi-

A cheese market in Alba, Cuneo province, Piedmont

GREAT FOOD FESTIVALS OF THE NORTH

One of the best ways to experience seasonal foods in northern Italy is to visit the festivals that celebrate the harvest.

ARIA DI FESTA *SAN DANIELE DEL FRIULI (Friuli).* Held the last weekend in June, this festival has workshops, tastings, factory visits, and more, all in praise of this prosciutto.

FESTA DELLA CASTAGNA *RONCEGNO (Trentino–Alto Adige).* Guided walks in the chestnut forests and a festive chestnut market in the piazza take place the third week of October.

FESTA DEL RISOTTO *VILLIMPENTA, MANTUA (Lombardy).* On the last Sunday in May, risotto is cooked for the entire town under tents in the main piazza.

FIERA INTERNAZIONALE DEL TARTUFO *ALBA (Piedmont).* Truffle specialties in all the city's restaurants, demonstrations and seminars on truffle hunting, and a truffle market are on offer in October and November.

POLENTATA *TOSSIGNANO (Emilia–Romagna).* Townspeople cook *polenta pasticciata* in situ over blazing wood fires in immense copper pots for anyone who wanders into the main piazza on the last Tuesday of Carnival.

SAGRA DEL PESCE *CAMOGLI (Liguria).* A community-wide fish fry in 12-foot frying pans takes place in the main square on the second Sunday in May.

VENERDÌ GNOCOLAR *VERONA (Veneto).* This rowdy procession in medieval costume—with colorful floats and jugglers led by the gnocchi king—is held on the last Friday of Carnival. It ends with a gnocchi-and-*pastissada* sauce pig-out provided by the city in Piazza San Zeno.

Papà del Gnoco, Verona's gnocchi king

---

nately in polenta. Indeed, the nickname for northerners is *polentoni*, polenta-heads. In the past the poor survived on corn polenta alone, leading to widespread pellagra. Today it is a primary starch. Buckwheat, rye, and other grains are also grown and find their way into pasta, breads, and cakes. In the richer north, fresh egg pasta made with soft flour is typically used in stuffed pasta dishes such as tortellini, versus the dried *maccheroni* made with semolina and water from the poorer south.

While grain has dominated the northern diet at different times and for different reasons, it's fair to say this is a land of dedicated carnivores. There is a long tradition of boiled, braised, and roasted meats cooked to the point of surrender. Root vegetables dominate the diet of the Alpine regions, but the Padan Plain produces a wider variety: beans (typically *borlotti* or Lamon varieties), fava beans, peas, asparagus, artichokes, various radicchios, tomatoes, berries, onions, and cardoons. The mountain valleys and foothills are home to spectacular hazelnuts, chestnuts, apricots, pears, plums, grapes that produce the best wines in the country, and apples (Alto Adige is the apple basket of Europe).

During la Serenessima, the Doge initiated St. Mark's day with a course of risi e bisi (rice and peas); if the first peas of spring were not yet ready for harvest, they were brought in from Genoa.

Rice, popularized throughout Italy after unification, remains an iconic staple of the northern regions. Some two dozen crossbreeds have been developed for diverse culinary purposes. The most prevalent are Arborio, Carnaroli, and Vialone Nano, grown in the Padan Plain. With their high starch content, they will dissolve into creamy risottos when stirred in liquid over low heat.

Four rice classifications are based on length, form, and cooking time required: *Riso comune* consists of cheap, short-grain types, often used for sweets. *Semifino* is medium length and plump, good for minestrone and the soupy rice dishes of Veneto. *Fino*, thick and tapered at the tips, is preferred for risotto and rice salads. *Superfino*, such as Arborio and Carnaroli, is suitable for everything from rice salads to *timballi*, but mostly it is risotto rice.

A Melting Pot of European Flavors

Overall, the more isolated areas such as Valle d'Aosta, Friuli, and Alto Adige produce a simpler cuisine that relies on foods sturdy enough to sustain a mountain lifestyle. Farther south, however, one finds a refinement in cooking long fostered in the wealthy regional capitals of Turin, Milan, Mantua, Genoa, Bologna, and Venice. But all regions share their culinary traditions with their neighbors: Piedmont's cuisine is refined, borrowing from the French; Valle d'Aosta shares food styles with Alpine France and Switzerland. Lombardy reflects its position as an international hub with dishes influenced by France and Germany. Alto Adigian foods are deeply connected to their Austrian neighbors, and Friuli–Venezia Giulia's cuisine is influenced by Eastern Europe and the Balkans. Veneto utilizes the fantastic array of imported goods made available by its great trading tradition, while in Emilia–Romagna the Emilia is influenced by foreign nobility (French, Spanish, and mid-European) and the Romagna by the Latin and central Italian cuisines. Finally, Liguria shares its dolce vita with the French Riviera.

Though northern Italy shares many qualities with other industrialized European cultures—efficiency, modernity, ambition, and recipes—it is, nonetheless, quintessentially Italian. Not only do northern Italians indulge with enthusiasm in the sweet life of food, wine, and company, but they also are quite sure they are the only ones who know how to do it properly.

Above: A grocer in Modena slices prosciutto on the Cadillac of meat slicers. Opposite: Morning mist over the Langhe, Piedmont, heart of the northern Italian wine scene

FROM BAROLO TO SOAVE

....

1. Piedmont is Italy's greatest wine region, home of two of the world's best reds: the aromatic Barolo and the velvety Barbaresco.

2. Valle d'Aosta, Italy's smallest wine region, produces mostly reds that are fresh and acidic, great with the region's robust buttery food.

3. Alto Adige has very special reds, most notably the inky Lagrein and spicy Schiava, and of the whites, the peppery Gewürztraminer.

4. Friuli–Venezia Giulia produces wines from local and international grapes. Most outstanding are their whites: the Pinot Bianco, Riesling, and Pinot Grigio, the delicate Tocai Friulano, sweet Romandolo, amber-colored Picolit, and the powerfully plummy red Refosco.

5. Lombardy makes white wines from Verdicchio and Pinot Bianco grapes, and a wonderful *spumante,* Francia-corta, which is only vintage-dated some years.

6. Veneto produces some of Italy's most famous wines: Soave, the peachy prosecco, the crisp red Valpolicella, and the raisiny Amarone.

7. Liguria grows the white Bosco, the Pigato (thought to be of Greek origin), and Spanish Vermentino grapes, which are tangy and lively.

8. Emilia–Romagna makes Lambrusco, which accounts for 5 percent of total wine produced in Italy.

Geography and Products of Northern Italy

Here geography dictates cuisine: mountains yielding superlative cheeses and meats, foothills hosting nut and fruit trees and wine grapes, and forests famous for mushrooms. The huge Po Valley remains a prolific producer of DOP grain and vegetable crops, freshwater fish and seafood along the littorals.

Lombardy
Bitto cheese DOP, Garda olive oil DOP, Gorgonzola DOP, Grana Padano DOP, Varesino honey DOP, Provolone Valpadana DOP, Brianza salami DOP, Taleggio cheese DOP, Cantello asparagus IGP, dried beef IGP, Valtellina apples IGP, Mantua melons and pears IGP, Trentino trout IGP, frogs

Valle d'Aosta
Fontina DOP, spicy cured ham DOP, cured and seasoned lard DOP, rye bread, cattle, butter, Rennet apples, Martin Sec pears, chestnuts

Piedmont
Bra cheese DOP, Crudo di Cuneo DOP, Gorgonzola DOP, Barraggia Biellese and Vercellese rice DOP, Robiola di Roccaverano cheese DOP, Taleggio DOP, brook trout, Asti Spumante DOP, Toma Piemontese cheese DOP, Cuneo beans IGP, Valle di Susa chestnuts IGP, Cuneo red apples IGP, hazelnuts IGP, white truffles, porcini mushrooms, vermouth

Liguria
Genovese basil DOP, Ligurian Riviera olive oil DOP, dried pasta, focaccia, apricots, oranges, chestnuts, *chinotti,* violet asparagus, tomatoes, spiny artichokes, garlic, saffron, potatoes, porcini mushrooms, honey, salted anchovies DOP

Map Labels

SWITZERLAND

FRANCE

Mont Blanc
15,774 ft
4,808 m

Saint-Rhémy

Aosta

VALLE D'AOSTA

Gran Paradiso
13,323 ft
4,061 m

Valley of Lys

Ossola Valley

Lake Maggiore

Lake Como

Lake Iseo

A

L

Saronno

Bergamo

Ivrea

Novara

Milan

LOMBARDY

Sesia

Dora Baltea

Turin

PIEDMONT

Ticino

Adda

Piacenza

Po

Asti

Tanaro

Bra

Alba

Po

A P P E N N N

LIGURIA

Genoa

Camogli

Rapallo

Portofino

Borgo San Dalmazzo

Limone
Piemonte

Colle di Tenda

Albenga

Riviera di Ponente

Cinque Terre

Campiglia

Pontedassio

Imperia

San Remo

Ventimiglia

Riviera di Ponente

LIGURIAN SEA

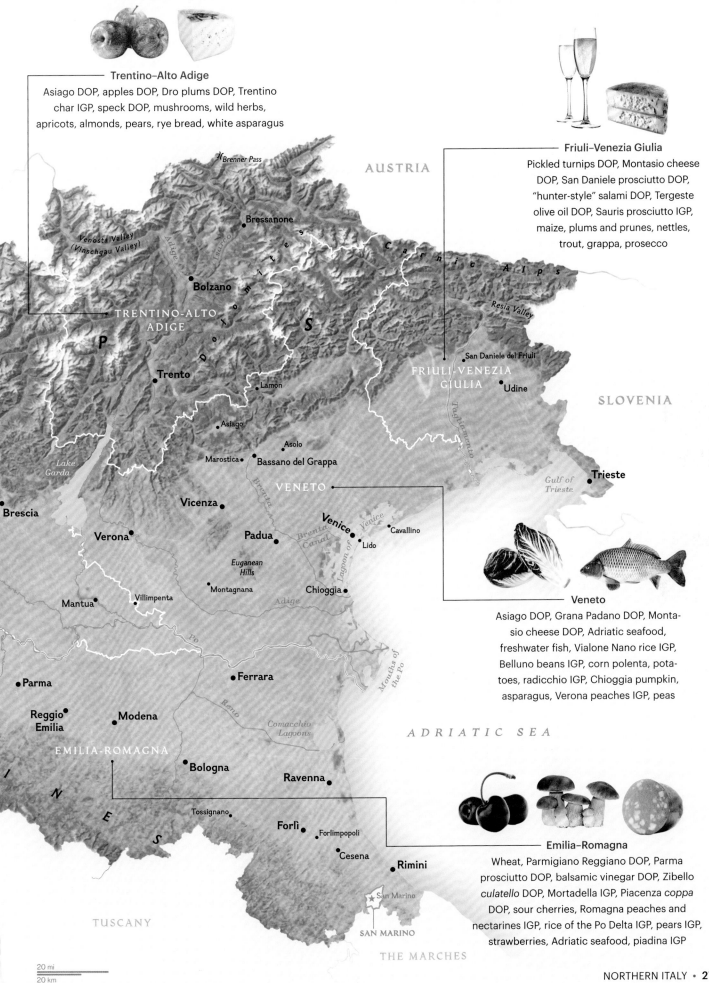

Trentino–Alto Adige
Asiago DOP, apples DOP, Dro plums DOP, Trentino char IGP, speck DOP, mushrooms, wild herbs, apricots, almonds, pears, rye bread, white asparagus

Friuli–Venezia Giulia
Pickled turnips DOP, Montasio cheese DOP, San Daniele prosciutto DOP, "hunter-style" salami DOP, Tergeste olive oil DOP, Sauris prosciutto IGP, maize, plums and prunes, nettles, trout, grappa, prosecco

Veneto
Asiago DOP, Grana Padano DOP, Montasio cheese DOP, Adriatic seafood, freshwater fish, Vialone Nano rice IGP, Belluno beans IGP, corn polenta, potatoes, radicchio IGP, Chioggia pumpkin, asparagus, Verona peaches IGP, peas

Emilia–Romagna
Wheat, Parmigiano Reggiano DOP, Parma prosciutto DOP, balsamic vinegar DOP, Zibello *culatello* DOP, Mortadella IGP, Piacenza *coppa* DOP, sour cherries, Romagna peaches and nectarines IGP, rice of the Po Delta IGP, pears IGP, strawberries, Adriatic seafood, piadina IGP

AUSTRIA

Brenner Pass

Venosta Valley
(Vinschgau Valley)

Bressanone

Bolzano

TRENTINO-ALTO ADIGE

Trento

Lamon

Asiago

Asolo

Marostica

Bassano del Grappa

VENETO

Vicenza

Lake Garda

Brescia

Verona

Padua

Venice

Cavallino

Lido

Euganean Hills

Montagnana

Chioggia

Mantua

Villimpenta

Parma

Ferrara

Reggio Emilia

Modena

EMILIA-ROMAGNA

Bologna

Ravenna

Tossignano

Forlì

Forlimpopoli

Cesena

Rimini

San Marino

SAN MARINO

TUSCANY

THE MARCHES

Carnic Alps

Resia Valley

San Daniele del Friuli

FRIULI-VENEZIA GIULIA

Udine

SLOVENIA

Trieste

Gulf of Trieste

Lagoon of Venice

Brenta Canal

Adige

Po

Reno

Comacchio Lagoons

Mouths of the Po

ADRIATIC SEA

Dolomites

Tagliamento

20 mi
20 km

Valle d'Aosta

Hearty Fare for Travelers

···

THERE IS A SAYING IN VALLE D'AOSTA: "The older the pot, the better the soup." In this remote yet well-traveled valley in the northwestern corner of Italy, there are two reasons to keep the soup pot simmering. Valle d'Aosta is cold and isolated, surrounded by Europe's grandest mountains—and soup keeps a body warm. But the region also sports mountain passes that access France and Switzerland. As a result, Valle d'Aosta is a historic layover for intracontinental travelers, who always have a cup of something hot on hand.

The valley penetrates into the Alps connecting Piedmont to central Europe. Its primary river, the Dora Baltea, flows out of the mountains, into Piedmont, and then all the way south to join the Po. Valle d'Aosta is actually a network of valleys. Beautiful small vales spring off to the east and west of the main valley like ribs, where castles overlook Alpine meadows filled with grazing piebald cattle and villages tucked among pink rhododendrons, oligotrophic lakes, and lichen-covered rocks.

Valle d'Aosta borders France and Switzerland to the west and north, and Piedmont to the east. It is Italy's smallest region, in both population and territory, but its historic importance lies in its position. The valley has been an important artery connecting central Europe and the Italian peninsula since Roman times. Valle d'Aosta is a long skinny valley; like a road, it's a place people travel along on their way to somewhere else. The local people, accustomed to travelers coming and going over the mountains, have for generations shared their hearty foods. Prime examples are the

Dairy cattle range freely in the high green valleys of Valle d'Aosta.

cold-weather soups they thrive on: *soeupa alla valpellinentze,* beef broth with cabbage and rye bread spread with melted Fontina on top; barley soup with pork (barley was probably introduced by the Romans); and milk soup with dried chestnuts, rice, and butter.

Today's visitors might revive themselves on this bulk-building cuisine after a day on the slopes. The valley hosts more than 150 ski lifts and some 500 miles of trails, mostly spread among the resorts of La Thuile, Courmayeur, Cervinia, Pila, Champoluc, and Gressoney.

Agriculture Among the Peaks

Valle d'Aosta is great for skiing because the high valleys have a snow season that lasts up to nine months. But that means there's not much time for agricultural pursuits. During the three months or so of summer, cattle, sheep, and goats are herded into the high mountain pastures to take advantage of the brief but rich vegetation. Dairy dominates the valley's agriculture, and its products are famous. Valle d'Aosta produces some of the best butter in northern Italy, and of its many cheeses it claims the original, internationally known Fontina as well as Fromadzo, a delicate cheese sometimes injected with aromatic mountain herbs.

What crops are grown are typical of a mountain ecology. Chestnut and fruit trees survive the chilly nights, and the region is particularly well known for its Rennet apples and small Martin Sec pears. Poached in red wine, these pears may be served with a local favorite, *tegole,* a thin crispy cookie made with nuts and egg whites. Rye and potatoes grow well in the poor soil, and lettuce is cultivated at the snow line, hence the name, snow lettuce. And true of any mountain culture, there is a long tradition of hunting the Alpine forests for wild goat, sheep, hare, boar, pheasant, and quail, as well as for mushrooms, the quiet hunt.

The ski scene supports high-end restaurants where almost all of the locally made wine is consumed, but the home cooking of Valle d'Aosta is based on caloric essentials: lard, butter, and cheese; cabbage, potatoes, and polenta; beef, bacon, and game; wine, chestnuts, and rye bread. These foods reflect a poverty of choice, but the dishes they make have evolved to satisfy these tough and sturdy people.

A Difficult Terrain, a Hardy People

Valdotians are like the mountains they live in. They are a people, said the writer David Lynch, who weather rather than age. This was originally the territory of the fierce Salassi tribe, whose origins likely were Celtic or Ligurian. The Salassi lands once spread as far south as the Dora Baltea's downstream gold washings at Ivrea (at the mouth of the valley and currently in Piedmont), or they did until the Romans took over by 25 B.C. They were one of the last tribes to succumb to Rome in the Mediterranean Basin, a reflection, perhaps, of the territory's difficult terrain and the hardiness of its people. Rome founded

---

LOCAL FLAVOR

FINDING FONTINA

In 1477 Pantaleone of Confienza wrote that in the Valley of Augustus (that is, Valle d'Aosta), "the cheeses are good." Indeed, they are. But Fontina is the star. Made from the milk of Valdostana cows that pasture in the high mountain meadows in the summer, Fontina is mild and fatty with a silky meltability. Facsimiles are produced in other regions, so to be sure you have the original, look for the DOP stamp on the rust-colored rind. Rich, yellow Fontina is the basis for *fonduta,* the signature melted cheese dish of Valle d'Aosta, a custard-like fondue enhanced with butter and egg yolks.

Snowshoeing in the Italian Alps at La Thuile: a winter sports lover's paradise

Augusta Praetoria Salassorum, currently the city of Aosta, which lent Valle d'Aosta, or the Valley of Augustus, its name.

Mountain Fare With European Flair

After the fall of Rome in the fifth century, Burgundians and Franks, and in the 11th century the French Savoy dynasty, dominated this strategic valley, and they left their mark. While the essential kitchen of Valle d'Aosta is mountain fare, you can nonetheless see the wine and cream influence of French and German cookery. Wild game that the Salassi probably hunted—such as chamois, ibex, hare, and pheasant—is commonly marinated in wine, herbs, and onions before cooking, and the region's very fine butter laces most dishes. For example, a local specialty, *carbonade valdostana,* is a stew of salt-cured beef, red wine, and butter, and the Valdotian version of *cotoletta,* the famous fried veal cutlet dish of Lombardy, gets a good dose of cream sauce. Ever popular with skiers, Valle d'Aosta is maybe best known for its *fonduta,* a type of fondue made with Fontina cheese that binds the region to its neighbors.

Valle d'Aosta has no provinces. It was itself a province of Piedmont until 1945, when it was granted independent recognition due to its unique linguistic and cultural

A network of paths allows the intrepid hiker to travel on foot around the entire perimeter of the Valle d'Aosta.

Tangy Bleu d'Aoste is one of many exceptional cheeses produced in the valley.

orientation. The valley is both Italian and French speaking, with more than half speaking a French Provençal language called Valdôtain; the adjacent Valley of Lys hosts German-speaking Swiss. Thus the valley, with its chalet-style architecture and its Euro-inflected mountain cuisine, is a mixed bag of cultural, linguistic, and culinary influences.

That's not to say Valle d'Aosta isn't indubitably Italian; it is. They cure pork as in every region, most famously the DOP-designated Jambon de Bosses, from the village of Saint-Rhémy-en-Bosses, and the sweet Lard d'Arnad, pork fat seasoned in wooden boxes. But these premier pork products are irrefutably Valdotian because they are flavored with local mountain herbs.

The Last Convivial Hearth

Geographically, Valle d'Aosta is the foyer of central Europe. It's where cultures meet and eat, where travelers have historically filled up on meals such as potato gnocchi or milk dumplings draped in a creamy robe of melted cheese, or ibex *bresaola,* sliced thin and eaten with black bread, butter, and a drizzle of the region's superb honey.

The valley is the last (or first, depending on your travel direction) welcoming home, where the weary can take a bracing shot of *genepy,* an herbal grappa flavored with the wormwood that grows in the mountains (although now mainly cultivated) before hitting the slopes. It is where travelers can warm themselves with a cup of broth from the eternally simmering pot on the stove before starting the next leg of their journey or venturing out into the snow.

A vineyard rises to the 12th-century castle of Saint-Pierre in the Aosta Valley.

LOCAL FLAVOR
THE *GROLLA*

Valdotians often share a coffee drink from a traditional wooden vessel called the *grolla.* Carved from walnut or maple (Valle d'Aosta is famous for its woodworkers), it looks like a round pot with four, six, or ten spouts. It is filled with a combination of hot coffee, lemon and orange zest, grappa, red wine, and sugar, and served on fire with sugar around the rim. Once the fire has burned out, the lid is put on and the cup is passed counterclockwise around the table, with each person drinking from a different spout. No one sets the cup down until the drink is finished. The Valdotians call it the cup of friendship, but the grolla is so much more: It is a symbol of Valle d'Aosta's unique place at a geographic and cultural crossroads.

Potato Gnocchi With Fontina Sauce

Gnocchi alla fontina · *Serves 4 to 6*

WHY THIS RECIPE WORKS: Potato gnocchi was originally born from frugality—just humble potatoes and flour added up to a meal. While a multitude of variations (made from other vegetables or flours, bread, or cheese, to name a few) exist across Italy, in Valle d'Aosta you'll most likely find potato gnocchi dressed simply with gooey, pungent fontina cheese—the pride of the region—and butter. Called *gnocchi alla fontina* or *gnocchi alla bava* ("drooling gnocchi," thanks to the melty cheese), the dish is warm and comforting. While some regional recipes bind the potatoes with buckwheat flour, all-purpose flour is equally traditional and readily available; we liked that it let the flavor of the fontina shine. For the potatoes, we went with starchy russets, which made for light dumplings. We baked rather than boiled the potatoes; this way they didn't absorb excess water and we could nail down an exact amount of flour to add—many recipes give a range, which can lead to dense dumplings. At their simplest and most traditional, recipes for the cheese component call for tossing chunks of butter and fontina with the hot gnocchi, but the cheese is prone to breaking. We found that whisking melted butter, fontina, and a bit of the gnocchi cooking water together prior to tossing resulted in a creamier, meltier sauce. A traditional pinch of freshly grated nutmeg in the sauce rounded out the flavors.

2 pounds russet potatoes, unpeeled
1 large egg, lightly beaten
¾ cup plus 1 tablespoon
    (4 ounces) all-purpose flour
Salt
3 tablespoons unsalted butter
4 ounces fontina cheese, shredded
    (1 cup)
⅛ teaspoon grated nutmeg

① Adjust oven rack to middle position and heat oven to 450 degrees. Poke each potato 8 times with paring knife. Microwave potatoes until slightly softened at ends, about 10 minutes, flipping potatoes halfway through microwaving. Transfer potatoes directly to oven rack and bake until skewer glides easily through flesh and potatoes yield to gentle pressure, 18 to 20 minutes.

② Holding potatoes with dish towel, peel with paring knife. Process potatoes through ricer or food mill onto rimmed baking sheet. Gently spread potatoes into even layer and let cool for 5 minutes.

③ Transfer 3 cups (16 ounces) warm potatoes to bowl; discard remaining potato or save for another use. Using fork, gently stir in egg until just combined. Sprinkle flour and 1 teaspoon salt over top and gently combine using fork until no pockets of dry flour remain. Press mixture into rough ball, transfer to lightly floured counter, and gently knead until smooth but slightly sticky, about 1 minute, lightly dusting counter with flour as needed to prevent sticking.

④ Line 2 rimmed baking sheets with parchment paper and dust liberally with flour. Divide dough into 8 pieces. Gently roll each piece of dough into ½-inch-thick rope on lightly floured counter, dusting with flour as needed to prevent sticking, then cut rope into ¾-inch lengths.

⑤ Holding fork with tines upside down in one hand, press each dough piece cut side down against tines with thumb of other hand to create indentation. Roll dough down tines to form ridges on sides. If dough sticks, dust thumb or fork with flour. Transfer gnocchi to prepared sheets.

⑥ Bring 4 quarts water to boil in large pot. Using parchment paper as sling, add half of gnocchi and 1 tablespoon salt and simmer gently, stirring occasionally, until firm and just cooked through, about 90 seconds (gnocchi should float to surface after about 1 minute).

⑦ Meanwhile, melt butter in 12-inch skillet over medium heat. Whisk in ¼ cup of cooking water, fontina, and nutmeg until cheese is melted and smooth. Using slotted spoon, transfer gnocchi to skillet and gently toss to coat; cover to keep warm. Return cooking water to boil and repeat cooking remaining gnocchi; transfer to skillet and gently toss to combine. Serve immediately.

MAKING RIDGES ON GNOCCHI

To make ridges on gnocchi, hold fork with tines facing down. Press each dough piece cut side down against tines with your thumb to make indentation. Roll dumpling down tines to create ridges on sides.

Savoy Cabbage Soup With Ham, Rye Bread, and Fontina

Soeupa alla valpellinentze · Serves 6 to 8

WHY THIS RECIPE WORKS: High in the Italian Alps, Valle d'Aosta is known for a regional wintertime dish, *soeupa alla valpellinentze*, a decadent combination of rich beef broth, pancetta, cabbage, rye bread, and nutty fontina cheese. While *soeupa* translates literally to soup, this dish is heartier—it reminded us of the cheesy top layer of French onion soup as we scooped out second helpings. Savoy cabbage is the regional favorite, and its subtly sweet flavor worked beautifully with the earthy rye bread that we cubed and dried at a low temperature in the oven. We built flavor and tenderized the cabbage by braising it with pancetta, onion, bay leaf, and beef broth before layering it in a casserole dish with the stale bread. The whole thing received a topping of cheese, which turned bubbly under the broiler. Any type of hearty rye bread will work well here. You will need a 13 by 9-inch broiler-safe baking dish for this recipe.

12 ounces hearty rye bread, cut into 1½-inch pieces
2 tablespoons extra-virgin olive oil
1 tablespoon unsalted butter
4 ounces pancetta, chopped fine
1 onion, halved and sliced thin
½ teaspoon salt
3 garlic cloves, minced
1 head savoy cabbage (1½ pounds), cored and cut into 1-inch pieces
4 cups beef broth
2 bay leaves
4 ounces fontina cheese, shredded (1 cup)
1 tablespoon chopped fresh parsley

❶ Adjust oven rack to middle position and heat oven to 250 degrees. Spread bread in even layer on rimmed baking sheet and bake, stirring occasionally, until dried and crisp throughout, about 45 minutes; let croutons cool completely.

❷ Heat oil and butter in Dutch oven over medium-low heat until butter is melted. Add pancetta and cook until browned and fat is rendered, about 8 minutes. Stir in onion and salt and cook over medium heat until softened and lightly browned, 5 to 7 minutes. Stir in garlic and cook until fragrant, about 30 seconds.

❸ Stir in cabbage, broth, and bay leaves and bring to boil. Reduce heat to low, cover, and simmer until cabbage is tender, about 45 minutes.

❹ Adjust oven rack 6 inches from broiler element and heat broiler. Discard bay leaves. Spread half of cabbage mixture evenly in bottom of 13 by 9-inch broiler-safe baking dish, then top with half of croutons. Repeat with remaining cabbage mixture and croutons. Gently press down on croutons with rubber spatula until thoroughly saturated. Sprinkle fontina over top and broil until melted and spotty brown, about 4 minutes. Sprinkle with parsley and serve.

Polenta With Cheese and Butter

Polenta concia · *Serves 6 to 8*

WHY THIS RECIPE WORKS: Polenta is a peasant dish enjoyed throughout Italy in many different forms, but the porridge traces its origins to the mountainous areas of northern Italy. It can be made with such grains as spelt, rye, or buckwheat, but it's most commonly made with cornmeal. *Polenta concia,* a version of the cornmeal porridge that's enriched with butter and cheese, is eaten widely in Valle d'Aosta. The traditional recipe is simple but time-consuming: Boil water, whisk in cornmeal, and stir like crazy for up to an hour to prevent lumps until the porridge has softened; then, whisk in cheese and butter. We wanted to reduce the time and exercise, so we added an unexpected and nontraditional ingredient: a pinch of baking soda, which broke down the corn's structure so it became creamy in less than half the time. The baking soda also helped the granules break down and release their starch in a uniform way, minimizing the need for stirring. Use coarse-ground cornmeal with grains the size of couscous. If the polenta bubbles or sputters even slightly after the first 10 minutes, the heat is too high and you may need a flame tamer. You can buy one or easily make your own: Shape a sheet of heavy-duty aluminum foil into a 1-inch-thick ring that fits on your burner, making sure the ring is of even thickness. Rich and satisfying, polenta concia can be a *primo* or a lovely base to a stew such as *Misto di funghi* (page 98); it also makes an ideal accompaniment to braised meat such as *Brasato al Barolo* (page 58).

7½ cups water
Salt and pepper
Pinch baking soda
1½ cups coarse-ground cornmeal
4 ounces Parmigiano Reggiano cheese, grated (2 cups), plus extra for serving
2 tablespoons unsalted butter

❶ Bring water to boil in large saucepan over medium-high heat. Stir in 1½ teaspoons salt and baking soda. Slowly pour cornmeal into water in steady stream while whisking constantly and bring to boil. Reduce heat to lowest possible setting, cover, and cook until grains of cornmeal are tender, about 30 minutes, stirring every few minutes. (Polenta should be loose and barely hold its shape; it will continue to thicken as it cools.)

❷ Off heat, whisk in Parmigiano and butter and season with pepper to taste. Cover and let sit for 5 minutes. Serve, passing extra Parmigiano separately.

Stuffed Veal Cutlets With Prosciutto and Fontina

Cotoletta alla valdostana · *Serves 4*

WHY THIS RECIPE WORKS: In the Alpine region of Valle d'Aosta, food is rich and hearty owing to its history: Substantial foods kept folks sated for the heavy lifting required of mountain living. Here, butter is preferred to olive oil and creamy cheeses—a product of the region's vast milk supply—are cherished. *Cotoletta alla valdostana* is a prime example of the hearty fare: A small amount of veal becomes a hearty meal when stuffed with decadent prosciutto and fontina cheese. While traditional recipes vary in preparation, we followed the neatest and simplest approach: We pounded a veal cutlet until thin and tender, topped it with cheese and prosciutto, and then placed another thin piece of veal on top. Once assembled, we breaded this veal "sandwich" and then cooked it in butter until crisp. Lemon wedges are the only accompaniment this satisfying dish needs, but you can also serve it on a bed of arugula.

4 (3-ounce) veal cutlets, about ¼ inch thick, halved crosswise
2 ounces fontina cheese, shredded (½ cup)
4 thin slices Prosciutto di Parma (2 ounces)
2 large eggs
2 tablespoons all-purpose flour
1½ cups panko bread crumbs
8 tablespoons unsalted butter
Salt and pepper
Lemon wedges

❶ Pat 2 cutlet halves dry with paper towels and place between 2 layers of plastic wrap. Pound cutlets into rough 5 by 4-inch rectangles, about ⅛ inch thick, using meat pounder. Place 2 tablespoons fontina in center of 1 cutlet half, leaving ¼-inch border around edge. Lay 1 slice prosciutto on top of fontina, folding it as needed to prevent any overhang. Place second cutlet half over prosciutto. Gently press down on cutlets to compress layers, then press along edges to seal. Repeat with remaining cutlet halves, fontina, and prosciutto.

❷ Whisk eggs and flour in shallow dish until smooth. Spread panko in second shallow dish. Working with 1 stuffed cutlet at a time, carefully dip in egg mixture, allowing excess to drip off. Dredge in panko to coat both sides, pressing gently so crumbs adhere. Place breaded cutlets in single layer on wire rack set in rimmed baking sheet and let sit for 5 minutes.

❸ Heat butter in 12-inch nonstick skillet over medium heat until foaming subsides (do not let butter brown). Place cutlets in skillet; cook until deep golden brown and crisp on first side, 3 to 6 minutes. Gently flip cutlets using 2 spatulas and continue to cook until deep golden brown and crisp on second side, about 4 minutes, adjusting burner as needed to prevent scorching. Transfer cutlets to paper towel–lined plate and blot dry. Season with salt and pepper to taste. Serve immediately with lemon wedges.

Piedmont

A Sophisticated Cuisine That Celebrates Its Rustic Roots

....

PIEDMONT IS ONE OF ITALY'S FIVE LANDLOCKED REGIONS, but if you visit the central provinces in spring you will encounter a land of shallow water shimmering with the reflections of poplars, red-tiled farmhouses, and blue sky. Piedmont's rice fields are located at the head of the glorious Po Valley, a huge tongue of fertile land that stretches east from Piedmont to the Adriatic Sea. The Po Valley is Europe's largest rice producer and more than half of that production is in Piedmont.

A Diverse Landscape

This is where the firm, starchy rice used to make that most silky of Italian dishes, risotto, is grown. While these farmlands and rice paddies are the heart of Piedmont, the region, which is about the size of Maryland (and Italy's second largest), is mostly mountains and hills. Piedmont is in the northwestern corner of Italy, cradled to the south, west, and north by the arc of the Ligurian Apennines and the western Alps, the source of rivers and Alpine lakes that drain into the Po. Piedmont derives its name from the medieval Latin *pedemontium*, or foothills, an homage to the spectacular mass of wavy hills south of the Po that are girded with Italy's most famous vineyards.

With this diverse geography comes a diverse agriculture. Beef and dairy cattle, particularly the almost-white native breed, the Piemontese, feed on subalpine meadows. The wild grass and herbs growing in these meadows are the foundation of a prosperous dairy industry and a local cuisine built on butter, cream, and cheese,

Visitors and locals dine alfresco at a restaurant in Turin.

including those with protected designations (DOP), such as the delicate and milky Bra, sweet Toma (a table and cooking cheese), and the luxurious Robiola. Trout are caught in the fast-moving streams, and game birds, truffles, and mushrooms hunted in the forests. Wine grapes and hazelnuts are grown in the hill country, and rice, wheat, and other cereals, as well as vegetables, are grown on the plains. This is the land of beef and rice, of cheese and truffles and red wine, of chocolate and hazelnuts (and yes, Nutella too).

A Cuisine of War and Peace

The mountain passes that connect Piedmont to Gaul have been both a liability and an asset. Celtic tribes were able to travel south over them with their herds and establish the proto-dairy culture of the region. But Rome also had its eye on those passes. It conquered the Celts in the Gallic Wars and extended the empire north, thereby gaining access to Gaul in what is France today. Though that access would influence the political and culinary future of Piedmont, once Rome fell in the fifth century, this strategically located region became the target of centuries of barbaric invasions. Piedmont fractured into autonomous city-states that were constantly at war; it was politically destabilizing, but it nurtured the specialization of eponymous foods such as Bra cheese from the town of Bra, and Asti Spumante from the town of Asti. By the 11th century, however, the region was largely unified by the House of Savoy, an ancient dynasty that originated in the western Alps where France, Italy, and Switzerland merge.

Piedmont experienced centuries of relative stability under the Savoys. The upper-

Racconigi Castle, one of the official residences of the House of Savoy

LOCAL FLAVOR

THE BATTLE OF THE ORANGES

Ivrea's Carnival used to be similar to others, with revelries and the elite throwing treats to the crowd from their balconies. The Battle of the Oranges, held during Carnival, is a colorful reenactment of a popular uprising. A hated tyrant had claimed his droit du seigneur with a miller's daughter. But rather than succumb, the rebellious girl cut off his head (or possibly his testicles, hence the oranges), thereby liberating the town from oppression. Today, thousands of townspeople battle carts full of helmeted men representing the tyrant's henchmen. Over three days of sticky street combat a million pounds of fresh oranges are thrown, and plenty of mulled wine is drunk.

Pasticceria Barbero in Cherasco, Cuneo, one of many places where Piedmont's marvelous chocolates are made

class Piedmontese who flourished then, particularly the residents of Turin, where the Savoys made their capital, didn't reject the hearty foods of the highland, nor the humble dishes of the lowland farms—they simply redesigned those dishes to reflect a more sumptuous and refined palate. For example, *bollito misto* is a boiled meat dish traditionally made from work animals after they have aged out of their jobs. The meat was tough and the boiling long. Modern bollito misto is still a boiled meat dinner, but composed of a grand array of beef, veal, poultry, and slices of sweet, chubby *cotechino* sausage, served with a variety of piquant sauces. In this way Piedmontese cooking is a melding of two traditions: simple robust country fare and sophisticated dishes developed in the kitchens of the aristocracy, which added French culinary influences to the native dairy-forward cuisine.

Today the region is a culinary leader with progressive ideas about protecting traditional foodways and supporting a new generation of farmers, vintners, and chefs. But then, Piedmont has a tradition of leadership. There is a saying that Piedmont gave birth to Italy. The region's numerous attempts to unify the country paid off with the crowning of their Savoy king, Victor Emmanuel II, as unified Italy's first monarch in 1861. The Savoys lost their crown with the creation of the Republic of Italy in 1946, but to the

The Ferrero Rocher factory in Alba produces 24 million chocolate-covered hazelnuts a day. About 3.6 billion are sold annually in 40 countries.

The international Slow Food movement, officially established in 1986, began out of Bra, a town and commune in Piedmont's Cuneo province.

delight of Italian gossip magazines, the family continues to argue among themselves as to who has the right to be the king of a throne that no longer exists.

There are eight provinces in modern Piedmont: Alessandria, Asti, and Cuneo are famous for their wines; Verbano-Cusio-Ossola, which includes the glorious Lake Maggiore, whose microclimate allows for Eden-like gardens of olive and lemon trees; Turin, the industrial heart of the region, with its coolly elegant capital city and delectable chocolatiers; and finally Novara, Vercelli, and Biella, home to so much Italian rice.

Rich, Refined, and Robust

No one is exactly sure how rice was brought to Italy, but it's widely believed the Spanish introduced it through the southern regions during the Middle Ages. Rice from Piedmont was so jealously guarded that it was illegal to take seed grain out of the country. Thomas Jefferson, though, apparently took the risk. He smuggled rice out of Piedmont in 1787 to see how it would grow in American soil. It grew very well.

In Piedmont rice is mainly consumed as risotto, where meat stock is slowly added while the rice is stirred, hastening the starch that binds the dish. Risotto is served soft enough to eat with a spoon, enriched with cheese or meat, red wine or truffles. Corn polenta, the other major starch of Piedmont, is dressed with cheese and flavored with a range of protein-rich tastes such as savory stewed meats and mushrooms. Soft wheat, grown in the north, is well suited to bread and leavened products such as cakes and pizza, and for making fresh egg pasta such as *agnolotti,* a ravioli-like pasta stuffed with braised or stewed meat. Another example is *tajarin,* a thin egg pasta simmered

Lakes Agnel and Serru and the Nivolet foothills within the Gracian Alps, Piedmont

libations: *SALUTE!* FROM TURIN

Piedmont has been an important producer of vermouth since the 1700s. Vermouth formulas themselves are closely held; the famous vermouth companies started as family enterprises, and for many decades they stayed that way to better protect their trade secrets. The basic recipe is a neutral white wine, like Moscato d'Asti, flavored with herbs, spices, roots, and wood, and alternately frozen and heated to create a 30-something proof fortified wine. The most well known producers, all originating in Turin, are Cinzano, Cora, and Martini & Rossi. Sweet vermouth, which acquires its red color from caramelized sugar, is key to a Manhattan cocktail, and dry vermouth to a martini.

A classic Manhattan cocktail

Truffles, the White Diamonds of Italy

What is it about the white truffle, *Tuber magnatum pico*, that makes people giddy with delight, pay as much as $3,600 a pound, and travel all the way to Alba in Piedmont just to taste a scraping or two on top of their risotto? In a word, the aroma. Truffles are mushrooms that evolved to grow underground (maybe to avoid environmental stresses), but when they did, they lost their primary means of spore dispersal, wind. To compensate, the truffle utilizes animal vectors. When the spores mature, the truffle emits volatile aromatic compounds that attract particular animals to dig it up, dispersing the spore in the process. There are many species of truffles, but the ones we like to eat evolved to attract swine. Truffle aroma is irresistible to pigs and humans because it is composed of chemicals that mimic mammalian reproductive pheromones. Sniffing a truffle is kind of like being drugged. But despite claims that they are aphrodisiacs, truffles won't attract your dining companion to you. They have evolved to attract her to it.

ALL ABOUT THE AROMA

Truffles are all about the aroma. When scraped over a fried egg, the heat lifts the scent to the diner's nose. But truffles only produce aroma for a few days—it's all timed to attract animals, remember—and once the aroma has dissipated, the unique flavor of the truffle is gone. Additionally, that aroma resists preservation. Most truffle products are flavored synthetically, with a chemical that imitates some of the truffle's complex aromatic compounds.

THE ULTIMATE SEASONAL FOOD

Truffles are the fruiting bodies of fungi that live in complex symbiotic relationships with living trees and the ecology of the soil around it, and while some truffle species have been cultivated in orchards, the *pico*, which grows on the roots of oak, willow, poplar, and hazelnut trees, has remained aloof. Which makes *Tuber magnatum pico* the ultimate seasonal food.

Opposite: A hunter compliments his dog on a good find: white truffles. Right: Black truffles are also found in Piedmont.

The Truffle Fair in Alba

On most food enthusiasts' bucket list is the International Truffle Fair, held in Alba in October and November when the truffles are collected. The fair, which dates to the 1920s, includes a donkey race, appearances by truffle hunters and their dogs, and a truffle market, where potential purchasers can sniff individual truffles placed in the bottom of wineglasses. There's also all manner of culinary hoopla where the province's great wines, cheeses, and hazelnuts are celebrated. Restaurants and food-stand menus feature truffle dishes, but for those on a budget, the entrance fee to the market is enough. Once inside you can sniff to your heart's content.

The Gancia family of Turin invented spumante in 1865; today the winery produces 20 million bottles of the bubbly a year.

in beef broth and smothered in butter, or cooked in a steaming pot of beans, onions, potatoes, and *lardo* (a type of cured pork fat so tasty some chefs call it white prosciutto). But Piedmont's most famous wheat-based product is *grissini,* the long skinny breadsticks from Turin that are ubiquitous on Italian restaurant tabletops all over the world.

The region is well known for its indulgent yet elegant beef and veal dishes, including *vitello tonnato,* delicate veal that has been simmered in broth, cooled, thinly sliced, and finished with a smooth mayonnaisey tuna sauce. Or try hearty *brasato al Barolo,* beef marinated in the supreme red wine of the region, then braised with herbs and vegetables. Organ meats are eaten here with relish: *fritto misto piemontese* is a mixed fry of meats, offal, vegetables, fruit, cheese, and even biscuits. Also popular is *finanziera,* a lip-smacking dish combining organ meats with Sicily's Marsala wine, garlic, and vinegar. Hare, goose, chicken, turkey, and donkey all find their way to the Piedmontese table, as well as pork dishes such as the rustic *puccia delle Langhe,* a cabbage and pork stew with corn and wheat polenta and beans. *Salumi* from Piedmont include tender prosciutto from the region of Cuneo and a *salame* aged in ceramic vessels filled with lard.

Turin, Piedmont's capital city and a bastion of refined cuisine, sparkles at dusk.

The *Amanita ceasarea* (Caesar's mushroom) has been prized for a millennium.

Sausages are stuffed with so much more than pork: trout, beef, goose, and even potatoes make their way into sausage casings.

There is not much of a traditional seafood culture here, though no landlocked region in Italy is very far from the sea. Nonetheless, one of the region's specialties is *bagna cauda,* a sauce made with anchovies, butter, and garlic served on raw vegetables. But the area's most renowned wild foods are without question mushrooms and truffles. Hunters gather porcini, a group of a few mushrooms in the *Boletus* genus, *Amanita caesarea* (Caesar's mushrooms), and other choice fungi, and with the help of their dogs, they find the *Tuber magnatum pico*, Piedmont's white truffle, the most expensive and arguably the most seductive species in the fungi kingdom. Porcini are eaten fresh or dried where their concentrated sugars powerfully enhance the umami flavor of meat braises and stews. Truffles are eaten raw, sliced paper-thin and scattered over cheese, eggs, rice, polenta, and pasta dishes, their aroma a surprisingly captivating combination of garlic, potatoes, and dirty socks.

Cultivars of beans and apples are specialties of Piedmont with their own DOP designations, but the region also produces cardoons, tree fruits, *cugnà* asparagus, and pumpkin, among many other vegetables. While the chestnuts of Cuneo have been lauded for centuries, maybe the most famous nut is the IGP-designated Nocciola del Piemonte (Piedmont Hazelnut), treasured for its delicate flavor and crisp pulp. Hazelnut cultivation has spread across the region, but it is concentrated in the provinces of Cuneo, Asti, and Alessandria. Most of the harvest is slated for the confectionaries of

LOCAL FLAVOR
NUTELLA, A WORLDWIDE ADDICTION

The hazelnut cocoa spread Nutella is the peanut butter of Italy, produced by the multibillion-dollar Ferrero Group, maker of Ferrero Rocher chocolates. Just after World War II, Italy experienced a period of hunger and deprivation. Chocolate was a rare treat, but there were hazelnuts growing in the Langhe. A century earlier the chocolatiers of Turin had developed an expensive concoction of chocolate and hazelnuts; Pietro Ferrero, Ferrero Group's founder, reimagined this confection with a lot more hazelnut, making it more affordable, and founded a company to sell it. In the 1960s the paste was reinvented again as a soft cream, renamed Nutella, and the product took off. Today one jar of Nutella is sold every 2.5 seconds.

The Swiss learned the art of making chocolate from the Piedmontese.

Alba, where they are made into the chocolate hazelnut spread Nutella as well as Ferrero Rocher chocolates. Not surprisingly, the Piedmontese love their sweets, with hazelnut chocolate cakes, candied chestnuts, and *panna cotta* among the many temptations.

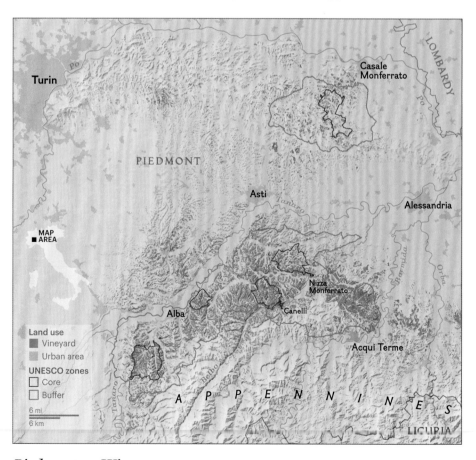

Chestnuts

Honoring the Past, Cooking Up the Future

The cuisine of Piedmont respects its heritage, but it is also forging a new identity as an exciting and dynamic restaurant culture. Turin is home to the University of Gastronomy, where chefs and food professionals from all over come to study the relationship between food and culture. Founded by Carlo Petrini, father of the Slow Food movement, this is the first university to graduate people skilled in the production, distribution, promotion, and communication of high-quality foods—professional gastronomes. It exists where it does because in Piedmont, food is more than sustenance; it's art.

The statues of Borromeo Palace on Isola Bella gaze across Lake Maggiore.

Piedmontese Wines The UNESCO World Heritage site of Langhe-Roero and Monferrato is a beautiful landscape showcasing the combined work of humans and nature.

Breadsticks

Grissini · *Makes 32 breadsticks*

WHY THIS RECIPE WORKS: Eat at a restaurant in Piedmont, and the first thing to come to the table will be a platter piled with long, slender hand-shaped breadsticks called *grissini*—the perfect antipasti accompaniment. While grissini can be found factory-made throughout Italy, the real deal is still handmade with care in its birthplace, Turin. More elegant than their doughy American counterparts, these airy, crisp Italian breadsticks taste purely of browned wheat, olive oil, and salt—and they're easy to make at home. The dough itself is a pizza dough, which we pulled together easily by kneading it in the food processor. Once we cut the dough into strips, we found it best to fold them in half vertically before rolling them; the doubled-up dough was less likely to break when stretched. A quick rest after folding relaxed the dough so it didn't snap back when we stretched it. Before baking, we brushed the sticks with olive oil and seasoned them with salt, pepper, and optional fennel seed. A moderate 350-degree oven delivered

perfectly crisp grissini that were lightly browned from tip to tip. These hand-rolled sticks naturally have thicker and thinner spots; extra cooling and drying time (about 2 hours) ensured thicker spots became totally dry.

> 2 cups (10 ounces) all-purpose flour
> 1 teaspoon instant or rapid-rise yeast
> ¾ teaspoon salt
> 1 tablespoon extra-virgin olive oil, plus extra for brushing
> ¾ cup ice water
> 1½ teaspoons coarse sea salt or kosher salt
> 1 teaspoon pepper
> ½ teaspoon fennel seeds, coarsely ground (optional)

❶ Pulse flour, yeast, and salt in food processor until combined, about 5 pulses. With processor running, add oil, then ice water, and process until rough ball forms, 30 to 40 seconds. Let dough rest for 2 minutes. Process 30 seconds longer.

❷ Transfer dough to lightly floured counter and knead by hand to form smooth, round ball, about 30 seconds. Place dough in lightly greased large bowl or container, cover tightly with plastic wrap, and let rise until doubled in size, 1½ to 2 hours. (Alternatively, refrigerate unrisen dough for at least 8 hours or up to 16 hours; let sit at room temperature for 30 minutes before deflating.)

❸ Adjust oven racks to upper-middle and lower-middle positions and heat oven to 350 degrees. Line 2 rimmed baking sheets with parchment paper. Combine sea salt, pepper, and fennel seeds, if using, in small bowl.

❹ Press down on dough to deflate. Transfer dough to clean counter and divide in half. Working with 1 piece of dough at a time (keep remaining piece covered with plastic), press and stretch dough into 12 by 8-inch rectangle, with long side parallel to counter edge. Using pizza cutter or chef's knife, cut dough vertically into 16 (8 by ¾-inch) strips; cover loosely with greased plastic. Fold each strip in half and gently roll into 4-inch-long log. Cover and let rest for 5 minutes.

❺ On slightly damp counter, stretch and roll each log into 20-inch stick and transfer to prepared sheets. Brush sticks with oil and sprinkle with sea salt mixture. Bake until golden brown, 25 to 30 minutes, switching and rotating sheets halfway through baking. Slide grissini, still on parchment, onto wire racks and let cool completely, about 2 hours, before serving. (Grissini can be stored at room temperature for up to 2 weeks.)

Warm Anchovy and Garlic Dipping Sauce

Bagna cauda · Serves 8

WHY THIS RECIPE WORKS: As warm and comforting as fondue but with the subtle funk of anchovy and garlic, *bagna cauda* (literally, "hot bath") is a dipping sauce originating in Piedmont that's often eaten on Christmas Eve throughout northern Italy. Historically, anchovies weren't widely available in Piedmont, but they made their way into kitchens through barter with Liguria. Although bagna cauda has peasant origins, the way it's eaten—diners gather round, dipping vegetables and bread into the warm sauce—feels special and celebratory. Perfumed with the flavors of anchovy and garlic and enriched with a base of warm olive oil or cream, bagna cauda can be one of the most glorious culinary experiences you'll ever have—if done well. Otherwise, it can taste overly fishy or have a slick, greasy texture. We liked a thicker base made from cream rather than the common oil, as it wasn't greasy and didn't separate, and clung better to the vegetables; cream also melded and mellowed the flavors of the anchovies and garlic as they cooked. Before cooking the sauce, we briefly processed the anchovies and cream in the blender, which broke up the fillets and infused the cream with their flavor. The sauce needed 15 to 20 minutes over medium-low heat to thicken to just the right consistency for elegantly coating whatever we dipped into it. This sauce should be served warm; you can keep it in a fondue pot or double boiler, if desired. Serve with crudités-style vegetables and either bread or *Grissini* (opposite).

1 cup heavy cream
3 ounces anchovy fillets, drained (about 35 fillets)
1 tablespoon extra-virgin olive oil
5 large garlic cloves, minced
Pinch cayenne pepper
Salt and pepper

❶ Process heavy cream and anchovy fillets in blender until smooth, about 5 seconds; set aside.

❷ Heat oil, garlic, and cayenne in small saucepan over medium heat until garlic is translucent, about 2 minutes. Reduce heat to medium-low and add anchovy-cream mixture. Cook, stirring occasionally, until mixture is slightly thickened, 15 to 20 minutes. Season with salt and pepper to taste. Serve warm.

Risotto With Sausage and Beans

Paniscia · *Serves 8*

WHY THIS RECIPE WORKS: One of the most iconic dishes of Piedmont is a rich risotto that unites four staples of the region: high-starch Carnaroli rice; thick-skinned, creamy cranberry beans (*borlotti* in Italian); salumi; and robust red wine. In the city of Novara, *paniscia* is made by creating a hearty, brothy vegetable and bean soup and incorporating it into a risotto flavored with *salam d'la duja*, a lard-cured salame. Salam d'la duja is difficult to find outside of Italy, so we used a mild, Italian-style salame in its place. This dish is traditionally prepared using Carnaroli rice, but you can substitute Arborio rice. A medium-bodied dry red wine such as Barbera works well here. You may have broth left over once the rice is finished cooking; different rice products cook differently, and we prefer to err on the side of slightly too much broth rather than too little. If you do use all the broth and the rice has not finished cooking, add hot water as needed.

BEANS AND BROTH

Salt and pepper
8 ounces (1¼ cups) dried cranberry
    beans, picked over and rinsed
1 tablespoon extra-virgin olive oil
2 ounces pancetta, chopped fine
1 leek, white and light green parts
    only, halved lengthwise, chopped
    fine, and washed thoroughly
1 carrot, peeled and chopped fine
1 celery rib, chopped fine
1 zucchini, cut into ½-inch pieces
1 cup shredded red cabbage
1 small sprig fresh rosemary

RISOTTO

2 tablespoons extra-virgin olive oil
1 small onion, chopped fine
2 (½-inch-thick) slices salame
    (6 ounces), cut into ½-inch
    pieces
Salt and pepper
1½ cups Carnaroli rice
1 tablespoon tomato paste
1 cup dry red wine
2 teaspoons red wine vinegar

❶ For the beans and broth: Dissolve 1½ tablespoons salt in 2 quarts cold water in large container. Add beans and soak at room temperature for at least 8 hours or up to 24 hours. Drain and rinse well.

❷ Cook oil and pancetta in large saucepan over medium-low heat until pancetta is browned and fat is rendered, 5 to 7 minutes. Stir in leek, carrot, celery, zucchini, and cabbage and cook over medium heat until softened and lightly browned, 5 to 7 minutes. Stir in beans, rosemary sprig, and 8 cups water and bring to boil. Reduce heat to medium-low, cover, and simmer, stirring occasionally, until beans are tender and liquid begins to thicken, 45 minutes to 1 hour.

❸ Strain bean-vegetable mixture through fine-mesh strainer into large bowl. Discard rosemary sprig and transfer bean-vegetable mixture to separate bowl; set aside. Return broth to now-empty saucepan, cover, and keep warm over low heat.

❹ For the risotto: Heat 1 tablespoon oil in Dutch oven over medium heat until shimmering. Add onion, salame, and ½ teaspoon salt and cook until onion is softened, about 5 minutes. Add rice and cook, stirring frequently, until grain edges begin to turn translucent, about 3 minutes.

❺ Stir in tomato paste and cook until fragrant, about 1 minute. Add wine and cook, stirring frequently, until fully absorbed, about 2 minutes. Stir in 2 cups warm broth, bring to simmer, and cook, stirring occasionally, until almost fully absorbed, about 5 minutes.

❻ Continue to cook rice, stirring frequently and adding warm broth, 1 cup at a time, every few minutes as liquid is absorbed, until rice is creamy and cooked through but still somewhat firm in center, 14 to 18 minutes.

❼ Off heat, stir in bean-vegetable mixture, cover, and let sit for 5 minutes. Adjust consistency with remaining warm broth as needed (you may have broth left over). Stir in vinegar and remaining 1 tablespoon oil and season with salt and pepper to taste. Serve.

Agnolotti

Agnolotti · Serves 8 to 10

WHY THIS RECIPE WORKS: Regional differences in the cuisine of Italy are many, but almost every region has a filled pasta. These stuffed specialties vary, but each tells a story: They often contain the prized ingredients of their respective regions. Rich, pillow-shaped agnolotti, which are stuffed with a comforting, meltingly tender braised Piemontese meat filling and simply tossed in browned butter, are a standout example. Legend has it that after a victorious battle, a nobleman requested a celebratory meal from his chef. With little food on hand, the chef used leftover braised meat to fill egg pasta. But while the filling for agnolotti traditionally is made from leftovers, we don't usually have braised beef on hand, so we started from scratch. We chose boneless beef short ribs for their rich flavor and tender texture. Savoy cabbage, butter, and rosemary, all Piedmontese ingredients, enhanced the texture and flavor of the filling. The traditional way of shaping agnolotti is the simplest: Rather than having to cut, fill, and shape each piece, long rows of pasta are piped with filling and then pinched and cut at individual intervals. Take care when shaping agnolotti; pinching the pasta too tightly may cause the final shape to burst open. You can find Grana Padano at most well-stocked cheese counters; if not, you can substitute Parmigiano Reggiano. Our favorite pasta machine is the Marcato Altas 150 Wellness Pasta Machine; the pasta will be thin and semi-transparent when rolled to setting 7. For more information on rolling pasta sheets, see page 365.

FILLING

- 1½ pounds boneless beef short ribs, trimmed and cut into 1½-inch pieces
- Salt and pepper
- 2 tablespoons unsalted butter
- 2 cups chopped savoy cabbage
- 1 onion, chopped
- 3 garlic cloves, minced
- 2 teaspoons minced fresh rosemary
- ½ cup dry red wine
- 2 cups beef broth
- 1 ounce Grana Padano cheese, grated (½ cup)
- 1 large egg
- ⅛ teaspoon ground nutmeg

PASTA AND SAUCE

- 1 recipe Fresh Egg Pasta (page 364)
- 8 tablespoons unsalted butter
- ¼ cup hazelnuts, toasted, skinned, and chopped coarse
- ¼ teaspoon salt
- 2 teaspoons red wine vinegar
- 2 tablespoons minced fresh parsley
- 1 tablespoon salt

❶ For the filling: Pat beef dry with paper towels and season with salt and pepper. Melt butter in Dutch oven over medium-high heat. Brown beef on all sides, 7 to 10 minutes; transfer to plate.

❷ Add cabbage and onion to fat left in pot and cook over medium heat until softened, about 3 minutes. Stir in garlic and rosemary and cook until fragrant, about 30 seconds. Stir in wine, scraping up any browned bits, then stir in broth. Return beef and any accumulated juices to pot and bring to simmer. Reduce heat to medium-low, cover, and simmer until beef is tender, about 1 hour.

3 Drain beef mixture in fine-mesh strainer set over bowl. Reserve ¼ cup cooking liquid; discard remaining liquid. Transfer beef mixture and liquid to food processor; process until finely ground, about 1 minute, scraping down sides of bowl as needed. Add Grana Padano, egg, and nutmeg and process until combined, about 30 seconds. Transfer filling to bowl; refrigerate for 30 minutes. (Filling can be refrigerated for up to 24 hours; bring to room temperature before proceeding with recipe.)

4 For the pasta and sauce: Transfer dough to clean counter, divide into 5 pieces, and cover with plastic wrap. Flatten 1 piece of dough into ½-inch-thick disk. Using pasta machine with rollers set to widest position, feed dough through rollers twice. Bring tapered ends of dough toward middle and press to seal. Feed dough seam side first through rollers again. Repeat feeding dough tapered end first through rollers set at widest position, without folding, until dough is smooth and barely tacky. (If dough sticks to fingers or rollers, lightly dust with flour and roll again.)

5 Narrow rollers to next setting and feed dough through rollers twice. Continue to progressively narrow rollers, feeding dough through each setting twice, until dough is very thin and semi-transparent. (If dough becomes too long to manage, halve crosswise.) Transfer sheet of pasta to liberally floured sheet of parchment paper. Cover with second sheet of parchment, followed by damp kitchen towel, to keep pasta from drying out. Repeat rolling with remaining 4 pieces of dough, stacking pasta sheets between floured layers of parchment.

6 Liberally dust 2 rimmed baking sheets with flour. Transfer filling to 1-gallon zipper-lock bag. Snip off 1 corner of bag to create ¾-inch opening. Position 1 pasta sheet on lightly floured counter with long side parallel to counter edge (keep remaining sheets covered). Using pizza cutter or sharp knife, trim pasta into uniform 4-inch-wide sheet. Pipe filling lengthwise down center of sheet, leaving 1-inch border at each end. Lightly brush edges with water. Fold bottom edge of pasta over filling until flush with top edge. Gently press to seal long edge of pasta flush to filling; leave narrow edges unsealed. With index finger and thumb of both your hands facing downward, pinch filled portion of pasta together at 1-inch increments to create individual sections (about 15).

7 Using fluted pastry wheel or pizza cutter, trim excess dough from filled pasta strip, leaving ¼-inch border on ends and 1-inch border on top. Starting at bottom edge of strip, roll pastry wheel away from you in one motion between pinched sections to fold and seal dough and separate agnolotti. Pinch edges of each agnolotto to reinforce seal, then transfer to prepared sheets. Repeat with filling and shaping remaining pasta sheets (you should have about 75 agnolotti). Let agnolotti sit uncovered until dry to touch and slightly stiffened, about 30 minutes. (Agnolotti can be wrapped with plastic and refrigerated for up to 4 hours or chilled in freezer until firm, then transferred to zipper-lock bag and frozen for up to 1 month. If frozen, do not thaw before cooking; increase simmering time to 4 to 5 minutes.)

8 Cook butter, hazelnuts, and ¼ teaspoon salt in 12-inch skillet over medium-high heat, swirling skillet constantly, until butter is melted, has golden-brown color, and releases nutty aroma, about 3 minutes. Off heat, stir in vinegar; set aside. Bring 4 quarts water to boil in large pot. Add half of agnolotti and 1 tablespoon salt and simmer gently, stirring often, until edges of pasta are al dente, 3 to 4 minutes. Using slotted spoon, transfer agnolotti to skillet, gently toss to coat, and cover. Return cooking water to boil and repeat cooking remaining agnolotti; transfer to skillet. Add 2 tablespoons cooking water and gently toss to coat. Sprinkle with parsley and serve immediately.

SHAPING AGNOLOTTI

1. Fold bottom edge of pasta sheet over filling until flush with top edge. Gently press to seal long edge of pasta flush to filling.

2. With index finger and thumb of both your hands facing downward, pinch filled portion of pasta together through filling at 1-inch increments.

3. Trim excess dough from filled pasta strip. Starting at bottom edge of strip, roll pastry wheel away from you in one motion between pinched sections to fold and seal dough and separate agnolotti. Pinch edges of each agnolotto to reinforce seal.

Beef Braised in Barolo

Brasato al Barolo · Serves 6

....

WHY THIS RECIPE WORKS: Beef in Barolo is a hearty yet elegant braise enjoyed in households across the Piedmont region for holidays and special occasions. This pot roast is supreme because it's cooked in a full bottle of Barolo, often called the king of wines. Rich, full-bodied, and velvety, the wine reduces to an ultraluxurious and complex-tasting sauce that can't be achieved with a lighter-bodied wine. But it's not just the regal wine that makes this dish special; as Piedmont is a cattle-grazing region, the meat is abundant and prized for its lean yet intensely flavorful qualities. *Brasato al Barolo*'s purpose is to highlight these two ingredients, so our goal was twofold: to produce tender meat using an American cut (while some specialty butchers supply Piemontese beef, it's difficult to find and expensive in the United States) and to create a superlatively rich, savory wine sauce. We started with our favorite cut for braises, chuck-eye roast, which is uniform in shape, well-marbled, deeply flavored, and doesn't dry out after a long braise. But it has a line of fat in the middle that doesn't easily break down. Separating the meat at the seam enabled us to discard excess fat before braising and create two roasts, which cooked quicker than one large roast. We kept the aromatics simple and poured in a whole bottle of Barolo. To temper its bold flavor, we also added a can of diced tomatoes, and just ½ teaspoon of sugar balanced the wine's acidity. After 3 hours of braising in a low oven (which provided even, consistent heat), a dark, full-flavored, and lustrous sauce bestowed nobility on our humble cut of meat. Use a Dutch oven that holds 7 quarts or more for this recipe.

1 (3½- to 4-pound) boneless beef chuck-eye roast, pulled apart at seams and trimmed
Salt and pepper
2 (¼-inch-thick) slices pancetta (4 ounces), cut into ¼-inch pieces
2 onions, chopped
2 carrots, peeled and chopped
2 celery ribs, chopped
3 garlic cloves, minced
1 tablespoon tomato paste
1 tablespoon all-purpose flour
½ teaspoon sugar
1 (750-ml) bottle Barolo wine
1 (14.5-ounce) can diced tomatoes, drained
10 sprigs fresh parsley
1 sprig fresh rosemary
1 sprig fresh thyme, plus 1 teaspoon minced

❶ Adjust oven rack to middle position and heat oven to 300 degrees. Pat beef dry with paper towels and season generously with pepper. Using 3 pieces of kitchen twine, tie each piece of beef crosswise to form even roasts.

❷ Cook pancetta in Dutch oven over medium-low heat until browned and fat is rendered, about 8 minutes. Using slotted spoon, transfer pancetta to bowl. Pour off all but 2 tablespoons fat from pot.

❸ Heat fat left in pot over medium-high heat until just smoking. Brown roasts well on all sides, about 8 minutes; transfer to plate.

❹ Add onions, carrots, and celery to fat left in pot and cook over medium heat until softened and lightly browned, 6 to 8 minutes. Stir in garlic, tomato paste, flour, sugar, and pancetta and cook until fragrant, about 1 minute. Slowly whisk in wine, scraping up any browned bits and smoothing out any lumps. Stir in tomatoes, parsley sprigs, rosemary sprig, and thyme sprig.

❺ Nestle roasts into pot along with any accumulated juices and bring to boil. Cover pot tightly with large piece of aluminum foil, then cover with lid; transfer pot to oven. Cook until beef is tender and fork slips easily in and out of meat, about 3 hours, turning roasts every 45 minutes.

❻ Transfer roasts to carving board, tent with foil, and let rest while finishing sauce. Let braising liquid settle for 5 minutes, then skim excess fat from surface using large spoon. Stir in minced thyme. Bring liquid to boil and cook, whisking vigorously to help vegetables break down, until thickened and reduced to about 3½ cups, about 18 minutes. Strain sauce through fine-mesh strainer into bowl, pressing on solids to extract as much liquid as possible; you should have about 1½ cups strained sauce (if necessary, return strained sauce to pot and continue to boil until sauce reduces to 1½ cups). Discard solids. Season sauce with salt and pepper to taste.

❼ Remove twine from roasts, slice against grain into ½-inch-thick slices, and transfer to serving dish. Spoon half of sauce over meat and serve, passing remaining sauce separately.

Chocolate-Hazelnut Cake

Torta gianduia · *Serves 8*

WHY THIS RECIPE WORKS: Hazelnuts from Piedmont are truly something special with their fine flavor and extremely crisp texture. Although they're beloved in many dishes, the flavor combination of hazelnuts and chocolate, called *gianduia*, is a Piedmontese favorite. Sometimes gianduia refers to a fudge-like confection that's sold in bar form, sometimes to a spread (think: Nutella), and sometimes to the popular gelato flavor. But it's also a favorite in cakes, and just about any cake from the region that features chocolate and hazelnuts might be called *torta gianduia*—some are dressed-up and multilayered, while others are low, lush, and glazed. We love the classic rustic version with a crackly, crisp top and a moist, dense interior that's something like a nutty flourless chocolate cake. The taste and texture are dependent on a delicate balance of whipped eggs (for structure and lift), butter, sugar, bittersweet chocolate, and ground hazelnuts. The quantity of nuts was of particular import. We started with 6 ounces of chocolate and 1 cup of nuts, but found the chocolate overpowered the more delicate hazelnut flavor and the texture was actually too moist and fudgy. One and a third cups of nuts was better, but we still felt the cake could be lighter; we found that replacing a small amount of the nuts with regular flour—2 tablespoons—provided a rich, melt-in-the-mouth cake that wasn't overly weighty. All this super-rich cake needed to finish was a dusting of powdered sugar for rustic charm. Serve with lightly sweetened whipped cream.

6 ounces bittersweet chocolate, chopped

1⅓ cups hazelnuts, toasted and skinned

1 cup (7 ounces) granulated sugar

2 tablespoons all-purpose flour

¼ teaspoon salt

5 large eggs, separated, plus 1 large yolk

Pinch cream of tartar

8 tablespoons unsalted butter, softened

Confectioners' sugar

❶ Adjust oven rack to middle position and heat oven to 350 degrees. Grease 9-inch springform pan, line with parchment, then grease pan sides only.

❷ Microwave chocolate in bowl at 50 percent power, stirring occasionally, until melted, 2 to 4 minutes; let cool completely. Pulse hazelnuts, ¼ cup granulated sugar, flour, and salt in food processor until finely ground, about 10 pulses; set aside.

❸ Using stand mixer fitted with whisk attachment, whip egg whites and cream of tartar on medium-low speed until foamy, about 1 minute. Increase speed to medium-high and whip until stiff peaks form, 3 to 4 minutes; transfer to large bowl.

❹ Return now-empty bowl to mixer and beat butter and remaining ¾ cup granulated sugar on medium-high speed until pale and fluffy, about 3 minutes. Add egg yolks, one at a time, and beat until combined. Reduce speed to low, add cooled chocolate, and mix until just combined. Add hazelnut mixture and mix until just combined, scraping down sides of bowl as needed.

❺ Using rubber spatula, stir one-third of whites into batter. Gently fold remaining whites into batter until no white streaks remain. Transfer batter to prepared pan, smooth top, and gently tap pan on counter to release air bubbles. Bake until toothpick inserted halfway between center and outer rim of cake comes out clean, 45 to 50 minutes. (Center of cake will still be moist.)

❻ Let cake cool completely in pan on wire rack, about 3 hours. (Cooled cake can be wrapped in plastic wrap and refrigerated for up to 4 days; let sit at room temperature for 30 minutes before serving.) Run paring knife around edge of cake to loosen, then remove sides of pan. Invert cake onto sheet of parchment paper. Peel off and discard parchment baked onto cake. Turn cake right side up onto serving dish. Dust with confectioners' sugar and serve.

Liguria

Italy's Northern Mediterranean Paradise

LIGURIA, A NARROW MOUNTAINOUS ARC of coastline strung between the French Riviera and the Tuscan frontier, overlooks 200-plus miles of the radiant Mediterranean, a blessing that has profoundly shaped its psyche. The excellence of its cooking can be understood by a look at medieval history when Genoa, its capital city, was one of the four most powerful sea-republics in the known world. *Lupi di mare*—sea wolves—are what the Italians call their stock, shrewd men of the sea. While others were answering the highest call of the ages to capture Christ's sepulcher from the infidel, the Genoese, along with the people of Venice, Amalfi, and Pisa, were renting ships to crusaders deploying to the Holy Land. Their acumen and sailors' grit endowed the Genoese with a taste for the best.

This is the Italian Riviera, which extends outward from Genoa to the west (*ponente*) and to the east (*levante*). On the Riviera di Ponente, a mere 10 miles from Monte Carlo, sprawl the glitz and glamour of San Remo and places like it. But there is a feral side: bays and gold-sand beaches with the scents of wild herbs upon them. The Riviera di Levante is all enchanting towns of pinks and ochers nestled into seaside cliffs, and shimmering bays of azure. Names like Golfo Paradiso, Portofino, Rapallo, Cinque Terre, and Gulf of Poets evoke its color and romance.

A Culture of Green

Ligurians still cultivate ancient crops on the narrow strip of earth pinched between the

The five ancient villages known as Cinque Terre are a UNESCO World Heritage site.

> *The difference between focaccia and pizza? Focaccia is cooked in a baking pan and cut into portions. Pizza is baked directly on the oven floor and served whole.*

sea and the hillsides. Here you will find Quarantina potatoes, Pignona onions, Seborga black tomatoes, and Orco Feglino red chickpeas, as well as violet asparagus, spiny artichokes, and garlic that are the pride of Albenga. Campiglia's terraces are colored with the purples of saffron crocuses, while Imperia is covered in fields of lavender. Once dominated by primeval chestnut forests, the slopes are now carpeted with

Lemons

olives, vines, and fruit trees—principally apricots, oranges, cherries, lemons, apples, figs, and *chinotti*—tiny bitter oranges used to flavor drinks. It is the landscape of Eden.

If this is one of Italy's smaller regions, its four provinces, sprawled over a steep and rugged terrain, are distinguished for exceptional products. Imperia's olive oil is renowned throughout Italy. Savona is covered with fragrant pine forests, the source of *Pinus pinea,* the coveted Mediterranean pine nut that enriches traditional pesto genovese, the Ligurian sauce that has made its way around the world. Because of its deep waters, Genoa's port could harbor Russian ships loaded with massive cargoes of Taganrog, the wheat necessary for dried pasta manufacture, and it has been known since the 19th century for its superior *maccheroni*. La Spezia is a mecca for plump mussels and other seafood.

La Cucina Ligure

The cooking of Liguria is quite unlike that of its northern neighbors, except around the near-tropical environments surrounding lakes Garda and Como. Shaped by the seamen and the women who waited for them, the region's soul, paradoxically, dwells in the garden. Its kitchen—dubbed *la cucina del ritorno*, or the cuisine of return—comforted the sailor weary of eating little else but fish and hardtack at sea. Spiked with the aromatics of the native terroir, *la cucina ligure* is a beguiling amalgam of French, Arab, Greek, and Spanish—a true pan-Mediterranean feast.

If Ligurians are lavish in their use of fresh herbs, their thrift is applied in an adroit use of ingredients. Consider stuffed cabbage—what could be more pedestrian? But here, leaves of savoy are filled with a stuffing of veal, *luganega,* mortadella, Parmigiano Reggiano, porcini, onion, and marjoram, and tied into bundles for braising in broth and wine with a touch of tomato.

An inviting bar in Genoa's old town

Overall, Ligurians are stuffers of all things. Such is their fetish, they even love the stuffing alone, forming it into such treats as *scarpassa,* aromatic eggplant fritters. The predilection reaches its apex in *cima alla genovese,* boned veal breast rolled around a bread-herb-pistachio stuffing, itself rolled around hard-cooked eggs, the lot tied up and braised. This makes for a resourceful use of meat, and a beauteous sight to behold when cooled and sliced—luxurious fare on a poor man's budget. Even breads and pies are stuffed, such as the savory *torta pasqualina,* an Easter pie of cooked chard, *prescinsêua* (a tangy fresh cheese), Parmigiano Reggiano, nutmeg, and egg. The original was enclosed in 33 layers of flaky crust to symbolize Jesus' years on earth, but modern versions hold at three, a holy number all the same. And there's the blissful paper-thin stuffed *focaccia di Recco,* filled with oozy *stracchino* cheese.

Like the rest of the Mediterranean, this is pasta and focaccia country, but with a Ligurian twist. *Croxetti* are thin disks of egg pasta stamped with royal insignia that hark back to their origins—dainties designed for noble weddings. Pillowy *pansöuti,* filled with the aforementioned *prescinsêua* and escarole or borage, may be the mother of all stuffed pastas if you consider that facsimiles—*agnolotti, cappelletti,* and the whole tribe—were called "gloves in the style of Genova" before aliases evolved. Focaccia can also take many forms, from the most simple, *fügassa al rosmarino,* a flatbread studded with rosemary sprigs, to *sardenara*—tomato, onion, and anchovy-topped flatbread created around 1500 for Adm. Andrea Doria—to *farinata* (*socca* in France), the flourless chickpea pancake redolent with rosemary.

Cured cod has been the staple stuff of maritime peoples at least since the first Viking hung a filet out to dry at sea. There are two types: *baccalà* and *stoccafisso.* The differences between them create endless confusion, confounded by the fact that even people who live on them refer to one as the other. For baccalà, the cod is gutted, skinned, boned, and cut into halves before being salted and dried. Stoccafisso is saltless; the fish cleaned and preserved skin-on, bone-in, and draped whole onto poles to dry in the wind. The first is more convenient, but the second is more delicate. Liguria cooks both in every way the imagination allows, using the spectrum of their aromatics. And naturally, they stuff it.

Touches of Genius

There is brilliance in the Ligurian "less is more" way of doing things. Take their ubiquitous *tõcchi* (touches), what we call sauces and what the Italians call *condimenti,* used for everything from topping pasta to flavoring fish dishes. Besides the queen of all, *pesto genovese,* there is *salsa di noci,* walnut sauce for stuffed pasta; *agliata,* a tangy garlic and vinegar condiment; *tõcco d'arrosto,* roasted meat drippings; and mushroom, artichoke, and baby clam variations. Liguria's cuisine is luxurious, like her pedigree, but like old money, resourceful and discriminating. *La necessità aguzza l'ingegno,* the Italians say, "Necessity sharpens ingenuity."

TERROIR TO TABLE
PESTO WITH A PEDIGREE

The very emblem and essence of Liguria's cooking is basil, an obsession that goes back to ancient times. A chronicler of the Holy Wars wrote that Genovese troops poised beneath the walls of Jerusalem during the First Crusade gave themselves away by its piercing smell on their breath. Returning home, they found their way to port following the scent of wild basil wafting from the hillsides—the same variety used in Genoa's pesto today. Lest you think all basil pesto is the same, the Ligurians will set you straight. There is *pesto genovese,* the real thing, and its pretenders. The Genovese Pesto Consortium, founded in 2011, has codified the true recipe. According to tradition, the correct pasta varieties to support the unctuous sauce are *trenette, trofie,* or potato gnocchi. *Basta.*

Rosemary Focaccia

Focaccia alla genovese · Makes two 9-inch round loaves

WHY THIS RECIPE WORKS: Centuries ago, focaccia began as a by-product: When bakers needed to gauge the heat of the wood-fired oven—focaccia stems from *focolare* and means "fireplace"—they would tear off a swatch of dough, flatten it, drizzle it with olive oil, and pop it into the hearth to bake as an edible oven thermometer. From there evolved countless variations on the theme—the stuffed pizza-like focaccia in Puglia and Calabria, the ring-shaped focaccia in Naples, focaccia made from rich or lean doughs, and even sweet versions. That said, it's the dimpled, chewy, herb-topped deep-dish *focaccia alla genovese* that's most fundamental. As is traditional, our recipe starts with a sponge—a mixture of flour, yeast, and water that ferments for at least 6 hours before it's added to the bulk dough. The sponge helps develop gluten (which gives breads structure and chew), depth of flavor, and a hint of tang. Rather than knead the dough, we simply used a series of gentle folds, which developed the gluten structure further while also incorporating air for a tender interior crumb. (This method was also helpful because our dough was quite wet and therefore difficult to knead; the more hydrated a bread dough, the more open and bubbly its crumb—a characteristic we were looking for in focaccia—because steam bubbles form and expand more readily.) Fruity olive oil is a requisite ingredient, but when we added it straight to the dough, it turned the bread dense and cakelike. Instead, we baked the bread in cake pans coated with a couple tablespoons of oil. Be sure to reduce the temperature immediately after putting the loaves in the oven.

SPONGE
½ cup (2½ ounces) all-purpose flour
⅓ cup water, room temperature
¼ teaspoon instant or rapid-rise yeast

DOUGH
2½ cups (12½ ounces) all-purpose flour
1¼ cups water, room temperature
1 teaspoon instant or rapid-rise yeast
Kosher salt
¼ cup extra-virgin olive oil
2 tablespoons chopped fresh rosemary

❶ For the sponge: Stir all ingredients in large bowl with wooden spoon until well combined. Cover tightly with plastic wrap and let sit at room temperature until sponge has risen and begins to collapse, about 6 hours (sponge can sit at room temperature for up to 24 hours).

❷ For the dough: Stir flour, water, and yeast into sponge with wooden spoon until well combined. Cover bowl tightly with plastic and let dough rest for 15 minutes.

❸ Stir 2 teaspoons salt into dough with wooden spoon until thoroughly incorporated, about 1 minute. Cover bowl tightly with plastic and let dough rest for 30 minutes.

❹ Using greased bowl scraper (or rubber spatula), fold dough over itself by gently lifting and folding edge of dough toward middle. Turn bowl 45 degrees and fold dough again; repeat turning bowl and folding dough 6 more times (total of 8 folds). Cover tightly with plastic and let rise for 30 minutes. Repeat folding and rising. Fold dough again, then cover bowl

tightly with plastic and let dough rise until nearly doubled in size, 30 minutes to 1 hour.

❺ One hour before baking, adjust oven rack to upper-middle position, place baking stone on rack, and heat oven to 500 degrees. Coat two 9-inch round cake pans with 2 tablespoons oil each. Sprinkle each pan with ½ teaspoon salt. Transfer dough to lightly floured counter and dust top with flour. Divide dough in half and cover loosely with greased plastic. Working with 1 piece of dough at a time (keep remaining piece covered), shape into 5-inch round by gently tucking under edges.

❻ Place dough rounds seam side up in prepared pans, coat bottoms and sides with oil, then flip rounds over. Cover loosely with greased plastic and let dough rest for 5 minutes.

❼ Using your fingertips, gently press each dough round into corners of pan, taking care not to tear dough. (If dough resists stretching, let it relax for 5 to 10 minutes before trying to stretch it again.) Using fork, poke surface of dough 25 to 30 times, popping any large bubbles. Sprinkle 1 tablespoon rosemary evenly over top of each loaf, cover loosely with greased plastic, and let dough rest until slightly bubbly, about 10 minutes.

❽ Place pans on baking stone and reduce oven temperature to 450 degrees. Bake until tops are golden brown, 25 to 30 minutes, rotating pans halfway through baking. Let loaves cool in pans for 5 minutes. Remove loaves from pans and transfer to wire rack. Brush tops with any oil remaining in pans and let cool for 30 minutes. Serve warm or at room temperature.

Chickpea Flour Pancake

Farinata · *Serves 6 to 8*

WHY THIS RECIPE WORKS: Stroll the narrow streets of Genoa and you're sure to spot golden *farinata* batter being poured across a wide, shallow copper pan and popped into a wood-burning pizza oven. Farinata is a savory chickpea flour pancake typically eaten as a mid-morning or midafternoon snack. The pan and the oven contribute to a pancake that's crispy and lacy at the edges—fried, almost—but that retains a creamy, custardy interior. The recipe itself is simple—a crêpe-like batter is made from just chickpea flour, water, and salt—but finding the right cooking method to replicate this dish in a home oven was a challenge. The key turned out to be cast iron—a preheated 12-inch cast-iron skillet was

the closest approximation we found to a traditional pan, and its excellent heat retention gave our pancake a wonderfully crisped bottom and edges, and an evenly cooked, custardy interior. Farinata is often served plain or with just one or two adornments. We preferred fresh rosemary and a sprinkling of freshly ground black pepper, both of which complemented the salty, savory pancake. Chickpea flour is also sold as garbanzo bean flour and is available in most well-stocked supermarkets. You will need a well-seasoned 12-inch cast-iron skillet for this recipe. To season your skillet, heat it over medium-low heat for 5 minutes, then add ½ teaspoon of vegetable oil and wipe the interior thoroughly with

paper towels until it is lightly covered with oil and turns dark and semi-glossy, with no uneven patches or excess oil. Let cool and proceed with recipe as directed.

> **1 cup (4½ ounces) chickpea (garbanzo bean) flour**
> **2 cups water**
> **¾ teaspoon salt**
> **3 tablespoons extra-virgin olive oil**
> **1 tablespoon chopped fresh rosemary**
> **Coarse sea salt**
> **Pepper**

❶ Whisk chickpea flour, water, and salt in large bowl until smooth. Cover and let sit at room temperature for at least 4 hours or up to 24 hours.

❷ Adjust oven rack to upper-middle position and heat oven to 400 degrees. Heat 12-inch cast-iron skillet over medium heat for 3 minutes. Add oil, swirl to coat evenly, and heat until shimmering. Add rosemary and cook until fragrant, about 30 seconds.

❸ Whisk batter to recombine and pour into skillet. Transfer skillet to oven and bake until top of pancake is dry and golden and edges begin to pull away from sides of skillet, 35 to 40 minutes. Remove skillet from oven and heat broiler.

❹ Return skillet to oven and broil until pancake is spotty brown, 1 to 2 minutes. Let pancake cool slightly in skillet on wire rack for 5 minutes. Using thin spatula, loosen edges and underside of pancake from skillet, then carefully slide pancake onto cutting board. Sprinkle with sea salt and pepper to taste. Cut into wedges and serve warm.

Pasta With Walnut Sauce

Pasta con salsa di noci · *Serves 6 to 8*

WHY THIS RECIPE WORKS: The temperate Mediterranean climate and forested hills of Liguria make it a perfect environment for a wide range of wild greens, herbs, and nuts to flourish. Some of these go into *salsa di noci*, a thick, rich, creamy pasta sauce made with walnuts and herbs. Some recipes include pine nuts (also plentiful nearby), but we preferred recipes that used only walnuts for clean, rounded walnut flavor. Toasting the walnuts gave the sauce greater depth, and using a combination of ground walnuts and coarsely chopped pieces offered a balance of background richness and textural contrast. Cooking the pasta just shy of al dente and then finishing it in the sauce—stirring it in with a generous amount of the pasta's starchy cooking water—ensured that every bite was perfectly tender and well-coated. A sprinkling of fresh marjoram, which grows freely on the region's hillsides, finished the dish with a soft herbal note. In Liguria, this sauce is traditionally served over a filled pasta called pansotti, or a ribbon-like pasta called trenette. Fettucine, linguine, and tagliatelle are wider than trenette, but work well as substitutes if you can't find trenette. We prefer the flavor and texture of fresh pasta here, but dried can be used as well. For more information on making your own fresh pasta, see page 364.

1½ cups walnuts, toasted
1¼ cups heavy cream
1 ounce Parmigiano Reggiano cheese, grated (½ cup)
Salt and pepper
1 pound fresh or dried trenette
1 teaspoon minced fresh marjoram or oregano, plus extra for serving

❶ Process 1 cup walnuts in food processor until finely ground, about 10 seconds; transfer to bowl. Pulse remaining ½ cup walnuts in now-empty processor until coarsely chopped, about 2 pulses.

❷ Bring cream to simmer in 12-inch skillet over medium heat and cook until thickened slightly, about 2 minutes. Whisk in ground and chopped walnuts, Parmigiano, ¾ teaspoon salt, and ½ teaspoon pepper; cover to keep warm.

❸ Meanwhile, bring 4 quarts water to boil in large pot. Add pasta and 1 tablespoon salt and cook, stirring often, until almost al dente. Reserve 1½ cups cooking water, then drain pasta and return it to pot. Add sauce, 1 cup reserved cooking water, and marjoram and toss to combine. Bring to simmer over medium heat and cook, tossing frequently, until pasta is tender and most of sauce has been absorbed, about 2 minutes. Adjust consistency with remaining ½ cup cooking water as needed. Season with salt and pepper to taste. Serve immediately in warmed bowls, sprinkling with extra marjoram.

Whole Roasted Branzino

Branzino al forno • *Serves 4*

WHY THIS RECIPE WORKS: Liguria's coastline is 220 miles long, so the region's culture is shaped by the sea. Although seafood surprisingly isn't always considered Ligurians' most prized meal—upon returning home, fishermen prefer food with a focus on the fresh produce that comes from the region's rich soil—salty air and al fresco dining make branzino, a European sea bass, a common dish in the region, as it is in coastal areas all over Italy. More so than in America, Italians favor cooking fish whole. Roasted whole, branzino is simplicity at its finest, and this easy technique delivers deep flavor to the mild white fish. Placing the fish on a rimmed baking sheet allowed for plenty of air circulation, which gave the branzino a firm, flaky texture, and a brief stint in a hot oven helped it stay moist. Shallow slashes in the skin ensured even cooking and seasoning, and also allowed us to gauge the doneness of the fish easily. We infused the branzino with flavor by rubbing it with an intense citrusy salt made from a combination of lemon zest, orange zest, salt, and pepper, and stuffing it with sliced oranges. We served it with a quick herby citrus vinaigrette. If branzino isn't available, you can substitute sea bass. Fish weighing more than 2 pounds will be hard to maneuver on the sheet and should be avoided.

6 tablespoons extra-virgin olive oil
¼ cup minced fresh parsley, stems reserved
2 teaspoons grated lemon zest plus 2 tablespoons juice
2 oranges (1 sliced into ¼-inch-thick rounds, 1 grated and juiced to yield 2 teaspoons zest and 2 tablespoons juice)
1 shallot, minced
⅛ teaspoon red pepper flakes
Salt and pepper
2 (1½- to 2-pound) whole branzino, scaled, gutted, fins snipped off with scissors

❶ Adjust oven rack to middle position and heat oven to 500 degrees. Line rimmed baking sheet with parchment paper and grease parchment. Whisk ¼ cup oil, minced parsley, lemon juice, orange juice, shallot, and pepper flakes together in bowl. Season with salt and pepper to taste; set aside for serving.

❷ Combine lemon zest, orange zest, 1½ teaspoons salt, and ½ teaspoon pepper in second bowl. Rinse each branzino under cold running water and pat dry with paper towels inside and out. Using sharp knife, make 3 or 4 shallow slashes, about 2 inches apart, on both sides of branzino. Open cavity of each branzino and sprinkle 1 teaspoon salt mixture on flesh. Stuff cavities with orange slices and parsley stems. Brush 1 tablespoon oil on outside of each branzino and season with remaining salt mixture; transfer to prepared sheet and let sit for 10 minutes.

❸ Roast until branzino flakes apart when gently prodded with paring knife and registers 140 degrees, 15 to 20 minutes.

❹ Carefully transfer branzino to cutting board and let rest for 5 minutes. Fillet branzino by making vertical cut just behind head from top of fish to belly; discard citrus slices. Make another cut along top of branzino from head to tail. Use spatula to lift meat from bones, starting at head end and running spatula over bones to lift out fillet. Repeat on other side of branzino. Discard head and skeleton. Whisk dressing to recombine and serve with branzino.

SERVING WHOLE FISH

1. Make vertical cut just behind head from top to belly, then cut along back of fish from head to tail.

2. Starting at head and working toward tail, use metal spatula to lift meat away from bones. Repeat on second side.

Trofie Pasta With Pesto, Potatoes, and Green Beans

Trofie alla genovese · *Serves 6 to 8*

WHY THIS RECIPE WORKS: Liguria is the land of herbs, and any dish labeled *alla genovese* (in the style of Genoa) will feature them—from *Focaccia alla genovese* (page 66), which is sprinkled with rosemary, to this pasta dish, which is coated in the most famous Ligurian herb recipe of all: basil pesto. *Trofie alla genovese* features intricate little twisted tubes of pasta that trap pesto in their coils, as well as green beans and potatoes—the former satisfying Ligurians' love for fresh, crisp vegetables, and the latter soaking up the flavorful pesto and bringing the dish together by lending the sauce body. The key to this dish lies in the treatment of the potatoes. The most successful recipes—those that turned out creamy and light versus dull and heavy—call for cutting the potatoes into chunks and then, once cooked, vigorously mixing them with the pasta and green beans. The agitation sloughs off their corners, which dissolve into the dish, pulling the pesto and cooking water together to form the sauce. We used lower-starch red potatoes rather than more conventional russets, whose tendency to cook up mealy gave the sauce a rough texture. Trofie is the traditional pasta for this dish, but spiraling gemelli works well as a substitute if you can't find trofie. We prefer the flavor and texture of fresh pasta here, but dried can be used as well.

12 ounces green beans, trimmed and cut into 1½-inch lengths
Salt and pepper
1 pound red potatoes, peeled and cut into ½-inch pieces
1 pound fresh or dried trofie
2 tablespoons unsalted butter, cut into ½-inch pieces and chilled
1 tablespoon lemon juice
¾ cup Pesto alla genovese (opposite)

❶ Bring 4 quarts water to boil in large pot. Add green beans and 1 tablespoon salt and cook until tender, 5 to 8 minutes. Using slotted spoon, transfer green beans to rimmed baking sheet.

❷ Return water to boil, add potatoes, and cook until tender but still hold their shape, 9 to 12 minutes. Using slotted spoon, transfer potatoes to sheet with green beans.

❸ Return water to boil, add pasta, and cook, stirring often, until al dente. Reserve 1½ cups cooking water, then drain pasta and return it to pot. Add butter, lemon juice, green beans, potatoes, pesto, ½ teaspoon pepper, and 1¼ cups reserved cooking water and stir vigorously with rubber spatula until sauce takes on creamy appearance. Adjust consistency with remaining ¼ cup cooking water as needed. Season with salt and pepper to taste. Serve immediately.

Basil Pesto

Pesto alla genovese · *Makes about 1½ cups; enough for 2 pounds pasta*

WHY THIS RECIPE WORKS: While variations on pesto in many regions feature a variety of herbs and nuts, the pure herbaceous basil sauce comes from Liguria, and this provenance is important. Seaside humidity and near-constant sunshine produce *basilico genovese*, which is superior to that found elsewhere; it has smaller leaves and is sweeter and free of any minty afterbite. And of course, *pesto alla genovese* includes the region's delicious olive oil. Traditional recipes call for pounding all the ingredients—basil, cheese, garlic, salt, and, sometimes, local pine nuts—with a mortar and pestle and making a paste with olive oil. (Pesto derives from the Italian verb *pestare*, which means "to pound.") Hoping to make quicker work of the recipe, we turned to the food processor; but, as Ligurians caution, the sauce was harsh. (The metal blades of a blender or food processor, they claim, ruin the flavor, as the pounding action of pesto processed by hand releases the basil's flavorful oils.) Fortunately, we found a perfect compromise: We gently pounded the basil to release those oils before processing it. A bit of parsley helped us replicate the fresher flavor of pesto made with sweeter Ligurian basil. While we liked a full garlic presence, we toasted the garlic to help tame its fiery flavor and keep our pesto as sweet as that found in Genoa. And where did we come down on nuts? Recipes vary between calling for pine nuts and walnuts; we thought pine nuts added nice richness and body, and we liked their sweetness, so we include a generous amount. When you're tossing the pesto with cooked pasta, it's important to add some pasta cooking water to achieve the proper sauce consistency.

6 garlic cloves, unpeeled
½ cup pine nuts
4 cups fresh basil leaves
¼ cup fresh parsley leaves
1 cup extra-virgin olive oil
1 ounce Parmigiano Reggiano
   cheese, grated fine (½ cup)
Salt and pepper

❶ Toast garlic in 8-inch skillet over medium heat, shaking skillet occasionally, until softened and spotty brown, about 8 minutes. When garlic is cool enough to handle, remove and discard skins and chop coarse. Meanwhile, toast pine nuts in now-empty skillet over medium heat, stirring often, until golden and fragrant, 4 to 5 minutes.

❷ Place basil and parsley in 1-gallon zipper-lock bag. Pound bag with flat side of meat pounder or with rolling pin until all leaves are bruised.

❸ Process garlic, pine nuts, and herbs in food processor until finely chopped, about 1 minute, scraping down sides of bowl as needed. With processor running, slowly add oil until incorporated. Transfer pesto to bowl, stir in Parmigiano, and season with salt and pepper to taste. (Pesto can be refrigerated for up to 3 days or frozen for up to 3 months. To prevent browning, press plastic wrap flush to surface or top with thin layer of olive oil. Bring to room temperature before using.)

Lombardy

Connoisseurs of Country Cuisine

···

LOMBARDY, THE INDUSTRIAL HEART OF ITALY, is all about business, and Milan, the regional capital, is all about the business of style. During fashion week, the chic restaurants are filled with glamorous Milanese wearing right-off-the-runway fashion. Swanky luncheon spots are packed shoulder pad to shoulder pad with elegantly suited men who dine on such regional specialties as *cotoletta alla milanese*, crispy veal rib chops on the bone, fried in butter. Milan, the seat of the Italian stock exchange, is dressy and

determined. The dialect is easy to understand, the people obey traffic laws, and the women wear high heels every day.

Lombardy is also a major agricultural area, one of the largest in Italy, producing a range of foods that are appreciated around the world. Their agricultural success is built on two factors: a variable ecology, with both mountains and plains nourished by a sophisticated water supply system, and a mind for marketing. A tradition of trade and a passion for commerce has supported Lombardy's specialties. Indeed, Lombards are connoisseurs of their regional foods.

Man-Made Paradise

Lombardy is about the size of Vermont, bordering Switzerland to the north, and kissing all the northern Italian regions except for remote Valle d'Aosta and Friuli–Venezia Giulia. Its northern half lies in the foothills and mountains of the Alps, home of exceptional

The elegant Galleria Vittorio Emanuele II embodies the grandeur of Milan.

A vineyard of Franciacorta DOCG, the sparkling wine of Lombardy

As payment for completing "The Last Supper" in Santa Maria delle Grazie church in 1497, Ludovico Sforza, the Duke of Milan, gifted Leonardo da Vinci a small vineyard across the street.

meat and dairy products. Lombardian cattle produce marvelous cheeses—including mascarpone, the secret to many Italian desserts—as well as unique meat products, such as *bresaola,* Lombardy's incomparable dried beef. The north is also home to the glacial lakes Como, Maggiore, Iseo, and the eastern bank of Lake Garda. Fresh fish—including carp, trout, eels, and caviar from sturgeon farms—are collected, and dishes such as *agoni,* little fishes dried and preserved with bay leaf, are served lakeside.

From these lakes the region's major rivers, the Sesia, Ticino, Adda, and Mincio, flow south to the massive Po. The lake regions enjoy dramatic Alpine scenery and exotic microclimates that allow for the quixotic cultivation of grapes, lemons, and olives. Studded with fancy villas owned by international celebrities and nobility, the lake district is what Winston Churchill once called "the last word in modern millionairism."

The southern half of the region is composed of soft hills, rich plains, and marshlands. Part of the sweeping Po Valley, the vast farms of Lombardy are managed by an irrigation system with ancient roots; some of the waterworks were designed by Leonardo da Vinci. This system ensured water was delivered to all viable corners of the region, and it fostered the development of villages, towns, and industry such as grain mills. Through the manipulation of water, the Lombards created a lush landscape that the writer Elena Kostioukovitch dubbed a "man-made paradise."

On these prosperous southern plains grow rice, wheat, corn, and buckwheat. In foggy Lombardy, as throughout the north, it is more common to eat polenta and rice than pasta, which only became popular after World War II. Lombardy, like Piedmont, grows a lot of rice for export, but also frequently uses it in soups and innumerable risotto recipes, from opulent dishes such as *risotto alla certosina,* rice cooked with frog's legs, crayfish, and perch fillets in a savory onion and leek sauce; to one of Lombardy's most famous dishes, *risotto alla milanese,* golden and aromatic with saffron; to simpler fare including *risotti rusti,* rice cooked with pork and beans. Maize flour makes polenta, which is combined with plenty of butter and cheese, and sauced with such tasty combinations as ground salt pork and fresh garlic. Lombards also grow buckwheat, called *grano saraceno,* or Saracen wheat, and use it in pasta dough and polenta. Lombardian farms produce an abundance of fruits specifically designated for their place of origin under DOP status, such as melons, apples, and pears, as well as vegetables, from pumpkins to asparagus. It is in Lombardy that Julius Caesar may have been introduced to asparagus with butter sauce.

From Herders to Kings

Lombardy's cuisine is the legacy of the herding peoples who populated the area after the fall of the Roman Empire. The most significant immigrants were the Lombards or Langobards (from the Old German for long beards), a Germanic tribe from the Rhineland that settled in the area in the sixth century. They gave the region its name and a cuisine based on butterfat. They also memorialized Italy's famous Easter sweet bread, the dove-shaped *colomba.* The story goes that the Lombardian king Alboin was set to

Milan's splendid Gothic cathedral took nearly 600 years to complete.

In elegant restaurants, bars, and cafés all over Lombardy glistening fruits are displayed in glass jars: tiny white pears, bloodred cherries, and segments of tangerine. This is *mostarda,* fruits preserved in simple syrup flavored with fiery mustard oil, a dramatic condiment served with cheese or boiled meats like *bollito misto.* There are regional *mostarde* in Lombardy, but the most famous, *mostarda di Cremona,* is made with whole fruits. *Mostarda* probably began as cooked grape must, called *mosto ardente—* the reduced remains of pressed grapes—which may be the origin of the word. On the other hand, "mostarda" means "mustard" in Italian and mustard seed has been on the peninsula a long time. Roman recipes called for mustard, and it's likely they exported the seed to Gaul, where it eventually made its way to Dijon.

Upon the advice of their doctors, royal households in Renaissance Milan coated their food with a dusting of gold as a remedy for heart ailments.

massacre the city of Pavia (founded by Romans and occupied by Latins), but was persuaded otherwise when a beautiful girl offered him the cake, shaped in the symbol of reconciliation. He ended up making Pavia his capital.

The Lombards were deposed by the Holy Roman Empire in the eighth century and city-based power struggles ushered in the era of autonomous city-states. Although their alienation from one another fomented constant war, it also allowed for the evolution of city-centric food specialties. Today there are 12 provinces in Lombardy—with Bergamo and Brescia being the biggest outside of Milan—and arguably 12 Lombardian cuisines.

During the Renaissance, the Milan and Mantua duchies dominated Lombardy, and in the 18th and 19th centuries, the French and Austrians dominated the land. Their influence on the local cuisine may be seen in the region's predilection for cream sauces and meats stewed and braised. In contrast to grilled and roasted meats, beef dishes such as *stufato* are stewed at length with wine and vegetables. The Milanese rose up and in 1861 helped crown Victor Emmanuel II, first king of a unified Italy. After the formation of the Italian Republic in 1946, Lombardy concentrated on business and finance.

A Wealth of Food, a Food of Wealth

Throughout its history Lombardy has been a busy marketplace and the cuisine here is a reflection of the populace's business-first culture. It's not uncommon for Lombards

The butchers at Peck, Milan's ultimate purveyor of meats, cheeses, and other fine Italian specialty products

Amaretto is a sweet liqueur flavored with apricot pits, almond pits, or both, from Saronno near Varese. Legend says the drink was invented in the 1500s by the lover of one of Leonardo da Vinci's pupils. (The brand Amaretto di Saronno, now known as Disaronno Originale, dates from 1851.) It is said Amaretti di Saronno, a similarly flavored almond cookie available internationally, was baked for the Cardinal of Milan's visit in 1719 by two lovers. They paired two of these dry, light, and marvelously crunchy macaroons in one package wrapped in colorful paper, representing their love. Other records suggest these cookies originated in Venice in the mid-1600s. Either way, the Lazzaroni family of Saronno controls the narrative: It has guarded the recipe since 1719.

Crunchy, sweet amaretto cookies

to grab food on the go—a *panino milanese* (fried chicken cutlet on a roll) perhaps, or a paper cone of *sciatt,* crispy buckwheat fritters filled with melted cheese, to eat standing up. But the cuisine of Lombardy is also characterized by the region's discernment, its ability, as a marketplace, to pick and choose. It has done so from within its own territory, conducting trade between the mountains and the plains, and with all its neighbors. Pavia was on the Venetian trade route where the Ticino meets the Po, and merchants from France, Spain, England, and Germany went there to buy goods imported by the Venetians.

Similarly, Milan lies between the Adda and the Ticino, where navigable canals were built as early as the 12th century connecting these rivers to the city and allowing for trade from the port of Venice all the way to the northern border lakes. Inter- and intra-regional commerce has been going on for so long that the trading mentality has become cultural.

Probably the ultimate example of this is the elegant Peck in Milan, founded in 1883. It's a fantastic emporium of *salumi,* cheese, and other exquisite food specialties representing the region's many products, including *violino di capra,* a goat meat prosciutto whose form resembles a violin (the violin-maker Stradivarius was from Cremona in Lombardy). Peck sells delicate Bitto cheese from the provinces of Sondrio and Bergamo, and sweet, creamy *stracchino* from Brescia. *Stracco* means "tired," and it refers to the state of the cows after making their migration from the high mountain meadows where they graze in the summer to the valleys for the winter. Grana Padano cheese from Lodi is also for sale at Peck. It's similar to Parmigiano Reggiano, but mistake the two in front of a northern Italian at your own risk. The true Gorgonzola from its namesake town in

Milan province is served throughout Lombardy, where stracchino and Gorgonzola are combined to make cheese sauce for pasta that is so creamy, savory, and salty it's practically immoral.

The Connoisseurs of a Farmhouse Cuisine

The Lombards may be gourmets, but they are nonetheless attached to their peasant cuisine. They prefer rib-sticking egg pasta dishes, such as *tortelli* or *cappellacci* filled with the famous pumpkin of Mantua and Ferrara, and *casonsei,* a kind of ravioli stuffed with sweet and savory ingredients such as ground beef, raisins, salumi, and crushed amaretto cookies. The same simple fare that is served on the farm is also in the restaurants, such as *pizzoccheri,* a wide buckwheat pasta tossed with chard and potatoes, creamy with cheese. Lombardian comfort food includes such dishes as *zuppa alla pavese,* beef stock with a raft of butter-fried bread and soft poached eggs, and *taroz,* a mash of onion, green beans, and potatoes.

Milanese sophisticates do enjoy their city's sleek eateries and the modern cuisines they serve, and that's in line with the Lombard's curatorial tastes. But it's the restaurants serving country dishes such as osso buco (crosscut veal shanks braised with carrots, onions, and celery, white wine, and broth) or beef stewed until it surrenders in Garda olive oil that are consistently crowded. It's Lombardian farm food that ultimately sustains the bankers in sunglasses and the editors in furs.

The charming harbor at Varenna, on glamorous Lake Como

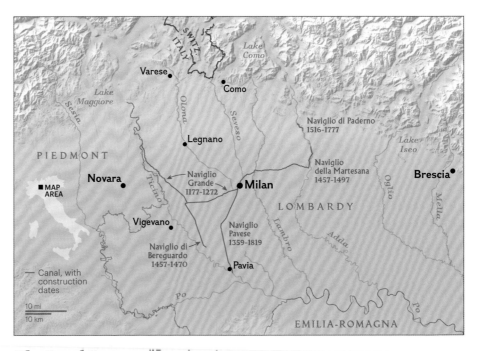

The Canal System of Lombardy During the Renaissance, Lombardy's canal system was the most extensive in Europe and transported goods and produce.

Dry-Aged Beef With Arugula and Parmigiano

Bresaola con rucola e Parmigiano • *Serves 6*

WHY THIS RECIPE WORKS: Bresaola is the sweet, ultrameaty, and aromatic result of dry-curing beef top round. True bresaola, made only in the Valtellina and Valchiavenna areas of Lombardy where the cool, dry climate is perfect for air-curing, now carries a protected geographic indication seal. Rich, salty bresaola is commonly served thinly sliced as part of a salumi board; however, we wanted a light, stand-alone bresaola antipasto. While you can make bresaola at home, the process is time-consuming and there's no mimicking the unique flavor with domestic meats, so finding true bresaola is worth the effort. We paired our star ingredient with just enough peppery arugula, which we tossed with fruity extra-virgin olive oil and bright lemon juice, to balance the meat's earthiness. We finished with some fresh cracked pepper and a healthy shaving of Parmigiano for a dish that's beautiful in its simplicity. You can find bresaola at most well-stocked deli counters.

4 ounces thinly sliced bresaola
1 cup baby arugula
2 teaspoons extra-virgin olive oil, plus extra for serving
1 teaspoon lemon juice, plus lemon wedges for serving
Salt and pepper
Shaved Parmigiano Reggiano cheese

Arrange bresaola in even layer over large serving dish, overlapping slices slightly. Toss arugula with oil and lemon juice and season with salt and pepper to taste. Top bresaola with arugula and Parmigiano and drizzle with extra oil. Serve with lemon wedges.

Braised Veal Shanks

Osso buco · *Serves 6*

WHY THIS RECIPE WORKS: Likely originating from farmhouse cooking in Lombardy in the 19th century, osso buco has been embraced all over Italy. In Milan, the recipe is a staple; it's traditionally served with *Risotto alla milanese* (opposite) for a rare *piatto unico* in Italy—a one-dish meal that combines both the primi and secondi courses. It's quite magical: Slow, steady cooking renders tough (but gelatin-rich) veal shanks (each diner is meant to get an individual one) remarkably tender and turns a simple broth of carrots, onion, celery, wine, and stock into a velvety sauce. For some, the best part is the luscious bone marrow, which diners extract using a small spoon. We sought to create a flavorful, foolproof braising liquid and cooking technique that produced a rich sauce true to this venerable recipe. First, we deepened the flavor of store-bought stock with lots of aromatics. We then oven-braised the shanks; this was the easiest method, and the natural reduction that took place left just the right amount of liquid in the pot. Finally, we stirred gremolata—a traditional accompaniment featuring minced garlic, parsley, and lemon zest—into the sauce to brighten the hearty dish.

VEAL SHANKS

6 (14- to 16-ounce) veal shanks,
   1½ inches thick
Salt and pepper
6 tablespoons extra-virgin olive oil
2½ cups dry white wine
2 onions, chopped
2 carrots, peeled and chopped
2 celery ribs, chopped
6 garlic cloves, minced
2 cups chicken broth
1 (14.5-ounce) can diced tomatoes,
   drained
2 bay leaves

GREMOLATA

¼ cup minced fresh parsley
3 garlic cloves, minced
2 teaspoons grated lemon zest

1 For the veal shanks: Adjust oven rack to lower-middle position and heat oven to 325 degrees. Pat shanks dry with paper towels and season with salt and pepper. Tie piece of twine around thickest portion of each shank to keep meat attached to bone while cooking. Heat 2 tablespoons oil in Dutch oven over medium-high heat until just smoking. Brown half of shanks on all sides, 8 to 10 minutes; transfer to large bowl. Repeat with 2 tablespoons oil and remaining shanks; transfer to bowl. Off heat, add 1½ cups wine to now-empty pot and scrape up any browned bits. Pour liquid into bowl with shanks.

2 Heat remaining 2 tablespoons oil in again-empty pot until shimmering. Add onions, carrots, and celery and cook until vegetables are softened and lightly browned, 8 to 10 minutes. Stir in garlic and cook until lightly browned, about 1 minute. Stir in broth, tomatoes, bay leaves, and remaining 1 cup wine and bring to simmer.

3 Nestle shanks into pot along with deglazing liquid. Cover pot, leaving lid slightly ajar, and transfer to oven. Cook until veal is tender and fork slips easily in and out of meat, but meat is not falling off bone, about 2 hours.

4 For the gremolata: Combine all ingredients in small bowl. Remove pot from oven and discard bay leaves. Stir half of gremolata into braising liquid and season with salt and pepper to taste. Let sit for 5 minutes.

5 Transfer shanks to individual bowls and discard twine. Ladle braising liquid over shanks and sprinkle with remaining gremolata. Serve.

Saffron Risotto

Risotto alla milanese • *Serves 6*

WHY THIS RECIPE WORKS: Risotto is a simple rice dish elevated beyond the prosaic by its voluptuously creamy texture. Of the many risotto dishes that dot northern Italy, *risotto alla milanese* is at once one of the simplest and most luxurious, because it's flavored with the most globally prized spice, saffron, which perfumes the dish with its floral aroma. The risotto is typically served on its own as a rich but delicate *primo* or as an accompaniment to *Osso buco* (opposite). The dish's origin is a subject of debate: One legend claims that it was invented in the 1500s by a Milanese glassmaker who earned the nickname "Zafferano" because he used saffron often to make gold stain. When he was jokingly challenged to add it to risotto, he did! However, the recipe's first appearance in an Italian cookbook wasn't until the 1800s. Perhaps it originated from Milan's ties to Spain, or a Milanese affinity for the golden color, or possibly the idea that saffron was beneficial to health. Risotto, Milanese or otherwise, achieves its creamy texture through constant stirring, which causes the rice to release its starch. We toasted the saffron in butter, which magnified its flavor, helped break up the threads, and distributed it throughout the rice. This dish is traditionally prepared using Carnaroli rice, but you can substitute Arborio rice. You may have broth left over once the rice is finished cooking; different rice products cook differently, and we prefer to err on the side of slightly too much broth rather than too little. If you do use all the broth and the rice has not finished cooking, add hot water as needed.

3½ cups chicken broth
3 cups water
4 tablespoons unsalted butter
1 onion, chopped fine
Salt and pepper
2 cups Carnaroli rice
¼ teaspoon saffron threads, crumbled
1 cup dry white wine
2 ounces Parmigiano Reggiano cheese, grated (1 cup)

❶ Bring broth and water to simmer in medium saucepan. Cover and keep warm over low heat.

❷ Melt butter in Dutch oven over medium heat. Add onion and ½ teaspoon salt and cook until softened, about 5 minutes. Add rice and saffron and cook, stirring frequently, until grain edges begin to turn translucent, about 5 minutes.

❸ Add wine and cook, stirring frequently, until fully absorbed, about 2 minutes. Stir in 3½ cups warm broth, bring to simmer, and cook, stirring occasionally, until almost fully absorbed, 10 to 12 minutes.

❹ Continue to cook rice, stirring frequently and adding warm broth, 1 cup at a time, every few minutes as liquid is absorbed, until rice is creamy and cooked through but still somewhat firm in center, 14 to 18 minutes. Remove pot from heat, cover, and let sit for 5 minutes. Adjust consistency with remaining warm broth as needed (you may have broth left over). Stir in Parmigiano and season with salt and pepper to taste before serving.

Buckwheat Pasta With Swiss Chard, Potatoes, and Taleggio

Pizzoccheri della Valtellina · *Serves 6*

WHY THIS RECIPE WORKS: Earthy and toothsome, *pizzoccheri* are short ribbons of fresh buckwheat pasta (a local specialty) that mingle with melted cheese, bitter greens, and soft potatoes in this traditional wintry dish from Valtellina. Wheat doesn't grow locally in the mountainous areas of Lombardy and other northern Italian regions, but buckwheat does. Despite its name, buckwheat isn't related to wheat; it's an herb, and its seeds are ground to make flour, which local cooks have historically used to make pasta. Because buckwheat flour contains no gluten, modern pasta

recipes combine it with white flour for a workable dough with pleasant chew. Rolling the pasta slightly thicker than most, like we do for lasagna noodles, and cooking the pasta briefly gave it a pleasant toothsomeness. Valtellina Casera, the alpine cheese commonly used in this dish, is hard to find in the United States. Taleggio, another cheese of Lombardy, was the perfect stand-in; it has a fruity tang and its strong yet milky flavor stood up to the earthy buckwheat; it also maintained a creamy consistency when melted. (Fontina, another frequently substituted cheese, became stretchy and rubbery when melted and wound up clumping in the greens.) Swiss chard and savoy cabbage are commonly used here; we loved chard's tender leaves and slightly bitter, vegetal flavor for our version. Finally, we cut russet potatoes into cubes; the starchy edges melted into and thickened the cheese sauce. Buckwheat flour can be found in natural food stores and well-stocked supermarkets. You can find Taleggio at most well-stocked cheese counters. Our favorite pasta machine is the Marcato Altas 150 Wellness Pasta Machine; the pasta will be thin but opaque when rolled to setting 6. For more information on rolling pasta sheets, see page 365.

PIZZOCCHERI

7½ ounces (1½ cups) all-purpose flour, plus extra as needed
2¾ ounces (½ cup) buckwheat flour
3 large eggs, lightly beaten

VEGETABLES AND SAUCE

3 tablespoons unsalted butter
1 tablespoon minced fresh sage
1 garlic clove, minced
2 pounds Swiss chard, stemmed and chopped coarse
8 ounces russet potatoes, peeled and cut into ½-inch pieces
Salt and pepper
6 ounces Taleggio cheese, rind removed, cut into ¼-inch pieces

1 For the pizzoccheri: Pulse all-purpose flour and buckwheat flour in food processor until combined, about 5 pulses. Add eggs and process until mixture forms cohesive dough that feels soft and is barely tacky to touch, about 45 seconds. (If dough sticks to fingers, add up to ¼ cup extra all-purpose flour, 1 tablespoon at a time, until barely tacky. If dough doesn't become cohesive, add up to 1 tablespoon water, 1 teaspoon at a time, until it just comes together; process 30 seconds longer.)

2 Transfer dough to clean counter and knead by hand to form smooth, round ball, about 2 minutes. Cover tightly with plastic wrap and let rest at room temperature for at least 15 minutes or up to 2 hours.

3 Transfer dough to clean counter, divide into 5 pieces, and cover with plastic. Flatten 1 piece of dough into ½-inch-thick disk. Using pasta machine with rollers set to widest position, feed dough through rollers twice. Bring tapered ends of dough toward middle and press to seal. Feed dough seam side first through rollers again. Repeat feeding dough tapered end first through rollers set at widest position, without folding, until dough is smooth and barely tacky. (If dough sticks to fingers or rollers, lightly dust with flour and roll again.)

4 Narrow rollers to next setting and feed dough through rollers twice. Continue to progressively narrow rollers, feeding dough through each setting twice, until dough is thin but opaque; transfer to lightly floured counter. (If dough becomes too long to manage, halve crosswise.) Let pasta sheet sit uncovered until dry to touch and slightly stiffened, about 10 minutes. Repeat rolling and drying remaining dough.

5 Using pizza cutter or sharp knife, cut pasta sheets into 2 by ¾-inch strips. Toss lightly with flour and transfer to rimmed baking sheet. (Pasta can be wrapped with plastic and refrigerated for up to 4 hours or chilled in freezer until firm, then transferred to zipper-lock bag and frozen for up to 1 month. If frozen, do not thaw before cooking.)

6 For the vegetables and sauce: Melt butter in Dutch oven over medium-high heat. Add sage and garlic and cook until fragrant, about 1 minute. Add chard, one handful at a time, and cook, stirring occasionally, until wilted and most liquid has evaporated, about 8 minutes. Cover and keep warm over low heat.

7 Meanwhile, bring 4 quarts water to boil in large pot. Add potatoes and 1 tablespoon salt and cook until just tender, 5 to 8 minutes. Using slotted spoon, transfer potatoes to bowl. Stir Taleggio, ¼ cup cooking water, and ½ teaspoon salt into chard until cheese is melted and sauce is smooth.

8 Return cooking water to boil. Add pasta and cook, stirring often, until al dente, 2 to 3 minutes. Reserve ¼ cup cooking water, then drain pasta. Add pasta and potatoes to chard mixture and gently toss to combine. Season with salt and pepper to taste. Adjust consistency with reserved cooking water as needed before serving.

Panettone

Panettone · Makes 2 loaves

WHY THIS RECIPE WORKS: Originating in Milan, panettone is a tall, luxurious, candied- and dried fruit–filled sweet bread that was once the bread of emperors and popes and made only during the Christmas season in northern Italy. Now you can find panettone even in American supermarkets, though these overly fluffy, preservative-filled versions pale in comparison to what's found in the bakeries of Italy. We wanted to develop a recipe that was worthy of its regal history but simple enough to make at home. All of the fat that makes panettone decadent—from butter, eggs, and extra yolks—can also make the bread dense and crumbly. To remedy this, we used high-protein bread flour and kneaded the dough in a stand mixer for 8 minutes before incorporating softened butter to ensure the dough had a strong gluten structure to support all that fat. We gave the rising dough a series of folds and let it rise overnight in the refrigerator; elongated fermentation maximized gas development from the yeast in the dough, resulting in a remarkably light, fluffy texture and slightly tangy flavor. You can find paper panettone molds online or at kitchen supply stores. Be sure to reduce the oven temperature immediately after putting the loaves in the oven.

1¼ cups (6¼ ounces) golden raisins

1½ tablespoons grated orange zest plus ¼ cup juice

5 cups (27½ ounces) bread flour

2 tablespoons instant or rapid-rise yeast

1½ teaspoons salt

2 cups whole milk, room temperature

4 large eggs plus 3 large yolks, room temperature

⅔ cup (1¾ ounces) sugar

2 teaspoons vanilla extract

1 teaspoon almond extract

8 tablespoons unsalted butter, cut into 8 pieces and softened

1¼ cups (6 ounces) finely chopped candied orange peel

1 Microwave raisins and orange juice in covered bowl until steaming, about 1 minute. Let sit until raisins have softened, about 15 minutes. Drain raisins and reserve orange juice.

2 Whisk flour, yeast, and salt together in bowl of stand mixer. Whisk milk, eggs and yolks, sugar, vanilla, almond extract, and reserved orange juice in 4-cup liquid measuring cup until sugar has dissolved. Using dough hook on low speed, slowly add milk mixture to flour mixture and mix until cohesive dough starts to form and no dry flour remains, about 5 minutes, scraping down bowl as needed.

3 Increase speed to medium-low and knead until dough is elastic but still sticks to sides of bowl, about 8 minutes. With mixer running, add butter, 1 tablespoon at a time, and knead until butter is fully incorporated, about 4 minutes. Continue to knead until dough is satiny and elastic and very sticky, about 3 minutes. Reduce speed to low, slowly add candied orange peel, raisins, and orange zest and mix until incorporated, about 3 minutes. Transfer dough to lightly greased large bowl or container, cover tightly with plastic wrap, and let rise for 30 minutes.

4 Using greased bowl scraper (or your fingertips), fold dough over itself by gently lifting and folding edge of dough toward middle. Turn bowl 90 degrees and fold dough again; repeat turning bowl and folding dough 2 more times (total of 4 folds). Cover tightly with plastic and let dough rise for 30 minutes. Fold dough again, then cover bowl tightly with

plastic and refrigerate for at least 16 hours or up to 48 hours.

5 Let dough sit at room temperature for 1½ hours. Press down on dough to deflate. Transfer dough to well-floured counter, divide in half, and cover loosely with greased plastic. Press 1 piece of dough (keep remaining piece covered) into 6-inch round. Working around circumference of dough, fold edges toward center until ball forms. Flip ball seam side down and, using your cupped hands, drag in small circles on counter until dough feels taut and round and all seams are secured on underside. Repeat with remaining piece of dough.

6 Place dough rounds into two 6 by 4-inch paper panettone molds, pressing dough gently into corners. Transfer to wire rack set in rimmed baking sheet, cover loosely with greased plastic, and let rise until loaves reach 2 inches above lip of molds and dough springs back minimally when poked gently with your knuckle, 3 to 4 hours.

7 Adjust oven rack to middle position and heat oven to 400 degrees. Using sharp paring knife or single-edge razor blade, make two 5-inch-long, ¼-inch-deep slashes with swift, fluid motion along top of each loaf to form cross.

8 Place baking sheet in oven and reduce oven temperature to 350 degrees. Bake until loaves are deep golden brown, about 40 minutes, rotating sheet halfway through baking. Tent loaves with aluminum foil and continue to bake until loaves register 190 to 195 degrees, 20 to 30 minutes. Let loaves cool completely on wire rack, about 3 hours, before serving.

Trentino–Alto Adige

Where the Foods of Austria and Italy Merge

DURING A PRESENTATION OF LOCAL HISTORY by the Trentino–Alto Adige Trade Commission, an audience of food journalists were shown a series of slides illustrating famous locals: a mountaineer, a rocket engineer, a "freedom fighter" who defied Napoleon when he tried to confiscate the local wine, and at the end, Ötzi, the mummy. • Ötzi, named after the Ötztal Alps in which he was found by a couple of German hikers in 1991, died around 3000 B.C. His well-preserved corpse has supplied a treasure trove of information about

what Neolithic Trentino–Alto Adigians were like and what they ate. Incredibly, it revealed a food still being enjoyed: Ötzi's last meal included smoked prosciutto, aka speck (or an early version of it), the region's most famous cured meat.

The Apple Basket of Europe

Ötzi's homeland is almost completely mountainous. The craggy Dolomites rise abruptly from lush valley floors and the nooks and crannies between peaks are dotted with small glacial lakes filled with salmon. Trentino–Alto Adige borders Austria to the north, Switzerland to the northwest, Lombardy to the west, and Veneto to the south. Today miles and miles of meticulously pruned orchards hug the highways, and vineyards climb the mountains' flanks. Medieval castles crumble on every promontory, isolated cabins seem airlifted into forests, and the farms and villages are charming and tidy. Even the cell phone stores sport window boxes full of flowers.

Bordering Austria and Switzerland, a place both Italian and Tyrolean

The Adige is the principal river (Alto Adige means "beyond the river") and it flows south through the region's two provinces: Bolzano in the north and Trento in the south, to Verona and the Lombardy Plain. Much of the region is forested, filled with wild mushrooms and herbs such as lady's mantle and tart wood sorrel, pine buds, and elderberry flowers that are used to flavor cheeses, soups, and sauces. But the valleys are populated and intensely cultivated. The Vinschgau Valley, between the Adige and Isarco Rivers, is Europe's largest self-contained apple-growing area, representing a third of all apples produced in Italy. This is the sunny side of the Alps, home to a small but well-regarded wine region. Cattle and dairy cows are raised on the valley slopes, producing cheeses such as the strong Puzzone di Moena and aromatic Stelvio. In the valley bottoms, rye is grown in the north, and corn and wheat in the south. In an ancient gruel called *mus,* cornmeal and wheat are combined with milk, and enriched with butter and cheese.

In the first century the Romans dominated here, and there are remnants of their culture, particularly in the Ladin, or pig Latin–speaking villages. But by 1027 the Holy Roman Empire had taken over and the region eventually became a bishopric of the Roman Catholic Church, attracting a large ecclesiastic population. They recognized so many holy days when meat was forbidden that the diet evolved to be grain-based. As a result, the region retains a grand tradition of bread and dumpling cookery.

But the primary foreign influence on Trentino–Alto Adigian culture and food is Austrian, which has had a presence in the region for over five centuries. The Dolomites are geographically and culturally at a crossroads between Italy to the south and Tyrol to the north. Indeed, Bolzano region is also known as Südtirol. The Adige River is an important passage connecting Italy to northern Europe, and the region, on the front lines between the Austria-Hungary border and Italy, saw heavy fighting during World War I. But after that war it was annexed by Italy, and after World War II, it gained autonomy, which pretty much freed it from the nuttiness of politics emanating from Rome.

Austrian-Italian Influences

Trentino–Alto Adige has evolved into a fascinating blend of cultures. Within an hour you can be sipping wine in a vineyard or climbing a glacier. The picturesque villages might have a sturdy Italian Gothic tower or an onion-domed Tyrolian steeple. Every sign is written in both German and Italian. That it's the best of both worlds becomes clear if you've ever tried to buy a stamp in Italy or pined for a little elegance in Austria. Here, the trains run on time and you can get fabulous panini in the station.

The food scene is derived from both Austrian and Italian culinary styles. The cuisine *di casa* tends to be heavy and simple, though in some restaurants modern sensibilities predominate. Here, you might be offered a shot glass of asparagus foam with speck chips by a waitress in a dirndl.

Of the two provinces, Bolzano trends more German—black bread prevails—and

Trento more Italian—white and yellow bread claim the majority. Bread overall is an important staple, and each valley has its own specialty. The most famous is *Schüttelbrot,* a thin crunchy bread made from leavened rye and flavored with caraway or fennel. These distinct breads happily make distinct bread crumbs, which find their way into softball-size *knödel* (aka *canederli*), boiled bread dumplings flavored with a range of ingredients including speck, cheese, nutmeg, and liver, then served in savory broths or with a silky butter sauce.

Speck, the region's tender and sweet smoked prosciutto

Ancient Trentino–Alto Adigian farmers only baked four times a year, so breads were made to last: Schüttelbrot has been known to last 20 years.

Vegetables here reflect the Austrian table more than the Italian. The region is famous for its white asparagus, thick as candles. Cabbage, parsnips, and potatoes are widely used, primarily in meat dishes such as goulash, sauerbraten, and potato and beef pies.

The Speck Smoking Tradition

In bars and trattorias all over the region one can make a meal of cheese, sliced apples, and the excellent speck, Trentino–Alto Adige's signature smoked prosciutto, served with a puff of grated horseradish. Lean and tasty, speck combines the good strong smoky quality of Germany's black forest ham with the yielding tenderness of Prosciutto di San Daniele. A visit to Bolzano's delicious, beery Speckfest in May celebrates the region's many producers and speck's many uses: as a flavoring in dumplings, for example; or wrapped around a trout and baked; on sandwiches with hard-cooked eggs; or served under a blanket of sliced porcini mushrooms from the forests.

In most traditional Ladin homes and in many contemporary hotels in Trentino–Alto Adige, the region's robust foods and great wines are enjoyed in the *stube,* a cozy, wood-paneled room with oompah-pah charm. Outfitted with hand-carved wooden chairs and tables, and warmed by a wood-burning stove, the stube was often the most important room in the house. Contemporary stubes would have seemed like a palace to Neolithic Ötzi. But under whatever circumstances he had his last meal, when he set out on his trek over the Dolomites, he stopped somewhere and ate wild herbs, cured meat, and bread—the Trentino–Alto Adige's eternal foods.

Half Moon Stuffed Pasta With Spinach and Ricotta

Mezzelune · Serves 6

WHY THIS RECIPE WORKS: The countries that border Trentino–Alto Adige have an undeniable influence on the local Alpine cuisine. But while this mountainous region is known for its cold, snowy winters and love of hearty pork-based dishes, it's actually a meat-free dish that stands out. *Mezzelune* is derived from the pierogi-like half-moon Austrian ravioli called *schlutzkrapfen* (the terms can be used interchangeably), and its simple filling of rich, soft

ricotta cheese and fresh spinach is a celebration of the region's ingredients. In our version, we stayed true to the recipe's roots and kept the filling simple; sautéed shallot was the only aromatic element our filling needed. We briefly cooked the minced spinach to rid it of excess water and avoid a soggy filling. We opted for frozen spinach over fresh spinach for its easy preparation, and tasters noted no difference in flavor. Rich ricotta cheese, sharp Asiago cheese, and an egg yolk for binding brought the filling together. Our favorite pasta machine is the Marcato Altas 150 Wellness Pasta Machine; the pasta will be thin and semi-transparent when rolled to setting 7. For more information on rolling pasta sheets, see page 365.

FILLING

- **2 tablespoons unsalted butter**
- **1 shallot, minced**
- **10 ounces frozen chopped spinach, thawed and squeezed dry**
- **Salt**
- **8 ounces (1 cup) whole-milk ricotta cheese**
- **1½ ounces Asiago cheese, grated (¾ cup), plus extra for serving**
- **1 large egg yolk**

MEZZELUNE

- **8 ounces Fresh Egg Pasta (page 364)**
- **6 tablespoons unsalted butter**
- **Salt**

1 For the filling: Melt butter in small saucepan over medium heat. Add shallot and cook until softened, about 3 minutes. Stir in spinach and ¼ teaspoon salt and cook until spinach is dry, about 1 minute; transfer to large bowl and let cool slightly. Stir in ricotta, Asiago, and egg yolk until well combined. Refrigerate until ready to use. (Filling can be refrigerated for up to 24 hours.)

2 For the mezzelune: Transfer dough to clean counter, divide into 3 pieces, and cover with plastic wrap. Flatten 1 piece of dough into ½-inch-thick disk. Using

pasta machine with rollers set to widest position, feed dough through rollers twice. Bring tapered ends of dough toward middle and press to seal. Feed dough seam side first through rollers again. Repeat feeding dough tapered ends first through rollers set at widest position, without folding, until dough is smooth and barely tacky. (If dough sticks to fingers or rollers, lightly dust with flour and roll again.)

3 Narrow rollers to next setting and feed dough through rollers twice. Continue to progressively narrow rollers, feeding dough through each setting twice, until dough is very thin and semi-transparent. (If dough becomes too long to manage, halve crosswise.) Transfer sheet of pasta to liberally floured sheet of parchment paper. Cover with second sheet of parchment, followed by damp kitchen towel, to keep pasta from drying out. Repeat rolling with remaining 2 pieces of dough, stacking pasta sheets between floured layers of parchment.

4 Liberally dust 2 rimmed baking sheets with flour. Cut 1 pasta sheet into rounds on lightly floured counter using 3-inch round cookie cutter (keep remaining sheets covered); discard scraps. Place 1½ teaspoons filling in center of each round. Working with 1 pasta round at a time, lightly brush edges with water. Fold bottom edge of pasta over filling until flush with top edge to form half-moon shape. Press to seal edges flush to filling and transfer to prepared sheets. Repeat cutting and filling remaining pasta (you should have about 30 mezzelune). Let mezzelune sit uncovered until dry to touch and slightly stiffened, about 30 minutes. (Mezzelune can be wrapped with plastic and refrigerated for up to 4 hours or chilled in freezer until firm, then transferred to zipper-lock bag and frozen for up to 1 month. If frozen, do not thaw before cooking; increase simmering time to 3 to 4 minutes.)

5 Melt butter in 12-inch skillet over medium heat; set aside. Bring 4 quarts water to boil in large pot. Add half of mezzelune and 1 tablespoon salt and simmer gently, stirring often, until edges of pasta are al dente, 2 to 3 minutes. Using slotted spoon, transfer mezzelune to skillet, gently toss to coat, and cover to keep warm. Return cooking water to boil and repeat cooking remaining mezzelune; transfer to skillet. Add ½ teaspoon salt and gently toss to coat. Top individual portions with extra Asiago before serving.

SHAPING MEZZELUNE

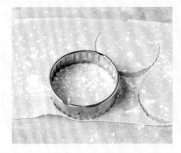

1. Cut pasta sheet into rounds on lightly floured counter using 3-inch round cookie cutter. Place 1½ teaspoons filling in center of each round.

2. Lightly brush edges of pasta round with water. Fold bottom edge of pasta over filling until flush with top edge to form half-moon shape. Press to seal edges flush to filling.

Bread Dumplings

Canederli · Serves 6

WHY THIS RECIPE WORKS: There aren't many dishes more humble and rustic than *canederli*, a typical dish of Trentino–Alto Adige in which stale bread is soaked in a flavorful egg, milk, and speck custard; formed into balls; and then boiled in broth. Remarkably similar to the classic German and Austrian dish *knödel*, the Italian riff features speck, which is arguably the region's most beloved addition to Italian cuisine. The cured-then-smoked ham lends richness, salinity, and a touch of smokiness to the dish. Waiting for bread to stale didn't sound very practical so we employed a shortcut: We baked sandwich bread in a 250-degree oven for 45 minutes to mimic the crisp, dry texture without the wait. Soaking the bread in a moderate amount of custard proved important (too much and the dumplings fell apart during cooking), as did allowing the bread enough time to soften (otherwise the bread wouldn't cohere into dumplings). We loved the idea of serving these dumplings in broth, but didn't want to spend hours creating one from scratch. Instead we fortified store-bought broth with more speck, parsley stems, and onion, giving it homemade flavor without all the hassle. You can find speck at most well-stocked deli counters, but you can also substitute an equal amount of plain bacon.

BROTH

4 cups chicken broth
1 onion, halved
1 ounce speck
5 parsley stems
Salt and pepper

DUMPLINGS

6 slices hearty white sandwich bread, cut into ½-inch pieces
1 tablespoon unsalted butter
1 small onion, chopped fine
4 ounces speck, chopped fine
Salt
⅛ teaspoon pepper
Pinch nutmeg
¾ cup whole milk
2 large eggs
2 tablespoons minced fresh chives
2 tablespoons minced fresh parsley

1 For the broth: Combine the chicken broth, onion, speck, and parsley in small saucepan and bring to simmer. Reduce heat to medium-low, cover, and cook for 15 minutes. Strain broth through fine-mesh strainer into bowl, pressing on solids with rubber spatula to extract as much liquid as possible; discard solids. (Broth can be refrigerated for up to 24 hours.) Return broth to now-empty saucepan, cover, and keep warm over low heat. Season with salt and pepper to taste.

2 For the dumplings: Adjust oven rack to middle position and heat oven to 250 degrees. Spread bread into even layer on rimmed baking sheet and bake, stirring occasionally, until dried and crisp throughout, about 45 minutes; let bread cool completely.

3 Melt butter in 12-inch skillet over medium heat. Add onion, speck, ¼ teaspoon salt, and pepper and cook until onion is softened, about 5 minutes. Stir in nutmeg and cook until fragrant, about 30 seconds; let cool slightly.

4 Whisk milk and eggs in large bowl until well combined. Stir in bread, onion mixture, 1 tablespoon chives, and 1 tablespoon parsley until well combined. Let bread mixture sit until softened, stirring occasionally, about 20 minutes.

5 Using your dampened hands, firmly pack bread mixture into rounded 2 tablespoon–size dumplings (about 18 dumplings) and transfer to large plate. (Dumplings can be refrigerated for up to 24 hours.)

6 Bring 4 quarts water to boil in large pot. Add 1 tablespoon salt, then carefully drop dumplings into water and simmer gently until tender and cooked through, 5 to 7 minutes. Using slotted spoon, transfer dumplings to paper towel–lined plate and let drain briefly. Transfer dumplings to individual bowls, spoon warm broth over top, and sprinkle with remaining 1 tablespoon chives and 1 tablespoon parsley. Serve.

Mushroom Ragù

Misto di funghi · *Serves 4*

WHY THIS RECIPE WORKS: The wooded north of Italy is a treasure trove of mushrooms: Beyond the famous white truffle, foragers hunt for countless wild edible varieties that can be found throughout Trentino–Alto Adige. The bounty is often stewed and served over soft polenta. To re-create this combination in our kitchen, we started with a mix of dried and fresh mushrooms. Dried porcini delivered depth of flavor similar to more obscure fresh Italian varieties, while a combination of chanterelle mushrooms—which are native to northern Italy and the very best wild mushrooms you can find in the U.S.—and portobellos provided deep, nutty flavor and meaty texture, respectively. Developing flavorful fond with 2 pounds of moisture-rich mushrooms took quite a lot of time, so we jump-started the cooking process in the microwave. After 6 minutes the mushrooms were tender and had released a fair amount of their juice (which we added to our deglazing liquid). Red wine, garlic, thyme, and canned diced tomatoes rounded out the flavors of our stew, which made an ideal topping for spooning over a bowl of *Polenta concia* (page 38). You can also serve the stew over pasta, although this preparation is not traditional. You can substitute any wild mushrooms for the chanterelles in this recipe.

1 pound portobello mushroom caps, gills removed, halved, and sliced ½ inch thick

18 ounces chanterelle mushrooms, trimmed and halved if small or quartered if large

2 tablespoons unsalted butter

1 onion, chopped fine

½ ounce dried porcini mushrooms, rinsed and minced

Salt and pepper

3 garlic cloves, minced

1 teaspoon minced fresh thyme or ¼ teaspoon dried

½ cup dry red wine

1 (14.5-ounce) can diced tomatoes, drained with juice reserved, chopped

2 tablespoons minced fresh parsley

1 recipe Polenta concia (page 38)

1 Microwave portobello mushrooms and chanterelle mushrooms in covered bowl, stirring occasionally, until tender and mushrooms have released their liquid, 6 to 8 minutes. Transfer mushrooms to colander set in bowl and let drain, reserving liquid.

2 Melt butter in Dutch oven over medium heat. Add onion, porcini, and ½ teaspoon salt and cook until softened and lightly browned, 5 to 7 minutes. Add mushrooms and cook, stirring often, until dry and lightly browned, about 5 minutes. Stir in garlic and thyme and cook until fragrant, about 30 seconds.

3 Stir in wine and reserved mushroom liquid, scraping up any browned bits. Stir in tomatoes and their juice, bring to simmer, and cook until ragù is slightly thickened, about 8 minutes. Off heat, stir in parsley and season with salt and pepper to taste. Serve over polenta.

Apple Strudel

Strudel di mele · *Serves 6*

WHY THIS RECIPE WORKS: Apple strudel, with its flaky pastry crust and lightly sweetened filling, may be more recognizable as a classic Austrian dessert, but it's also made in northern Italy and holds a special place in the cuisine of Trentino–Alto Adige. Something like half of all apples sold in Italy come from the small area known as Val di Non, so it's no wonder that this Alpine region produces a *strudel di mele* to rival any produced by its northern neighbor. Traditional recipes are laborious, calling for kneading an unleavened dough that's rolled, stretched until it's so thin it's transparent, and then wrapped around a filling of chopped apples (tossed with sugar, cinnamon, a handful of dried fruit, and a distinctly Italian addition, pine nuts). Store-bought phyllo dough was a winning replacement for the handmade dough; it's far easier to work with and produced equally crispy layers. For the filling, we employed a trick we've used for other apple desserts to ensure the apples didn't end up mushy. Parcooking the apple pieces in the microwave set off an enzymatic reaction that caused the pectin in the fruit to set, ensuring the apple pieces would hold their shape while also releasing some of their liquid (which we captured to brush on the strudel just before baking). Some panko bread crumbs absorbed any extra moisture. Finally, slicing each strudel into thirds after baking allowed excess steam to escape and ensured the phyllo remained flaky. Gala apples can be substituted for the Golden Delicious apples. Phyllo dough is also available in larger 18 by 14-inch sheets; if using, cut them in half to make 14 by 9-inch sheets. Thaw phyllo in the refrigerator overnight or on the counter for 4 to 5 hours; don't thaw it in the microwave.

1¾ pounds Golden Delicious apples, peeled, cored, and cut into ½-inch pieces
3 tablespoons granulated sugar
½ teaspoon grated lemon zest plus 1½ teaspoons juice
¼ teaspoon ground cinnamon
Salt
½ cup pine nuts, toasted and chopped
3 tablespoons golden raisins
1½ tablespoons panko bread crumbs
7 tablespoons unsalted butter, melted
14 (14 by 9-inch) phyllo sheets, thawed
1 tablespoon confectioners' sugar, plus extra for serving

1 Toss apples, granulated sugar, lemon zest and juice, cinnamon, and ⅛ teaspoon salt together in large bowl. Cover and microwave until apples are warm to touch, about 2 minutes, stirring once halfway through microwaving. Let apples sit, covered, for 5 minutes. Transfer apples to colander set in second bowl and let drain, reserving liquid. Combine apples, pine nuts, raisins, and panko in now-empty bowl.

2 Adjust oven rack to upper-middle position and heat oven to 375 degrees. Spray rimmed baking sheet with vegetable oil spray. Stir ⅛ teaspoon salt into melted butter.

3 Place 16½ by 12-inch sheet of parchment paper on counter with long side parallel to counter edge. Place 1 phyllo sheet on parchment with long side parallel to counter edge. Place 1½ teaspoons confectioners' sugar in fine-mesh strainer (rest strainer in bowl to prevent making a mess). Lightly brush sheet with melted butter and dust sparingly with confectioners' sugar. Repeat with 6 more phyllo sheets, melted butter, and confectioners' sugar, stacking sheets one on top of the other as you go.

4 Arrange half of apple mixture in 2 ½ by 10-inch rectangle 2 inches from bottom of phyllo and about 2 inches from each side. Using parchment, fold sides of phyllo over filling, then fold bottom edge of phyllo over filling. Brush folded portions of phyllo with reserved apple liquid. Fold top edge over filling, making sure top and bottom edges overlap by about 1 inch. (If they do not overlap, unfold, rearrange filling into slightly narrower strip, and refold.) Press firmly to seal. Using thin metal spatula, transfer strudel to 1 side of prepared sheet, facing seam toward center of sheet. Lightly brush top and sides of strudel with half of reserved apple liquid. Repeat process with remaining phyllo, melted butter, confectioners' sugar, filling, and apple liquid. Place second strudel on other side of prepared sheet, with seam facing center of sheet.

5 Bake until golden brown, 27 to 35 minutes, rotating sheet halfway through baking. Using thin metal spatula, immediately transfer strudels to cutting board. Let cool for 3 minutes. Slice each strudel into thirds and let cool for at least 20 minutes. Serve warm or at room temperature, dusting with extra confectioners' sugar before serving.

Veneto

La Serenissima and Her Bounteous Region

....

"HEAVEN IS LOCATED SOMEWHERE IN THE HILLS OF ASOLO." So said the writer Mary McCarthy on the paintings of the Venetian masters, all sons of Veneto immortalizing their homeland. Bellini's landscapes are heavenly visions: lofty villages lit by halos; faraway peaks fused with the sky. The saturated colors of Titian, the ethereal lagoon views of Canaletto— paradise seems to reside here. Indeed, nature has bestowed this corner of northeast Italy with some of the most blissful and bounteous scenery, rich and varied, all in one region.

Lay of the Land

There is the sea and its fabled offspring, Venice, created when the fluvial sediments of three mighty Alpine rivers met the currents of the Adriatic. A bulwark of barrier reefs was formed that cradled the lagoon, a sea within a sea, like a fairy vision but throbbing with natural life. The Adriatic that laps 100 miles of Veneto's shores delivers the coveted "rich fish"—sole, sea bass, turbot, mullet, John Dory. The majestic Alps on the northern border are visible from as far away as Venice. Between their forbidding peaks huddle valleys planted with crops that sustain the mountain people. The Padan Plain, arguably the richest earth in Italy, covers half the region. Rivers, streams, and canals cut through the land everywhere like glittery ribbons. Amid it all, there shimmers Garda, the biggest lake in Italy, which provides 35 species of freshwater fish and an environment for lemons and olives.

This is soil for growing maize and *vialone nano,* the rice variety that melts into the

Dining at twilight, overlooking Venice's central Grand Canal

creamiest risottos the way the Venetians like it—*all'onda*, literally "like a wave." The celebrated Bardolino, Soave, and Valpolicella vineyards are scattered in the lake region, giving birth to wines that inspired Cassiodorus, in 1583, to compare them with lilies. "[They are] of an incredible sweetness and softness . . . an almost meaty liquid . . . a drink that you could almost eat," he sings.

Fare of the Region

From the bucolic countryside scattered with picturesque towns and magnificent 17th-century Palladian villas to the tidy timber chalets with their neat stacks of cut wood and roaring hearths, Veneto's varying landscapes furnish a diversity and abundance of products that is hardly matched elsewhere in Italy. The hills that slope toward the sea, fanned by the salt-laden air of the Adriatic, are a natural environment for curing world-class cheeses such as Grana Padano (produced across the Po Valley), Asiago, Montasio, and Piave, as well as Berico-Euganeo hams and succulent *soppressa* and other sausages. Garda produces a naturally delicate extra-virgin, one of the few oils of the north. San Zeno is famous for chestnuts, Chioggia for sugary pumpkins, and Bassano del Grappa for white asparagus

Venice Begot Veneto

A remarkable history also shapes the foods of Veneto. The Euganei, the indigenous Bronze Age inhabitants, share the name of the volcanic hills south of Padua that boast 13 wines, the Colli Euganei. In the 12th century B.C. they were conquered by the Adriatic Veneti, men of the plow with a shrewd flair for trading who bonded with the Romans. When, beginning in the fifth century A.D., successive waves of Vandals fell from the

---

libations: VENICE'S COCKTAIL HOUR

In the evening, the ritual of *andare a cicheto*—going for a nibble—goes hand in hand with *andare per l'ombra*—going for a shade (from *ombra*, shadow), which is a glass of wine, prosecco, or prosecco-based cocktails. They can include the Bellini, prosecco flavored with peach puree; the Tiziano, blended with grape juice; the Tintoretto, tinted with pomegranate; and the Rossini, mixed with strawberry. Enjoy these with cicheti, finger foods: anything from *salumi* to tidbits of cheese to sundry fritters, deep-fried savories of seafood, squash flowers, or vegetables, all sold from walk-up windows in the numerous trattorias, *osterie*, and *bacari* (wine bars offering snacks eaten standing up), where locals can be seen lining up after work.

Cicheti of little toasts topped with anchovies

The Cadore region in the Dolomites, birthplace of Titian and, purportedly, gelato. Monte Antelao rises majestically in the distance.

north, they fled to the remote lagoon where some 200 islands provided natural protection. Once merchants and farmers, they erected houses on piles, fished, mined salt, and built boats. They cultivated the islands of Mazzorbo and Sant'Erasmo where lagoon dwellers today still trap fish, plant vines, tend fruit orchards, and grow vegetables. Famous among these are the violet artichokes *(castraure),* the "castrated" artichoke, so-named for the pruning the first floral shoots get when they are at their most tender. (A castraure festival is still held on Sant'Erasmo on the second Sunday of every May.)

While the gastronomic flame flickered on *terraferma* for five centuries, in Venice it burned brightly. During the first eight centuries of her history, she was transformed, in the words of Goethe, from "a republic of beavers" into the supreme sea power of her day. Venice was called La Serenissima, the "most serene republic," and she dominated the trade routes to Persia, India, and China. The city was the crossroads of civilization, art, and commerce. Through her ports passed galleons loaded with olive oil and wine and the merchandise and curiosities of all the world—wild animals, priceless works of art plundered from Constantinople (most famously, the gilded horses of St. Mark's), and foods that transformed eating habits throughout Europe. The city's mercantile character made Venetians curious, open-minded, and pragmatic. Foreigners who lived in their midst exchanged not only goods and money but also ideas about cooking. Years away from their homelands, they brought servants and cooks with

With the explorations of the Americas in the 15th and 16th centuries and competition from new rivals in the West, Venice's trading dominance whittled away. She turned toward the territory from which her forebears had fled and annexed a mainland empire that reached to Lombardy. Wealthy Venetians subsidized by the republic reclaimed marshlands and the agricultural revolution, sparked from the top down, paid off handsomely for both.

The ruling class passed its time shuttling between its regal Palladian farmhouses and the dolce vita of Venice, spawning the famous *carnevale* that epitomized its excess. La Serenissima was a tottering grande dame by the time Napoleon sailed past her once impenetrable ramparts in 1797, facing barely any resistance. The provinces endured as the breadbasket of Venice, or more accurately, the "rice dish" and the "polenta pot."

Carving fish at the table, Mistrà trattoria on the Giudecca, Venice

---

TERROIR TO TABLE
A PASSION FOR PUMPKIN

Of Italy's 20 gastronomically diverse regions, none raises the pumpkin to such culinary heights as Veneto. The favorite variety is *marina di Chioggia*, also known as sea pumpkin, after its native town in the lagoon. Dense, flavorful, and silky, it is no wonder so many delicious recipes have been derived from it. Called *suca baruca* (warty pumpkin) in the Venetian dialect, the slightly squashed sphere with gnarled, dark green skin and vibrant orange flesh is rich and sweet enough, once cooked, to eat as a confection. Vendors with their big golden wedges of pumpkin still ply the markets from the Rialto to Sicily.

Saltwater Fish and Seafood of the Adriatic

The fish and bivalves, cephalopods, and crustaceans of the Adriatic Sea are key to the numerous delectable dishes prepared all along Italy's eastern coast.

- **eel** (*anguilla* aka *bisato*)
- **turbot** (*rombo*)
- **sole** (*sogliola*)
- **gilt-head bream** (*orata*)
- **sea bass** (*branzino* or *spigola*)
- **John Dory aka St. Peter's fish** (*pesce San Pietro*)
- **anglerfish** (*coda di rospo*

- **mullet** (*muggine*)
- **gray mullet** (*cefalo*)
- **red mullet** (*triglia*)
- **sardines** (*sardine*)
- **anchovies** (*acciughe*)
- **scallop** (*capesante*)
- **spider crab** (*granseola* in Venetian dialect)

- **miniature octopus** (*moscardini*)
- ***canocchio*** (a kind of prawn)
- **cuttlefish** (*seppia*)
- **mussels** (*mitili*)
- **oysters** (*ostriche*)
- **schie** (*tiny lagoon shrimp*)

Polenta, Granoturco— America's Gift

Of Veneto's staple foods, polenta made from corn is the most emblematic. Its origins have a long history that reaches back to the ancient *puls* of the Romans—barley meal, ground fava beans, or buckwheat cooked into porridge.

Rovigo, the site of a big polenta *sagra* each year, is where Italians first attempted to plant corn in 1554, soon after Columbus returned with it from the New World. (Its Italian doppelgänger, *granoturco* [Turkish grain], is a misnomer, originating in the days of the republic when exotic new foods were given the perfunctory tag "Turkish.") Experts say that the first plants were the ancestors of Eight Row Flint, a native American variety considered "the most flavorful polenta corn on the planet," says Glenn Roberts, a collector of rare seeds. The Italian south was too hot and the mountain areas were too cold, but it grew fast and well on the fertile Po Plain. More economical than bread and less laborious to prepare, polenta took its place.

After taking firm root in the soils of northern Italy, corn became the primary staple. It wasn't eaten fresh, but rather dried and ground before boiling. For four centuries, polenta alone kept the wolf from the door of the common people. In the mountains, it was the sole staple, often eaten three times a day. The poor ate it plain—or with cheese, if there was any. The upper class added condiments or made it into elaborate baked dishes called *pasticci*. In the 18th century, polenta was common street food in Venice, where sellers cooked it in cauldrons and hawked it topped with butter and cheese to passersby.

Eventually, corn polenta infiltrated central and southern Italy, but nowhere was it more popular than in the so-called northern polenta belt, illustrated in the true story of a benevolent 19th-century nobleman who gave a generous portion of meat from his pantry to each of his peasants only to discover soon after that they sold their meat to buy polenta instead.

The mountains prefer coarse-ground yellow polenta. The lowlands like fine-ground white polenta, smooth as butter.

Polenta Dishes of the Veneto

Polenta is the rogue of the Veneto table. It doesn't fit in any course category, but it shows up in everything from appetizers to sweets. It might be served as a loose porridge, alongside a dish that will flavor its edges with gravy or sauce—such as Vicenza's exalted *baccalà alla vicentina*, creamy rehydrated salt cod braised in milk. Or it might be baked with alternating layers of a sauce (with meat or meatless) and a melting cheese. It is a stalwart ingredient in all kinds of sweets, including *torta sabbiosa* (sandy cake) and Venice's favorite golden cookies, *zaletti* (literally, "little yellow ones").

The Fare of Venice and the Provinces

The island city and her coastline eat more fish and seafood than anywhere else on the peninsula, fish that is considered superior for its delicate flesh, due in part to the lower salt content of Adriatic waters. As everywhere on the coast, it revels in the fish fry: *fritto misto alla veneziana,* with its sweet Adriatic calamari, prawns, small fry, and little cubes of crispy golden polenta, is a triumph. Of course, not all seafood is fried, most famously *granseola alla veneziana,* stuffed spider crab; *canocchie,* sweet mantis shrimp, often served raw; and tiny shrimp called *schie* that Venetians consider the caviar of the lagoon. Of all Venice's tasty *baccalà* specialties, creamy whipped *baccalà mantecato,* mother of the *brandade de morue* of France, just might be the most delectable. The region's only signature meat dish, *fegato alla veneziana,* is a revelation: calf's liver sautéed quickly with caramelized onion and served alongside slices of crispy fried polenta.

There are some provincial distinctions. The refinement of Verona's cooking harks back to the Renaissance tables of the Scaligeri family, once powerful lords. The province, immersed in the rice culture of Isola della Scala is inspired in its risotto kitchen. It also makes long, round, noodles called *bigoli.* Most of all, the local cuisine elevates cloudlike potato gnocchi with *pastissada*—a beguiling meat sauce spiked with cinna-

The picturesque Soave vineyards and castle in the medieval village of Soave, Veneto

mon and the splendid Amarone wine of the region. The duet is celebrated every year on the last Friday of carnival week in a raucous festival led by the Papà del Gnoco, a gnocchi king elected based on the closest resemblance among the candidates to a hoary gnome.

Breathtaking Vicenza province, with its Palladian villas tucked into the soft hills, is genteel with a cuisine to match—tasty duck and goose dishes come to mind. The adage "life is a bowl of cherries" must have originated in Marostica, near Vicenza, famous all over Italy for its sweet and fleshy crop, which is celebrated with harvest *sagre* (festivals) in the province throughout June.

Fringed by the beaches of the Adriatic, the picturesque province of Padua is known for its 800-year-old university (where Galileo lectured), for its Montagnana hams, and its poultry, not necessarily in that order. Its aristocratic past and proximity to Venice are reflected in the elegance of many of its dishes, such as *risotto ricco* (rich risotto), so-called because it holds twice as much chicken and mushrooms as rice. The road along the Brenta Canal is not to be missed, as it is lined with splendid patrician villas and excellent fish restaurants.

Treviso prides itself on rich but refined cooking. There is the famous "flower that you eat," as the locals affectionately call their world-famous radicchio, to which colorful harvest festivals are dedicated. They stuff it; caramelize it for saucing pasta or topping focaccia; melt it into a buttery risotto; and coat it in batter to fry. Of the numerous varieties, *tardivo* (which means "late blooming") is the most beautiful, if not the most toothsome. Another native food that has traveled the world is tiramisu, an inspired trifle with its coffee, mascarpone, and spirit-soaked ladyfingers thought to have been invented here in the 1970s.

Both carpaccio and the Bellini cocktail were invented at Harry's Bar, a favorite Venetian hangout of the rich and famous.

To the north, in mountainous Belluno, cooking could almost be called Austrian. Consider *casunzièi,* pretty pink potato-beet-filled ravioli under a veil of melted butter, aged smoked ricotta, and poppy seeds. The beautiful town of Lamon, known for its eponymous bean, likewise doesn't disappoint with its lusty rendition of *pasta e fagioli,* a sturdy *zuppa* fortified with prosciutto. Another dish to get the local cheese treatment is *skiz con polenta,* when skiz, a lovely soft cheese, is sautéed to a golden brown and subjected to a dousing of thick, fresh cream while still hot in the pan, then served over slabs of steaming polenta.

Four ingredients—corn polenta, beans, baccalà, rice—are the great unifiers of the cooking of Veneto. How Venetian—with all the fantastic recipes and exotic flavors that the empire once indulged in—that the lighthearted dishes of the commoner have endured.

A Venetian's daily produce shopping leads canalside rather than to a grocery store.

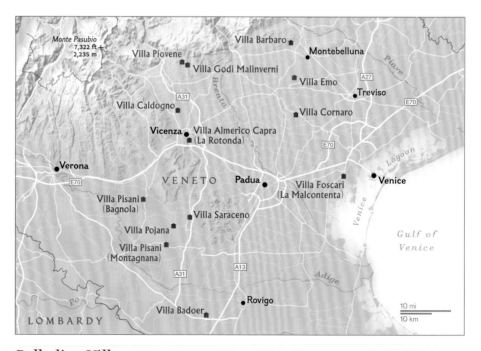

Palladian Villas Andrea Palladio's 16th-century glorified farmhouses dot the Veneto. Many are restored and open to the public.

Grilled Radicchio

Radicchio alla griglia · *Serves 4*

WHY THIS RECIPE WORKS: While it's true that radicchio is a salad green, that doesn't mean it's just a salad ingredient. Grown all over the Veneto region and coming in many varieties, the striking leaves are not just eaten raw but also cooked in an enormous variety of ways. Grilling is a particularly simple and delicious option: The purple leaves become lightly crisp and smoky-tasting, providing a nice complement to the radicchio's bitterness. The main challenge is ensuring the layers don't fall apart on the grill. Cutting the radicchio heads through the core, first in half and then in quarters, created thick wedges that held together. While we wanted char on our radicchio leaves, we didn't want to burn them; brushing them with a liberal amount of good olive oil added flavor and richness, and prevented burning. We wanted to expose as much surface area to the grill as possible for maximum flavor, so we turned each wedge twice so both sides of the wedge spent ample time facing the fire. Grilled radicchio makes an especially fine accompaniment to meat, poultry, or fish. Use common round heads of radicchio (radicchio di Chioggia) for this recipe.

3 heads radicchio, cut into quarters through core
¼ cup extra-virgin olive oil
Salt and pepper
Balsamic vinegar

❶ Place radicchio wedges on baking sheet, brush with oil, and season with salt and pepper.

❷A For a charcoal grill: Open bottom vent completely. Light large chimney starter three-quarters filled with charcoal briquettes (4½ quarts). When top coals are partially covered with ash, pour evenly over grill. Set cooking grate in place, cover, and open lid vent completely. Heat grill until hot, about 5 minutes.

B For a gas grill: Turn all burners to high, cover, and heat grill until hot, about 15 minutes. Turn all burners to medium-high.

❸ Clean and oil cooking grate. Grill radicchio, turning every 1½ minutes, until edges are browned and wilted but center remains slightly firm, about 5 minutes. Transfer radicchio to serving dish, drizzle with vinegar, and serve immediately.

Rice and Peas

Risi e bisi · *Serves 4 to 6*

WHY THIS RECIPE WORKS: Venetians have a centuries-old tradition of dishing up *risi e bisi* (rice and peas) every April 25, St. Mark's Day, to celebrate spring's first peas and to honor rice production in the Veneto region. Thinner than traditional risotto yet thicker than soup, the dish's unique consistency and fresh flavors make it an ambassador for the season: a light and vibrant—yet still satisfying—escape from heavier winter fare. Most recipes adhere to the long-established risotto method of vigorously stirring broth into the rice in multiple additions, but since our goal was not to create a dish with such a velvety consistency, we could jettison the routine and simply cook the dish like soup. We reached for frozen peas; processed soon after harvest, frozen peas retain their sugars. The rice will quickly absorb the soup's liquid as it sits, so add more liquid if necessary. This dish is traditionally prepared using Vialone Nano rice, but you can substitute Carnaroli or Arborio rice. We use frozen petite peas here, but regular frozen peas can be substituted, if desired. For the proper consistency, cook the rice at a gentle boil.

4 cups chicken broth
1½ cups water
3 tablespoons extra-virgin olive oil
2 ounces pancetta, chopped fine
1 onion, chopped fine
2 garlic cloves, minced
1 cup Vialone Nano rice
2 cups frozen petite peas, thawed
1 ounce Parmigiano Reggiano cheese, grated (½ cup), plus extra for serving
3 tablespoons minced fresh parsley
1 teaspoon lemon juice, plus lemon wedges for serving
Salt and pepper

❶ Bring broth and water to boil in large saucepan over high heat. Remove from heat and cover to keep warm.

❷ Cook oil and pancetta in Dutch oven over medium-low heat until pancetta is browned and fat is rendered, 5 to 7 minutes. Add onion and cook over medium heat until softened, about 5 minutes. Stir in garlic and cook until fragrant, about 30 seconds. Add rice and stir to coat, about 1 minute.

❸ Stir in 5 cups warm broth mixture and bring to boil. Reduce heat to medium-low, cover, and simmer, stirring occasionally, until rice is tender but not mushy, about 15 minutes.

❹ Off heat, whisk rice vigorously until broth has thickened slightly, about 15 seconds. Stir in peas, Parmigiano, parsley, and lemon juice. Season with salt and pepper to taste. Adjust consistency with remaining ½ cup warm broth mixture as needed. Serve, passing extra Parmigiano and lemon wedges separately.

115

Whipped Salt Cod Spread

Baccalà mantecato · Makes about 2 cups

WHY THIS RECIPE WORKS: Dried and salted cod may not seem like an obvious favorite in the Veneto given its access to fresh seafood. But the region's status as a trading hub made residents aware of this inexpensive and reliable method for preserving fish. There are said to be upwards of 150 dishes featuring *baccalà* in the Veneto, and one of the most beloved is *baccalà mantecato*—literally, creamed cod. The preserved cod is soaked to remove salt and then cooked in milk to tenderize before being whipped with olive oil to create a luscious, creamy spread. A sachet of aromatics added to the cooking liquid imparted a delicate sweetness that balanced the salty cod. Pureed in the food processor, the cod became creamy without losing its texture entirely. You can find salt cod in most fish markets and some well-stocked supermarkets. It is shelf stable and typically packaged in a wooden box or plastic bag. Be sure to change the water when soaking the salt cod in step 1, or the spread will taste unpalatably salty. This dish is traditionally served on small pieces of *Polenta grigliata* (opposite), but it can also be served on crostini or with crudités.

1 pound salt cod, checked for bones and rinsed thoroughly
½ onion, cut into 1-inch pieces
1 celery rib, cut into 1-inch pieces
3 garlic cloves, peeled and smashed
2 tablespoons minced fresh parsley, stems reserved
1 bay leaf
2 cups whole milk
½ cup extra-virgin olive oil
⅔ cup heavy cream
Salt and pepper

❶ Submerge salt cod in large bowl of cold water and refrigerate until cod is soft enough to break apart easily with your fingers, about 24 hours, changing water twice during soaking.

❷ Wrap onion, celery, garlic, parsley stems, and bay leaf in piece of cheesecloth and secure with kitchen twine. Drain cod and transfer to large saucepan along with cheesecloth bundle, milk, and 2 cups water. Bring to simmer, then reduce heat to low, cover, and simmer gently until cod begins to flake apart when gently prodded with paring knife, about 30 minutes.

❸ Discard cheesecloth bundle. Drain cod, spread evenly over large plate, and let cool completely. Pulse cod in food processor until coarsely chopped, about 8 pulses. With processor running, slowly add oil, then cream and process until mixture is smooth and lightly whipped, about 1 minute, scraping down sides of bowl as needed. Add minced parsley and pulse until combined, about 4 pulses. Season with salt and pepper to taste. Serve at room temperature or chilled. (Spread can be refrigerated for up to 2 days; bring to room temperature and vigorously stir to recombine before serving.)

Grilled Polenta

Polenta grigliata · *Serves 4*

WHY THIS RECIPE WORKS: Versatile polenta isn't just eaten as a porridge like our *Polenta concia* (page 38). Grilling slabs of firm polenta is a popular treatment in the Veneto. The challenge is ensuring the polenta maintains a nice creamy consistency while being sturdy enough to hold together during grilling. To do this we reduced the liquid-to-corn ratio for our classic porridge to the minimum amount of liquid needed to hydrate the corn. We cooked the polenta on the stovetop until it was fully hydrated and then stirred in a few tablespoons of oil, which contributed richness and kept the polenta from being sticky. After chilling in an 8 by 8-inch baking pan, the polenta was firm enough to slice into portions. We then grilled it over a hot fire until crispy on the outside but creamy on the inside. Use coarse-ground cornmeal with grains the size of couscous in this recipe. If the polenta bubbles or sputters even slightly after the first 10 minutes, the heat is too high and you may need a flame tamer (see page 38).

2 cups water
½ teaspoon salt
Pinch baking soda
1 cup coarse-ground cornmeal
3 tablespoons extra-virgin olive oil

❶ Grease 8-inch square baking pan, line with parchment paper, and grease parchment. Bring water to boil in large saucepan over medium-high heat. Stir in salt and baking soda. Slowly pour cornmeal into water in steady stream while whisking constantly and return to boil. Reduce heat to lowest possible setting, cover, and cook until grains of cornmeal are tender, about 30 minutes, stirring every few minutes. (Polenta should be very thick.) Off heat, whisk in oil and pour polenta into prepared pan, smooth top, and let cool completely, about 30 minutes. Wrap tightly in plastic wrap and refrigerate until polenta is very firm, at least 2 hours or up to 3 days.

❷ Run knife around edge of polenta, then flip onto cutting board; discard parchment. Slice polenta into 4 squares and refrigerate until ready to grill.

❸ A For a charcoal grill: Open bottom vent completely. Light large chimney starter filled with charcoal briquettes (6 quarts). When top coals are partially covered with ash, pour evenly over half of grill. Set cooking grate in place, cover, and open lid vent completely. Heat grill until hot, about 5 minutes.

B For a gas grill: Turn all burners to high, cover, and heat grill until hot, about 15 minutes. Leave primary burner on high and turn off other burner(s).

❹ Clean and oil cooking grate, then repeatedly brush grate with well-oiled paper towels until grate is black and glossy, 5 to 10 times. Place polenta on hotter side of grill and cook (covered if using gas) until polenta is lightly charred on first side, 6 to 8 minutes. Using 2 spatulas, gently flip polenta, and continue to cook until lightly charred on second side, 6 to 8 minutes. Serve.

Spaghettini With Shrimp

Spaghettini con le schie · Serves 6 to 8

WHY THIS RECIPE WORKS: Seafood has always been central to Venetian cuisine. The earliest Venetians were skilled fishermen and their diet relied heavily on the bounty found in the city's lagoon ecosystem. And while the Veneto may not be as famous for pasta dishes as some other regions, *spaghettini con le schie* is a Venetian celebration of the uniquely delicious small shrimp found in their waters. While shrimp of this size found stateside are often unappealing (lacking in flavor and quality), we loved the sweet, briny flavors and ease of this dish and decided to develop a simple shrimp pasta that would taste just as good in our kitchens. We began by halving large shrimp, which have reliably good flavor. We then reinforced the shrimp presence by first cooking the shrimp shells in oil and wine. Shrimp shells are rich in glutamates, which add meaty depth, as well as volatile fatty acids, which generate fresh, delicate flavors when cooked. The result was a deeply flavored shrimp sauce. Some garlic, butter, lemon zest, and fresh parsley were all we needed to finish this flavorful weeknight dish.

⅓ cup extra-virgin olive oil

2 pounds large shrimp (26 to 30 per pound), peeled, deveined, and halved crosswise, shells reserved

1 cup dry white wine

5 garlic cloves, minced

Salt and pepper

¼ cup minced fresh parsley

4 tablespoons unsalted butter, cut into 4 pieces

1½ teaspoons grated lemon zest, plus lemon wedges for serving

1 pound spaghettini or thin spaghetti

1 Heat ¼ cup oil in 12-inch skillet over high heat until shimmering. Add shrimp shells and cook, stirring frequently, until they begin to turn spotty brown, 2 to 4 minutes. Off heat, carefully add wine. Once bubbling subsides, return skillet to medium heat and simmer for 5 minutes. Strain wine mixture through fine-mesh strainer into large bowl, pressing on solids to extract as much liquid as possible; discard solids. (You should have about ⅔ cup wine mixture.) Wipe skillet clean with paper towels.

2 Heat remaining oil and garlic in now-empty skillet over medium-low heat, stirring occasionally, until garlic is fragrant and just beginning to brown, about 30 seconds. Add reserved wine mixture and ½ teaspoon salt and bring to simmer. Add shrimp, cover, and cook, stirring occasionally, until just opaque, about 2 minutes. Off heat, stir in parsley, butter, and lemon zest.

3 Meanwhile, bring 4 quarts water to boil in large pot. Add pasta and 1 tablespoon salt and cook, stirring often, until al dente. Reserve ½ cup cooking water, then drain pasta and return it to pot. Add sauce and toss to coat. Adjust consistency with reserved cooking water as needed. Season with pepper to taste. Serve with lemon wedges.

Seafood Risotto

Risotto alla pescatora · *Serves 6 to 8*

WHY THIS RECIPE WORKS: The risottos of Veneto are among its culinary glories. One of our favorites is seafood risotto, a classic Venetian dish that uses its vast sea treasures to create a luxurious mix of flavors and textures against a lush backdrop of creamy short-grain rice, which is fortified with the region's fine wines. Venetians are known for enjoying their risottos *all'onda*, meaning they are wavier, more fluid, and looser than in other Italian regions. With a wide array of seafood to choose from, the preparation can easily become overloaded, so we decided to set some limits. We chose universally appealing shrimp and made a quick seafood broth by simmering the shrimp shells in a base of bottled clam juice, chicken broth, and water, to which we added bay leaves and canned tomatoes. Once the risotto was fully cooked, we stirred in the shrimp along with mussels and squid and allowed them to steam gently in the warm rice, resulting in flawlessly tender seafood. Do not buy peeled shrimp; you'll need the shrimp shells to make the broth. This dish is traditionally prepared using Vialone Nano rice, but you can substitute Carnaroli or Arborio rice. You may have broth left over once the rice is finished cooking; different rice products cook differently, and we prefer to err on the side of slightly too much broth rather than too little. If you do use all the broth and the rice has not finished cooking, add hot water.

12 ounces large shrimp (26 to 30 per pound), peeled and deveined, shells reserved
2 cups chicken broth
3½ cups water
4 (8-ounce) bottles clam juice
1 (14.5-ounce) can diced tomatoes, drained
2 bay leaves
5 tablespoons unsalted butter, cut into 5 pieces
1 onion, chopped fine
2 cups Vialone Nano rice
5 garlic cloves, minced
1 teaspoon minced fresh thyme or ¼ teaspoon dried
1 cup dry white wine
12 mussels, scrubbed and debearded
8 ounces squid, bodies sliced crosswise into ¼-inch-thick rings, tentacles halved
2 tablespoons minced fresh parsley
1 tablespoon lemon juice
Salt and pepper

❶ Bring shrimp shells, broth, water, clam juice, tomatoes, and bay leaves to boil in large saucepan. Reduce to simmer and cook for 20 minutes. Strain mixture through fine-mesh strainer into large bowl, pressing on solids to extract as much liquid as possible; discard solids. Return broth to now-empty saucepan, cover, and keep warm over low heat.

❷ Melt 2 tablespoons butter in Dutch oven over medium heat. Add onion and cook until softened, about 5 minutes. Add rice, garlic, and thyme and cook, stirring frequently, until grain edges begin to turn translucent, about 5 minutes.

❸ Add wine and cook, stirring frequently, until fully absorbed, about 2 minutes. Stir in 3½ cups warm broth, bring to simmer, and cook, stirring occasionally, until almost fully absorbed, 10 to 12 minutes.

❹ Continue to cook rice, stirring frequently and adding warm broth, 1 cup at a time, every few minutes as liquid is absorbed, until rice is creamy and loose and cooked through but still slightly firm in center, 14 to 18 minutes.

❺ Stir in shrimp, mussels, squid, and 1 cup broth and cook, stirring frequently, until shrimp and squid are opaque throughout, about 3 minutes. Remove pot from heat, cover, and let sit until all mussels have opened, about 5 minutes; discard any mussels that have not opened. Adjust consistency with remaining warm broth as needed. (Risotto should be somewhat loose; you may have broth left over). Stir in remaining 3 tablespoons butter, parsley, and lemon juice and season with salt and pepper to taste. Serve immediately.

Tiramisu

Tiramisù · Serves 10 to 12

WHY THIS RECIPE WORKS: With its boozy, coffee-soaked ladyfingers and sweet, creamy filling, it's no wonder *tiramisù* is Italian for "pick me up." Instead of making a custard filling, we simply whipped egg yolks, sugar, salt, rum, and mascarpone together and lightened it with whipped cream. We briefly moistened the ladyfingers in a mixture of coffee, espresso powder, and more rum. We prefer a tiramisu with a pronounced rum flavor; for a less potent rum flavor, reduce the amount of rum in the coffee mixture. Brandy or whiskey can be substituted for the rum. Don't let the mascarpone warm to room temperature before whipping. Dried ladyfingers are also called *savoiardi;* you will need between 42 and 60, depending on their size and the brand.

- 2½ cups strong brewed coffee, room temperature
- 1½ tablespoons instant espresso powder
- 9 tablespoons dark rum
- 6 large egg yolks
- ⅔ cup (4⅔ ounces) sugar
- ¼ teaspoon salt
- 1½ pounds (3 cups) mascarpone cheese, chilled
- ¾ cup heavy cream, chilled
- 14 ounces dried ladyfingers
- 3½ tablespoons unsweetened cocoa powder
- ¼ cup grated semisweet or bittersweet chocolate (optional)

❶ Combine coffee, espresso powder, and 5 tablespoons rum in wide bowl or baking dish until espresso dissolves.

❷ Using stand mixer fitted with whisk attachment, mix egg yolks at low speed until just combined. Add sugar and salt and mix at medium-high speed until pale yellow, 1½ to 2 minutes, scraping down sides of bowl as needed. Reduce speed to medium, add remaining ¼ cup rum, and mix at medium speed until just combined, 20 to 30 seconds; scrape bowl. Add mascarpone and mix until no lumps remain, 30 to 45 seconds, scraping down bowl as needed. Transfer mixture to large bowl.

❸ In now-empty mixer bowl (no need to clean mixer bowl), whip cream on medium-low speed until foamy, about 1 minute. Increase speed to high and whip until stiff peaks form, 1 to 3 minutes. Using rubber spatula, fold one-third of the whipped cream into mascarpone mixture to lighten, then gently fold in remaining whipped cream until no white streaks remain.

❹ Working with 1 ladyfinger at a time, drop half of ladyfingers into coffee mixture, roll, remove, and transfer to 13 by 9-inch baking dish. (Do not submerge ladyfingers in coffee mixture; entire process should take no longer than 2 to 3 seconds for each cookie.) Arrange soaked cookies in single layer in baking dish, breaking or trimming ladyfingers as needed to fit neatly into dish.

❺ Spread half of mascarpone mixture over ladyfingers, spreading it to sides and into corners of dish, and smooth top. Place 2 tablespoons cocoa in fine-mesh strainer and dust cocoa over mascarpone. Repeat with remaining ladyfingers, mascarpone, and 1½ tablespoons cocoa to make second layer. Clean edges of dish, cover with plastic wrap, and refrigerate until set, at least 6 hours or up to 24 hours. Before serving, sprinkle with grated chocolate, if using.

Friuli–Venezia Giulia

Homeland With a Pan-European Cuisine

....

FRIULI–VENEZIA GIULIA LIES in the northeastern corner of Italy, bordering Austria and Slovenia to the north and east, Veneto to the west, and the Adriatic Sea to the south. The northern half of the region is composed of the rough and crumbly Carnic Alps and foothills, where snowmelt-filled creeks tumble into deep lakes. Friuli–Venezia Giulia has the longest, snowiest winters in Italy, but warm weather reveals a verdant Alpine landscape of mountain meadows, piney forests, and chilly streams. • Game, trout, mushrooms, and

herbs including nettles, silene, and wild spinach are gathered in these mountains, and meat and dairy cattle forage in the high meadows. They are the source of Friuli's wonderful cheeses, most famously, the soft and delicate Montasio, eaten fresh or used to make *frico*, a chewy frittata-like cake of cheese, potatoes, and onions. (There are as many variations of frico as there are farmhouses, but the common thread is melted Montasio.) In the foothills the days are warm, the nights cold, and winds blow south from the Alps and north from the sea. This well-ventilated area produces the region's great wines, tree fruit, and cured meats. The smoky Prosciutto di Sauris is a regional favorite, and the superlative Prosciutto di San Daniele, which is preserved in sea salt, is considered the best in Italy.

A Tradition of Invasion

If you ask a Friulian for directions to the train station, don't expect to be invited home

Though in many ways a modern city, Udine retains its old-world charm.

Friuli–Venezia Giulia is grappa country, a marc-derived eau-de-vie deemed country swill until repackaged as a luxury drink in the 1980s.

for lunch, as you might in the south. These are a people whose land has been invaded by wave upon wave of barbarians, or folks acting barbaric: Huns, Goths, Langobards, Turks, Venetians, Austrians, Napoleon, Hapsburgs, Slavs, and Nazis. Strangers traditionally are, well, a problem.

They have endured domination and war, poverty and disease for almost all of their past, surviving in a nominally fertile land with a history of seismic catastrophe. Yet despite their misfortunes the Friulians have maintained their cultural identity, even their unique language, by absorbing—not being absorbed by—their occupiers' cultures, DNA, and cuisines. Friuli–Venezia Giulia, about the size of Puerto Rico, calls itself a *piccola patria* (small homeland) that lies at the geographic center of Europe. So does its cooking.

From the Carnic Alps and hills spills the Tagliamento River, a grand system of braided streams that reaches into the heart of the region. The valley provides irrigation water to the central plains where vegetables and grains are grown, most importantly, maize. Farther south, the river feeds marshlands and rice fields, eventually draining into the sea. The coastal area to the west dissolves into shallow lagoons, and rises to bright white limestone cliffs in the east. Trieste, the regional capital, is on the Gulf of Trieste at the foot of these cliffs. Fishing boats supply the region's seafood from the grand Port of Trieste, as do the more modest seafarers of the lagoon.

The regal church of Sant'Antonio Taumaturgo presides over Trieste's Grand Canal.

A Melting Pot

Prehistoric people here came from the south by sea and over the mountains in the north (Alpine tribes have been credited with introducing meat curing to the area), but by the second century B.C. Rome had colonized the region—hence the name. Friuli comes from Forum Julii and Venezia Giulia from Julian's Venice. The Romans introduced vegetable fermentation, a legacy evident in the regional specialty, *brovada,* shredded turnips fermented in marc until tender and sour. (Marc is the solid remains of pressed grapes or other fruit. It's also used to make grappa and eau-de-vie.)

After the fall of the empire, Friuli fell prey to waves of invading forces, absorbing the culture of each to become a melting pot of European genes and recipes. To their Latin culinary vernacular Friulians integrated Hungarian, Austrian, and Slavic dishes, such as paprika-spiked goulash and *gubana,* a tender brioche-like cake filled with a sticky sweetened nut mixture.

Venice exploited the region from the 14th to 18th centuries, leading to widespread hunger. The Friulians were saved from starvation by the introduction of corn—and thus polenta—in the 16th century, though many suffered debilitating vitamin deficiency. The region eventually recovered, but to this day polenta is eaten regularly. It is plated in a warm puddle or firm, in wedges sliced with a thread, and the leftovers are grilled and served beside meats. The Friulians also co-opted Venetian dishes, for example, giving the classic Venetian soup *risi e bisi* a caloric upgrade with rice and peas mashed together and served with egg pasta.

Life was different in Trieste. Coddled by its Austro-Hungarian occupiers who valued its port, the city's flavors evolved in more of a side-by-side approach. In Trieste you can eat Venetian-type dishes such as *risotto maranese*, with shrimp, squid, and mussels, followed by a slice of black Sacher torte. Your espresso (Illy is from Trieste) is served with a dollop of whipped cream on the side. Friuli–Venezia Giulia joined the Italian Republic after World War I, sharing the destiny of all Italy thereafter, with the exception of the rather constant unpredictability of their unruly Balkan neighbors.

Cuisine of Many Parents

Today the area called Friuli constitutes the largest part of the region, mainly in the south, west, and north. The Venezia Giulia part is in the east and includes Trieste. There are four provinces: Udine to the east, which stretches from the Alps to the sea; Pordenone to the west; tiny Gorizia to the east (a great wine region); and Trieste, primarily the city and such coastal towns as Prosecco, which gave its name to the popular sparkling white wine.

The food of Friuli–Venezia Giulia is an aggregate. To wit, Austrian Liptauer cheese gets jazzed up with anchovy while lasagna gets dressed with poppy seeds, and dumplings with smoked ricotta. The Friulians love gnocchi, or dumplings, and their many versions reflect both Austrian and Italian kitchens. Gnocchi, for example, may be fla-

LOCAL FLAVOR
THE *FRASCA* TABLE

With their language and traditions forged in isolated mountain valleys periodically overrun by marauding invaders, it is no wonder the Friulians are tough customers. But one way they welcome visitors is by sharing wine and traditional foods at the *frasca* table. *Frasca* means "branch," from the tradition of hanging a laurel branch at an intersection of roads pointing the way to a vineyard with new wine to sell. *Frasche* are working vineyards and farms, mainly in the hill country, with a special license to sell wine and food. The good news is the food they serve must be produced on the premises: cheesy *frico* made with their own cheese, featherlight gnocchi, fatty sausages (from their own pigs) cooked in vinegar and onions, grilled wedges of polenta, and pitchers of fizzy new wine.

> *Polenta is all about the stirring. To get started on the right foot, the traditional cook begins by tracing the sign of the cross with her ladle.*

vored with wild herbs, potato, prune, plum, raisin, pumpkin, or apricot. A specialty is *cjarsons* (or *cjalsons*), pierogi-like pasta filled with a sweet and savory combination of potatoes and onions and a dizzying variety of counterintuitive ingredients such as lemon balm and amaretto cookie crumbles.

Meat such as *pezzata rossa friulana* veal, *lujanis* sausage, and *cevaps* (spicy pork and beef patties) are typically grilled. The stewy dishes of central Europe are thoroughly integrated in Friulian cuisine, including *ramnasici* (stuffed cabbage), and *porzino* (boiled pork with mustard). Vegetables are less prominent, reflecting both the limited land resources and the northern European palate. There are exceptional asparagus, however, and radicchio, Jerusalem artichokes, and garlic from the Resia Valley, but the primary vegetables are white turnips, cabbage, potatoes, and beans. The small, red *fasuj* bean is used in dishes such as the rich *Jota,* a sauerkraut and bean soup. Breads and sweets also reflect the consortium of European food styles: *Strucolo* is the Friulian strudel, with a single layer of pastry dough wrapping a mass of chopped fruit, while *crostata,* a short crust jam tart, is similar to the Austrian linzer torte.

Friulians have instituted a Committee for the Defense of Traditions that focuses on supporting *osterie,* taverns where local wine and foods are served. These aren't just places to eat a succulent slice of *porchetta* with grated horseradish on a poppy seed bun; they are repositories of the region's folk recipes, an edible record of its trials and tribulations, and a testament to the Friulian's perseverance.

Cool mountain air is the secret to curing Sauris's exceptional prosciutto.

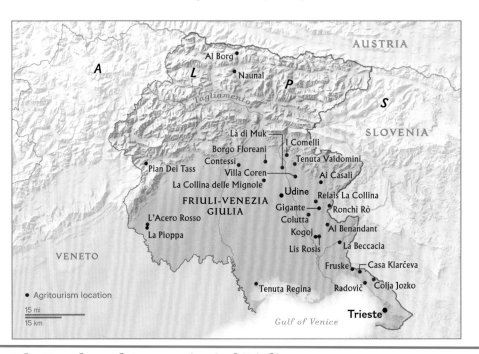

The Frasche and Agrotourismi of Friuli The Friulians love dining alfresco at farms and vineyards that serve their beloved regional specialties.

Cheese Wafers

Frico friabile · *Makes 8 large wafers*

WHY THIS RECIPE WORKS: *Frico friabile* is a one-ingredient wonder and a delightful antipasto—especially alongside a glass of chilled white wine from the region. Nothing more than grated cheese that is melted and then browned to create a light, airy, crisp, and impressively sized wafer, this simple snack highlights the intense flavor of the cheese. But despite their simplicity, these wafers can turn out bitter, and too salty, without the crispness we preferred. Some recipes cook the cheese in butter or olive oil, but using a 10-inch nonstick skillet eliminated the need for any fat. To flip the round without it tearing or stretching, we removed the pan from the heat for several seconds to cool; allowing a few moments for the cheese wafer to set up made it easy to flip. Cooking the cheese at high heat caused it to brown too fast and become bitter, but at low heat it took too long and dried out. A combination of medium and medium-high heat was best. Serve frico with drinks and other antipasti bites such as olives and tomatoes. Montasio cheese is worth tracking down; if you can't find it, substitute Asiago.

1 pound Montasio or aged Asiago cheese, shredded (4 cups)

Sprinkle ½ cup cheese over bottom of 10-inch nonstick skillet. Cook over medium-high heat, shaking skillet occasionally to ensure even distribution of cheese over bottom of skillet, until edges are lacy and toasted, about 4 minutes. As cheese begins to melt, use spatula to tidy lacy outer edges of cheese and prevent them from burning. Remove skillet from heat and allow cheese to set, about 30 seconds. Using fork and spatula, carefully flip cheese wafer over and return skillet to medium-high heat. Cook until second side is golden brown, about 2 minutes. Slide cheese wafer out of skillet onto plate. Repeat with remaining cheese. Serve.

Barley and Bean Soup

Minestra di orzo e fasio ·
Serves 4 to 6

....

WHY THIS RECIPE WORKS: In Italy, *orzo*—what Americans think of as a rice-shaped pasta—is the word for barley, and it's one of the most important ingredients in Friuli, where the high altitude of the mountainous areas facilitates its cultivation. It's found in risotto-like dishes, but it's also frequently combined with hearty beans for a soup that makes a warming winter staple. This Friulian alternative to *pasta e fagioli* was once a peasant dish but has become a recognized culinary specialty of the region. We started with dried cranberry (aka *borlotti*) beans, a common Friulian ingredient, that we soaked overnight in salted water so they cooked up with soft skins. Next we rendered the fat from flavorful pancetta (cut into spoon-friendly bites) before adding onion, garlic, and bay leaves along with water and the soaked beans. We added the barley to the soup for the last hour of cooking and simmered it until both the beans and grains were tender and thickened to a porridge-like consistency. This soup is traditionally served very thick; adjust consistency with additional hot water as needed. Do not substitute hulled, hull-less, quick-cooking, or pre-steamed barley (read the ingredient list on the package to determine this) in this recipe.

Salt and pepper
8 ounces (1¼ cups) dried cranberry beans, picked over and rinsed
1 tablespoon extra-virgin olive oil, plus extra for serving
4 ounces pancetta, cut into ¼-inch pieces
1 onion, chopped fine
3 garlic cloves, minced
2 bay leaves
1 cup pearl barley
¼ cup minced fresh parsley
1 tablespoon red wine vinegar

❶ Dissolve 1½ tablespoons salt in 2 quarts cold water in large container. Add beans and soak at room temperature for at least 8 hours or up to 24 hours. Drain and rinse well.

❷ Heat oil in large saucepan over medium-high heat until shimmering.
Add pancetta and cook until browned and fat is rendered, 5 to 7 minutes. Add onion and 1 teaspoon salt and cook until softened and lightly browned, 5 to 7 minutes. Stir in garlic and cook until fragrant, about 30 seconds.

❸ Stir in beans, 12 cups water, and bay leaves and bring to boil. Reduce heat to medium-low and cover, leaving lid slightly ajar. Simmer, stirring occasionally, until beans are tender, about 1 hour.

❹ Stir in barley and simmer, uncovered, stirring occasionally, until barley is tender, beans begin to break down, and soup has thickened, about 1 hour.

❺ Discard bay leaves. Stir in parsley and vinegar and season with salt and pepper to taste. Adjust consistency with hot water as needed. Drizzle individual portions with extra oil before serving.

Grilled Cornish Game Hens

Pollastrella alla griglia · *Serves 4*

WHY THIS RECIPE WORKS: Friulians take the simplest of ingredients and transform them into delicious and uncomplicated meals. Wild game birds, for example, are hunted and then cooked over an open flame, embellished with nothing more than salt and pepper. As we would need to work with what we could buy in an American supermarket, we chose easy-to-find Cornish game hens, which are small birds with robustly flavored meat. We butterflied the hens, creating a uniform thickness for even cooking, and we sprinkled them with salt and pepper. We then set up a half-grill fire and started cooking the hens skin side up over the cooler side of the grill so the fatty skin had time to slowly render while the meat cooked. To finish, we flipped them skin side down and placed them over the hotter side, which crisped the skin in a few minutes. The juicy, flavorful meat pairs well with a traditional side dish of *Polenta grigliata* (page 117). While the hens rest, you can grill the polenta on the hotter side of the grill.

4 Cornish game hens (1¼ to
   1½ pounds each), giblets
   discarded
Salt and pepper
Lemon wedges

1 Working with 1 hen at a time, place breast side down on cutting board and use kitchen shears to cut through bones on either side of backbone; discard backbone. Flip hen and press on breastbone to flatten. Trim any excess fat and skin.

2 A For a charcoal grill: Open bottom vent completely. Light large chimney starter filled with charcoal briquettes (6 quarts). When top coals are partially covered with ash, pour evenly over half of grill. Set cooking grate in place, cover, and open lid vent completely. Heat grill until hot, about 5 minutes.

B For a gas grill: Turn all burners to high, cover, and heat grill until hot, about 15 minutes. Leave primary burner on high and turn off other burner(s). Adjust primary burner (or, if using three-burner grill, primary burner and second burner) as needed to maintain grill temperature between 400 and 450 degrees.

3 Clean and oil cooking grate. Tuck wingtips behind backs and turn legs so drumsticks face inward toward breasts. Season hens with salt and pepper. Place hens skin side up on cooler side of grill (if using charcoal, arrange hens so that legs and thighs are facing coals). Cover and cook until skin is browned and breasts register 145 to 150 degrees, 30 to 35 minutes, rotating hens halfway through cooking.

4 Using tongs, carefully flip hens skin side down and move to hotter side of grill. Cover and cook until skin is crisp and deeply browned and breasts register 160 degrees, 3 to 5 minutes, being careful to avoid burning. Transfer hens skin side up to cutting board, tent with aluminum foil, and let rest for 5 to 10 minutes. Cut each hen in half or into quarters and serve with lemon wedges.

Braised Savoy Cabbage With Pancetta

Verza stufata · *Serves 4 to 6*

WHY THIS RECIPE WORKS: Savoy cabbage, known as *cavolo verza*, is a major staple in northern Italy; "Savoy" refers to the historical land bordering France, Switzerland, and northwest Italy where the cabbage grows abundantly. Milder than green or red cabbage with a light, feathery texture, earthy savoy cabbage is used in creative ways throughout Italy, and Friulians are known for braising it with subtly spiced pancetta. The method for this comforting dish is straightforward: The pancetta is cooked to render some of its fat and then the cabbage is added along with liquid (usually stock), at which point the pot is partially covered so the cabbage braises until it's tender and the liquid has evaporated. But while many Italian recipes call for little beyond cabbage and pancetta, we felt the dish needed a bit more depth: Sautéed onion bolstered the sweetness, garlic accented the cabbage's earthiness, and minced parsley, stirred in at the end, added welcome freshness.

2 tablespoons unsalted butter
4 ounces pancetta, chopped fine
1 onion, halved and sliced thin
4 garlic cloves, sliced thin
1 head savoy cabbage (1½ pounds), cored and sliced thin
2 cups chicken broth
1 bay leaf
2 tablespoons minced fresh parsley
Salt and pepper

❶ Melt butter in Dutch oven over medium heat. Add pancetta and cook until browned and fat is rendered, 5 to 7 minutes. Add onion and cook until softened and lightly browned, 5 to 7 minutes. Stir in garlic and cook until fragrant, about 30 seconds.

❷ Stir in cabbage, broth, and bay leaf and bring to boil. Reduce heat to medium-low and cover, leaving lid slightly ajar. Simmer until cabbage is tender and no broth remains, about 45 minutes. Discard bay leaf. Stir in parsley and season with salt and pepper to taste. Serve.

Emilia–Romagna

Porky Pleasures and Epicurean Delights

···

TO CONNOISSEURS, EMILIA–ROMAGNA'S CAPITAL CITY, nicknamed "Bologna the Fat," is most significant not for its ancient university founded in 1088 (the first in Europe), but for its food. • According to some guidebooks, the cooking of Emilia and that of Romagna, once separate states, have become seamless. But this is not so. Emilia's traditions have a blue-blood streak; Romagna's are rooted in popular cooking. What we can agree on is that in both parts, the masses share the *cucina povera* with Tuscany across the border.

The region's temperament—practical and cool, if graceful—belongs to the north. If Bologna is fabled for its culinary treasures, so are the other provinces in the Padan Plain, the great plain of the Po River—places with names like Modena, Parma, and Ferrara that roll off the tongues of food lovers everywhere. This is cattle and hog country, land of silky hams, famed cheeses, and the most delicate of pastas with whimsical names— *cappelletti,* little hats; *tortelli,* pies; *tortelli con la coda,* pies with tails—all lubricated with good wine.

Crossroads of the Ancients

Celts, Umbri, Etruscans, Gauls, ancient Romans, the infernal Lombards—everyone who came here coveted this benevolent valley. But the region's etymology is a result of the merger of two important Roman roads, Via Emilia, named for Marcus Aemilius Lepidus, the consul who built it, and Via Romea, the passage to the Eternal City. The first is a

Eating alfresco under the arcade, Piazza Maggiore, Bologna

LOCAL FLAVOR
BLOOD TYPE:
RAGÙ

Few vapors are as intoxicating as those emanating from *ragù* simmering in a pot. All of Italy's provinces make the celebrated *salsa*, each town or cook with their own version, but Bologna owns it. This is not the meat sauce parading on menus abroad as the topping for "spaghetti Bolognaise" (Bologna does not make spaghetti, nor is the spelling Italian). The real thing, *Salsa Bolognese*, designed for anointing the region's fresh egg pasta, is a heady, butter-based meat sauce scented with wine and nutmeg. It simmers at a lazy bubble—sometimes up to five hours—before, perhaps, being finished with a touch of cream or shaved truffle. One humorist has suggested that the leaning stone towers that have become a symbol of the city were put up for the citizens to better whiff the vapors of their splendid ragù cooking in every pot.

border. Along the way, it connects the remarkable cities and the gastronomies that distinguish them like a string of pearls: Cesena, Forlì, Bologna, Modena, and Parma. The second road runs north to south, connecting Rimini to Rome. If they are beset with the din of transport trucks and roaring of motorcycles today, they once carried chariots going to and fro with the stuff of empire for a period of a thousand years. Wagons drawn by oxen transported hams, olive oil, wine, grains, and produce grown in the countryside to the towns along their routes.

Exuberant Food From the Prodigal Land

Emilia, the upland, flat and fertile like a Midwest prairie, stretches from the Adriatic nearly across the entire shaft of Italy's boot, its westernmost corner ending in the Apennines where Liguria begins. Covered with alluvial soil formed millions of years ago when the area between the Adriatic and the Mediterranean was under seawater, this is some of Italy's most productive farmland. It leads Italy in growing *grano tenero,* the soft wheat used for its outstanding *sfoglia* (leaf, or sheet) egg pasta. This is the near-transparent, handmade dough that envelopes plump stuffed pasta creations, and forms paper-thin tagliatelle, *garganelli*, and all the rest.

Wander through this vast garden, perfumed with its famous orchards, and you will understand why it is considered the fruit bowl of Italy. The cherries, peaches, and pears are coveted not only as table fruit but also for making their famed preserves and gelatos.

A fruit stall in Parma flush at the height of tomato season

Farmers in the Parmigiano Reggiano areas pamper the dairy cows that provide the milk for the most famous cheese in the world.

Several thousand dairy farms on the plain supply milk to over 300 *casari*, cheese-makers who produce Parmigiano Reggiano, Italy's majestic cow's-milk cheese. Whey, the by-product of cheesemaking, is fed to Emilian hogs, pampered porkers that turn up in sublime *salumi,* considered the best in the world. The same milk is the source of distinctive butter, the traditional cooking fat here. Its deep, round flavor transforms even the simplest dish into a triumph, whether melted for the classic *burro oro e salvia*, or golden butter and sage, a sauce that coddles everything from fettuccine to potato gnocchi—or dolloped onto a heap of boiled lentils.

Romagna, the eastern half, runs the length of the coast as far as Le Marche. No doubt about it—this is Roman Italy. Before that, beginning in the 12th century B.C., it was Etruscan Italy. The Romans obliterated the Etruscans, but the mythical Etruscan taste for the good life endures. Rimini, which spawned none other than Federico Fellini, embraces the dolce vita with its colorful beach towns and open-air trattorias, as well as a four-day international gelato competition held every two years in a park bearing Fellini's name. It was the infamous film director who once said, "It is easier to be faithful to a restaurant than to a woman." You can visit the Fellini Museum in the historic town center.

Another word Italians use for salumi, *dry-cured meats, is* insaccati, *meaning meat "in a sack."*

BREEZY PROSCIUTTO DI PARMA

Salt-cured and air-dried Prosciutto di Parma DOP, the most sought-after ham in the world, needs four essential ingredients: wholesome hogs well fed on whey (a by-product of Parmigiano Reggiano cheese), barley, corn, and fruit; dry mountain air; salt; and know-how. Parma province has it all. Steady air currents rise from the Versilia River and blow through the Apennines. By the time they reach the spacious *prosciuttifici* in the round hills where the rear legs of 10-month porkers are salted, hung, and periodically massaged, they have picked up the perfumes of olive groves, chestnut woods, and pine forests along the way— terroir in a slice.

Marriage of Blue Blood and Country Stock

Emilia–Romagna's love of lavish eating can be attributed to nurture as much as nature. It was reared on the patrician sensibilities of powerful ruling families. Following the collapse of the Roman Empire, feudal lords battled to control the bountiful flatlands and foothills. Their feast continued in the Renaissance courts of the Este of Ferrara, the Bentivoglio of Bologna, the Maletesta of Rimini, the Farnese of Parma and Piacenza—and well into the 18th century when Parma was ruled by the Hapsburg duchess Marie-Louise (second wife of Napoleon). Empress of France, she brought Paris's sauces and pastries to her new Emilia home. These 400 years of court food became the forerunner of today's cooking. Ferrara's *torta di farro Messisbugo*, a velvety cheese tart rimmed with a golden, saffron-tinged crust, was the masterpiece of Cristoforo di Messisbugo. Steward of the 16th-century Este court, his documentation of its cooking earned him a noble title.

The region's country cooking evolved over centuries, too, especially during frigid winters when people gathered around the hearth, conjuring tasty fare that endures in robust polentas, rustic country breads, and savory pies.

Provincial Nuances

There are more similarities than differences in the cooking of the region's nine provinces, but each has distinctive specialties. Bologna is the rightful seat of Mortadella Bologna. With its silky, peony-pink-petal-colored meat, the real thing looks—and tastes—more German wurst than Italian sausage, leading one to wonder if it wasn't originally the brainchild of some *wurstmacher* during the prosperous days of Liutprand, the eighth-century Lombard king.

Modena, home of Ferrari, Pavarotti, exquisite salumi, and *aceto balsamico*—more a sacrament than a vinegar in these parts—is synonymous with excellence. Every Emilian province has its version of *bollito misto,* the grand boiled dinner reserved for special occasions. But Modena's, with its famed *zampone* among the 10 different meats, is the ultimate (three different sauces are served on the side).

Aristocratic Ferrara has a rich roster of local quiddities, most famously *cappellacci di zucca* IGP, feather-light pasta envelopes stuffed with a nutmeg-scented pumpkin filling. A tradition of Jewish cooking includes goose prosciutto and elaborate marzipan confections. Reggio Emilia, known for its stews and *scarpazzone,* chard pie, has a Hebraic tradition, too. If you are there on a Thursday, you might find *polpettone di tacchino,* turkey and veal meatloaf, for sale in specialty shops, prepared in advance for the Sabbath.

The cultured city of Parma, birthplace of Verdi and Toscanini, makes music in many ways. Its province, namesake of Parmigiano Reggiano, is considered the food capital of Italy for its refined cuisine and high-profile foods. Two millennia of tradition go into making its prestigious hams, using as little salt as necessary for buttery meat, a method

Laura Maioli and her assistant create traditional *cappelletti* at Pasta Fresca Laura.

Parmigiano Reggiano, The Real Deal

Parmigiano Reggiano, despite its name, is made throughout the Po Valley. Even if the designated production zone extends to Modena and parts of Bologna and Lombardy, the spread is the result of a compromise struck only in the last century between the cheesemakers of Parma and Reggio Emilia next door. The soil, season, climate, air, vegetation, and cattle-raising traditions of the five provinces are as essential to the character of this cheese as the dedication of those producing it.

Even if some *casari* have fine-tuned their modern operations to resemble more of a Ferrari shop floor than the simple *caseifici* (dairies) of yesterday, the process remains unchanged. Family cheesemakers devote their entire lives to these norms, rising early to collect the morning milk from which the cheese must be made. In such caseifici, a worker might tell you that he has no time for taking a honeymoon after his upcoming nuptials—the cheese requires as much tender, loving care as any offspring he might produce for future generations of casari. Large operation or small, what remains consistent are strict protocols following tradition that prevent

the prospect of its production from ever becoming industrial.

As the cheese ages for 18 months to four years, its flavor intensifies, so that when these wheels the color of burnished gold are cleaved open, their aroma conveys no less than the life and memories of whole villages. So valuable are they that in the bigger operations you might see guards equipped with machine guns supervising their transfer to armored trucks destined for market.

A nugget of bona fide Parmigiano Reggiano is a rich straw color as well as firm, moist, flaky, and possessing a slightly granular texture. Freshly grated, its flavor elevates so many of Emilia–Romagna's dishes from what might otherwise be merely great to simply magnficent. To understand why, eat it on its own as a starter for its full bouquet and complex texture, which are released slowly as the grains dissolve in your mouth and layer after layer of flavor is revealed.

A cheesemaker tends to his stock of precious Parmigiano Reggiano in an aging room at Caseificio Gennari.

Secrets of the Rind

To be sure you are getting authentic Parmigiano Reggiano and not an imitation, buy a block of cheese recently pried from the whole wheel. Look for the black riddled markings on the rind that brand the name Parmigiano Reggiano and show the date of production. Younger cheeses may be served on their own, but it is the more aged, known as *stravecchio* (very mature), that when grated are essential to the region's opulent pasta dishes.

Grate the cheese as close to use as possible to preserve its moisture and flavor. A word to the wise: Pulverized Parmesan (actually a French term) is about as genuine as the green can it comes in.

that remains practically unchanged. Salt-cured and air-dried Prosciutto di Parma, produced at a rate of nearly nine million a year in a process defined and protected with a DOP seal, is a craft with a lineage that the locals say goes back to the Etruscans. This is also the realm of *culatello,* a boneless ham filet distinct from the whole hind legs of Parma prosciutti. The art of its curing is practiced in cellars along the Po River, which envelop the "little bottoms" with a beguiling umami.

At the western extremity of Emilia–Romagna, stretched between the Po on its northern border and the Ligurian Appenines to the southwest, lies the province of Piacenza. Once a crossroads of travel between north and south, this was vital Roman territory and a thriving trade juncture. Today, it is famous gastronomically for both growing rice, a culinary obsession it shares with Lombardy, and making sausages. The first is evidenced in *bomba di riso,* a dome of rice molded around a rich ragù, the second in a varied and impressive production of salumi, with DOP applied to Coppa Piacentina, cured and subtly spiced pork shoulder (*capocollo* in the southern regions). Its eponymous capital, a walled Roman city on the left bank of the Po, is considered the jewel of the Renaissance. Not to be outdone by any of its rival cities, Piacenza has a unique variation on the theme of *pasta e fagioli* called *pisarei e faso,* a dish of miniature bread dumplings simmered with other types of gnocchi and joined with a tomato sauce and tender borlotti beans.

Upper Crust and Griddle Bread Meet

Romagna, which became more southern in character after the Papal States annexed it to central Italy, has something else that Emilia doesn't have: the sea. This is the home of *brodetto,* Romagna's dense fish soup, and *canocchie ripiene ai ferri,* the delicate mantis shrimp, stuffed with crumbs and herbs before grilling. Forlimpopoli, farther inland,

---

the truth about: TRADITIONAL BALSAMIC VINEGAR

Italians disagree that imitation is the best form of flattery, particularly with regard to Modena's miracle, *aceto balsamico tradizionale* (also made in Reggio Emilia). The "balsamic" used on salad is an industrial product that has become ubiquitous even where sweetness doesn't belong. The real thing is meticulous handiwork steeped in time-honored methods to transform indigenous grapes into a precious condiment, a cordial, an elixir—a process that takes 12 to 25 years. A judicious drop anoints a roast or a risotto, a peach, or a dish of strawberries, imbuing flesh or grain, fruit or vegetable, cheese or sweet, with its inimitable sweet-tart mystery.

True aged balsamic vinegar is thick, syrupy, sweet, and tart.

San Leo, Rimini, 10th-century capital of the Italian kingdom under the Lombard king Berengar II

deserves a mention for its cooking school, Casa Artusi, named after native son Pellegrino Artusi. The first to collect recipes (790 of them) from a united Italy after the Risorgimento, his cookbook was a recognition of the concept of "Italian cooking." The school is an ideal setting for immersion in the techniques of its humble, signature griddle bread called *piadina;* garganelli, quill-shaped fresh egg pasta formed on a comb; and other Romagnoli dishes, and for tastings of handcrafted cheeses that are not so easy to find abroad. Examples include *Squacquerone* and *Raviggiolo,* delectable fresh cheeses that have DOP designations but don't travel well because of their perishability.

Coasting the Olive Hills

The Adriatic hills of Forlì-Cesena and Rimini, catching the warm currents off the coast, have been a source of extra-virgin olive oil since the Etruscans planted the first groves on the hillsides. The oil has the intensity of the best from farther south, imbuing the food with profound *amaro,* bitter tones considered attributes to the initiated palate, whether for cooking or finishing.

The Apennines on the region's southern fringe, shared with Tuscany and Le Marche, are forbidding if you don't know your way. But for locals they mean truffles, lots of them, both white and black, and a surfeit of mushrooms, including the peerless porcini. Here you'll find wood-roasted meats and winey game braises with mountain herbs upon

For cutting Parmigiano Reggiano, use a small, blunt, spade-shaped knife with a bulbous handle designed to keep its grainy texture (actual crystals of protein) intact.

The famed cherries of Romagna, handpicked for market

them. The coastal and mountain cuisine spills over into San Marino, the curious republic of hilltop castles about the size of the Vatican state rising from the Romagna flatlands and framed entirely by Italian territory. Should you find yourself in Rimini for the aforementioned Gelato World Cup, San Marino is a 30-minute jaunt south by car for a panoramic view and doppelgängers of Romagna's piadina and the perfunctory braised rabbit with fennel.

Probably no other place can prepare you for the sumptuous feast of Emilia–Romagna. If you partake of its table, you will understand the difference between a glutton and a gourmand. Here is a land that understands that we are not only what we eat, to borrow a few words from the old lawyer-gastronome Brillat-Savarin, but also, how we eat.

Opposite: A spin past Modena's Duomo on the Piazza Grande

A Tale of Two Cheeses Grana Padano was the first cheese exported to the United States. Its vast production area is far bigger than the more recognized Parmigiano Reggiano's.

Stuffed Flatbreads

Piadine romagnole · *Makes 6 sandwiches*

WHY THIS RECIPE WORKS: What was once a poor man's bread in Emilia–Romagna, *piadina* is now found at the table in most restaurants. And when stuffed with various cheeses and cured meats and griddled, it's the region's best street and festival food. The texture is bready yet tender, with a short crumb. Delicate in flavor and easy to eat, it's perfect for folding around flavorful fillings for the ultimate sandwich. We started with the traditional technique of cutting lard into flour and then stirring in milk, but this first attempt resulted in piadine that were too thin and overly chewy and bready. A little baking soda helped puff the flatbreads ever so slightly. To simplify things, we moved our mixture to the food processor, drizzling in melted lard so it coated the flour particles; this prevented too much gluten from forming. We chose to fill our piadine with mild, melty mozzarella, which paired well with thinly sliced prosciutto, mortadella, or coppa—all delicious pork products of the region. Arugula provided fresh, peppery bite. Extra-virgin olive oil can be substituted for lard; however, the flatbreads will be slightly more chewy. A nonstick skillet can be used in place of the cast-iron skillet; preheat the empty nonstick skillet with 1 teaspoon oil, then wipe out oil before proceeding with the recipe.

2 cups (10 ounces) all-purpose flour
½ teaspoon salt
¼ teaspoon baking soda
1 tablespoon lard, melted
¾ cup whole milk
6 ounces thinly sliced Prosciutto di Parma, mortadella, or coppa
6 ounces mozzarella cheese, shredded (1½ cups)
2 ounces (2 cups) baby arugula

1 Pulse flour, salt, and baking soda in food processor until combined, about 5 pulses. With processor running, slowly add lard until incorporated, then add milk and process until dough forms tacky ball, about 5 seconds. Transfer dough to lightly floured counter and knead by hand to form smooth, round ball, about 3 minutes.

2 Divide dough into 6 equal pieces and cover loosely with greased plastic wrap. Working with 1 piece of dough at a time (keep remaining pieces covered), place ball seam side down on clean counter and, using your cupped hand, drag in small circles until dough feels taut and round. Let dough balls rest for 30 minutes.

3 Roll 1 ball of dough into 8-inch round of even thickness (about 1⁄16 inch thick) on lightly floured counter. Cover loosely with plastic and repeat with remaining dough balls.

4 Heat 12-inch cast-iron skillet over medium heat for 3 minutes. Carefully place 1 dough round in skillet and prick in several places with fork. Cook until spotty golden, 1 to 3 minutes per side, popping any large bubbles that form with fork. Transfer piadina to rimmed baking sheet and cover with clean dish towel; repeat with remaining dough rounds, stacking them under towel as they finish. (Cooled piadine can be stored in zipper-lock bag for up to 2 days; microwave for 30 seconds to soften before proceeding with recipe.)

5 Heat now-empty skillet over medium-low heat for 2 minutes. Evenly layer prosciutto, mozzarella, and arugula on half of each piadina, leaving ½-inch border at edge. Working with 2 filled piadine at a time, fold other half of flatbread over filling, then place cheese side down in skillet and press lightly with back of spatula to compress layers. Cook until cheese is melted and piadine are warmed through, 1 to 3 minutes per side. Repeat folding and cooking remaining piadine in 2 batches. Serve immediately.

Milk-Braised Pork Roast

Arrosto di maiale al latte • *Serves 4 to 6*

WHY THIS RECIPE WORKS: Cooking meat in milk is a classic braising treatment for pork loin in Emilia–Romagna—and for good reason. The milk tenderizes the pork and the meat soaks up the flavors of the resulting sweet, nutty sauce. Bolognese families often prepare this hearty dish on Sundays in the winter. As you'd expect, the milk curdles; Italians don't mind, but we wanted to make the sauce more attractive. We minimized curdling (and amped up flavor) by adding a touch of fat from rendered salt pork; the fat coats the casein proteins in milk and prevents them from bonding. A small amount of baking soda raised the pH of the sauce to create conditions more favorable for Maillard browning, a series of reactions that create flavorful aromatic compounds. The milk will bubble up when added to the pot. If necessary, remove the pot from the heat and stir to break up the foam before returning it to the heat. We prefer natural pork, but if your pork is enhanced (injected with a salt solution), do not brine.

Salt and pepper
½ cup sugar
1 (2- to 2½-pound) boneless pork loin roast, trimmed
2 ounces salt pork, chopped coarse
3 cups whole milk
5 garlic cloves, peeled
1 teaspoon minced fresh sage
½ teaspoon baking soda
½ cup dry white wine
3 tablespoons chopped fresh parsley
1 teaspoon Dijon mustard

❶ Dissolve ¼ cup salt and sugar in 2 quarts cold water in large container. Submerge roast in brine, cover, and refrigerate for at least 1½ hours or up to 2 hours. Remove roast from brine and pat dry with paper towels.

❷ Adjust oven rack to middle position and heat oven to 275 degrees. Bring salt pork and ½ cup water to simmer in Dutch oven over medium heat. Simmer until water evaporates and salt pork begins to sizzle, 5 to 6 minutes. Continue to cook, stirring frequently, until salt pork is lightly browned and fat has rendered, 2 to 3 minutes. Using slotted spoon, discard salt pork, leaving fat in pot.

❸ Increase heat to medium-high, add roast to pot, and brown on all sides, 8 to 10 minutes. Transfer roast to large plate. Add milk, garlic, sage, and baking soda to pot and bring to simmer, scraping up any browned bits. Cook, stirring frequently, until milk is lightly browned and has consistency of heavy cream, 14 to 16 minutes. Reduce heat to medium-low and continue to cook, stirring and scraping bottom of pot constantly, until milk thickens to consistency of thin batter, 1 to 3 minutes. Remove pot from heat.

❹ Return roast to pot, cover, and transfer to oven. Cook until pork registers 140 degrees, 40 to 50 minutes, flipping roast once halfway through cooking. Transfer roast to carving board, tent with aluminum foil, and let rest for 20 to 25 minutes.

❺ Once roast has rested, pour any accumulated juices into pot. Add wine and return sauce to simmer over medium-high heat, whisking vigorously to smooth out sauce. Simmer until sauce has consistency of thin gravy, 2 to 3 minutes. Off heat, stir in 2 tablespoons parsley and mustard and season with salt and pepper to taste. Slice roast into ¼-inch-thick slices and transfer to serving dish. Spoon sauce over pork, sprinkle with remaining 1 tablespoon parsley, and serve.

Tortellini in Broth

Tortellini in brodo · *Serves 8 to 10*

WHY THIS RECIPE WORKS: *Tortellini in brodo* is a treasured dish of pasta-loving Emilia–Romagna. Deceptively simple, it's nothing more than filled pasta barely swimming in a basic broth. But it achieves complexity for a few reasons: The delicate pasta shapes are tiny and intricately folded, the flavors inside are rich and meaty, and the broth is light but has a nuanced flavor. This preparation might be the best way to fully appreciate the eggy softness of fresh pasta and the meaty, rich flavors of the region's prime ingredients in its filling. Tortellini, when prepared at home, is typically served as a special occasion *primo*, although it's a staple on many trattoria menus at all times. Both pork loin and chicken are traditional filling ingredients; we opted for ground chicken because it offered a good balance of fatty and lean meat. In addition, the rich, salty qualities of the region's cured meats, Prosciutto di Parma and mortadella, helped create a smooth, robust filling. Parmigiano, parsley, and nutmeg rounded out the flavors. Letting the raw tortellini dry for 30 minutes helped them hold their shape once cooked. You can make homemade broth, but given that shaping tortellini is a time-consuming process, we found we could infuse store-bought broth with some of our ground chicken, onion, garlic, and more nutmeg for superb flavor. Be sure to use ground chicken, not ground chicken breast (also labeled

99 percent fat free). Our favorite pasta machine is the Marcato Altas 150 Wellness Pasta Machine; the pasta will be thin and semi-transparent when rolled to setting 7. For more information on rolling pasta sheets, see page 365.

BROTH

- 8 ounces ground chicken
- 2 cups chicken broth
- ½ onion, peeled
- 3 garlic cloves, peeled and smashed
- 4 parsley stems
- ¼ teaspoon salt
- ¼ teaspoon ground nutmeg

TORTELLINI

- 4 ounces ground chicken
- 2 ounces mortadella, chopped coarse
- 1 ounce Prosciutto di Parma, chopped coarse
- 2 tablespoons grated Parmigiano Reggiano cheese
- 2 tablespoons chopped fresh parsley
- 2 tablespoons extra-virgin olive oil
- ¼ teaspoon ground nutmeg
- 8 ounces Fresh Egg Pasta (page 364)
- 1 tablespoon salt

1 For the broth: Bring all ingredients to simmer in small saucepan. Reduce heat to medium-low, cover, and cook until flavors meld, about 15 minutes. Strain broth through fine-mesh strainer into bowl, pressing on solids with rubber spatula to extract as much liquid as possible; discard solids. (Broth can be refrigerated for up to 24 hours.) Return broth to now-empty saucepan, cover, and keep warm over low heat.

2 For the tortellini: Process ground chicken, mortadella, prosciutto, Parmigiano, parsley, oil, nutmeg, and 1 tablespoon warm broth in food processor until smooth, 30 to 45 seconds, scraping down sides of bowl as needed. Transfer mixture to bowl, cover, and refrigerate until chilled, about 30 minutes.

3 Transfer dough to clean counter, divide into 3 pieces, and cover with plastic wrap. Flatten 1 piece of dough into ½-inch-thick disk. Using pasta machine with rollers set to widest position, feed dough through rollers twice. Bring tapered ends of dough toward middle and press to seal. Feed dough seam side first through rollers again. Repeat feeding dough tapered end first through rollers set at widest position, without folding, until dough is smooth and barely tacky. (If dough sticks to fingers or rollers, lightly dust with flour and roll again.)

4 Narrow rollers to next setting and feed dough through rollers twice. Continue to progressively narrow rollers, feeding dough through each setting twice, until dough is very thin and semi-transparent. (If dough becomes too long to manage, halve crosswise.) Transfer sheet of pasta to liberally floured sheet of parchment paper. Cover with second sheet of parchment, followed by damp kitchen towel, to keep pasta from drying out. Repeat rolling with remaining 2 pieces of dough, stacking pasta sheets between floured layers of parchment.

5 Liberally dust rimmed baking sheet with flour. Cut 1 pasta sheet into rounds on lightly floured counter using 2½-inch round cookie cutter (keep remaining sheets covered); discard scraps. Place ½ teaspoon filling in center of each round. Working with 1 pasta round at a time, lightly brush edges with water. Fold bottom edge of pasta over filling until flush with top edge to form half-moon shape. Press to seal edges flush to filling.

6 With folded edge of filled pasta facing you, pull corners together below filling until slightly overlapped to create tortellini with cupped outer edge and dimpled center. Press to seal overlapping edges and transfer to prepared sheet. Repeat cutting and filling remaining pasta (you should have about 60 tortellini). Let tortellini sit uncovered until dry to touch and slightly stiffened, about 30 minutes. (Tortellini can be wrapped with plastic

and refrigerated for up to 4 hours or chilled in freezer until firm, then transferred to zipper-lock bag and frozen for up to 1 month. If frozen, do not thaw before cooking; increase simmering time to 3 to 4 minutes.)

7 Bring 4 quarts water to boil in large pot. Add tortellini and salt and simmer gently, stirring often, until edges of tortellini are al dente, 2 to 3 minute. Using slotted spoon, transfer tortellini to individual bowls. Spoon warm broth over top and serve.

SHAPING TORTELLINI

1. Fold bottom edge of pasta over filling until flush with top edge to form half-moon shape. Press to seal edges flush to filling.

2. Pull corners together below filling until slightly overlapped to create tortellini with cupped outer edge and dimpled center. Press to seal overlapping edges.

Swiss Chard Pie

Erbazzone • *Serves 12*

....

WHY THIS RECIPE WORKS: The city of Reggio Emilia is the birthplace of the most satisfying of snacks: *erbazzone*, a hearty, savory pie packed with tender greens. It originated as a peasant picnic dish called *scarpazzoun*, which used the stems of beet or chard greens (referred to as *scarpa*, which literally translates to "shoe"), since greens were always plentiful in gardens of the region. Eventually, the pie became commonly known as erbazzone (herb pie), which signifies that it's packed with greens, usually Swiss chard. The greens are cooked down, flavored with the region's famous pork and plenty of Parmigiano Reggiano cheese, and wrapped in a flaky crust. Variations abound—some call for egg in the filling, and some are shaped into rectangles while others are shaped into circles—but the one controversial ingredient is ricotta. Many recipes don't include it, while others claim it's not erbazzone without it. We liked the cleaner, earthier taste of the erbazzone without the ricotta, but if you prefer a cheesier filling we've provided the option. This dough will be moister than most pie doughs; as the dough chills it will absorb any excess moisture, leaving it supple and workable.

CRUST
- 20 tablespoons (2½ sticks) cold unsalted butter
- 2½ cups (12½ ounces) all-purpose flour
- 1 teaspoon salt
- ½ cup ice water

FILLING
- 1 tablespoon extra-virgin olive oil
- 3 ounces pancetta, chopped fine (⅔ cup)
- 1 onion, chopped fine
- 4 garlic cloves, minced
- 3 pounds Swiss chard, stemmed and cut into 1-inch pieces
- 4 ounces Parmigiano Reggiano cheese, grated (2 cups)
- 6 ounces (¾ cup) whole-milk ricotta cheese (optional)
- 1 large egg, lightly beaten

1 For the crust: Grate half stick butter using coarse holes on box grater and place in freezer. Cut remaining 2 sticks butter into ½-inch pieces.

2 Pulse 1½ cups flour and salt in food processor until combined, about 4 pulses. Add butter pieces and process until homogenous dough forms, about 30 seconds. Using hands, carefully break dough into 2-inch chunks and redistribute evenly around processor blade. Add remaining 1 cup flour and pulse until mixture is broken into pieces no larger than 1 inch (most pieces will be much smaller), 4 to 5 pulses. Empty mixture into medium bowl. Add grated butter and toss until butter pieces are separated and coated with flour.

3 Sprinkle ¼ cup ice water over mixture. Toss with rubber spatula until mixture is evenly moistened. Sprinkle remaining ¼ cup ice water over mixture and toss to combine. Press dough with spatula until dough sticks together. Divide dough in half and transfer to sheets of plastic wrap. Draw edges of plastic wrap over first dough half and press firmly on sides and top to form compact, fissure-free mass. Flatten to form 5-inch square. Repeat with second dough half. Refrigerate for at least 2 hours or up to 2 days. Let chilled dough sit on counter to soften slightly, about 10 minutes, before rolling.

4 For the filling: Adjust oven rack to lower-middle position and heat oven to 400 degrees. Cook oil and ⅓ cup pancetta in Dutch oven over medium-low heat until pancetta is browned and fat is rendered, 5 to 7 minutes. Using slotted spoon, transfer pancetta to bowl. Pour off all but 1 tablespoon fat from pot.

5 Add onion to fat left in pot and cook over medium heat until softened, about 5 minutes. Stir in garlic and cook until fragrant, about 30 seconds. Increase heat to high; add chard, 1 handful at a time, and cook until beginning to wilt, about 1 minute. Cover and continue to cook, stirring occasionally, until chard is wilted but still bright green, 2 to 4 minutes. Uncover and continue to cook until liquid evaporates, about 5 minutes. Transfer chard to large bowl and let cool to room temperature, about 30 minutes.

6 Grease rimmed baking sheet. Stir Parmigiano, ricotta, if using, and pancetta into chard. Roll 1 dough square into 14 by 10-inch rectangle on well-floured counter. Loosely roll dough around rolling pin and unroll it onto prepared sheet. Spread chard mixture evenly over crust, leaving 1-inch border around edges. Brush edges of crust with egg.

7 Roll remaining dough square into 14 by 10-inch rectangle on lightly floured counter. Loosely roll dough around rolling pin and unroll it over filling. Press edges of crusts together to seal. Roll edges inward and use your fingers to crimp. Using sharp knife, cut through top crust into 12 equal squares (do not cut through filling). Brush with remaining egg and sprinkle with remaining ⅓ cup pancetta.

8 Bake until pie is golden brown and pancetta is crisp, 30 to 35 minutes, rotating sheet halfway through baking. Transfer sheet to wire rack and let pie cool completely, about 30 minutes. Transfer pie to cutting board, cut into squares, and serve.

Green Lasagna With Meat Sauce

Lasagne verdi alla bolognese · *Serves 10 to 12*

WHY THIS RECIPE WORKS: Emilia–Romagna is home to the quintessential Italian lasagna, the celebrated and celebratory *lasagne verdi alla bolognese*. Served at holidays or other special occasions, this showstopper is a decadent combination of meaty *Ragù alla bolognese* (page 160); velvety, creamy béchamel sauce; and lots of Parmigiano Reggiano, all layered between thin sheets of vibrant green spinach pasta. Preparing spinach pasta dough sounded daunting, but we found that frozen spinach worked just as well as fresh spinach; we simply pureed it in the food processor with the eggs. Knowing our rich, flavorful meat sauce would be a bit of a project (albeit well worth the work), we looked to simplify the béchamel. To avoid the hassle of cooking milk, butter, and flour, we turned to an unorthodox option: cottage cheese. Cottage cheese turns creamy (instead of grainy like ricotta) in the oven. We whisked it with cream, Parmigiano, and a touch of cornstarch (to prevent curdling) for a surprisingly lush no-cook cream sauce. We finished our lasagna with a sprinkling of Parmigiano over a final layer of cream sauce, which baked into a gooey, crisp-edged, golden-brown top. Our favorite pasta machine is the Marcato Altas 150 Wellness Pasta Machine; the pasta will be thin but opaque when rolled to setting 6. For more information on rolling pasta sheets, see page 365.

PASTA SHEETS

- 5 ounces frozen chopped spinach, thawed and squeezed dry
- 3 large eggs
- 2 cups (10 ounces) all-purpose flour, plus extra as needed
- 1 tablespoon salt
- 1 tablespoon extra-virgin olive oil

LASAGNA

- 6½ ounces Parmigiano Reggiano cheese, grated (3¼ cups)
- 8 ounces (1 cup) whole-milk cottage cheese
- 1 cup heavy cream
- 2 garlic cloves, minced
- 1 tablespoon cornstarch
- ½ teaspoon pepper
- ¼ teaspoon salt
- 3 cups Ragù alla bolognese (page 160), room temperature

1 For the pasta sheets: Process spinach and eggs in food processor until spinach is finely chopped, about 30 seconds, scraping down sides of bowl as needed. Add flour and process until mixture forms cohesive dough that feels soft and is barely tacky to touch, about 45 seconds. (If dough sticks to fingers, add up to ¼ cup extra flour, 1 tablespoon at a time, until barely tacky.)

2 Transfer dough to clean counter and knead by hand to form smooth, round ball, about 2 minutes. Cover tightly with plastic wrap and let rest at room temperature for at least 15 minutes or up to 2 hours.

3 Transfer dough to clean counter, divide into 10 pieces (about 2¾ ounces each), and cover with plastic. Flatten 1 piece of dough into ½-inch-thick disk. Using pasta machine with rollers set to widest position, feed dough through rollers twice. Bring tapered ends of dough toward middle and press to seal. Feed dough seam side first through rollers again. Repeat feeding dough tapered end first through rollers set at widest position, without folding, until dough is smooth. (If dough sticks to fingers or rollers, lightly dust with flour and roll again.)

4 Narrow rollers to next setting and feed dough through rollers twice. Continue to progressively narrow rollers, feeding dough through each setting twice, until dough is thin but still sturdy; transfer to lightly floured counter. Using pizza cutter or sharp knife, trim pasta sheet into 11 by 3 ½-inch rectangle; discard scraps. Let lasagna noodle sit uncovered on counter while rolling remaining 9 pieces of dough (do not overlap noodles as they may stick together).

5 Bring 4 quarts water to boil in large pot. Add noodles and salt and cook, stirring often, until just tender, 2 to 3 minutes. Drain noodles and toss with oil. Using tongs, lay noodles flat over 2 rimmed baking sheets, overlapping as needed, and let cool slightly.

6 For the lasagna: Adjust oven rack to middle position and heat oven to 425 degrees. Grease 13 by 9-inch baking dish. Stir 3 cups Parmigiano, cottage cheese, cream, garlic, cornstarch, pepper, and salt together in bowl.

7 Spread 1 cup ragù in bottom of prepared dish. Lay 2 noodles lengthwise in dish, trimming edges as needed to fit. Spread 1 cup cream sauce over top, followed by second layer of noodles. Spread 1 cup ragù over top, followed by third layer of noodles. Repeat layering of cream sauce, noodles, and ragù, ending with fifth layer of noodles. Spread remaining cream sauce over top and sprinkle with remaining ¼ cup Parmigiano. Spray sheet of aluminum foil with vegetable oil spray and cover lasagna. (Lasagna can be refrigerated for up to 24 hours.)

8 Bake until bubbling around edges, about 30 minutes. Remove foil and continue to bake until top is spotty brown, about 10 minutes. Let lasagna cool for 45 minutes. Cut into pieces and serve.

Squash-Filled Pasta

Cappellacci di zucca · *Serves 6*

....

WHY THIS RECIPE WORKS: The artful *cappellacci* ("big hats") are another of the glorious filled pastas of Emilia–Romagna. They're similar in shape to jumbo tortellini, but they sport a pointed top. The Italian pumpkin *zucca* is plentiful in Emilia–Romagna, and when combined with the region's Parmigiano Reggiano it serves as a luscious, rich filling for *cappellacci di zucca*, a beloved, signature dish of the city of Ferrara. We found that butternut squash is the best stateside substitute for the sweet-fleshed zucca. Variations of the filling often incorporate *mostarda* (a fruit and mustard condiment) or crumbled amaretti cookies. To streamline the grocery list, we omitted these additions, but we did like the brightness that the assertive, acidic mostarda contributed. A simple drizzle of high-quality balsamic vinegar, an esteemed product of the region, brought a similar balance to the dish. Because the cappellacci were relatively large, the seams and folds where the dough is pinched together remained chewy and undercooked in early tests. To fix this, we rolled the pasta until it was paper thin (translucent enough to see your hand through the dough). This way, even at its bulkiest folded parts, the pasta cooked up tender and supple in a matter of minutes. All these pasta pillows needed for sauce was a toss in melted sage butter. Do not use frozen squash here. Our favorite pasta machine is the Marcato

Atlas 150 Wellness Pasta Machine; the pasta will be thin and semi-transparent when rolled to setting 8. For more information on rolling pasta sheets, see page 364.

FILLING

- **1½ pounds butternut squash, peeled, seeded, and cut into 1-inch pieces (3½ cups)**
- **6 tablespoons unsalted butter**
- **2½ ounces Parmigiano Reggiano cheese, grated (1¼ cups)**
- **Salt and pepper**
- **Pinch ground nutmeg**

CAPPELLACCI

- **1 recipe Fresh Egg Pasta (page 364)**
- **6 tablespoons unsalted butter**
- **1 tablespoon minced fresh sage**
- **Salt**
- **Balsamic vinegar**
- **Shaved Parmigiano Reggiano cheese**

1 For the filling: Microwave squash in covered bowl until very soft and easily pierced with fork, 15 to 18 minutes, stirring halfway through microwaving. Carefully remove cover, allowing steam to escape away from you, and drain squash.

2 Process squash, butter, Parmigiano, ¼ teaspoon salt, ⅛ teaspoon pepper, and nutmeg in food processor until smooth, about 1 minute, scraping down sides of bowl as needed. Transfer filling to bowl and refrigerate for 30 minutes. (Filling can be refrigerated for up to 24 hours.)

3 For the cappellacci: Transfer dough to clean counter, divide into 6 pieces, and cover with plastic wrap. Flatten 1 piece of dough into ½-inch-thick disk. Using pasta machine with rollers set to widest position, feed dough through rollers twice. Bring tapered ends of dough toward middle and press to seal. Feed dough seam side first through rollers again. Repeat feeding dough tapered ends first through rollers set at widest position, without folding, until dough is

smooth and barely tacky. (If dough sticks to fingers or rollers, lightly dust with flour and roll again.)

4 Narrow rollers to next setting and feed dough through rollers twice. Continue to progressively narrow rollers, feeding dough through each setting twice, until dough is paper thin, transparent, and delicate. (Pasta sheet should be about 5 inches wide; if not, fold sheet in half crosswise and roll again.) Transfer sheet of pasta to liberally floured sheet of parchment paper. Cover with second sheet of parchment, followed by damp kitchen towel, to keep pasta from drying out. Repeat rolling with remaining 5 pieces of dough, stacking pasta sheets between floured layers of parchment.

5 Liberally dust rimmed baking sheet with flour. Using pizza cutter or sharp knife, cut 1 pasta sheet into 5-inch squares on lightly floured counter (keep remaining sheets covered); discard scraps. Place 1 rounded tablespoon filling in center of each square. Working with 1 pasta square at a time, lightly brush edges with water. With one corner of pasta square facing you, fold bottom corner of pasta over filling until flush with top corner to form triangle shape. Press to seal edges flush to filling. Trim any uneven edges.

6 With folded edge of filled pasta facing you, pull corners together below filling until slightly overlapped to create cappellacci with cupped outer edge and dimpled center. Press to seal overlapping edges and transfer to prepared sheet. Repeat cutting and filling remaining pasta (you should have about 18 cappellacci). Let cappellacci sit uncovered until dry to touch and slightly stiffened, about 30 minutes. (Cappellacci can be wrapped with plastic and refrigerated for up to 4 hours or chilled in freezer until firm, then transferred to zipper-lock bag and frozen for up to 1 month. If frozen, do not thaw before cooking; increase simmering time to 6 to 8 minutes.)

7 Melt butter in 12-inch skillet over medium heat. Off heat, stir in sage and ¼ teaspoon salt; set aside. Bring 4 quarts water to boil in large pot. Add half of cappellacci and 1 tablespoon salt and simmer gently, stirring often, until edges of cappellacci are al dente, 4 to 6 minutes. Using slotted spoon, transfer cappellacci to skillet, gently toss to coat, and cover to keep warm. Return cooking water to boil and repeat cooking remaining cappellacci; transfer to skillet and gently toss to coat. Drizzle individual portions with balsamic vinegar and top with Parmigiano before serving.

SHAPING CAPPELLACCI

1. Fold bottom corner of pasta over filling until flush with top corner to form triangle shape. Press to seal edges flush to filling.

2. Pull corners together below filling until slightly overlapped to create cappellacci with cupped outer edge and dimpled center. Press to seal overlapping edges.

Bolognese Sauce

Ragù alla bolognese · Serves 6 to 8

WHY THIS RECIPE WORKS: When tossed with strands of fresh tagliatelle pasta, *ragù alla bolognese* constitutes the essential comfort food of Emilia–Romagna. In fact, it's codified as such: The Accademia Italiana della Cucina has defined what ingredients go into the most typical ragù alla bolognese. However, the dish still lends itself to interpretation (and hearty debate) by Bolognesi. Recipes differ from family to family in the fat used for cooking, the choices of meat, the cooking liquid, whether tomato is used or not, and whether milk is involved and when it's added. If there's one consensus, however, it's that a good bolognese should always be hearty and rich but not cloying, with a velvety texture that clings lightly to the noodles. We utilized six types of meat for ultrarich, complex flavor: ground beef, pork, and veal; pancetta; mortadella; and pureed chicken livers, which added a subtle gamy flavor that elevated the dish. A combination of red wine and tomato paste created a sauce with balanced acidity. What was missing, however, was the ultraglossy cling of the best Bolognese sauces. Many Italian recipes call for homemade beef broth; the gelatin rendered from the bones in the broth makes the sauce glossy and viscous. To short-cut the time-consuming step of preparing homemade broth, we dissolved gelatin in store-bought broth for a sauce that was super silky. As for the milk, we found it muted the meaty flavor, so we departed from what some Bolognesi cooks consider tradition and left it out. But how could any version be Bolognese without a little controversy? This recipe makes enough sauce to coat 2 pounds of pasta; leftover sauce may be refrigerated for up to 3 days or frozen for up to 1 month. Eight teaspoons of gelatin is equivalent to one (1-ounce) box of gelatin.

1 cup chicken broth
1 cup beef broth
8 teaspoons unflavored gelatin
1 onion, chopped coarse
1 large carrot, peeled and
    chopped coarse
1 celery rib, chopped coarse
4 ounces pancetta, chopped
4 ounces mortadella, chopped
6 ounces chicken livers, trimmed
3 tablespoons extra-virgin olive oil
12 ounces 85 percent lean
    ground beef
12 ounces ground veal
12 ounces ground pork
3 tablespoons minced fresh sage
1 (6-ounce) can tomato paste
2 cups dry red wine
Salt and pepper
1 pound Fresh Egg Pasta
    (page 364)

1 Combine chicken broth and beef broth in bowl; sprinkle gelatin over top and let sit until softened, about 5 minutes.

2 Pulse onion, carrot, and celery in food processor until finely chopped, about 10 pulses, scraping down sides of bowl as needed; transfer to separate bowl. Pulse pancetta and mortadella in now-empty processor until finely chopped, about 25 pulses; transfer to third bowl. Process chicken livers in again-empty processor until pureed, about 5 seconds; refrigerate until ready to use.

3 Heat oil in Dutch oven over medium-high heat until shimmering. Add ground beef, veal, and pork and cook, breaking up meat with wooden spoon, until all liquid has evaporated and meat begins to sizzle, 10 to 15 minutes. Stir in pancetta mixture and sage and cook until pancetta is translucent, 5 to 7 minutes, adjusting heat as needed to keep fond from burning. Stir in chopped vegetables and cook until softened, 5 to 7 minutes. Stir in tomato paste and cook until rust-colored and fragrant, about 3 minutes.

4 Stir in wine, scraping up any browned bits, and simmer until thickened, about 5 minutes. Stir in broth mixture, return to bare simmer, and cook until sauce has thickened (wooden spoon should leave trail when dragged through sauce), about 1½ hours.

5 Stir in chicken livers and bring to brief simmer. Season with salt and pepper to taste.

6 Meanwhile, bring 4 quarts water to boil in large pot. Add pasta and 1 tablespoon salt and cook, stirring often, until al dente. Reserve 1 cup cooking water, then drain pasta and return it to pot. Add half of sauce and ½ cup reserved cooking water and toss to combine. Before serving, adjust consistency with remaining ½ cup reserved cooking water as needed.

The city of Florence, capital of
the Renaissance, is a work of art.

PART TWO

Central Italy

An archaic culture of wealth and luxury established the culinary traditions of the central regions.

From Ancient Roots, a Superlative Cuisine

NEITHER THE COOL, COSMOPOLITAN NORTH, nor the hot, passionate south, central Italy strikes just the right balance for discerning travelers and their palates. The landscape seems quintessentially Italian: a rumpled quilt of rolling hills, intensely cultivated and dominated by small farms, tall cypress trees along ancient roads, terra cotta–tiled farmhouses, and exquisite cities including Rome, Orvieto, Urbino, and Florence. • Central Italy, its mountains, plains, valleys, and merry coastline, is

both civilized and down to earth. Home of the Renaissance, this most visited part of Italy, along with its celebrated culture and cuisine, is what most travelers think of as "Italian." Indeed, the central Italian kitchen, which takes simplicity to a higher level, characterizes much of what generally makes Italian food so special. That finesse is derived from two things: an ancient cosmopolitan heritage and a fidelity to the high-quality ingredients that are locally grown or produced.

Ancient Origins, Contemporary Customs

The most significant influence on the foods of central Italy comes from the Etruscans, who may have arisen from Italian soil or migrated to Italy from the East. Their culture was powerful and wealthy by the sixth century B.C., leading to the founding of many still standing cities, including Viterbo, Arezzo, and Perugia. They also introduced land improvements, including river flow regulation, land reclamation, and irrigation systems, some of which are still working today.

Many of the same mother crops grown by the Etruscans remain staples here, such as olives—ancient Etruria was one of the first areas in Italy to cultivate olive trees—as

Great ingredients make great dishes.

well as barley, fava beans, legumes, sesame, peas, *Triticum durum* wheat, and farro, an ancient grain that has made a comeback. They farmed fish (as did the Romans, and as the central Italians still do), particularly sturgeon and eel. This ancient people planted grapes and were prolific wine traders who profited from the thirsty Gauls, with ports along the northern Mediterranean and trading posts in the Po Valley.

Red garlic

So much of what we consider Italian can be traced to the posh, sophisticated Etruscans, such as the extended courses in an Italian meal and the large midday meal. Contrary to the enduring myth that the Italians learned about pasta from the Chinese, archaeological evidence suggests the Etruscans were making pasta as far back as the fourth century B.C. Tellingly, Roman chronicles show the Etruscans dressed it *all'olio,* with olive oil and garlic, just as it is prepared in central Italian kitchens today.

Other Italic peoples dominated the eastern slopes of the Apennines to the Adriatic Sea, such as the Umbri, Piceni, and Samnites. But eventually they were all either defeated or absorbed by Rome and made citizens. Ancient central Italy was heavily wooded, with game predominant in the diet. Boar, for example, was cooked on a spit with myrtle and other feral herbs. Today's version of this roasted pig with herbs, *porchetta,* is claimed by every central region.

A pause for refreshments at a restaurant in Rome

FESTIVALS OF THE CENTRAL REGIONS

Some festivals go back to pagan harvest rites. Others promote local foods. These are among the most ancient and the most curious.

FESTA DEL DUCA *URBINO (LE MARCHE).* A three-day mid-August celebration of city history with pageantry, games, and traditional food.

FIERA DEL CACIO *PIENZA (TUSCANY).* On the first Sunday of September, this 100-year-old pecorino fair features music and games with a wheel of cheese made more hilarious by the ample wine.

MERCATO DELLE GAITE *BEVAGNA (UMBRIA).* In late June, in a time warp back to the Middle Ages, citizens go about in medieval dress and practice ancient trades as taverns serve medieval food.

RASSEGNA DEI CUOCHI *SANTA MARIA (ABRUZZO).* A two-day street banquet held by local cooks in mid-October in a town famous for supplying Rome's restaurants with chefs.

SAGRA DELLE FRAGOLE *NEMI (LAZIO).* To celebrate this town's famous strawberry harvest, revelers wear the period costume of pickers on the second Sunday in June.

At Nemi's strawberry festival

Ample Resources, Refined Palates

A plethora of foods are grown and raised in Italy's central provinces, leading to a broad choice of ingredients for its cuisine. This diversity is a reflection of the area's varied climates, from frosty temperatures that allow for the development of flavor in calciferous vegetables, to such hot-weather foods as tomatoes and chile peppers. Additionally, the historic tradition of the small farm endures, preventing big agricultural concerns from supplanting the local cultivars that are exquisitely attuned to their place of origin. Lazio, for example, is famous for its artichokes and peas; Tuscany for beans and black cabbage; and the uplands of Umbria, Le Marche, Abruzzo, and Molise for lentils, chickpeas, and potatoes. In the woods throughout the central Apennines grow a variety of truffles, and exceptional olive oil is made throughout the central hills. It is said in Italy that there are as many different sheep cheeses as there are shepherds, and indeed the mountainous areas produce pecorino of great variety and quality, key to the tangy pasta dishes that characterize the region, perhaps most famously Pecorino Romano.

All six regions in central Italy prepare olive oil–based cuisines that focus on grains, seasonal produce, and—in the richer areas—plentiful meat. Lamb and pork are dominant in the steeper country, while veal and beef favor the gentler slopes and plains, primarily in Tuscany. Foods tend to be prepared quickly on top of the stove in Lazio,

Truffles are commonly found in central Italy. Indeed, Umbria supplies Italy with 80 percent of the country's truffles, primarily black summer truffles.

Le Marche, Abruzzo, and Molise, while slow-cooked dishes prevail in Umbria and Tuscany, though all the central regions roast and grill meat, and on the coast, fish. Fresh seafood is confined to coastal areas, and each port boasts its own fish stew, called *brodetto* on the Adriatic and *cacciucco* on the Tyrrhenian Sea. Inland in landlocked Umbria, cooks make use of sweetwater lake and river fish along with the usual preserved saltwater varieties—anchovies, tuna, sardines, and salt cod—that are ubiquitous throughout Italy.

The ancient grain farro is still used in soups, as is chestnut flour, once a leading staple in the upland Apennines. Chestnut flour is also used to make polenta, flatbreads, and sweets. Today wheat is the base of pasta and bread, including the unsalted loaves of Umbria, Tuscany, and Le Marche. Pasta is split between dried and fresh in the central regions, where rice and corn polenta play secondary roles.

But what binds all these regional foods together is the central Italian tendency toward culinary simplicity and balance, a cooking style that navigates the European influences of the buttery north with the exuberant and often fiery flavors of the south. As with the character of central Italians today, the cooking here is a product of its location and history. This is the home of an independent-minded people, as secure in their identity as the original Italians. At least, the central Italians will say so.

Above: The dramatic cliffside town of Pitigliano, Tuscany. **Opposite:** Tasting room in the Marchesi Antinori winery in the Chianti hills south of Florence.

WINES OF CENTRAL ITALY

SPICY REDS AND CRISP WHITES

....

1. Tuscany: The second most important wine region in Italy produces dense, delicious reds from Sangiovese and other grapes, such as Chianti and Brunello di Montalcino, and crisp whites including Trebbiano and Vernaccia. "Super Tuscans" rank among the most refined.

2. Umbria: The famous Orvieto Classico white wine is made from Trebbiano grapes. Of the reds, Sangiovese grapes are in the best Umbrian wines, such as the earthy Lungarotti; Sagrantino is a native grape with exotic spice flavors.

3. Le Marche: Verdicchio is the region's great grape, a white with green fruit aroma and almond flavors. Verdicchio dei Castelli di Jesi is exceptional. Reds include the easy drinking Rosso Piceno and Rosso Conero, a mix of Sangiovese and Montepulciano grapes.

4. Lazio: The reds are primarily French grapes, though Cesanese, which makes Cesanese del Piglio, is native and a favorite of popes. Crisp dry whites like the great Frascati are made from the Malvasia grape and delicate Trebbiano.

5. Abruzzo: The grape *is* the wine here. Trebbiano d'Abruzzo is the primary white, dry and light. Montepulciano d'Abruzzo makes the primary red, tannic and fruity.

6. Molise: Molise grows the same grapes as Abruzzo, but its rustic winemaking style is influenced by its neighbors to the south, Campania and Apulia.

LIGURIA

EMILIA-ROMAGNA

Carrara
marble
mines

LIGURIAN
SEA

A

P

P

SAN
MARINO
San Marino ★

Matraia

Lucca

Pisa

Prato

Florence   Fiesole

Arno

Urbino

E

Livorno

Gorgona

San Gimignano

Chianti

Arezzo

N

Gubbio

Siena

TUSCANY

Magione

Perugia   Assisi

Capraia

Populonia

M

A

R

E

Pienza

Ombrone

Lago
Trasimeno

Spello

Deruta   Bevagna

San Terenziano

Trevi

UMBRIA

Elba

Pianosa

TUSCAN
ARCHIPELAGO

Montecristo

Giglio

Giannutri

M

M

A

Orvieto

Lago di
Bolsena

Terni

Nera

Viterbo

Lago di
Bracciano

Tiber

Civitavecchia

Cerveteri

LAZIO

Rome
VATICAN ★
CITY

Castelli
Romani

Ostia Antica

Nemi

Alban Hills

Anzio

TYRRHENIAN

SEA

Tuscany

Chianina beef, Cantuccini cookies IGP, Chianti Classico, oil
DOP, Sorana beans IGP, farro grain IGP, Finocchiona sau-
sage IGP, Colonnata lard IGP, Cinta Senese swine DOP,
Lucca oil DOP, chestnuts DOP, Lunigiana apples DOP,
Mortadella cold cuts IGP, Tuscan bread DOP, pecorino,
saffron DOP, Leghorn chicken, Tuscan kale

Lazio

Pecorino Romano DOP, baby lamb IGP, suckling pig, Ariccia
porchetta IGP, Romanesco artichoke IGP, fava beans,
chickpeas, Catalan chicory, ewe's-milk ricotta DOP, Buffalo
Mozzarella of Campania DOP, offal, extra-virgin olive oil of
Sabina DOP, Pontecorvo pepper DOP, white veal of central
Apennines IGP, freshwater fish and seafood, zucchini, potatoes,
white celery, Vallerano chestnuts DOP, pizza by the meter

Geography and Products of Central Italy

The Apennines divide this region west and east, with verdant lands and fertile forests falling off the mountains. Sheep reign in the heights, pigs populate small estate farms, and vegetables of all sorts grow in a climate that becomes increasingly Mediterranean as the land slopes to the seas, where fisheries abound.

Le Marche

Ascoli olives DOP, Cartoceto oil DOP, Casciotta cheese DOP, anisette, seafood, lentils, chickpeas, red potatoes, *ciauscolo* sausage, sour cherries, apricots, peaches, *maccheroncini* of Campofilone (pasta), marjoram

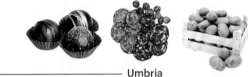

Umbria

Umbrian extra-virgin olive oil DOP, black truffles, *salumi,* freshwater fish, lentils of Castelluccio IGP, red potatoes of Colfiorito IGP, pecorino, pork, white veal of central Apennines IGP, lamb IGP, farro DOP, game, *torta al testo,* chocolate, onions, "black" celery, saffron, *porchetta,* wild mushrooms

Abruzzo and Molise

Lamb IGP, arrosticini, Aprutino Pescarese oil DOP, Colline Teatine oil DOP, Fucino potatoes IGP, saffron DOP, Fucino carrots IGP, sheep's-milk cheese, freshwater fish and seafood, eel, licorice, turkey, Paganica beans, garlic, onions, white celery, sugared almonds

Fano

Ancona

THE MARCHES (LE MARCHE)

Gualdo Tadino

Camerino

Colfiorito

Fermo

San Benedetto del Tronto

Porto d'Ascoli

Norcia

Esino

Tenna

Tronto

ADRIATIC SEA

Canzano

Amatrice

GRAN SASSO E MONTI DELLA

Campotosto

Gran Sasso d'Italia

NATIONAL

Pescara

Corno Grande 9,554 ft 2,912 m

PARK

L'Aquila

Santo Stefano di Sessanio

Capestrano

Pescara

ABRUZZO

Navelli

Aterno

Montagna della Maiella

Sangro

Conca del Fucino

Cocullo

Sulmona

Termoli

Pettorano sul Gizio

Villa Santa Maria

Biferno

Isernia

MOLISE

APULIA

Campobasso

Latina

CAMPANIA

+ Mount Cicero 1,775 ft 541 m

Gulf of Gaeta

15 mi

15 km

Tuscany

Simple, Excellent, and Essential

....

TUSCANY IS ITALY'S ICONIC LANDSCAPE, a rumpled quilt of small, intensely cultivated green and gold fields, and vineyards heavy with dusty purple fruit. As poet Dylan Thomas wrote, "The pine hills are endless, the cypresses at the hilltop tell one all about the length of death, and the woods are deep as love." • The woodlands are indeed dark and cool, filled with porcini mushrooms and truffles, chestnuts and game. On top of each little hill sits a red-tiled farmhouse, a stony church, or a village with winding medieval streets.

The towns and cities are home to exquisite cathedrals and crumbling palazzos, and shops whose display windows, whether they sell shoes or sausages, are artfully styled. This is the scenery of the great Renaissance painters, the environment that embodies the romance of Italy. But the deeper source of Tuscany's appeal is its ancient and enduring sophistication. Tuscan standards of excellence—in food and art and science— have always set the bar for the country.

The Heart of Italy, in the Heart of Italy

Tuscany is the heartland of Italy, although not located in its dead center (Umbria is). Two-thirds of the region flaunts fertile rolling hill country, captured between the Tuscan-Emilian Apennines and the Tyrrhenian Sea. About the size of New Hampshire, Tuscany shares its mountainous border with Emilia-Romagna to the east and Liguria to the north. Here are Tuscany's great marble mines of Massa-Carrara, where the

A timeless Tuscan landscape in the Val d'Orcia

SIENA'S 800-YEAR-OLD FRUITCAKE

Chewy, spicy, riddled with almonds and dusted with powdered sugar—the panforte (strong bread) of Siena is similar to a fruitcake. Its history may date to the 13th century, when records show townspeople donated it to the Abbey of Montecelso. Then, it was called *panes pepatos et melatos* (bread with pepper and honey) because the dough included spices with presumed medicinal attributes. The recipe stayed the same until 1879, when Queen Margherita of Savoy visited Siena. In honor of her visit, a local spice seller made a version with an icing of sugar instead of black pepper. This "white version" is the one made today.

Prosciutto and melon, an ancient pairing

province's awesome spiced pork fat, Lardo di Colonnata, is aged in white marble sarcophagi. Le Marche lies to the east, and Umbria and Lazio to the south. The southwest of the region contains the coastal Maremma, once a malarial marsh, now drained and home to rich agricultural fields. Tuscany's primary river is the Arno, and most of the region's great cities are on its banks. To the west, the seven islands of the Tuscan archipelago include Elba, famous for its resident exile, Napoleon Bonaparte, and a cult dessert wine called Aleatico.

The agriculture of Tuscany is a reflection of its hot and cold climate, its small farms of mixed crops, as well as its large operations. The region's principal products are wine—particularly in Chianti—and wheat. Soft fruit and vegetables such as tomatoes and melons flourish in the central Arezzo and Siena provinces, as do the remarkable Chianina beef cattle and the Cinta Senese, a free-range pig raised on acorns, beechnuts, and fruit. Tuscans produce many types of pork products, including the fennel-scented *finocchiona* and Prosciutto Toscano. The delectable and ubiquitous appetizer prosciutto and melon is a Tuscan invention. Olives, especially around Lucca, make exceptional oil, the primary fat in the Tuscan kitchen. Cold inland winters are ideal for growing leafy vegetables whose flavor is enhanced by a frost, such as cabbage, Tuscan kale, and spinach.

While Tuscany is known for its meat culture, particularly beef and boar, it does have a substantial coast and, at different times in its history, hosted major ports of trade. Livorno, for example, was a free port in the 16th century, known for its social diversity.

Indeed, *cacciucco alla livornese*, a luscious fish stew usually spooned over bread, is sometimes served on a fluffy pile of couscous, a legacy of the city's Arab Jews.

300 Generations of Tuscans

Fertile, sun-soaked Tuscany has been continually inhabited for thousands of years. Archeological remains suggest the earliest residents ate fungi, nuts, game, and grilled meat—much the way Tuscans still do today. For example, ancient Tuscans depended on chestnuts to make bread. That's never gone away: Most wine bars in Florence still offer *necci*, thin chestnut flour pancakes, with your glass of Chianti.

But the Tuscan identity really starts with the Etruscans, an ancient people whose culture emerged about 1200 B.C., hitting their zenith in the sixth century B.C. Early farming communities moved between the low-country villages, where they maintained agricultural plots, and the hills where they grazed small herds of sheep. The latter likely began the tradition of Pecorino Toscano, a hard ewe's-milk cheese Tuscans still enjoy in an age-old pairing with raw fava beans.

By the beginning of 1000 B.C. the industrious Etruscans had built larger towns such

Tuscany was a major producer of saffron in the Middle Ages, especially the mountain town of San Gimignano, where it's been revived as Zafferano di San Gimignano DOP.

Brunelleschi's triumph: the dome of Cattedrale di Santa Maria del Fiore in Florence

The phrase alla fiorentina *often implies a dish contains spinach, but not always: Arista alla fiorentina is pork roasted with garlic and rosemary.*

as Orvieto, Fiesole, Perugia, and Pisa, and established ports at Cerveteri, Populonia, and the island of Elba, among others. At its height, Etruria—as the Etruscan lands were called—consisted of all present-day Tuscany and part of Umbria and Lazio, as well as colonies in the Po Valley. For the next 700 years Etruscan cities grew rich on minerals and trade networks throughout the Mediterranean Basin and the Baltics. Trade was governed by religious sensibilities, an influence still evident today: Many Tuscan markets are held on saint's days. The legacy of Etruscan cookery, on the other hand, can be found in the region's flavorful and robust approach to cooking, as in the *battuto*, the onion or garlic, parsley, and celery combo that is the base of many dishes. Even some Etruscan recipes remain, such as pigeon cooked with rosemary and beans, and porcini mushrooms wrapped in grape leaves and grilled over coals.

The name Tuscany derives from Tusci, the Roman name for the Etruscans. Rome overran Etruria in the second century B.C., their troops nourished by the Tuscan farro fields, an ancient indigenous grain still used in soups and stews. Despite a thousand years of barbarian occupation following the fall of the Roman Empire, Tuscan cities became rich—so rich that by the 12th century they had the resources to vie among themselves for dominance. Florence and Pisa were two such rivals. Before the mouth of the Arno silted up, Pisa was a major conduit for foreign goods, such as the spices that flavored Siena's beloved panforte cake. Lore says the reason why the Tuscan bread *filone* is unsalted is because the Pisans placed an embargo on salt. Undaunted, the Florentines responded by going without.

A vendor sells *salumi* and cheeses from his food truck in Tuscany.

the truth about: FORK IT OVER

If you talk to a French chef, she will say that Renaissance France had a cuisine sophisticated enough to stand up to the Italians. Talk to an Italian, and the French back then were barely civilized enough to sit at a table. When 14-year-old Catherine de Médicis married Henry II of France, she brought many Tuscan customs with her. She has been variously credited with introducing the French to artichokes, aspics, baby peas, broccoli, cakes, candied vegetables, cream puffs, custards, frangipane, ices, lettuce, macaroons, milk-fed veal, parsley, pasta, quenelles, scaloppine, sherbet, spinach, sweetbreads, truffles and zabaglione, flowers on the table, sugar sculptures, olive oil, Chianti wine, béchamel, white beans, and duck à l'orange. She may even have suggested savory and sweet flavors be separated. The French don't concur, although both acknowledge her role in encouraging use of the fork.

Lucca's Liquid Gold

Almost every region in Italy grows olives, but a few locales are especially famous for the aromatic, rich extra-virgin oil they produce. Tuscany is one of those places, and within Tuscany, the extra-virgin of Lucca near the Tyrrhenian coast is among the best of all. Founded by the Etruscans, picturesque Lucca is an ancient walled city surrounded by rolling hills hazy with the silvery foliage of olive trees. As early as the 14th century olive oil obtained from the groves north of the city, in the area called Matraia, was the most prized. The south-facing slopes of these hills are home to a number of mills where the olives were pressed between traditional grinding stones. While the techniques have modernized somewhat, the oil from this part of Lucca is still the liquid gold of Tuscany. Lucchese extra-virgin olive oil refers to oil extracted from the first pressing of fruit from olive trees located within a six-mile radius of the city's famous fortified walls. The extra-virgin of Lucca, which is typically made from a blend of olives, is yellow-green, light, and fluid. It has been described as grassy and herbaceous, with a peppery finish and hints of artichoke, cardoon, and almond.

The olive plant, which probably originated in the Middle East, has been cultivated for 6,000 years. Its use for culinary, religious, and medicinal purposes has grown side by side with the great cultures of the Mediterranean basin. There are 700-plus varietals, and because the trees may live many centuries, and take as many as 40 years just to reach full production, many older varieties remain in orchards today. But not all is rooted in the past: Lucca has the largest concentration of biodynamic farmers in Italy. This system, while cutting into yields, produces exceptional olives. To make extra-virgin olive oil, the olives are harvested by hand without breaking the fruit skins, and pressed within 24 hours under cool conditions.

When Italians speak of olive oil, they are referring exclusively to extra-virgin oil. By EU law extra-virgin oil may be produced by mechanical means only and can contain no more than 0.8 percent free oleic acid, a reflection of the fruit's condition at pressing. True extra-virgin olive oil is costly and labor-intensive to make and its handcrafted production is naturally limited—but it is essential to Tuscan cuisine, indeed to the culinary cultures of all Mediterranean regions. A drizzle is often the only flavoring used to fortify Tuscany's simple bean dishes or humble, rib-sticking *ribollita*. Even a juicy Chianina steak reaches new heights garnished with a swirl of Lucchese liquid gold.

Opposite: A farmer harvests the tiny, flavorful olives that make delicious Lucca oil (right).

Decoding Oil Labels

Fraud is rampant in the Italian olive oil industry, and so is confusion abroad. Here are some tips for selecting the real thing. Look for a harvest, not a "best by" date, a specific producer's name, and where the oil comes from. "Packed" or "Bottled in Italy" does not mean it's Italian. Look, too, for the DOP or IGP seal or some other printed certification by olive oil associations such as the IOOC. Note that organic certification doesn't always offer assurances of quality. Unfiltered oil is not more authentic than filtered. And finally, pay attention to price: Premium olive oil rarely costs under $20 a liter, no matter what the label says.

In 1953 the National Florentine Steak Party campaigned on the promise of a minimum steak of 450 grams for every person. Their slogan? "Better a steak today than an empire tomorrow."

A Cuisine Born of Equality

Not only were medieval Tuscan cities at odds, but within the cities noble families staked out neighborhood territories and squabbled among themselves, shooting at each other from their fortified residences and tall stone towers. Fifteen of these striking strongholds remain in the town of San Gimignano. Perhaps the most vivid display of *contrade* rivalry can be seen in the nearby elegant town of Siena, with the Palio di Siena, a "horse race so epic," described one young observer, "it blurs the line between enthusiasm and clinical insanity." Eventually the unhinged noble classes, whose violent feuding terrorized the local people, were displaced by a merchant class, among them the Florentine Medici bankers who would come to dominate Tuscan politics for 300 years. These were the *popolo grasso*, the fat people whose extravagant spending was curbed by laws restricting the kinds and amounts of food that could be served at a single meal. A grand austerity arrived with the Renaissance in the 15th century, reflected in the region's magnificent yet sober architecture and a simple but highly finessed cuisine.

During its period of dominance over the region in the 18th century, the Austrian Empire modernized the local government and Tuscany emerged as a unified modern state. However, the tradition of the *mezzadria*, a medieval form of sharecropping, con-

A vineyard of Sangiovese grapes, in Colombaia, Siena province

tinued. Eventually landlord neglect led to a decline in productivity, which is why the countryside looks so traditional today.

Bread, Beans, and Beef

Unlike other parts of Italy, Tuscany didn't experience hierarchies based on court-appointed favoritism. Over the centuries this fostered a self-confidence that resonates in the Tuscan character and kitchen still. The Tuscans like their company straightforward and cultured, and likewise their food made of prime ingredients and with a mini-

Borlotti, also known as cranberry beans

mum of fuss. If there ever was a metaphor for the unpretentious yet demanding Tuscan, it is their diet, dominated by bread and beans and meat.

Bread is key to Tuscan cuisine. The typical starter is crostini, grilled bread topped with aromatic mashed beans, chicken livers, or white truffles creamed with butter. Bread also finds its way into another favorite: *panzanella,* a salad of stale bread, fresh tomatoes, cucumbers, and onions tossed in olive oil and lemon juice (though there are many variations). Bread is used in soups, most notably *acquacotta* (cooked water), which is a savory broth poured over bread, maybe thickened with egg and cheese; and *pappa al pomodoro,* tomato soup enriched with bread and laced with olive oil.

But beans are just as important here. Indeed, Tuscans are called *mangiafagioli*—bean eaters—by other Italians. Alessandro de' Medici, Duke of Florence, started the bean mania in the 16th century, and they've been ubiquitous in Tuscan kitchens ever since. Fava, *sorana,* borlotti, and cannellini beans all find their way into Tuscan pasta and soups, such as that ultimate comfort food *pasta e fagioli* and the hearty vegetable stew *ribollita.* Beans are tossed in salads, perhaps with tuna and raw red onions, and served as *contorni* (side dishes), including the memorable *fagioli al fiasco:* beans with olive oil and herbs simmered until tender in a Chianti bottle over hot coals.

Beans are always served with the region's marvelous grilled meats, most necessarily, *bistecca alla fiorentina,* made from Tuscany's famous Chianina beef. But equally loved are rich pork loin roasts, often cooked with rosemary, as well as grilled butterflied chicken—preferably a Leghorn hen from Livorno, which is white with yellow legs.

The double boiler was invented by Tuscan alchemist Maria de' Cleofa. Her invention, which became known as "Mary's bath," is called **bagno maria** *in Italian and* **bain-Marie** *in French.*

The Cinta Senese pigs of Tuscany

(In Italy, if you are referring to a sophisticated person, you might say he has yellow legs.) Game birds may be skewered and grilled with sage leaves, while boar is formed into tiny mahogany sausages or prepared *all'agrodolce,* stewed in red wine and an intoxicating combination of unsweetened chocolate, cinnamon, and salty cured black olives.

These dishes, and many others, such as *pici,* a thick soft spaghetti tossed with a rich ragù, and tripe simmered in tomato, can be found in the fanciest restaurants and the humblest *buchi.* Regardless of the recipe or the setting, the main thing that matters to the exacting Tuscan is a rare steak, and a job well done.

Piazza San Michele in Lucca, on the site of an ancient Roman forum

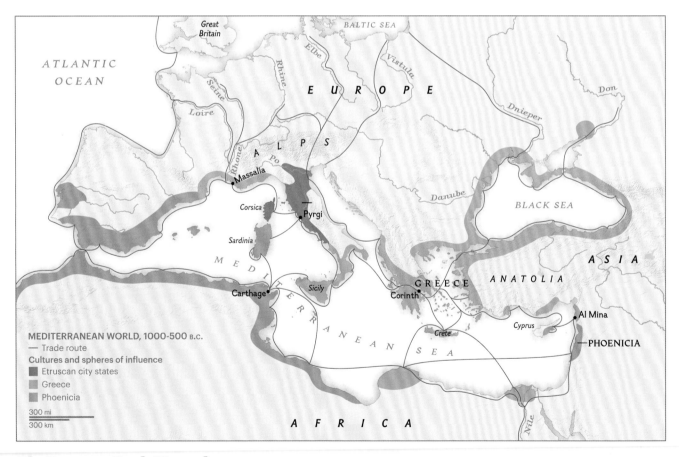

The Etruscan Trade Network Central Italy's early peoples created significant trade networks that moved Tuscan wine, black pottery, and minerals around the Mediterranean and as far north as Great Britain.

Crostini With Chicken Liver Spread

Crostini di fegatini • *Serves 8 to 10*

WHY THIS RECIPE WORKS: No Tuscan antipasto course would be complete without *crostini di fegatini*, which you'll often find served alongside a charcuterie platter and a glass of wine. Unlike French liver pâtés, which are smooth and creamy, Italian liver spreads have a chunky texture—their rustic nature is characteristic of the region's cuisine. Variations on flavors abound, but all have a signature salty element to complement the liver. We chose capers over anchovies for this component, preferring their briny bite. White wine (options such as red wine and vin santo overpowered the other flavors of the dish), sage, and onion were welcome additions. Many recipes cook the livers through until they're no longer pink, but we found that they produced a much better spread when they cooked for only a few minutes and maintained a rosy interior; when cooked quickly, the liver retains its soft, creamy texture and a clean, mellow flavor that blends easily with the other ingredients. We prefer to serve this spread warm; however, it can be refrigerated for up to 24 hours and brought to room temperature before serving.

1 (10 by 5-inch) loaf rustic Italian bread, ends discarded, halved lengthwise and sliced ¾ inch thick
1 large garlic clove, peeled
6 tablespoons unsalted butter
1 small onion, chopped fine
1 tablespoon chopped fresh sage
Salt and pepper
1 pound chicken livers, rinsed, patted dry, and trimmed
½ cup dry white wine
2 tablespoons capers, rinsed
2 tablespoons minced fresh parsley

❶ Adjust oven rack to middle position and heat oven to 400 degrees. Arrange bread slices in single layer on rimmed baking sheet and bake until dry and crisp, 8 to 10 minutes, flipping slices halfway through baking. While still hot, rub each slice of bread with garlic clove; set aside for serving.

❷ Melt butter in 12-inch skillet over medium-high heat. Add onion, sage, and ¼ teaspoon salt and cook until softened and lightly browned, about 5 minutes. Stir in livers and cook until exteriors are no longer pink, about 1 minute. Add wine and capers and simmer until liquid is syrupy and livers are slightly firm to touch but still have rosy interiors, 2 to 4 minutes.

❸ Transfer liver mixture to food processor and pulse until coarsely chopped, 5 to 7 pulses, scraping down sides of bowl as needed. Season with salt and pepper to taste. Spread liver mixture on each piece of toast and sprinkle with parsley. Serve.

Tuscan White Bean Stew

Zuppa di fagioli alla toscana • *Serves 8*

WHY THIS RECIPE WORKS: The people of Tuscany are known as *mangiafagioli,* or "bean eaters," a nod to the prominent role beans play in their cuisine. Cannellini (white kidney) beans are the region's most famous legume, and Tuscan cooks go to extremes to ensure these beans are cooked perfectly, from simmering them in rainwater to slow-cooking them overnight in a wine bottle in a fire's dying embers. *Zuppa di fagioli alla toscana* is a quintessential bean dish featuring an aromatic base, hearty greens, tomatoes, pancetta, and, of course, creamy, buttery beans. Soaking the beans overnight was essential to soften them so their interiors cooked up creamy. And salting the soaking water—essentially brining—softened the skins until they were barely perceptible for ultratender beans. After experimenting with cooking times and temperatures, we found that a vigorous stovetop simmer caused some beans to explode, so we gently cooked them in a 250-degree oven for even results. Adding the tomatoes toward the end of cooking ensured their acidity wouldn't toughen the beans.

Salt and pepper
1 pound (2½ cups) dried cannellini beans, picked over and rinsed
6 ounces pancetta, cut into ¼-inch pieces
1 tablespoon extra-virgin olive oil, plus extra for serving
1 onion, chopped
2 carrots, peeled and cut into ½-inch pieces
2 celery ribs, cut into ½-inch pieces
8 garlic cloves, peeled and smashed
4 cups chicken broth
Water
2 bay leaves
1 pound kale or collard greens, stemmed and chopped
1 (14.5-ounce) can diced tomatoes, drained
1 sprig fresh rosemary

❶ Dissolve 3 tablespoons salt in 4 quarts cold water in large container. Add beans and soak at room temperature for at least 8 hours or up to 24 hours. Drain and rinse well.

❷ Adjust oven rack to lower-middle position and heat oven to 250 degrees. Cook pancetta and oil in Dutch oven over medium heat, stirring occasionally, until pancetta is lightly browned and fat is rendered, 6 to 10 minutes. Stir in onion, carrots, and celery and cook until softened and lightly browned, 10 to 16 minutes. Stir in garlic and cook until fragrant, about 1 minute. Stir in broth, 3 cups water, bay leaves, and beans and bring to boil. Cover, transfer pot to oven, and cook until beans are almost tender (very center of beans will still be firm), 45 minutes to 1 hour.

❸ Stir in kale and tomatoes, cover, and cook until beans and greens are fully tender, 30 to 40 minutes.

❹ Remove pot from oven and submerge rosemary sprig in stew. Cover and let sit for 15 minutes. Discard bay leaves and rosemary sprig and season stew with salt and pepper to taste. If desired, use back of spoon to press some beans against side of pot to thicken stew. Drizzle individual portions with extra oil before serving.

Chicken Under a Brick

Pollo al mattone · *Serves 4 to 6*

WHY THIS RECIPE WORKS: In Tuscany, whole chicken is often spatchcocked (that is, the backbone is removed and the bird is opened and flattened) and then grilled *al mattone*, or "under a brick." The term refers to the beautifully made terra-cotta tiles from Imprunta, a town near Florence, that were originally used for this technique. Weighing down the spatchcocked bird accomplishes a few goals: It ensures even cooking of all the parts, it speeds up the cooking process, and it maximizes contact with the cooking grate for perfectly crisp skin. We started by salting the bird so it would retain its juices, even while being pressed and cooked over a hot flame. We gave the chicken a couple of flips on the grill to further ensure evenly cooked meat, and loosening the chicken's skin from the meat guaranteed that an ultracrisp sheath developed. Preheated foil-wrapped bricks provided a scorching start by delivering heat from above, and using two of them distributed the weight evenly. Rosemary, garlic, and lemon are typical flavorings for this dish; we tried adding them to a wet marinade, but it foiled our efforts for crispy skin. Instead, we utilized a homemade garlic-and-herb-infused oil; we strained the solids from the oil, rubbed them like a paste on the chicken's flesh, and whisked the

flavorful oil with lemon juice to make a sauce for serving. This recipe calls for two standard-size bricks. (A cast-iron skillet or other heavy pan can be used in place of the bricks.) Use a potholder or dish towel to safely grip and maneuver the hot bricks onto the chicken. The hot bricks ensure that the chicken's skin will be evenly browned and well rendered.

⅓ cup extra-virgin olive oil
8 garlic cloves, minced
1 teaspoon grated lemon zest plus 2 tablespoons juice
Pinch red pepper flakes
4 teaspoons minced fresh thyme
1 tablespoon minced fresh rosemary
1 (3½- to 4-pound) whole chicken, giblets discarded
Salt and pepper

1 Heat oil, garlic, lemon zest, and pepper flakes in small saucepan over medium-low heat until sizzling, about 3 minutes. Stir in 1 tablespoon thyme and 2 teaspoons rosemary and continue to cook 30 seconds longer. Strain mixture through fine-mesh strainer set over small bowl, pushing on solids to extract oil. Transfer garlic-herb mixture to second bowl and let cool; set aside oil and garlic-herb mixture.

2 With chicken breast side down, using kitchen shears, cut through bones on either side of backbone; discard backbone. Flip chicken over and press on breastbone to flatten. Tuck wings behind back. Using your fingers, gently loosen skin covering breast and thighs and remove any excess fat.

3 Combine 1½ teaspoons salt and 1 teaspoon pepper in bowl. Mix 2 teaspoons salt mixture into cooled garlic-herb mixture. Spread garlic-herb mixture evenly under skin of breast and thighs. Flip chicken and spread remaining ½ teaspoon salt mixture on bone side. Place chicken, skin side up, on wire rack set in rimmed baking sheet and refrigerate for 1 to 2 hours.

4 A For a charcoal grill: Open bottom vent halfway. Light large chimney starter three-quarters filled with charcoal briquettes (4½ quarts). When top coals are partially covered with ash, pour evenly over half of grill. Set cooking grate in place, wrap 2 bricks tightly in aluminum foil, and place bricks on cooking grate. Cover and open lid vent halfway. Heat grill until hot, about 5 minutes.

B For a gas grill: Wrap 2 bricks tightly in aluminum foil and place on cooking grate. Turn all burners to high, cover, and heat grill until hot, about 15 minutes. Leave primary burner on high and turn off other burner(s). (Adjust primary burner as needed to maintain grill temperature of about 350 degrees.)

5 Clean and oil cooking grate. Place chicken on cooler side of grill, skin side down, with legs facing coals. Place 1 hot brick lengthwise over each breast half, cover, and cook until skin is lightly browned and faint grill marks appear, 22 to 25 minutes. Remove bricks. Using tongs, grip legs and flip chicken (chicken should release freely from grill; use thin metal spatula to loosen if stuck), then transfer, skin side up, to hotter side of grill. Place bricks over breast, cover, and cook until chicken is well browned, 12 to 15 minutes.

6 Remove bricks, flip chicken, skin side down, and continue to cook until skin is well browned and breast registers 160 degrees and thighs register 175 degrees, 5 to 10 minutes longer. Transfer chicken to carving board, tent with foil, and let rest for 15 minutes.

7 Whisk lemon juice, remaining 1 teaspoon thyme, and remaining 1 teaspoon rosemary into reserved oil and season with salt and pepper to taste. Carve chicken and serve, passing sauce separately.

BUTTERFLYING CHICKEN

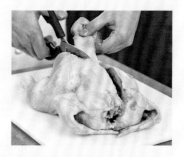

1. Cut through bones on either side of backbone and trim any excess fat and skin around neck.

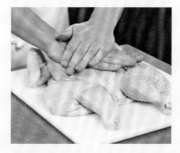

2. Flip chicken over and use heel of your hand to flatten breastbone.

Grilled Steak With Olive Oil and Lemon

Bistecca alla fiorentina · *Serves 6 to 8*

WHY THIS RECIPE WORKS: Simple preparation is a hallmark of Tuscan cooking; the Tuscans teach us that with little fuss and few ingredients, the results can be transcendent. Tuscany's famous steak, *bistecca alla fiorentina*, is a great example of this approach. For this dish, the star ingredient, a ruby-red thick-cut porterhouse steak, is always sourced from the Chianina cows of Valdichiana, whose meat is of impeccable quality. Rather than slather the rare steak with rich sauces or compound butters, the Tuscans simply (of course) and lavishly drizzle the meat with their regional olive oil and serve it with lemon. We take the intimidation out of grilling thick-cut porterhouse steaks with a dependable method that makes our steak taste just as good as Chianina beef. Salting the steaks and letting them rest before cooking enabled the salt to penetrate the meat, boosting flavor from crust to bone. Setting up a half-grill fire with a cooler side and a hotter side allowed us to control the amount of crusty exterior and achieve rosy interiors for our steaks. We grilled the steaks directly over the coals to char them before moving them to the cooler side of the grill to finish cooking. To protect the leaner, quicker-cooking tenderloin portion of the porterhouse, we positioned the steaks with the tenderloins facing the cooler side of the grill. The T-shaped bone in the middle of the steaks acts as a heat shield, further protecting the tenderloins from the heat. We drizzled on the oil after slicing—just before serving—to preserve its delicate flavors and aromas. Flare-ups may occur when grilling over charcoal. If the flames become constant, slide the steaks to the cooler side of the grill until the flames die down.

2 (2½- to 3-pound) porterhouse steaks, 2 inches thick, fat trimmed to ¼ inch
Kosher salt and pepper
4 teaspoons extra-virgin olive oil (if using gas), plus extra for drizzling
Lemon wedges

❶ Pat steaks dry with paper towels and sprinkle each side of each steak with 1 teaspoon salt. Transfer steaks to large plate and refrigerate, uncovered, for at least 1 hour or up to 24 hours.

❷ **A** For a charcoal grill: Open bottom vent completely. Light large chimney starter filled with charcoal briquettes (6 quarts). When top coals are partially covered with ash, pour evenly over half of grill. Set cooking grate in place, cover, and open lid vent completely. Heat grill until hot, about 5 minutes.

B For a gas grill: Turn all burners to high, cover, and heat grill until hot, about 15 minutes. Leave primary burner on high and turn off other burner(s). (Adjust primary burner or, if using three-burner grill, primary burner and second burner as needed to maintain grill temperature of 450 degrees.)

❸ Pat steaks dry with paper towels. If using gas, brush each side of each steak with 1 teaspoon oil. Sprinkle each side of each steak with ½ teaspoon pepper.

❹ Clean and oil cooking grate. Place steaks on hotter side of grill, with tenderloins facing cooler side. Cook (covered if using gas) until evenly charred on first side, 6 to 8 minutes. Flip steaks and position so tenderloins are still facing cooler side of grill. Continue to cook (covered if using gas) until evenly charred on second side, 6 to 8 minutes.

❺ Flip steaks and transfer to cooler side of grill, with bone side facing hotter side. Cover and cook until thermometer inserted 3 inches from tip of strip side of steak registers 115 to 120 degrees (for medium-rare), 8 to 12 minutes, flipping steaks halfway through cooking. Transfer steaks to wire rack set in rimmed baking sheet, tent with aluminum foil, and let rest for 10 to 15 minutes.

❻ Transfer steaks to carving board. Carve strips and tenderloins from bones. Place bones on serving dish. Slice steaks thin against grain, then reassemble sliced steaks around bones. Drizzle with extra olive oil and season with salt and pepper to taste. Serve with lemon wedges.

Tuscan Tomato and Bread Soup

Pappa al pomodoro · *Serves 6*

WHY THIS RECIPE WORKS: In Tuscany, it's a high sin to throw away stale bread. The region's saltless bread is a staple, eaten more frequently than pasta or rice. The bread is baked once a week and enjoyed throughout the day, every day. Religious themes, in addition to a basic desire not to waste, inspired the creation of many Tuscan recipes using bread, including soup. On paper, *pappa al pomodoro* is a tomato-bread soup finished with basil; but in the pot, the ingredients meld to form a fragrant porridge-like stew that's downright luxurious. At its best, it displays the tangy-sweet flavor of tomatoes, which become elevated with a swirl of olive oil. We knew that picking the right type of tomato and processing it properly would be key. We tested every manner of canned tomatoes and pureed them, but this resulted in an acidic slurry that was just too tomatoey. However, fresh tomatoes were wan if not perfectly ripe. For an all-season soup, we returned to canned; as it turned out, it wasn't the tomatoes but our handling of them that was giving us inferior results. Chopping canned whole tomatoes (which we liked for their sweetness), rather than pureeing them, worked much better, giving us a soup with a balanced profile and texture.

6 ounces rustic Italian bread, crusts removed, cut into 1-inch pieces (about 3 cups)

¼ cup extra-virgin olive oil, plus extra for serving

1 red onion, chopped fine

Salt and pepper

3 garlic cloves, minced

¼ teaspoon red pepper flakes

6 cups chicken broth

2 (28-ounce) cans whole peeled tomatoes, drained and chopped coarse

½ cup chopped fresh basil

Parmigiano Reggiano cheese, for serving

❶ Adjust oven rack to middle position and heat oven to 225 degrees. Arrange bread in single layer on rimmed baking sheet and bake, stirring occasionally, until dry and crisp, about 40 minutes.

❷ Heat oil in Dutch oven over medium heat until shimmering. Add onion and ½ teaspoon salt and cook until softened, about 5 minutes. Stir in garlic and pepper flakes and cook until fragrant, about 30 seconds. Stir in broth and tomatoes and bring to simmer. Reduce heat to medium-low, cover, and cook until tomatoes are softened, about 20 minutes.

❸ Stir in bread, pressing on cubes to submerge in liquid. Cover and cook until bread is softened, about 15 minutes. Off heat, whisk soup vigorously until bread is completely broken down and soup is thickened. Stir in basil. Season with salt and pepper to taste. Drizzle individual portions with extra oil and serve, passing Parmigiano separately.

Bread Salad

Panzanella · Serves 4

WHY THIS RECIPE WORKS: Like Tuscan *Pappa al pomodoro* (opposite), *panzanella*—a salad of fresh tomatoes and bread—is another way the Tuscans make use of their precious loaves. One of the earliest mentions was by the 14th-century Florentine author Giovanni Boccaccio in his collection of novellas, *Il Decameron*. He called it *pan lavato*, or washed bread, and this early version didn't include tomatoes; the stale bread was simply soaked in water and any vegetables were tossed in. The version that's popular today is a chunky salad in which croutons act as a sponge for sweet tomato juice and bright vinaigrette, so the croutons become flavorful, soft, and just a little chewy. We wanted bread that was lightly moistened, not unpleasantly soggy. Toasting fresh bread in the oven worked better than using stale bread (which is less common in American kitchens anyway); the bread lost enough moisture in the oven to absorb the dressing without becoming waterlogged. A 10-minute soak yielded perfectly moistened bread ready to be tossed with the tomatoes, which we salted to intensify their flavor and draw out their juice, and some cucumber, which is optional but we liked for cool crunch. A thinly sliced shallot for bite plus a handful of chopped fresh basil perfected our salad.

1 pound rustic Italian bread, cut into 1-inch pieces (6 cups)
½ cup extra-virgin olive oil
Salt and pepper
1½ pounds ripe tomatoes, cored, seeded, and cut into 1-inch pieces
3 tablespoons red wine vinegar
1 cucumber, peeled, halved lengthwise, seeded, and sliced thin (optional)
1 shallot, sliced thin
¼ cup chopped fresh basil

❶ Adjust oven rack to middle position and heat oven to 400 degrees. Toss bread pieces with 2 tablespoons oil and ¼ teaspoon salt in bowl and spread in single layer on rimmed baking sheet. Bake bread until just starting to turn light golden, 15 to 20 minutes, stirring halfway through baking. Let cool completely.

❷ Meanwhile, gently toss tomatoes with ½ teaspoon salt in large bowl. Transfer to colander set over now-empty bowl and let drain for 15 minutes, tossing occasionally.

❸ Whisk remaining 6 tablespoons oil, vinegar, and ¼ teaspoon pepper into drained tomato juices. Add bread, toss to coat, and let sit for 10 minutes, tossing occasionally. Add drained tomatoes, cucumber, if using, shallot, and basil and toss to combine. Season with salt and pepper to taste. Serve immediately.

Almond Biscotti

Cantucci · Makes 30

WHY THIS RECIPE WORKS: The famous Italian cookies, biscotti (meaning "twice-cooked"), first appeared in the Roman empire as a dry food that provided easy nourishment on long journeys—and that was their sole purpose until the Renaissance when they reemerged in Tuscany in the town of Prato and became the treasure they are today. The *biscotti di Prato* are known in Tuscany as *cantucci,* with the term biscotti having evolved into a more generic word for a cookie or biscuit. The twice-baked Tuscan cantucci are extra-crunchy; the dough is formed into a loaf and baked and then sliced on the bias into planks, which are returned to the oven to dry. The result: nutty cookies that are perfect served alongside coffee—or, in Tuscany, dipped in a glass of vin santo, a regional fortified wine, to moisten the dry, hard biscuits. In Prato, cantucci are always flavored with almonds, which grow abundantly there. But while Tuscans like their cantucci dry and hard, Americans tend to favor a buttery, more tender version. We wanted a cookie that fell somewhere in between, one that had plenty of crunch but wasn't tooth-breaking. Batches of cantucci made with little (or no) fat were hard as rocks, while doughs enriched with a full stick of butter baked up much too soft. Four tablespoons of butter struck just the right balance, for a cookie that was both crunchy and tender. Whipping the eggs before adding the other ingredients provided lift, and swapping out ¼ cup of flour for an equal amount of ground almonds made the cookies more tender by breaking up the crumb and interrupting gluten development. The almonds will continue to toast during baking, so toast them just until they're fragrant.

1 ¼ cups whole almonds, lightly toasted
1 ¾ cups (8¾ ounces) all-purpose flour
2 teaspoons baking powder
¼ teaspoon salt
2 large eggs, plus 1 large white beaten with pinch salt
1 cup (7 ounces) sugar
4 tablespoons unsalted butter, melted and cooled
1½ teaspoons almond extract
½ teaspoon vanilla extract
Vegetable oil spray

❶ Adjust oven rack to middle position and heat oven to 325 degrees. Using ruler and pencil, draw two 8 by 3-inch rectangles, spaced 4 inches apart, on piece of parchment paper. Grease baking sheet and place parchment on it, marked side down.

❷ Pulse 1 cup almonds in food processor until coarsely chopped, 8 to 10 pulses; transfer to bowl and set aside. Process remaining ¼ cup almonds in now-empty food processor until finely ground, about 45 seconds. Add flour, baking powder, and salt; process to combine, about 15 seconds. Transfer flour mixture to second bowl. Process 2 eggs in now-empty food processor until lightened in color and almost doubled in volume, about 3 minutes. With processor running, slowly add sugar until thoroughly combined, about 15 seconds. Add melted butter, almond extract, and vanilla and process until combined, about 10 seconds. Transfer egg mixture to bowl. Sprinkle half of flour mixture over egg mixture and, using spatula, gently fold until just combined. Add remaining flour mixture and chopped almonds and gently fold until just combined.

❸ Divide dough in half. Using floured hands, form each half into 8 by 3-inch rectangle, using lines on parchment as guide. Spray each loaf lightly with oil spray. Using rubber spatula lightly coated with oil spray, smooth tops and sides of loaves. Gently brush tops of loaves with egg white beaten with salt.

❹ Bake until loaves are golden and just beginning to crack on top, 25 to 30 minutes, rotating sheet halfway through baking. Let loaves cool on sheet for 30 minutes, then transfer to cutting board. Using serrated knife, slice each loaf on slight bias into ½-inch-thick pieces. Set wire rack in rimmed baking sheet. Space slices, cut side down, about ¼ inch apart on prepared rack. Bake until crisp and golden brown on both sides, about 35 minutes, flipping slices halfway through baking. Let cool completely before serving. (Biscotti can be stored at room temperature for up to 1 month.)

Umbria

Italy's Heart and Soul

KNOWN AS A SACRED LAND FOR THE SAINTS, monasteries, and mystics that it has spawned, Umbria is the heart and the soul of Italy. Revered for its pristine Apennine landscape—a refuge to rare flora and fauna that have become extinct elsewhere on the continent—Umbria has been muse to writers, poets, and painters who have tried to capture its enchantment. Indeed, anyone wandering its landscape would have reason to believe that she is finding herself momentarily dreaming or in front of theatrical scenery. Instead, it is there, firm and fixed.

Umbria is a grateful recipient of the bounties of this dramatic landscape, home to olives and vines, hogs and game—and most spectacularly, six species of prodigious truffles, predominantly black. These foods have inspired its native cooking, one rustic and rich in flavor.

Earthly Riches, Culinary Simplicity

Less known than neighboring Tuscany, Umbria is like the overlooked second child, diminutive (it ranks 16th out of Italy's 20 regions in size, 17th in population), shining quietly with a brilliance and beauty uniquely its own. As if an expression of its introversion—or its cause, perhaps—Umbria is the one central Italian region that does not touch the sea.

To the east rise the highest peaks of the central Apennines, shared with Le Marche.

Inside the Basilica di San Francesco d'Assisi, restored after the 1997 earthquake

Umbria's predilection for goose dates to the Etruscans, who valued the fowl not only as food but also as a symbol of domestic tranquillity and maternal protection.

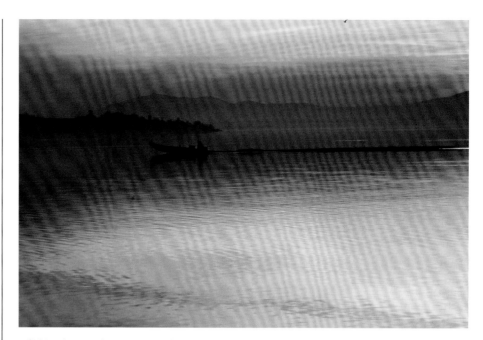

A fishing boat makes its way at dawn on Lake Trasimeno.

While rugged, Umbria is not barren; rather, it is forested and fruitful with many wild harvests including field asparagus, berries, hazelnuts, and game.

To the west sparkles Lake Trasimeno, the fourth largest body of water in Italy, brimming with such fish as perch and tench, as well as giant carp that can grow bigger than a suckling pig. The microclimate here, sheltered by hills encircling the lake's western shores, is warm enough for the kinds of crops that flourish in warmer climes, including citrus fruits and almonds.

The impression visitors have upon arriving in Umbria from Lazio on the southern border, or from Tuscany to the west, is one of a series of wide basins. These are the fertile river valleys of the Tiber and its tributaries, notably the Nera, which water the land and provide trout as well as eel, once the passion of Rome's popes and emperors and still a favorite for its rich, compact flesh. The surrounding farmland displays its prosperity in well-tilled fields of wheat, corn, and varied produce, including seemingly endless rows of wine varietals, red and white.

Pagans and Saints

Umbria is part of the Etruscan heartland, even if the Umbri, an Italic tribe that migrated to central Italy at the beginning of the Bronze Age, planted their feet here even earlier. While we know little about them, we are certain that their capital was Gubbio, and that their name stuck.

Umbria's story is more gruesome than most, colored with the blood from epic battles against the papacy and the savage feuding of its ruling families. But the land, deeply connected with nature's equilibrium, radiates with timeless grace. Hills are speckled with ancient towns, high-hung convents, and castles mounted upon the crests. Gorgeous Orvieto, Perugia, and Assisi cannot escape mention, nor Spello, Bevagna, and Montefalco, which are especially enchanting (and their cooking, curiously, particularly delicious). Its golden cities, surrounded by olive trees and immortalized by Giotto, Lorenzetti, Perugino, and Pinturicchio, jut out of tufa rock into the dreamy skyline. As journalist H. V. Morton observed, "The city of Perugia, seated upon its mountain like the Ark on Ararat, looks as it did in the Middle Ages." In some ways, it remains in a time warp.

Umbria is blood-linked to its pagan progenitors through its traditions—and food. How can it not be? In the cellars beneath the medieval houses they live in, modern people stumble on Etruscan tunnels even now; some store their wine there. Farmers still turn up ancient artifacts in the soil and tell stories about apparitions of Etruscan warriors in their fields. Inherent in this mystical link is a palpable respect for the generous land that has sustained them, perhaps more so than in the bigger agricultural regions to the north where people live faster lives and their connection to their prodigal land is more distant.

Olives and Old Ways

There is a saying in Umbria that good olive oil is a product of its mother. The territory's sheltered valleys, plus rocky slopes with good drainage, rich soil, and golden weather provide the perfect environment for exceptional olives and their oil. Not coincidentally, every year Ercole Olivario, the prestigious national competition for olive oil excellence—a big deal in Italy—is held in Perugia.

Organic farming and local agriculture are not new ideas in this region, where people have long developed a taste for wholesome products and animals bred on mountain herbs. Shepherds tend their flocks on the flanks of the mountain pastures untouched by chemical fertilizers; the flocks themselves descend from the central Apennine race that provided Italic shepherds with milk for cheese, wool for clothing, and fresh meat for the spit, the same as now.

The Prodigal Pig and Other Products

The pig is another story. A formidable reserve of meat and fat, it has always been the protein bank of central Italy, providing nourishment throughout the year in the form of both fresh and preserved meat. The local tradition of pork butchery dates as far back as the first-century Roman emperor Vespasian, who held vast swaths of land here for breeding pigs. After his conquest of Jerusalem, he imported Jewish slaves to farm the animals, knowing their dietary laws would ensure they wouldn't eat the meat themselves.

Related to pork but unlike it in flavor is wild boar, which roam the countryside and decimate crops throughout central Italy. Every farmer hunts these brutes. Their meat is savored as much as their presence is loathed, cooked fresh in ragù, or put to use in

TERROIR TO TABLE
NORCINI, THE MASTER BUTCHERS

In Norcia, where hogs feast on acorns and truffles, *norcino* has come to define the very profession of fine sausage making for some 500 years. Once these butchers, called *maestri norcini* even in Roman times, also practiced surgery, dentistry, and bone setting, their skills honed in one of Italy's first medical schools, located here. Norcini are expert at utilizing the animal from nose to tail for fresh cuts, sausages, and *salumi* such as *capocollo*, *barbozzo (guanciale)*, *mazzafegati* (liver sausages studded with orange peel and dried fruit), immense mortadellas, and the delectable Prosciutto di Norcia.

Chef Maria Luisa Scolastra cooks at Villa Roncali.

salumi. Besides small game, domesticated rabbit, duck, and guinea hen *(faraona)* have a special place on the Umbrian table. Finally, there is the marked taste for the goose *(oca)*, a fetish that harks back to Etruria.

As for produce, the plump and tiny lentils of the Castelluccio plateau are an ancient, uninterrupted crop, a humble legume that becomes divine when braised in meat juices and topped with Umbria's plump sausages. The Colfiorito plateau is famous for its buttery, pink-skinned potatoes, while mushrooms and chestnuts abound in the mountains. Two notable crops are the Cannara onion, and the "black" celery of Trevi. The first has been cultivated for centuries in the porous, sandy soil of that area. The second, so-called because it turns dark if not properly cultivated, is actually pale green with a tender heart, and free of fibers.

Umbria is not without industry, food products especially. This includes Perugia's chocolate, celebrated in a nine-day festival each year. To grace its tables, world-class pottery is made in Deruta, Gubbio, Orvieto, and Gualdo Tadino, each town's output discernable with an emblematic palette and style. While the best representation of this ancient art is practiced by masters of the genre, a wide range of pleasing ceramics are produced to suit every budget.

Umbria at Table

Umbria's legendary chef Angelo Paracucchi once said that the holy trinity of flavors in Umbrian cooking is olive oil, vinegar, and wine. Indeed, perhaps nothing better describes the region's rich yet simple essence than the delicate yet vivid quality of pungent, genuine olive oil, the bite of vinegar, the baritone notes of wine in cooking, epitomized in meats roasted *alla ghiotta,* with a basting liquid that includes all three along with garlic and a profusion of wild herbs.

This is the "happy reign of the *spiedo*," or the spit, as the Italian gastronome Felice Cùnsolo called it, but also the grill and the oven—modern adaptations of hearth cooking, once the center of life here. Most everything is cooked on the fire, famously, *porchetta.* This is not to say that Umbria doesn't practice stovetop cooking, which it certainly does, notably in the form of rib-sticking stews such as *coniglio alla cacciatora,* hunter's-style rabbit, or *tegamaccio,* Trasimeno's answer to *zuppa di pesce.* Perhaps the most quintessential epicurean examples of this lush land of porky pleasures and endless vineyards is *salsicce all'uva,* pan-roasted sausages with grapes, a succulent dish that joins two of their gastronomical obsessions.

Pasta making in Etruria goes back to antiquity. This includes *umbricelli,* called *ciriole* in the province of Terni (indistinguishable from the *bigoli* of Veneto), rolled, handmade noodles long and thick enough to wrap around your waist. Also called *penci,* a version of Tuscan *pici,* these are fresh wheat or farro noodles incorporating little or no egg. Consequently, the dough must be prepared *culu mossu,* which in the local dialect means a continual movement of the (cook's) rump. There are also *strangozzi,* alias *strangolapreti* (the unappetizingly named "priest stranglers"), long narrow flat strands of egg-based fresh pasta indistinguishable from tagliatelle. *Umbricelli al sugo d'oca,* noodles with a tomatoey goose ragù, is a classic pairing during carnival time.

The ancients' zest for life and the refinement and naturalness of Umbrian culture survived the Roman conquest, the Vandals, and the Dark Ages to resurface in central Italy when plagues and wars dwindled and secure agrarian life came about in the late Middle Ages. Umbria's cuisine is still Etruscan at heart, with its excesses tempered, perhaps, in the spirit of its most famous saint. The contemporary Umbrian kitchen is nothing if not simple, honest, and wholesome, in a word, Franciscan.

Unlike other truffle-producing regions, Umbria is generous with its treasure, showering black gold on its dishes when the fungi are in season.

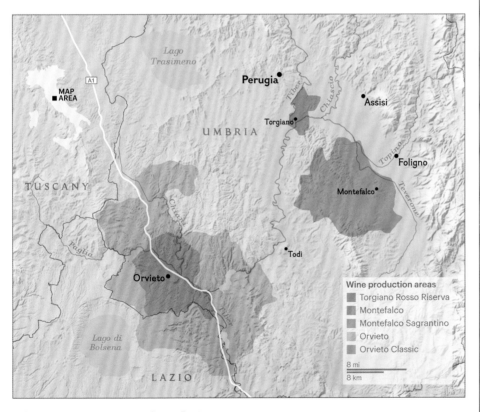

The Wine Regions of Umbria Umbria's significant DOC and DOCG wine areas include Orvieto, Montefalco, and Torgiano, home to the renowned Museo del Vino.

Orecchiette With Sausage and Cream

Orecchiette alla Norcina · *Serves 6 to 8*

WHY THIS RECIPE WORKS: The black pigs of Umbria are prized for their superlative flavor, owing to their diet of plants, herbs, and truffles that thrive in the region's mountains. In the Middle Ages, butchers in the Umbrian village of Norcia became so adept at cutting, salting, and curing the meat from these pigs that the products they produced—sausage, bacon, prosciutto, and capocolloi, to name a few—became legendary. Still named after the small town to this day, most pork butcher shops throughout Italy are called *norcinerie,* and pork butchers bear the title of *norcino.* It's no surprise, then, that sausage is beloved in Umbria, and *pasta alla Norcina*—a dish of fresh sausage and creamy sauce tossed with pasta—is a great use of it. To re-create this dish, we wanted a rich-tasting, moist, and appropriately flavored sausage; store-bought links wouldn't cut it. Fortunately, going the handmade route turned out to be surprisingly easy (no meat grinder needed) and allowed us to incorporate Umbrian seasonings. We started with ground pork. To give it savory flavor and a tender, more cohesive texture, we folded in some salt and an unlikely ingredient, baking soda, and let the pork sit for 10 minutes. The salt dissolved some of the pork's protein fibers, and the baking soda raised the pH of the meat and improved its water-holding capacity so it stayed juicy like Umbrian pork. We flavored the mix traditionally, with rosemary, nutmeg, and garlic. Since browning crumbled sausage virtually guarantees dry nuggets of meat, we formed our pork into one big patty, browned it on both sides, and chopped it up; the sausage pieces finished cooking through in the sauce, which guaranteed moist, tender meat. Mushrooms are a debated addition, but we liked how some browned chopped mushrooms bolstered the dish's earthy flavors. White mushrooms may be substituted for the cremini. We liked the way our homemade orecchiette (small ears of pasta) captured the sausage in its bowls. We prefer the flavor and texture of fresh pasta here, but dried can be used as well. For more information on making your own fresh orecchiette, see page 366.

Salt and pepper
¼ teaspoon baking soda
8 ounces ground pork
3 garlic cloves, minced
1¼ teaspoons minced fresh
   rosemary
⅛ teaspoon ground nutmeg
8 ounces cremini mushrooms,
   trimmed
7 teaspoons extra-virgin olive oil
1 pound fresh or dried orecchiette
½ cup dry white wine
¾ cup heavy cream
1½ ounces Pecorino Romano
   cheese, grated (¾ cup)
3 tablespoons minced fresh parsley
1 tablespoon lemon juice

❶ Spray large plate with vegetable oil spray. Dissolve ½ teaspoon salt and baking soda in 4 teaspoons water in medium bowl. Gently fold in pork until combined and let sit for 10 minutes. Add one-third of garlic, ¾ teaspoon rosemary, nutmeg, and ¾ teaspoon pepper and smear with rubber spatula until well combined and tacky, 10 to 15 seconds. Transfer sausage mixture to prepared plate and form into rough 6-inch patty. Pulse mushrooms in food processor until finely chopped, 10 to 12 pulses.

❷ Heat 2 teaspoons oil in 12-inch skillet over medium-high heat until just smoking. Add patty and cook, without moving, until browned, 2 to 3 minutes. Flip and continue to cook until well browned on second side, 2 to 3 minutes (very center will be raw). Transfer patty to cutting board and chop into ⅛- to ¼-inch pieces.

❸ Bring 4 quarts water to boil in large pot. Add pasta and 1 tablespoon salt and cook, stirring often, until al dente. Reserve 1½ cups cooking water, then drain pasta and return it to pot.

❹ Meanwhile, heat 1 tablespoon oil in now-empty skillet over medium heat. Add mushrooms and pinch salt and cook, stirring frequently, until browned, 5 to 7 minutes. Stir in remaining 2 teaspoons oil, remaining garlic, remaining ½ teaspoon rosemary, and ½ teaspoon pepper and cook until fragrant, about 30 seconds. Stir in wine, scraping up any browned bits, and cook until completely evaporated, 1 to 2 minutes. Stir in sausage, cream, and ¾ cup pasta cooking water and simmer until meat is no longer pink, 1 to 3 minutes. Off heat, stir in Pecorino Romano until smooth.

❺ Add sauce, parsley, and lemon juice to pasta and toss to coat. Adjust consistency with reserved cooking water as needed. Season with salt and pepper to taste. Serve immediately.

Lentil and Escarole Soup

Minestra di lenticchie e scarola · *Serves 6*

WHY THIS RECIPE WORKS: Tiny, deep green, and fragrant, lentils from the high, dry plains of Castelluccio in Umbria are considered some of the world's best: They're packed with minerals and are especially tender. However, these superior lentils aren't abundant—a factor that contributes to their prized status. Often paired with the region's exceptional sausage, they're also commonplace in soup, a favorite wintertime primo. Because Umbrian lentils hold their shape particularly well during cooking, the soup remains brothy rather than thick and creamy. Supporting ingredients vary from town to town, but we particularly liked escarole, a common hearty choice. We also included canned diced tomatoes—a classic addition—and a couple bay leaves for warmth. While many lentil and escarole soup recipes call for a long simmering time once the escarole is added, we chose to add it toward the end of cooking so the leaves retained some of their character. Finally, adding a rind of Parmigiano Reggiano to the simmering soup gave the broth a super-savory backbone. Umbrian lentils are our preferred choice for this recipe, but brown lentils are fine, too (note that cooking time will vary).

¼ cup extra-virgin olive oil, plus extra for drizzling
1 onion, chopped fine
1 carrot, peeled and chopped fine
1 celery rib, chopped fine
Salt and pepper
6 garlic cloves, sliced thin
2 tablespoons minced fresh parsley
4 cups chicken broth, plus extra as needed
3 cups water
8 ounces (1¼ cups) Umbrian lentils, picked over and rinsed
1 (14.5-ounce) can diced tomatoes
1 Parmigiano Reggiano cheese rind (optional), plus grated Parmigiano Reggiano for serving
2 bay leaves
½ head escarole (8 ounces), trimmed and cut into ½-inch pieces

❶ Heat oil in Dutch oven over medium heat until shimmering. Add onion, carrot, celery, and ½ teaspoon salt and cook until softened and lightly browned, 8 to 10 minutes. Stir in garlic and parsley and cook until fragrant, about 30 seconds. Stir in broth, water, lentils, tomatoes and their juice, Parmigiano rind, if using, and bay leaves and bring to simmer. Reduce heat to medium-low and cover, leaving lid slightly ajar. Simmer until lentils are tender, 1 to 1¼ hours.

❷ Discard Parmigiano rind, if using, and bay leaves. Stir in escarole, one handful at a time, and cook until wilted, about 5 minutes. Adjust consistency with extra hot broth as needed. Season with salt and pepper to taste. Drizzle individual portions with extra oil and serve, passing grated Parmigiano separately.

Sausage With Grapes
Salsiccia all'uva • *Serves 4 to 6*

WHY THIS RECIPE WORKS: Making use of the very special Umbrian sausage and the plentiful wine grapes of the harvest season, *salsiccia all'uva* is a humble dish that originated as a quick meal for vineyard laborers. Rich, juicy, and well browned, the sausages are a great match for grapes that soften and caramelize in the pan; we tie the dish together with a tangy-sweet vinegar-based sauce. Since this skillet dish is so simple, it is important that the sausages are cooked perfectly—we wanted them nicely browned yet still plump and juicy. To achieve this, we used a combination of sautéing and steaming: First, we browned the sausages; we then added onion (we liked the depth this nontraditional ingredient added) and seedless red grapes (their dark pigment looked nicer with the inky balsamic vinegar than pale green grapes did) along with a small amount of water, covered the skillet, and cooked the links through. The result was nicely browned sausages whose casings didn't burst and let out moisture. We removed the cooked links to build a sweet but complex sauce in the same skillet. A combination of white wine and balsamic vinegar lent the dish acidity and complemented the grapes. Oregano and pepper contributed earthiness and a touch of spice, while a finish of fresh mint added brightness. Serve with crusty bread for a heartier meal.

1 tablespoon extra-virgin olive oil
1½ pounds sweet Italian sausage
1 pound seedless red grapes, halved lengthwise (3 cups)
1 onion, halved and sliced thin
¼ cup water
¼ teaspoon pepper
⅛ teaspoon salt
¼ cup dry white wine
1 tablespoon chopped fresh oregano
2 teaspoons balsamic vinegar
2 tablespoons chopped fresh mint

❶ Heat oil in 12-inch skillet over medium heat until shimmering. Arrange sausages in skillet and cook, turning once, until browned on 2 sides, about 5 minutes. Tilt skillet and carefully remove excess fat with paper towel. Distribute grapes and onion over and around sausages. Add water and immediately cover. Cook, turning sausages once, until they register between 160 and 165 degrees and onion and grapes have softened, about 10 minutes.

❷ Transfer sausages to paper towel–lined plate and tent with aluminum foil. Return skillet to medium-high heat and stir pepper and salt into grape-onion mixture. Spread grape-onion mixture in even layer in skillet and cook without stirring until browned, 3 to 5 minutes. Continue to cook, stirring frequently, until mixture is well browned and grapes are soft but still retain their shape, 3 to 5 minutes. Stir in wine and oregano, scraping up any browned bits, and cook over medium heat until wine is reduced by half, 30 to 60 seconds. Off heat, stir in vinegar.

❸ Arrange sausages on serving dish and spoon grape-onion mixture over top. Sprinkle with mint and serve.

Vegetable and Farro Soup

Minestra di farro · *Serves 6 to 8*

WHY THIS RECIPE WORKS: Farro is a staple of Umbria, where it actually predates common wheat. The Umbrians use humble ingredients to build a rich cuisine, and employ the good-for-you grain both whole and as flour, which they use to make gnocchi, pasta, and even crêpes. Umbrians also use coarsely ground farro to thicken and flavor soups like the classic *minestra di farro*, an incomparably hearty soup in which the nutty flavor of farro shines above all else. While ground farro isn't readily available in most American grocery stores, we were happy to discover that it's simple to create your own; six pulses in a blender were enough to break up the grain into smaller pieces. While a prosciutto bone may be a traditional flavor booster for this soup, we used readily accessible pancetta to deliver a similarly rich, salty note. Leeks, celery, and carrot contributed sweetness, and we loved that even the dark green parts of the leek softened in the time it took the farro to cook through. A sprinkling of fresh parsley and some freshly grated Pecorino Romano finished this humble soup. Use the entire leek (dark and light green parts) in this recipe. We prefer the flavor and texture of whole farro. Do not use quick-cooking, presteamed, or pearled farro (read the ingredient list on the package to determine this) in this recipe.

1 cup whole farro, rinsed and dried
3 ounces pancetta, chopped fine
1 pound whole leeks, trimmed, chopped, and washed thoroughly
2 carrots, peeled and chopped
1 celery rib, chopped
8 cups chicken broth
2 tablespoons minced fresh parsley
Salt and pepper
Grated Pecorino Romano cheese

❶ Pulse farro in blender until about half of grains are broken into smaller pieces, about 6 pulses; set aside.

❷ Cook pancetta in Dutch oven over medium-low heat until browned and fat is rendered, about 5 minutes. Stir in leeks, carrots, and celery and cook until softened and lightly browned, 5 to 7 minutes.

❸ Stir in broth and farro, bring to simmer, and cook until farro is tender with slight chew, 15 to 30 minutes. Stir in parsley and season with salt and pepper to taste. Serve with Pecorino.

Le Marche

A Cuisine of Sea and Mountains

LE MARCHE IS OFTEN TOUTED as a place on the verge of discovery, yet this small, bucolic region is accustomed to being off the radar. The Marchigiani are hard-working, earnest people known for their labor-intensive foods. If there is a food metaphor for the Marchigiano state of mind, it is the complicated and luscious lasagna called *vincisgrassi*—made with a ragù of chicken giblets, sweetbreads or bone marrow, and truffles—possibly created to impress an Austrian general who beat back Napoleon's army in Le Marche.

Every Inch Cultivated

Le Marche lies between Umbria in the north and Abruzzo in the south, sandwiched between the Apennine mountain range and the Adriatic Sea. Countless inland farms spread over honey-colored hills rounded by thousands of years under the plow, each surmounted by a farmhouse, a church, or an ancient fortified village where crafts such as lacemaking and traditional cooking have been preserved. Peppered throughout the region are small picturesque cities such as Urbino, a Renaissance treasure and UNESCO World Heritage site. Numerous rivers flow to the sea, and the valleys are intensely cultivated. Even the highway meridians are filled with tomato lattices. The coast itself is mostly limestone cliffs, sandy beaches, and busy ports such as the regional capital, Ancona.

Upland, the winters can be harsh, but as the land tumbles toward the Adriatic it becomes increasingly Mediterranean. Marchigiani farmers produce cereals such as wheat, beans, lentils (the exquisite Lenticchia di Castelluccio di Norcia, for example),

Sunset falls on Urbino, Le Marche's walled city, a UNESCO World Heritage site.

> *The Romans paid their soldiers in salt from the Adriatic Sea, leading to the word "salary," from sale, or salt.*

and vegetables of all sorts, most exceptionally, the red potato, Patata Rossa di Colfiorito. Small holding farms, many organic, raise their own hogs and produce a range of pork products including the fatty, spreadable *ciauscolo* sausage. Of the cheese products, both locals and visitors vie for the white spring pecorino, sweetly sour as a baby's milky burp, and Formaggio di Fossa, which is aged in limestone caves.

Black figs

Grapes (most famously, Verdicchio) and tree fruit including olives are grown throughout the region, especially the Ascolana del Piceno olive, a large, mild olive treasured by the Romans.

Fishing is a major source of income. Most of the Adriatic fish are small, oily, and bony, such as sardines and anchovies (a typical starter is *alici marinate*, tiny silver anchovies boned and marinated in vinegar), lionfish, and scorpionfish. Also found are the local crustaceans and mollusks, such as the tiny, tender clam known as *vongole veraci*. These may be boiled in vinegar and hot pepper, or used in a spaghetti with clam sauce that is so delicious it will ruin your taste for all others.

Slumbering Borderlands, Busy Marchigiani

The region that became Le Marche was originally the home to the Iron Age Piceni and Umbri tribes, as well as refugees from Syracuse who founded Ancona in the fourth century B.C. and Gauls. But all fell under Roman administration by the third century B.C. Rome built two famous roads to Le Marche: The Via Flamina connected Rome to Fano in the north, and the Via Salaria, the salt road, connected Rome to the Porto d'Ascoli and the Adriatic salt flats in the south.

After the fall of the Roman Empire, Le Marche was sacked by Goths, Vandals, Ostrogoths, Lombards, and finally the Holy Roman Empire, which reigned for a thousand years. But with its focus on battles elsewhere, cities such as Ancona became independently powerful. The name Le Marche, a medieval term for borderland, originally referred to the lands controlled

A welcoming wine bar

by Ancona, Camerino, and Fermo. By the 17th century, Le Marche was a papal state, and left to its own devices by the Vatican, it slumbered until reunification.

Mare e Monte

Perhaps this history is why Le Marche is always on the verge of being discovered: It has abided, without much fanfare, for so long. Le Marche is a small region with five provinces. Each province is composed of upland and coast, and produces dishes from both sea and mountains, with local variations. Every province along the coast specializes in *bordetto,* a tangy fish stew made of a varying number of crustaceans and Adriatic fish, but the dish flaunts distinctive flavors depending on where you eat it.

Inland, pastas and meat reign. The hill country fare is ample, savory, and rich, embodied by dishes such as chicken or rabbit prepared *al potacchio,* braised in garlic, onions, sometimes tomatoes, wine, olive oil, and rosemary or fennel. There is also a cross cultivation of recipes from the coastal and inland tables: *Stoccafisso,* air-dried codfish, is cooked al potacchio, too. The ultralight *maccheroncini di Campofilone,* a durum-wheat pasta made with eggs (but no water or oil), is sauced with a chicken giblet ragù inland but a fish-flavored marinara on the coast. Likewise, inland Ascoli olives are stuffed with meat; but on the coast, they are stuffed with tender, white-fleshed fish.

Marchigiana sweets reflect the same values evident elsewhere in the cuisine: The Marchigiani love to make complicated desserts. One specialty is *salame di fico,* a log of dried figs, nuts, and spices such as star anise, wrapped in fig leaves and tied. However, despite this tendency toward the complex, Le Marche is ultimately a modest place. Which is why, for the Marchigiani, the best dessert of all may be a fresh peach cut directly into a glass of wine.

---

libations: COFFEE, CORRECTED

Caffè corretto is a shot of espresso coffee with a splash of liquor. While typical all over Italy, it reaches a new level with a local drink, *moretta,* in Fano in northern Le Marche. To make a moretta, add equal parts anise (typically, Meletti from Ascoli), rum, and brandy with sugar, lemon zest, and espresso coffee (or hot water in the evenings before bed). It is always served in a small, clear glass, and in three layers: liquor, coffee, and *schiumetta del caffè,* or the coffee foam. The drink may have been invented to keep the port of Fano fishermen and sailors warm at work.

A dynamic duo: coffee beans and anisette liqueur

Fried Stuffed Olives

Olive all'ascolana • *Makes 40*

WHY THIS RECIPE WORKS: Attend a festival in Le Marche, and you may sample one of the greatest snacks you'll ever have: *olive all'ascolana*. Crisp-coated, salty fried olives stuffed with a rich meat filling are a culinary marvel of taste and texture that originated in the town of Ascoli Piceno. We just had to try making these delightful bites, but we suspected it might be a challenge—after all, we'd have to figure out how to pit and stuff an olive! We tried starting with pitted olives as a short-cut, but found them lacking in color, texture, and overall olive flavor. Instead we used large, mild-flavored Cerignola olives, which are easy to find in delis and prepared food places. To remove the pits, we left the olive flesh in one piece, slicing down one side of the olive and cutting around the pit with a paring knife as if we were peeling an apple. We were pleasantly surprised to find that the process went quickly after we got used to pitting the first few. With these olives, the filling shares the spotlight, and we found a lot of impractical recipes calling for a menagerie of meat scraps or specialty cuts. We started with ground pork; while uninspiring by itself, additions of prosciutto, sautéed carrot, and shallot built beautiful layers of flavor. A little nutmeg provided the classic warm spice and aroma, while wine added brightness. One large yolk and Parmigiano gave the filling richness and a creamy texture. We prefer to use Cerignola olives, but other large brine-cured green olives will work, too. To allow for practice, the recipe calls for extra olives.

2 tablespoons plus 3 cups extra-virgin olive oil
1 carrot, chopped
1 shallot, chopped
⅛ teaspoon salt
⅛ teaspoon pepper
4 ounces ground pork

1 ounce Prosciutto di Parma, chopped
⅛ teaspoon ground nutmeg
¼ cup dry white wine
¼ cup grated Parmigiano Reggiano cheese
1 large egg yolk, plus 2 large eggs
¼ teaspoon grated lemon zest
45 large brine-cured green olives with pits
1½ cups panko bread crumbs
1 cup all-purpose flour

❶ Heat 2 tablespoons oil in 12-inch skillet over medium heat until shimmering. Add carrot, shallot, salt, and pepper and cook until softened and lightly browned, 3 to 5 minutes. Add pork and cook, breaking up meat with wooden spoon, until browned, about 4 minutes. Stir in prosciutto and nutmeg and cook until fragrant, about 30 seconds. Stir in wine and cook until nearly evaporated, about 1 minute. Process pork mixture in food processor until smooth, about 2 minutes, scraping down sides of bowl as needed. Add Parmigiano, egg yolk, and lemon zest and pulse to combine, about 5 pulses. Transfer filling to bowl and let cool slightly. (Filling can be refrigerated for up to 2 days.)

❷ Working with 1 olive at a time, use paring knife to cut lengthwise down one side of pit (do not cut through olive). Continue to cut around pit until released, rotating olive as needed and keeping as much of olive intact as possible. Spoon scant 1 teaspoon filling into each olive (olives should be full but not overflowing), then close sides around filling, gently squeezing to seal.

❸ Line rimmed baking sheet with triple layer of paper towels. Process panko in clean food processor to fine crumbs, about 20 seconds; transfer to shallow dish. Spread flour in second shallow dish. Beat eggs in third shallow dish. Working with several olives at a time, dredge in flour, dip in egg, and coat with panko, pressing firmly to adhere. Transfer to large plate and let sit for 5 minutes.

❹ Heat remaining 3 cups oil in Dutch oven over medium-high heat to 375 degrees. Add half of olives and cook, stirring occasionally to prevent sticking, until golden brown and crisp, about 2 minutes. Using wire skimmer or slotted spoon, transfer olives to prepared sheet and let drain. Return oil to 375 degrees and repeat with remaining olives. Serve.

PREPARING STUFFED OLIVES

1. After making cut lengthwise down one side of pit, continue to cut around pit until released.

2. Spoon scant 1 teaspoon filling into olive, then close sides around filling, gently squeezing to seal.

Seafood Soup

Brodetto all'anconetana • *Serves 6*

··

WHY THIS RECIPE WORKS: Jutting into the Adriatic Sea, Ancona, the capital city of Le Marche, has a vibrant maritime culture. A trademark dish, *brodetto all'anconetana*, is a seafood lover's dream and has long served as a way for fishermen to use the bycatch remaining after selling the day's haul. Though once a humble dish of seafood scraps, the soup has evolved from fisherman fare to regional delicacy. Showcasing the diversity of the seafood found off the coast, traditional recipes are prepared with 13 types—one for each attendee of the Last Supper. Mediterranean flavors of tomatoes, onions, parsley, garlic, vinegar, and oil meld to create a bright, complex broth, anointed with more fruity olive oil. We wanted to remain true to the spirit of the original dish, but we also hoped to make our soup with a more reasonable number of ingredients. Our seafood choices provide a good mix of textures and flavors. For the fish, halibut fillets were tender and had just enough heft so they didn't flake apart. For the cephalopod component, we chose squid over octopus for its milder taste and attainability. Finally, for the shellfish, a combination of briny littleneck clams, savory mussels, and sweet shrimp provided the diversity we sought. We cooked the seafood in a careful sequence to ensure plump and tender results: First, we simmered the squid in the Dutch oven until it was two-thirds done. Halibut was next, which we cooked until it reached 135 degrees. To prevent the shrimp from overcooking, we added them to the simmering broth just 2 minutes before serving. Finally, we steamed the clams and mussels in a separate pan, removing them as they opened to ensure ideal doneness for each. For a spicier soup, use more red pepper flakes. Trim any squid tentacles longer than 3 inches. Serve with crusty bread.

½ cup extra-virgin olive oil, plus extra for drizzling
2 large onions, chopped fine
Salt and pepper
4 garlic cloves, minced
⅛ to ¼ teaspoon red pepper flakes
1 (28-ounce) can whole peeled tomatoes, drained with juice reserved, chopped coarse
1 (8-ounce) bottle clam juice
¾ cup water
1 pound squid, bodies sliced crosswise into ½-inch-thick rings, tentacles left whole, patted dry
1 (1-pound) skinless halibut fillet, ¾ to 1 inch thick, cut into 6 pieces
1¼ cups dry white wine
1 pound littleneck clams, scrubbed
8 ounces mussels, scrubbed and debearded
8 ounces large shrimp (26 to 30 per pound), peeled, deveined, and tails removed
¼ cup chopped fresh parsley

❶ Heat ¼ cup oil in Dutch oven over medium heat until shimmering. Add onions, ½ teaspoon salt, and ½ teaspoon pepper and cook until softened and lightly browned, 8 to 10 minutes. Stir in garlic and pepper flakes and cook until fragrant, about 30 seconds. Stir in tomatoes and reserved juice, clam juice, and water and bring to simmer. Stir in squid, reduce heat to medium-low, cover, and cook for 30 minutes.

❷ Nestle halibut into broth, cover, and cook until fish registers 135 to 140 degrees, 10 to 14 minutes. Off heat, transfer halibut to plate with slotted spoon; cover to keep warm and set aside.

❸ Bring wine and remaining ¼ cup oil to boil in 12-inch skillet over high heat. Add clams, cover, and cook, shaking skillet occasionally, until clams have just opened, 6 to 8 minutes. Transfer clams to large bowl, discarding any that haven't opened, and cover to keep warm. Add mussels to skillet with wine mixture and cook, shaking skillet occasionally, until mussels have just opened, 2 to 4 minutes. Transfer mussels to bowl with clams, discarding any that haven't opened, and cover to keep warm.

❹ Pour cooking liquid from skillet into pot, being careful not to pour any grit from skillet into pot. Return broth to simmer over medium heat. Add shrimp, cover, and cook until just opaque, about 2 minutes.

❺ Off heat, stir in clam-mussel mixture and parsley and season with salt and pepper to taste. Divide halibut, clams, mussels, squid, and shrimp among individual serving bowls. Ladle broth over top. Drizzle with extra oil before serving.

Hunter's-Style Chicken

Pollo alla cacciatora · Serves 4 to 6

WHY THIS RECIPE WORKS: In Italy, anything cooked *alla cacciatora* is cooked "the hunter's way." Hunters in central regions like Le Marche would braise their fresh-killed game simply, until super-tender and enveloped in a savory sauce. Given the dish's throw-together nature, there isn't one recipe. What is always standard: The meat (typically rabbit or poultry) is first sautéed and then cooked slowly with a selection of vegetables, which are often foraged. Many know only of the Italian-American version, which features chicken in a thick marinara-like sauce. We wanted something you'd find in central Italy, with a sauce that is just substantial enough to cling to the chicken. Tomatoes were in, as we liked their sweetness and acidity, and our wine of choice was white for its lighter profile. To keep this mix from being too harsh we cut it with chicken broth, which buffered the presence of the wine and rounded the savory flavors. The flavors of garlic and rosemary complemented the poultry. For even cooking, we sautéed the chicken on the stove and then transferred it to the oven to finish cooking through gently. As the chicken rested, we reduced the infused broth to form a flavorful sauce.

4 pounds bone-in chicken pieces (2 split breasts cut in half cross-wise, 2 drumsticks, and 2 thighs)
Salt and pepper
2 tablespoons extra-virgin olive oil
1 onion, chopped
1 carrot, peeled and chopped
1 celery rib, chopped
2 garlic cloves, minced
1½ teaspoons minced fresh rosemary
½ cup dry white wine
½ cup chicken broth
1 (14.5-ounce) can diced tomatoes, drained
1 tablespoon minced fresh parsley

❶ Adjust oven rack to middle position and heat oven to 325 degrees. Pat chicken dry with paper towels and season with salt and pepper. Heat oil in Dutch oven over medium-high heat until just smoking. Brown half of chicken on all sides, 8 to 10 minutes; transfer to plate. Repeat with remaining chicken; transfer to plate.

❷ Add onion, carrot, and celery to fat left in pot and cook over medium heat until softened and lightly browned, 6 to 8 minutes. Stir in garlic and rosemary and cook until fragrant, about 30 seconds. Stir in wine, scraping up any browned bits, and cook until almost completely evaporated, about 2 minutes. Stir in broth and tomatoes and bring to simmer.

❸ Return chicken to pot along with any accumulated juices. Cover, transfer pot to oven, and cook until breasts register 160 degrees and drumsticks/thighs register 175 degrees, 35 to 40 minutes, turning chicken halfway through cooking.

❹ Remove pot from oven. Transfer chicken to serving dish and tent with aluminum foil. Bring sauce to simmer over medium-high heat and cook until reduced to about 2 cups, 5 to 8 minutes. Season with salt and pepper to taste. Spoon sauce over chicken and sprinkle with parsley. Serve.

Lazio

The Eternal City and Its Environs: In a Word, Lusty

EVEN IF LAZIO IS GROUPED with central Italy geographically, it is here that the south begins in spirit—baroque, ebullient, volatile, colorful, chaotic, exasperating, and sometimes tragic—the converse of cool-headed, prosperous northern Italy. • If bards and philosophers have waxed poetic over the region's magic, a true geographical description goes something like this: Lazio sprawls along the shore of the Tyrrhenian Sea, tumbling down from the wild and wind-whipped Maremma on the Tuscan frontier to meet

Campania's fabled coastline. According to Virgil, it was here in the ancient land of Latina, where six volcanic islands are flung like pearls into the sea and Mount Circeo juts into the Gulf of Gaeta, that Ulysses' men were transmuted into swine by the nymph Circe. And it was here, on the limestone bluffs of this enchanting, if not enchanted, beach that Roman emperors built their summer villas. Inland the topography is rich in lakes and watered with rivers, principally the Tiber, as it alternates between flat and hilly.

Squarely in the middle is Rome, where some 80 percent of Lazio's population lives, one of the world's oldest cities and epicenter of Western culture. The surrounding intensely cultivated countryside, the *agro romano*, is where most of the region's food is grown. Though Lazio's hinterlands have always been in Rome's shadow, they retain their provincial differences. The province of Viterbo shares Tuscany's Etruscan heritage in most things, including the cult of the olive and its oil, on which its cooking is based

A seasoned server with drinks on the threshold of Osteria delle Coppelle

THE ART OF NOSE-TO-TAIL

All of Italy eats meat "nose-to-tail," but nowhere is the concept carried out more imaginatively than in Rome. The city and its region dote on the *quinto quarto,* fifth quarter—the organs and trimmings of a butchered animal. The head and tail and parts in between —heart, feet, kidneys, cartilage—were historically left to the masses after the choicer cuts were set aside for the nobles, the clergy, the bourgeoisie, and the soldiers, in that order. Many iconic dishes originated in Testaccio, site of the city's slaughterhouses. Nearby trattorias made good use of these parts in recipes such as *coda alla vaccinara,* a heady braise of oxtail simmered in a ragù enriched with bitter chocolate, sultanas, and pine nuts; *trippa alla romana,* tomato-simmered tender veal tripe with mint; or *pajata,* veal chitterlings cooked in prosciutto fat, tomato, and white wine.

(the rest of Lazio traditionally relied on pork fat). Rieti, land of the ancient Sabine, was originally part of Abruzzo. It remains connected in spirit and cookery, sharing, for example, the tradition of *jaccoli,* a doppelgänger of the yards-long hand-pulled fresh pasta of Abruzzo. Parts of Latina and Frosinone once held allegiance to the Kingdom of Naples and remain in its sphere, producing mozzarella from the milk of the water buffalo that inhabit the coastal wetlands Lazio and Campania share.

Roman Roots

The Etruscans are invariably credited with being the first to put down roots here, but by the time they arrived it was already a confusion of Italic tribes. Most important of these were the Latini, who first attached their name to it and built fortified settlements between the Tiber River and the Alban Hills. One of the small cities they founded, in the ninth century B.C., formed the nucleus of what became Rome.

Chronicles of ancient Roman cuisine conjure up a civilization whose gastronomical feats, designed to impress as much as to sate voracious appetites, were as fantastic as its military ones. They tell of multiple courses of elaborate (if ridiculous) dishes, from live birds concealed in pies to roasted peacocks served in their plumage. When Rome was lost to the Vandals, rich and poor alike came back to the humble dishes that were dear to the shepherds and the country people. In time, these became the basis of the *cucina romana* that remains.

Green onions and *pomodorini*

The cooking of Lazio today is still connected to what Romans call *roba nostrana,* local "stuff," and keenly in tune with the change of seasons. Descended from ancient Etruscan cooking, it too is based on pork fat or olive oil and flavored with many of the same aromatics the ancients used, notably, onion, garlic, parsley, and celery. Rosemary, mint, sage, basil, and marjoram are the predominant *odori,* or herbs; cloves and cinnamon are the favored spices.

This is meat country, with locally bred lamb and pork preferred, but also veal, poultry, and game available. Italy's love affair with *baccalà* (salt cod) is alive and well here. So is a predilection for

The lush landscape of Viterbo in springtime

freshwater fish, including eel and pike, a habit formed in past times when transporting seafood to Rome was difficult. Saltwater fish continue to be brought in through Civitavecchia, Ostia Antica, and Anzio—ports older than Rome itself. The fastidious Romans like to go out for seafood here, rather than stink up their homes by cooking it themselves.

Lazio's countryside, renowned since antiquity for its phosphorus-rich volcanic soil, grows exceptional produce and unique strains of plants. Whenever you see the word *romanesco* fastened to a variety, you'll know it is their brainchild. Think extraterrestrial-looking green cauliflowers with pointed heads; meaty, striped zucchini that are tastier and less watery than any other; and the flat, foot-long green beans popular now—naturally buttery when cooked the Roman way, tender, not crunchy. They're all Lazio babies.

La Cucina Romana, Bold and Beguiling

There is a local saying: "May heaven deliver us to a place where we can eat." In other words, Romans love to eat. Their kitchen is lusty and unrestrained, extroverted, at once

Caesar salad has no relation to any Roman caesar, or to Roman cooking. It was invented during Prohibition by an Italian-American restaurateur in Tijuana.

Think of the old adage that all roads lead to Rome, and imagine that along all those roads there were osterie for the streams of visitors. You then might understand why it is a city of hospitality. But the culture of eating out has even deeper roots, to when cooking indoors was prohibited in the city's crowded tenements, which frequently collapsed. Or, as one Roman writer posits, "The women, fiery and combative like their men, were maladapted to standing in front of the stove." People lived their lives in the streets, taking meals in informal eateries at appointed times. Romans still love to eat out, and you will find them enjoying themselves noisily at bars, cafés, and trattorias at all times of day, gesticulating wildly and arguing passionately. As Italian food writer Bruno Rossi once said, "The way to know Romans best is to meet them at dinner."

Rome, the "great beauty," queen of cities, in all her sparkle—potent, fabled, eternal

earthy and beguiling, like the city herself. If you ask locals to explain their cooking, they might respond as did Alessio Liberatore, proprietor of Rome's popular Taverna dei Fori Imperiali: "[O]ur food has *profumi*," meaning that its flavor is derived from the natural essences of the ingredients themselves. It is a cuisine designed to sate the carnivore, the fish lover, the vegetable lover, the pasta lover, the polenta lover, and the rice lover alike. It is cooking born of a region whose capital city was once the center of the world, home not only to swollen, mad emperors and deified popes but also to commoners, country people, pilgrims, foreigners, and eaters of all stripes.

Part of its culinary charm is that for all its savor, preparation is carried off seemingly effortlessly—a few ingredients, a secret or two, a little magic. Go out to any restaurant and the delivery says it all: The waiter needs no pen and paper, no tablet in hand to remember your order, but course after course arrives with a knowing nod and a flourish. The Italians call it *sprezzatura*, a word invented by Baldassare Castiglione in the 16th century to describe the art of the courtier, one that defines famous Roman hospitality. Romans are seasoned *osti*, or hosts, who have been cooking for the traveler, for an audience, for millennia.

Food Specialties of Rome and Lazio

Even a casual look at a Roman menu will make it plain that meat is king. Rome likes its meat young—very young—eating *maialino* (suckling pig) and *capretto* (kid) barely

The Roman bar is a neighborhood hub in which to pass the time and grab a quick espresso.

Rome Is for Artichokes

Lazio's delicate-fleshed, violet globe artichoke, *carciofo romanesco,* is the very symbol of Rome. Also known as *cimarolo* (from *cima,* meaning "top") or *mammola,* a variety without thorns or choke, it is the product of careful pruning. As a result each plant produces a single shoot, the most prime specimen on the stalk. Cultivated in the provinces of Viterbo, Rome, and Latina, where the volcanic soil imparts a particular flavor, it is supplemented with other varieties throughout the season.

If you are in Rome between late February and mid-April, you might very well see big bouquets of the plant's showy thistles set out at the entrances of the trattorias, beckoning you to step in. Once inside, you will no doubt be greeted at the antipasto table with *carciofi alla romana,* the artichokes, trimmed and braised whole, displayed on immense platters, their leggy stems upright like a company of chorus girls. In an elaborated version, garlic and mint are tucked between the leaves before cooking, and wine added to the bath.

There are infinite recipes. *Carciofi alla matticella*—from *matticella,* or pruned grape shoots—is a spring ritual that goes back to Etruscan times in the Castelli Romani: artichokes bathed in olive oil and roasted in the open

fields (or on a backyard grill) over dried shoots pruned from the grapevines. One dish not to be missed is the simple but blissful *carciofi a spicchi,* artichoke hearts sliced and braised in olive oil with garlic and parsley. Other gastronomic delights include delicious braises composed of the artichokes with sweetbreads or *coratella* (peppery lamb lung, liver, heart, spleen); or with *abbacchio* (baby lamb); or with green onion, fava beans, peas, and tender beet greens in the much anticipated *vignarola,* a triumph of tender spring vegetables perfectly seasoned.

A specialty of the city's historic Jewish ghetto is the *carciofi alla giudia,* twice-fried artichokes "in the Jewish style," flattened and crunchy. Fresh artichokes are themselves tender enough to be eaten raw, grazed with good olive oil. At the end of the season, smaller artichoke heads that remain are trimmed, pickled, and conserved whole in olive oil for enjoyment in the long winter months.

Opposite: A springtime passion in the Roman countryside: *carciofi alla matticella.* Right: Roman violet globe artichokes

Artichoke Artistry

Rome's imaginative vegetable cookery stems from the resourcefulness of a Jewish enclave confined by papal decree to a squalid ghetto in 1555 for over three centuries until its liberation in 1870. Restricted to the cheap and plentiful ingredients that Jewish peddlers were permitted to sell, including lowly artichokes, alliums, and lettuces, and following the dietary laws of kashruth, they created a remarkable vegetable cuisine suffused with the seasonings of the Spanish Jews living in their midst. From this came *carciofi alla giudia, carciofi con lattuga* (artichokes and lettuce braised with garlic and onion), and *pasticcio di cervello* (artichokes cooked with brain), dishes that were absorbed into Lazio's cuisine.

bigger than a hare when it's butchered. *Abbacchio,* lamb between 20 days and six weeks, is an obsession. When cooked, it goes down the throat like butter. Lazio is one of the few regions that bothers much with chicken, free-range that is, not "machine-made," as they are wont to call cage-farmed animals. If the Roman palate considers it bland, it nonetheless comes to life in *pollo alla romana,* braised chicken with bell peppers. Food writer Maurizio Pelli tells us that it was considered plebeian food in ancient Rome, the food of slaves, servants, and soldiers; the legions brought chicken coops with them on their campaigns.

The region is a virtual lambscape, so sheep cheese is central. Most distinctive of its fresh, unfermented *latticini,* or local dairy products, is *ricotta romana* made from the milk of designated breeds of sheep, giving it a deeper, tangier flavor than the cow's-milk ricotta familiar to Americans. This is what makes *maccheroni alla pastora* and other Lazian pasta dishes, or its ricotta desserts such as *crostata di ricotta,* so exceptional.

The tradition of salting meats in this porky land is older than Lazio itself, going at least as far back as the Greeks and Etruscans and probably further, to the Phoenicians, who first harvested salt from the sea and used it to preserve meats and fish. Fine *prosciutti crudi,* salted and air-cured hams, come from Bassiano and Guarcino. The region's famed *guanciale,* air-cured pork jowl, is indispensable for many of its dishes, including Rieti's *bucatini all'amatriciana.*

Lazio isn't world-famous for its olive oil, but it should be. Because its olive lands are hilly, the harvesting has to be done largely by hand, and the output is small, and special. The extra-virgins of Canino and Sabina were the first in Italy to get DOP status.

No one, simply no one, has the same devotion to vegetables as the Romans. You

the truth about: GELATO VS. ICE CREAM

Rome is a temple to gelato, with some 2,500 *gelaterie* around the city. What's the difference between gelato and ice cream? Simply put, gelato is creamier but lower in fat and added sugar, sweetened by the products that define its flavors. Chilled and churned, ideally in situ and in small batches to preserve its taste and silkiness, it is produced, and eaten, the day it is made. The best Roman *gelatai* prepare their confections in-house, using fresh dairy and quality raw ingredients for their artisanal scoops—seasonal, local fruits, premium chocolate, local nuts—and, often, fine wines and spirits. Try an exquisite favorite flavor, *gelato di ricotta alla romana,* made from the day's fresh local ricotta.

Delectable offerings at a Roman *gelateria*

Campo de' Fiori, Rome's most famous open market, is known for elaborate produce displays and boisterous vendors.

can see it in their riotous market displays—the bewildering variety of their famed brassicas and lettuces, baby zucchini with their perky blossoms still connected, and clusters of candy-sweet tomatoes still attached to their umbilical vines. The many kinds and colors of peppers, both sweet and fiery, are put to good use in classic dishes such as *capretto all'arrabbiata,* "angry" goat. The brief spring growing season for fava beans is eagerly anticipated, as is that for *puntarelle* (Catalan chicory hearts), and for fennel, *finocchio,* which they love to eat *in pinzimonio*—raw, dipped in extra-virgin olive oil with salt and pepper. Whether due to the boisterous Roman vendors, who seem louder and shriller than those elsewhere, or to the perfect proportions of the Roman piazza, Rome's famous and boisterous near-daily outdoor market at Campo de' Fiori ("the flowering field") is theater.

Also apparent is a love for legumes that has no bounds—lentils, *borlotti,* and all the others that are the basis for so many of their bold *zuppe* (soups) and pasta

The ancient Romans invented "takeout" and the "doggy bag," an outgrowth of the restriction against cooking inside their fire-prone tenements.

dishes. The aforementioned Mr. Pelli tells us that so important were chickpeas to the ancient Roman diet that *cece*, chickpea in Latin, was given as a family name, viz. the orator Cicero.

Lazio does wonderful things with pasta, a habit encouraged by its proximity to Campania, the *maccheroni* capital of Italy. Roman restaurants make *spaghetti alla carbonara* and *spaghetti cacio e pepe* (with sheep cheese and lots of black pepper) rock-star dishes even if restaurants abroad most often bastardize them. But these are a mere sampling of the region's sensational pasta repertoire.

Whatever the dish, somehow, everything tastes better in Rome—or so many foreigners say. Is it true, or is it imagined? Maybe it doesn't matter. Romance is a sauce (a word invented, incidentally, by the Romans), and Rome is, if nothing else, romantic. Indeed, Roman cooking—Lazian cooking—can be thrilling. It is all about intense flavors, about combinations of ingredients that, however uncomplicated, deliver a heightened experience of taste and an endless feast for the senses. "Sitting in front of a plate of Roman food can revive the dead," wrote Roman author Giuliano Malizia, "because the official host is *gioia di vivere*," joy of life.

The 18th-century Trevi Fountain marked the terminus of the Roman aqueduct system.

The Via Francigena This historic pilgrimage route, popular with travelers today, begins in Canterbury, England, passes through France and Switzerland, and ends in Rome.

Spaghetti With Cheese and Pepper

Cacio e pepe • *Serves 6 to 8*

WHY THIS RECIPE WORKS: Romans love pasta and are known to eat spaghetti in extravagant amounts. *Cacio e pepe,* one of Rome's famed pasta dishes, combines spaghetti with salty Pecorino Romano (*cacio* is another word for cheese used in central and southern Italy) and fresh-cracked black pepper (*pepe*) in a creamy, intensely flavored sauce. Now popularly thrown together at home to cap off a late night on the town, it originated as a meal for traveling shepherds, as they always had cheese, pepper, and dried pasta with them. In theory, the sauce forms itself when cheese and some cooking water are stirred with the pasta, as the starch in the cooking water prevents the cheese's proteins from clumping together. In practice, however, we found that this wasn't enough; the cheese still clumped. For a more foolproof route to an ultrasmooth sauce, we cut the amount of cooking water in half when boiling the pasta; this upped the starch level in the water, providing more of a safeguard. But we still needed help: A couple spoonfuls of heavy cream further ensured a fluid sauce (the cream contains molecules called lipoproteins that act as a sort of liaison between protein and fat, keeping them emulsified). Do not adjust the amount of water for cooking the pasta; the amount used is critical to the success of the recipe. Make sure to stir the pasta frequently while cooking so that it doesn't stick to the pot. Draining the pasta water into the serving bowl warms the bowl and helps keep the dish hot until it is served. Letting the dish rest briefly before serving allows the flavors to develop and the sauce to thicken to the right consistency.

6 ounces Pecorino Romano cheese, 4 ounces grated fine (2 cups) and 2 ounces grated coarse (1 cup)
1 pound dried spaghetti
1½ teaspoons salt
2 tablespoons heavy cream
2 teaspoons extra-virgin olive oil
1½ teaspoons pepper

❶ Place finely grated Pecorino in medium bowl. Set colander in large serving bowl.

❷ Meanwhile, bring 2 quarts water to boil in large pot. Add pasta and salt and cook, stirring often, until al dente. Drain pasta in prepared colander, reserving cooking water. Pour 1½ cups cooking water into 2-cup liquid measuring cup and discard remainder. Return pasta to now-empty bowl.

❸ Slowly whisk 1 cup reserved cooking water into finely grated Pecorino until smooth, then whisk in cream, oil, and pepper. Gradually pour Pecorino mixture over pasta, tossing to coat. Let pasta rest for 1 to 2 minutes, tossing frequently and adjusting consistency with remaining reserved cooking water as needed. Serve immediately, passing coarsely grated Pecorino separately.

Jewish-Style Artichokes

Carciofi alla giudia ·
Serves 4 to 6

WHY THIS RECIPE WORKS: Today, *carciofi alla giudia* is considered a traditional Roman dish, but its name reveals a more nuanced history. Translating to "Jewish-style artichokes," this dish was born in the isolated Jewish ghetto of Rome (first established by decree of the Pope in 1555), and as such is a simple and unaltered example of truly traditional Jewish-Italian cuisine. It's nothing more than baby artichokes—a prominent vegetable in Roman cuisine—that are pared down to their tender core and delicate inner leaves, cooked in hot extra-virgin olive oil until crispy and browned, and then sprinkled with sea salt and served with lemon. Such simple dishes usually rely on the quality of their ingredients, and this classic is no different. Baby artichokes are a must here, as their tender hearts cook quickly and their soft leaves become shatteringly crisp. The leaves of the larger globe artichokes were tough by the time they were golden, and the larger heart didn't have the same creamy interior. The cooking method proved just as important: Dropping the prepped artichokes in hot oil produced scorched, bitter-tasting leaves, while starting them in cold oil produced spotty browning. Instead, we landed on an approach somewhere in the middle. We started the artichokes in a pot of extra-virgin olive oil heated to a moderate 300 degrees until the hearts were just cooked through; we then removed them while we increased the heat to 325 degrees. The artichokes required just 1 or 2 minutes in the hotter oil to develop golden, super-crisp leaves. While we prefer the flavor of extra-virgin olive oil, you can use vegetable, canola, or peanut oil to fry the artichokes.

1 lemon, halved, plus lemon wedges
 for serving
2 pounds baby artichokes
Extra-virgin olive oil
Flake sea salt

❶ Squeeze lemon halves into 4 cups cold water in large bowl; add spent halves. Working with 1 artichoke at a time, peel and trim stem to remove dark green layer, then cut off top quarter of artichoke. Break off tough outer leaves by pulling them downward until you reach delicate yellow leaves. Cut artichoke in half lengthwise and submerge in water.

❷ Line rimmed baking sheet with kitchen towel. Remove artichokes from lemon water, shaking off excess water, and transfer to prepared sheet; discard water and spent halves. Thoroughly pat artichokes dry and transfer to clean bowl.

❸ Set wire rack in now-empty rimmed baking sheet and line with triple layer of paper towels. Add oil to large Dutch oven until it measures about 2 inches deep and heat over medium-high heat to 300 degrees. Carefully add artichokes to oil and cook until tender, pale green, and edges of leaves just begin to brown, 2 to 3 minutes. Using spider or slotted spoon, transfer artichokes to prepared sheet.

❹ Heat oil over medium-high heat to 325 degrees. Return artichokes to oil and cook until golden and crisp, 1 to 2 minutes. Using skimmer or slotted spoon, transfer artichokes to sheet. Season with salt to taste. Serve with lemon wedges.

233

Braised Oxtails

Coda alla vaccinara • *Serves 6 to 8*

WHY THIS RECIPE WORKS: A classic Roman peasant meal, *coda alla vaccinara* is a lush braise originally prepared by slaughtermen *(vaccinari)* who were often paid with the undesirable parts of the animal. It's from these parts, like oxtail, that they made delicious dishes and proved the underestimated worth of these inexpensive cuts. Coda alla vaccinara is still served in Roman trattorias. When simmered slowly—traditionally for 5 to 6 hours—the tough, fatty oxtails transform into meltingly tender meat coated by a rich, deeply flavored sauce that is thicker than that of a stew. Tomatoes, tomato paste, and a touch of wine, along with a sautéed soffritto (onion, carrot, and celery, cut large to have presence in the final dish) make the base of a sauce that's elevated to lustrous as the oxtails braise in it. Sometimes chocolate is added, but we found the oxtails enriched the sauce more than enough on their own. Clove contributes comforting warmth and raisins introduce the agrodolce (sour and sweet) notes that Italians favor. To be sure our braise didn't turn out greasy, we started by roasting the oxtails for an hour rather than quickly browning them on the stovetop; this allowed a significant amount of fat (about a half cup) to be rendered and discarded. We set aside the oxtails while we deglazed the roasting pan with chicken broth, added this mixture to the braising liquid, and then nestled the oxtails in the sauce. We found our oxtails needed 3 hours in the moderate heat of a 300-degree oven to become fork tender. After braising, we were careful to remove the fat (about another half cup) from the cooking liquid using a fat separator. A sprinkling of pine nuts is common and added crunch and visual appeal. Try to buy oxtails that are approximately 2 inches thick and 2 to 4 inches in diameter. Oxtails can often be found in the freezer section of the grocery store; if using frozen oxtails, be sure to thaw them completely before using.

4 pounds oxtails, trimmed
Salt and pepper
4 cups chicken broth
2 tablespoons extra-virgin olive oil
1 onion, chopped fine
1 carrot, peeled and chopped fine
2 celery ribs, cut into 1-inch lengths
2 tablespoons tomato paste
3 garlic cloves, minced
⅛ teaspoon ground clove
½ cup dry white wine
1 (28-ounce) can whole peeled tomatoes, drained with juice reserved and chopped
2 tablespoons raisins, chopped
¼ cup pine nuts, toasted

❶ Adjust oven rack to lower-middle position and heat oven to 450 degrees. Pat oxtails dry with paper towels and season with salt and pepper. Arrange oxtails cut side down in single layer in large roasting pan and roast until meat begins to brown, about 45 minutes.

❷ Discard any accumulated fat and juices in pan and continue to roast until meat is well browned, 15 to 20 minutes. Transfer oxtails to bowl; set aside. Stir broth into pan, scraping up any browned bits; set aside.

❸ Reduce oven temperature to 300 degrees. Heat oil in Dutch oven over medium heat until shimmering. Add onion, carrot, and celery and cook until softened, about 5 minutes. Stir in tomato paste, garlic, and clove and cook until fragrant, about 30 seconds.

❹ Stir in wine and cook until nearly all liquid is evaporated, about 2 minutes. Stir in broth mixture from roasting pan, tomatoes and their juice, and raisins and bring to simmer. Nestle oxtails into pot and bring to simmer. Cover, transfer pot to oven, and cook until oxtails are tender and fork slips easily in and out of meat, about 3 hours.

❺ Transfer oxtails to serving dish and tent loosely with aluminum foil. Strain braising liquid through fine-mesh strainer into fat separator; return solids to now-empty pot. Let braising liquid settle for 5 minutes, then pour defatted liquid into pot with solids. Season with salt and pepper to taste. Spoon 1 cup sauce over top of oxtails and sprinkle with pine nuts. Serve, passing remaining sauce separately.

Roman Gnocchi

Gnocchi alla romana · *Serves 4 to 6*

. . . .

WHY THIS RECIPE WORKS: In Roman times, gnocchi were made from semolina flour—no potatoes, ricotta, or other flours here. As versions from other regions emerged, Romans continued to make their dumplings this way, and for good reason: Semolina gnocchi is particularly comforting because it's appealingly creamy and slightly dense, similar to polenta. To make it, a sort of semolina porridge is cooked, spread into a thin layer, cooled, cut, and baked rather than boiled. We found the key was getting the ratio of liquid to semolina just right. If the mixture was too loose it took a long time to set up, and even then, cleanly cutting out the dumplings was difficult. Plus, the gnocchi fused together in the heat of the oven. A mixture made with 2½ cups of milk and 1 cup of semolina was stiff enough that we could shape the dumplings immediately—no cooling required. And instead of stamping out rounds, which wasted much of the semolina mixture, we simply portioned dumplings straight from the pot using a measuring cup. Refrigerating them before baking allowed a skin to form on the outside of each dumpling, ensuring that they held their shape and could be lifted out of the dish cleanly to be served individually. An egg provided binding power and, along with a little baking powder, lift. Parmigiano Reggiano and some rosemary contributed plenty of flavor. A sprinkling of Parmigiano over the shingled dumplings

before baking developed into an irresistable golden-brown top. You can find fine semolina (sometimes labeled *semola rimacinata*) in most Italian markets or in the international aisle of some well-stocked supermarkets. Avoid conventional semolina, which is too coarse for this recipe and will not work.

2½ cups whole milk
½ teaspoon salt
Pinch ground nutmeg
1 cup (5¾ ounces) fine semolina flour
4 tablespoons unsalted butter, cut into 4 pieces
1 large egg, lightly beaten
2 ounces Parmigiano Reggiano cheese, grated (1 cup)
1 teaspoon minced fresh rosemary
½ teaspoon baking powder

1 Adjust oven rack to middle position and heat oven to 400 degrees. Heat milk, salt, and nutmeg in medium saucepan over medium-low heat until bubbles form around edges of saucepan. Slowly pour semolina into milk mixture in steady stream while whisking constantly. Reduce heat to low and cook, stirring often with rubber spatula, until mixture

forms stiff mass that pulls away from sides when stirring, 3 to 5 minutes. Remove saucepan from heat and let semolina mixture cool for 5 minutes.

2 Stir 3 tablespoons butter and egg into semolina mixture until incorporated. (Mixture will appear separated at first but will become smooth and somewhat shiny.) Stir in ¾ cup Parmigiano, rosemary, and baking powder until incorporated.

3 Fill small bowl with water. Moisten ¼-cup dry measuring cup with water and scoop even portion of semolina mixture. Invert gnocchi onto tray or large plate. Repeat, moistening measuring cup between scoops to prevent sticking. Refrigerate gnocchi, uncovered, for 30 minutes. (Gnocchi can be refrigerated, covered, for up to 24 hours.)

4 Grease 8-inch square baking dish with remaining 1 tablespoon butter. Shingle gnocchi in prepared dish, creating 3 rows of 4 gnocchi each. Sprinkle gnocchi with remaining ¼ cup Parmigiano and bake until tops of gnocchi are golden brown, 35 to 40 minutes. Let cool for 15 minutes before serving.

Spaghetti With Amatriciana Sauce

Spaghetti all'amatriciana · *Serves 6 to 8*

· ·

WHY THIS RECIPE WORKS: *Spaghetti all'amatriciana* is more than a recipe; the dish is the legacy of a village. On August 24, 2016 (three days before the town's festival to celebrate its famed dish), an earthquake devastated Amatrice, leaving it very much in ruin. Spaghetti all'amatriciana is popular throughout Lazio and in Rome, helping to preserve the culture. It calls for spaghetti, tomatoes, hot red peppers, guanciale, Pecorino Romano, and white wine, which balances the bold flavors of the dish. Departing slightly from tradition, we used red wine, which provided a richer flavor, but we touched little else. Guanciale is undoubtedly the star player here: Pig jowl that's simply salt-cured, not smoked, it provides pure pork flavor and bits of texture as well as rendered fat that enriches the tomato sauce. We decided to stretch its magic even further: To keep the cheese from clumping, we mixed it with some rendered guanciale fat, which coated the proteins and prevented them from bonding. You can substitute an equal amount of salt pork, rind removed, rinsed, and patted dry, for the guanciale. Like guanciale, salt pork (from the pig's belly) isn't smoked. Don't opt for pancetta, another common substitute, as it gives the dish an odd sour taste. Look for salt pork that's roughly 70 percent fat and 30 percent lean meat; leaner salt pork may not render enough fat. If the guanciale is difficult to slice, put it in the freezer for 15 minutes to firm up.

8 ounces guanciale
½ cup water
½ teaspoon red pepper flakes
2 tablespoons tomato paste
¼ cup red wine
1 (28-ounce) can diced tomatoes
2 ounces Pecorino Romano cheese, grated (1 cup)
1 pound dried spaghetti
1 tablespoon salt

❶ Slice guanciale into ¼-inch-thick strips, then cut each strip crosswise into ¼-inch pieces. Bring pork and water to simmer in 10-inch nonstick skillet over medium heat and cook until water evaporates and guanciale begins to sizzle, 5 to 8 minutes. Reduce heat to medium-low and continue to cook, stirring frequently, until fat renders and guanciale turns golden, 5 to 8 minutes. Using slotted spoon, transfer pork to bowl. Pour all but 1 tablespoon fat from skillet into second bowl and reserve.

❷ Add pepper flakes and tomato paste to fat left in skillet and cook, stirring constantly, for 20 seconds. Stir in wine and cook for 30 seconds. Stir in tomatoes and their juice and guanciale and bring to simmer. Cook, stirring frequently, until thickened, 12 to 16 minutes. While sauce simmers, smear 2 tablespoons reserved fat and ½ cup Pecorino together in bowl to form paste.

❸ Meanwhile, bring 4 quarts water to boil in large pot. Add pasta and salt and cook, stirring often, until al dente. Reserve 1 cup cooking water, then drain pasta and return it to pot.

❹ Add sauce, ⅓ cup reserved cooking water, and Pecorino-fat mixture and toss well to coat. Adjust consistency with remaining reserved cooking water as needed. Serve, passing remaining ½ cup Pecorino separately.

Spaghetti Carbonara

Spaghetti alla carbonara • *Serves 6 to 8*

....

WHY THIS RECIPE WORKS: Another minimalist Roman pasta made from pantry staples (cured pork, eggs, Pecorino), *spaghetti alla carbonara* is an indulgent dish with a foggy history. While the word *carbonaro* means "charcoal burner" and could point to the dish being eaten by charcoal workers, some think it was dreamed up during the Allied liberation of Rome, during which Romans were supplied bacon and eggs from the Americans. Others theorize that this dish, like *cacio e pepe* (page 232), was made by meandering shepherds. Whatever the origin, spaghetti carbonara may seem simple but can be devilishly hard to get right: The finicky sauce relies on the heat of the pasta to become lush and glossy, but all too often the eggs scramble and the cheese clumps. Looking for a way to keep the sauce reliably fluid, we reduced the amount of pasta cooking water by half as we did for cacio e pepe. In addition to preventing clumping, the starch in this concentrated liquid worked in concert with the egg proteins to lend viscosity to the sauce. While some recipes use all egg yolks for custardy richness, we found their powerful emulsifying and thickening capabilities turned the sauce into glue just minutes after serving. Three whites and four yolks gave us a sauce with the flavor we were after and an ideal thickness during a 15-minute serving window. It's important to work quickly in steps 2 and 3. The heat from the cooking water and the hot spaghetti will "cook" the sauce only if used immediately. Warming the mixing and serving bowls helps the sauce stay creamy. You can substitute an equal amount of bacon for the guanciale.

8 ounces guanciale, cut into ½-inch pieces
½ cup water
3 garlic cloves, minced
2½ ounces Pecorino Romano, grated (1¼ cups)
3 large eggs plus 1 large yolk
1 teaspoon pepper
1 pound dried spaghetti
1 tablespoon salt

❶ Bring guanciale and water to simmer in 10-inch nonstick skillet over medium heat and cook until water evaporates and guanciale begins to sizzle, about 8 minutes. Reduce heat to medium-low and continue to cook until fat renders and guanciale browns, 5 to 8 minutes. Add garlic and cook, stirring constantly, until fragrant, about 30 seconds. Strain guanciale mixture through fine-mesh strainer set in bowl. Set aside guanciale mixture. Measure out 1 tablespoon fat and place in bowl; discard remaining fat. Whisk Pecorino, eggs and yolk, and pepper into fat until combined.

❷ Meanwhile, set colander in large serving bowl. Bring 2 quarts water to boil in large pot. Add spaghetti and salt and cook, stirring often, until al dente. Drain pasta in prepared colander, reserving cooking water. Pour 1 cup cooking water into liquid measuring cup and discard remainder. Return pasta to now-empty bowl.

❸ Slowly whisk ½ cup reserved cooking water into Pecorino mixture until smooth. Gradually pour Pecorino mixture over pasta, tossing to coat. Add guanciale mixture and toss to combine. Let pasta rest, tossing frequently, until sauce has thickened slightly and coats pasta, 2 to 4 minutes, adjusting consistency with remaining reserved cooking water as needed. Serve immediately in warmed serving bowls.

239

Herb-Roasted Pork

Porchetta · Serves 10 to 12

WHY THIS RECIPE WORKS: *Porchetta*—fall-apart tender, rich pieces of slow-cooked pork, infused with the flavors of garlic, fennel, rosemary, and thyme and served with pieces of crisp skin on a crusty roll—is one of Italy's greatest street foods. In Lazio, it's also eaten for holidays or festivals. Traditionally a whole pig is boned and the meat is rubbed with an herb-spice paste. The pig is then tied around a spit and allowed to sit overnight. The next day, it's slow-roasted over a wood fire until the meat is ultratender and the skin is burnished and crackling-crisp. We made some tweaks to transition it from the street to the home as a centerpiece roast. Easy-to-find pork butt offered the right balance of meat and fatty richness. For quicker cooking, we cut the roast into two pieces and tied each into a compact cylinder. To season the meat, we cut slits in the exterior and then coated it with salt and an intensely flavored paste of garlic, rosemary,

thyme, and fennel. We also cut a crosshatch in the fat cap and rubbed it with a mixture of salt and baking soda before letting it sit overnight in the refrigerator; these steps helped the exterior dry out and crisp up. A two-stage cooking method gave us the perfect combination of moist, juicy meat and crispy crust. Pork butt roast is often labeled Boston butt in the supermarket. Look for a roast with a substantial fat cap. If fennel seeds are unavailable, substitute ¼ cup of ground fennel.

3 tablespoons fennel seeds
½ cup fresh rosemary leaves (2 bunches)
¼ cup fresh thyme leaves (2 bunches)
12 garlic cloves, peeled
Kosher salt and pepper
½ cup extra-virgin olive oil
1 (5- to 6-pound) boneless pork butt roast, trimmed
¼ teaspoon baking soda

❶ Grind fennel seeds in spice grinder or mortar and pestle until finely ground. Transfer ground fennel to food processor and add rosemary, thyme, garlic, 1 tablespoon pepper, and 2 teaspoons salt. Pulse mixture until finely chopped, 10 to 15 pulses. Add oil and process until smooth paste forms, 20 to 30 seconds.

❷ Using sharp knife, cut slits in surface fat of roast, spaced 1 inch apart, in crosshatch pattern, being careful not to cut into meat. Cut roast in half with grain into 2 equal pieces.

❸ Turn each roast on its side so fat cap is facing away from you, bottom of roast is facing toward you, and newly cut side is facing up. Starting 1 inch from short end of each roast, use boning or paring knife to make a slit that starts 1 inch from top of roast and ends 1 inch from bottom, pushing knife completely

through roast. Repeat making slits, spaced 1 to 1½ inches apart, along length of each roast, stopping 1 inch from opposite end (you should have 6 to 8 slits, depending on size of roast).

❹ Turn roast so fat cap is facing down. Rub sides and bottom of each roast with 2 teaspoons salt, taking care to work salt into slits from both sides. Rub herb paste onto sides and bottom of each roast, taking care to work paste into slits from both sides. Flip roast so that fat cap is facing up. Using 3 pieces of kitchen twine per roast, tie each roast into compact cylinder.

❺ Combine 1 tablespoon salt, 1 teaspoon pepper, and baking soda in small bowl. Rub fat cap of each roast with salt–baking soda mixture, taking care to work mixture into crosshatches. Transfer roasts to wire rack set in rimmed baking sheet and refrigerate, uncovered, for at least 6 hours or up to 24 hours.

❻ Adjust oven rack to middle position and heat oven to 325 degrees. Transfer roasts, fat side up, to large roasting pan, leaving at least 2 inches between roasts. Cover tightly with aluminum foil. Cook until pork registers 180 degrees, 2 to 2½ hours.

❼ Remove pan from oven and increase oven temperature to 500 degrees. Carefully remove and discard foil and transfer roasts to large plate. Discard liquid in pan. Line pan with foil. Remove twine from roasts; return roasts to pan, directly on foil; and return pan to oven. Cook until exteriors of roasts are well browned and interiors register 190 degrees, 20 to 30 minutes.

❽ Transfer roasts to carving board and let rest for 20 minutes. Slice roasts into ½-inch-thick slices, transfer to serving dish, and serve.

READYING TWO ROASTS FOR PORCHETTA

1. After crosshatching surface, halve pork butt, creating two smaller roasts.

2. Cut deep slits into sides of roasts, then rub salt and herb paste over roasts and into slits.

3. Using 3 pieces of kitchen twine per roast, tie each roast into a compact cylinder.

Abruzzo & Molise

Where the Chefs Come From

....

ABRUZZO AND ITS SISTER REGION MOLISE are fiercely independent, rugged places with a long history of resistance and banditry. And yet the area produces more chefs than any other region in Italy. That may be because Abruzzo is the historic home of the profession in Italy. But it may also be due to the region's simple yet highly flavored foods. The Abruzzesi, isolated in their mountain retreats, spent a millennium cooking with the same ingredients. The results are a cuisine that is ingenious and intense: It makes a lot out of little.

A Rugged and Isolated Land

Central Italy lies on the edge of the Eurasian and African continental plates, and as a result earthquakes perpetually menace the region, including in 2009 when the capital of Abruzzo, L'Aquila, was devastated. But its location is also why Abruzzo and Molise are torn and tough places, high and wild with daunting and dramatic beauty. Three-quarters of the land is mountainous, culminating in the 9,554-foot Corno Grande.

Abruzzo and Molise are also known as the greenest regions, with about a third of their combined territory protected as national parks or nature reserves. The Gran Sasso e Monti della Laga National Park, for example, is home to many animals that are rare in Italy, such as bears, lynx, and golden eagles. Shepherds graze their sheep on the lower slopes of the cool Gran Sasso in the summer, and in the winter move them down to the hot plains of Puglia along ancient transhumant routes.

To the south of the Gran Sasso lie the Majella mountains, a mystical range to the

An overlook of beautiful Anversa, a typical hill town in Abruzzo

Lunchtime near the Sarracco Fountain in Scanno, L'Aquila

superstitious Abruzzesi. Here caves and grottoes, waterfalls, and hidden hermitages are tucked between verdant pastures of medicinal and culinary herbs such as myrtle, willow, capers, rosemary, and licorice. Equally magical is Molise's Matese massif, home to orchids, wolves, and groves of 100-foot beech trees. Several rivers drain the mountains to the east, the largest being the Aterno-Pescara and the Sangro in Abruzzo, and the Biferno in Molise. The warm, fertile river valleys are cultivated with wheat, legumes, and vegetables; aromatic pine groves grow along the narrow coast of white beaches, cheerful summer resorts, and gritty fishing towns.

Simple, Outstanding Provisions

Abruzzo borders Lazio to the west, Le Marche to the north, Molise to the south, and the Adriatic Sea to the east. Molise became an independent region in 1963 but is otherwise geographically and culturally similar to Abruzzo. It borders Lazio (marginally) to the west, Puglia to the southeast, and Campania to the southwest. Both regions are influenced by their neighbors, and yet they belong only to themselves—an independence fostered by a mountainous territory that hindered development. Indeed, until the 20th century Abruzzo and Molise were primarily isolated sheepherding regions. In the 1960s, however, highways and a tunnel through the Gran Sasso opened the territory to the rest of Italy and Europe. Even still, much of the local agriculture continues to be small-scale farming, sheepherding, and fishing.

The patron saint of chefs throughout the world, according to the Holy See, is St. Francis Caracciolo, a monk born in the Abruzzese town of Villa Santa Maria.

Today there are four provinces in Abruzzo, named for their main cities: Teramo, Pescara, Chieti, and the landlocked L'Aquila. Molise's two provinces—Campobasso to the east and Isernia to the west—both produce a wealth of proteins mainly for local consumption, mostly lamb and mutton (*spiedini,* savory grilled lamb kebabs, are a staple), but also beef and goat. Like other central Italian regions, Abruzzo and Molise make their own aromatic version of *porchetta* (boned roasted pig with crushed fennel seeds), and *salame,* such as a mortadella from Campotosto known as "mule's balls," and *salame alla cacciatora,* called hunter's salami because they were small enough for a hunter to pack in his pocket. Where there are herds there are curds, so it's not surprising that sheep's-milk pecorino and cow's-milk *caciocavallo* are key cheeses, as are goat's-milk *caprino* and the stretchy *scamorza,* eaten smoked, grilled, and fresh.

With 100 miles of coast, fishing plays a big role in the local economy. From the port towns of Pescara, Ortona, and Termoli, for example, fishermen catch red mullet, anchovies, squid, octopuses, and crabs, and collect clams and sea snails. These are key for the local *brodetto vastese* (the essential brodetto of the Adriatic, it uses nothing but oil, fish, garlic, parsley, salt, and pepper); *polipi in purgatorio*, a light, spicy octopus stew; and the heavenly *scapece*, fish fillets fried and preserved in vinegar flavored with saffron.

The woods and pastures are hunted for game, mushrooms, and wild herbs, while the streams and lakes yield eel, trout, and crayfish. Farmlands produce almond and fruit trees, grapes, and olives (which make excellent olive oil), and a wide variety of vegetables from artichokes to zucchini. Only a few products are exported, including saffron, licorice—and chefs.

The valleys carve the region up into small locations, leading to each town having its own food specialties. These are simple provisions of outstanding quality, which, over the centuries of isolation, the Abruzzesi have figured out how to cook to perfection. For example, excellent pork products come from Campotosto, chickpeas and saffron from Navelli, lentils from Santo Stefano di Sessanio, white beans from Capestrano, onions from Isernia, and giant white celery from Campobasso.

A Cuisine Born of Independence

While humans have been living on these lands for 700,000 years, Abruzzo and Molise's first known ethnic identity is Samnite, an Iron Age tribe of pastoral warriors. The Samnites lived in isolated quarrelsome communities, which eventually became unified through trade and their hatred of Rome. The Romans did not conquer the Samnites easily. The mountains between their lands are high and the locals were ferocious. By the third century B.C., rather than deal with their relentless insurrections, the Romans conceded full citizenship to the tribes (the *Lex Julia*).

Indeed, the history of Abruzzo and Molise is one of resistance and self-reliance. Following the fall of the Roman Empire in the fifth century, the invading Goths were, in turn, harassed by the locals here just as the Romans were. By the 12th century the

LOCAL FLAVOR
VIRTUES OF
VIRTÙ

Virtù soup is the Abruzzese pantry's version of spring-cleaning. By May, the larder likely has only lentils, some chickpeas, bits and ends of dried pasta, and the last not-so-prime cuts of pork. At the same time, the first vegetables are coming in: sweet peas, tender favas, and wild herbs. Root vegetables such as onions and carrots may be wrinkled but are still good. Combine them all in a robust soup and the result is virtù, or virtue (a more stew-like version is called *vignole*). Tradition has it that 28 ingredients, both fresh and preserved, go into its making, each ingredient with its own cooking time. Virtù, which can take hours to create, is robust and sublime, rich and light, intense and delicate, just like spring.

THE THICK AND
THE THIN

Two very different types of pasta define Abruzzese cooking: *maccheroni alla molinara* (known as *jàccoli* or *a fezze* across the border in Lazio), long, fat noodles shaped by hand, and *maccheroni alla chitarra*, thin, square spaghetti pressed through a wooden frame strung with metal wires. Both are made with flour, eggs, and water. *Alla molinara*, meaning "miller's wife's," dates to the mid-14th century and the introduction of flour mills. *Alla chitarra* means "guitar," a name referring to its preparation. Both pastas are commonly served with a tomato sauce flavored with savory meats such as chicken feet.

Separating saffron threads in L'Aquila, painstaking work

Normans had added these regions to their Kingdom of Naples, which included southern Italy and Sicily and lasted until Italian unification. Control of the kingdom, however, was tossed from German to French to Spanish dynasties (the Spanish notably introducing saffron to the area in the 1300s). But they suffered constant harassment by local militias hiding out in the Majella, living off sheep, game, and herbs. One theory for the origin of *pasta alla carbonara* comes from the *carbonari*, freedom fighters who hid in the forests and made the dish with salt pork, goat cheese, and wild quail eggs.

A Culinary Intelligence

Abruzzese and Molisana cooking is not so much influenced by its neighbors, various occupiers, and trading partners as by its many centuries of isolation and reliance on limited ingredients. The basic flavors are olive oil, tomatoes, maybe minced salt pork, and hot pepper, all cooked quickly to preserve the fresh taste of the ingredients, with herbs of different sorts. The cuisine is fabulously savory; for example, *potacchio* dishes like those in Le Marche are made here, but with the flavor amped up by adding local capers, olives, and more hot pepper. Recipes are rarely complex, but the results are always articulate. You can taste everything in these dishes.

The food of Abruzzo and Molise is like the perfect curse word—it accomplishes so much with so little. Take, for example, *scrippelle*, delicate egg and parsley omelets thin as crepes that are rolled and placed in the bottom of a soup bowl, over which hot capon

The elaborate doorway of the Basilica di Santa Maria di Collemaggio, L'Aquila

broth is poured. Or the lip-smacking spiny lobster poached in vinegar, or lamb cooked in earthenware with olive oil, black olives, lemon, oregano, and hot pepper. *Zuppa di lenticche e castagne* is made with tiny lentils and fresh chestnuts, tomatoes, salt pork, and mountain herbs. And *schiacciata*, a flatbread baked with wine grapes and sugar, is a sure sign the grape harvests are on. And don't forget dessert, often a surprising combination, such as ricotta cheese drizzled with honey and dusted with saffron, or fried sweet ravioli stuffed with grape must and nutmeats. Only a few ingredients are used, but they are ingeniously combined. The resulting complex flavors portray what the author Elena Kostioukovitch calls the regions' "subtle flair and culinary intelligence."

Vegetables play a big role in the cooking of Abruzzo and Molise, as they do in every less-than-rich area. Here, peas are cooked with *guanciale*; giant cardoons are cooked in a soup with tomatoes and salt pork; and potatoes are sliced and laid on a hearth and pressed with a *coppo,* an iron lid that is piled with live coals, and then, when tender, dressed with oil and vinegar. Intrepid combinations of flavors and unusual techniques are why the Abruzzesi chefs are so famous.

But those chefs have pedigree, too. In the 16th century Ferrante Caracciolo, a nobleman and epicurean from the Abruzzese municipality Villa Santa Maria, taught his staff how to cook. For generations the teaching here continued, and from this historical kitchen, chefs were sent to work for other nobles and heads of state, spreading the reputation of Abruzzesi chefs far and wide. Today Villa Santa Maria is home to the seminal Istituto Alberghiero, a culinary and hotel management school. The chefs it produces are descended from a long line of cooks that predate the 1500s. Their heritage reaches back to the Samnite shepherds, to the bandits and resistance fighters who spent their years in camps and hideouts, grilling *spiedini* to perfection over an open fire.

A *trabocco*, the traditional fishing hut, built over the sea along the Abruzzo coast

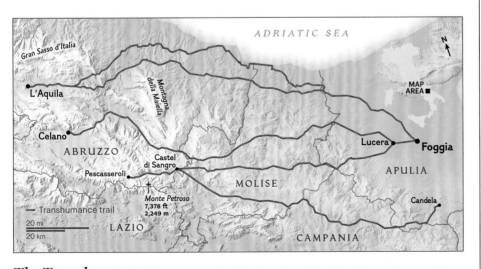

The Transhumance The annual trek of shepherds and their flocks from the mountain pastures of Abruzzo south to Puglia (Apulia) for the winter is an age-old migration.

Chitarra Pasta With Lamb Ragù

Maccheroni alla chitarra con ragù di agnello • *Serves 6 to 8*

WHY THIS RECIPE WORKS: In the rugged mountains of Abruzzo, many shepherds practice transhumance (*transumanza* in Italian), or the seasonal movement of sheep between alpine summer pastures and lowland winter pastures. This custom enables the sheep to graze on a wide array of grasses and flowers, and as a result they produce particularly aromatic milk and meat. It's no wonder that a simple lamb ragù,

perfumed with mountain herbs and saffron (cultivated by a mere few families on the plains of Abruzzo), is a staple of this region. After testing our way through traditional recipes that called for braising or stewing various cuts of lamb, we found that braising large (3-inch) chunks of boneless lamb shoulder, shredding them, and then returning them to the cooking liquid yielded far and away the best result: meltingly tender and deeply

flavorful bits of lamb in a rich sauce. This classic Abruzzese ragù is most often paired with a unique pasta known locally as *maccheroni alla chitarra*—a rich egg dough rolled into thick sheets and cut into attractive squared-off strands on a cutter called a *chitarra* ("guitar" in Italian) that resembles a stringed musical instrument. Until recently, the chitarra was difficult to find outside of Abruzzo, but it's now available through specialty vendors

and online. If you cannot find a chitarra to cut your own pasta, you can substitute 1 pound dried maccheroni alla chitarra (also known as *spaghetti alla chitarra* or *pasta alla chitarra*) for the fresh maccheroni. Fresh or dried linguine or spaghetti can also be used. You can substitute 2 pounds lamb shoulder chops (blade or round bone) for the lamb shoulder. Guanciale is traditional in this recipe, but an equal amount of salt pork, rind removed, rinsed, can be substituted. If it's difficult to chop the guanciale, put it in the freezer for 15 minutes to firm up. If your chitarra has more than one set of strings, choose the set that are spaced approximately ⅛ inch apart.

RAGÙ

- 1½ pounds boneless lamb shoulder, trimmed and cut into 3-inch pieces
- Salt and pepper
- 1 tablespoon extra-virgin olive oil
- 2 ounces guanciale, chopped fine
- 1 onion, chopped fine
- 1 carrot, peeled and chopped fine
- 1 celery rib, minced
- 3 garlic cloves, minced
- 1 tablespoon tomato paste
- 2 teaspoons minced fresh rosemary
- ½ teaspoon saffron threads, crumbled
- ¼ teaspoon red pepper flakes
- ½ cup dry white wine
- 1 (28-ounce) can whole peeled tomatoes

MACCHERONI

- 1 pound Fresh Egg Pasta (page 364)
- Salt and pepper
- Grated Pecorino Romano cheese

1 For the ragù: Adjust oven rack to lower-middle position and heat oven to 300 degrees. Pat lamb dry with paper towels and season with salt and pepper. Heat oil in Dutch oven over medium-high heat until just smoking. Brown lamb on all sides, about 8 minutes; transfer to plate. Pour off all but 1 tablespoon fat from pot and let pot cool slightly.

2 Add guanciale to fat left in pot and cook over medium-low heat until fat is rendered, about 2 minutes. Stir in onion, carrot, and celery, increase heat to medium, and cook until softened and lightly browned, 6 to 8 minutes. Stir in garlic, tomato paste, rosemary, saffron, and pepper flakes and cook until fragrant, about 30 seconds.

3 Stir in wine, scraping up any browned bits, and cook until reduced by half, about 3 minutes. Stir in tomatoes and their juice, breaking up tomatoes into rough 1-inch pieces with wooden spoon, and bring to simmer. Nestle lamb into pot along with any accumulated juices and return to simmer. Cover, transfer pot to oven, and cook until lamb is very tender, 2 to 2½ hours, turning lamb halfway through cooking.

4 Remove pot from oven. Transfer lamb to cutting board, let cool slightly, then shred into bite-size pieces using 2 forks; discard excess fat. Stir lamb and any accumulated juices into sauce and let sit until heated through, about 5 minutes. Season with salt and pepper to taste. Cover to keep warm. (Ragù can be refrigerated for up to 3 days; gently reheat before using.)

5 For the maccheroni: Transfer dough to clean counter, divide into 5 pieces, and cover with plastic wrap. Flatten 1 piece of dough into ½-inch-thick disk. Using pasta machine with rollers set to widest position, feed dough through rollers twice. Bring tapered ends of dough toward middle and press to seal. Feed dough seam side first through rollers again. Repeat feeding dough tapered ends first through rollers set at widest position, without folding, until dough is smooth and barely tacky. (If dough sticks to fingers or rollers, lightly dust with flour and roll again.)

6 Narrow rollers to next setting and feed dough through rollers twice. Continue to progressively narrow rollers, feeding dough through each setting twice, until dough is ⅛ inch thick. (If dough becomes too long to manage, halve crosswise.) Transfer sheet of pasta to lightly floured counter and repeat rolling with remaining 4 pieces of dough; do not overlap pasta sheets. Let pasta sheets sit until dry to touch, about 15 minutes.

7 Line 2 rimmed baking sheets with parchment paper and liberally dust with flour. Liberally dust pasta sheets with flour and cut into lengths approximately 2 inches shorter than length of strings on chitarra. Lay 1 pasta sheet on top of chitarra strings and firmly roll floured rolling pin over pasta to cut into strands. Liberally dust maccheroni with flour and arrange in small bundles on prepared sheets. Repeat with remaining pasta sheets. (Maccheroni can be held at room temperature for up to 30 minutes, refrigerated for up to 4 hours, or chilled in freezer until firm, then transferred to zipper-lock bag and frozen for up to 1 month. If frozen, do not thaw before cooking.)

8 Bring 4 quarts water to boil in large pot. Add pasta and 1 tablespoon salt and cook, stirring often, until al dente. Reserve ½ cup cooking water, then drain pasta and return it to pot. Add sauce and toss to combine. Adjust consistency with reserved cooking water as needed. Season with salt and pepper to taste. Serve with Pecorino.

Linguine With Seafood

Linguine allo scoglio · *Serves 6 to 8*

WHY THIS RECIPE WORKS: While pasta with seafood isn't limited to a specific region, it's enjoyed with particular delight on the coast of Abruzzo and Molise—a prime spot for enjoying the crustaceous fruits of the Adriatic Sea. To create a seafood pasta dish with rich, savory seafood flavor in every bite (not just in the pieces of shellfish), we made a sauce with clam juice and four minced anchovies, which fortified the juices released by the shellfish. Cooking the ingredients in a careful sequence—adding hardier clams and mussels first and reserving the shrimp and squid for the final few minutes of cooking—ensured that every piece was plump and tender. We parboiled the linguine and then finished cooking it directly in the sauce. The noodles soaked up flavor while shedding starches, which thickened the sauce so that it clung well to the pasta. Cherry tomatoes, lots of garlic, fresh herbs, and lemon made for a bright, clean, complex-tasting sauce. And it wouldn't be an Abruzzese dish without the vibrant jolt of some pepper flakes. For a simpler version of this dish, you can omit the clams and squid and increase the amounts of mussels and shrimp to 1½ pounds each; you'll also need to increase the amount of salt in step 2 to ¾ teaspoon.

6 tablespoons extra-virgin olive oil
12 garlic cloves, minced
¼ teaspoon red pepper flakes
1 pound littleneck clams, scrubbed
1 pound mussels, scrubbed and debearded
1¼ pounds cherry tomatoes (10 ounces whole, 10 ounces halved)
1 (8-ounce) bottle clam juice
1 cup dry white wine
1 cup minced fresh parsley
1 tablespoon tomato paste
4 anchovy fillets, rinsed, patted dry, and minced
1 teaspoon minced fresh thyme
Salt and pepper
1 pound dried linguine
1 pound extra-large shrimp (21 to 25 per pound), peeled, deveined, and tails removed
8 ounces squid bodies, sliced crosswise into ½-inch-thick rings
2 teaspoons grated lemon zest, plus lemon wedges for serving

❶ Heat ¼ cup oil in Dutch oven over medium-high heat until shimmering. Add garlic and pepper flakes and cook until fragrant, about 1 minute. Add clams, cover, and cook, shaking pot occasionally, for 4 minutes. Add mussels, cover, and continue to cook, shaking pot occasionally, until clams and mussels have opened, 3 to 4 minutes. Transfer clams and mussels to bowl, discarding any that haven't opened, and cover to keep warm; leave any broth in pot.

❷ Add whole tomatoes, clam juice, wine, ½ cup parsley, tomato paste, anchovies, thyme, and ½ teaspoon salt to pot. Bring to simmer and cook, stirring occasionally, until tomatoes have started to break down and sauce is reduced by one-third, about 10 minutes.

❸ Meanwhile, bring 4 quarts water to boil in large pot. Add pasta and 1 tablespoon salt and cook, stirring often, for 7 minutes. Reserve ½ cup cooking water, then drain pasta.

❹ Add pasta to sauce in Dutch oven and cook over medium heat, stirring gently, for 2 minutes. Reduce heat to medium-low, stir in shrimp, cover, and cook for 4 minutes. Stir in squid, lemon zest, halved tomatoes, and remaining ½ cup parsley. Cover and continue to cook until shrimp and squid are just cooked through, about 2 minutes. Gently stir in clams and mussels. Remove pot from heat, cover, and let sit until clams and mussels are warmed through, about 2 minutes. Adjust consistency with reserved cooking water as needed. Season with salt and pepper to taste. Transfer to large serving dish, drizzle with remaining 2 tablespoons oil, and serve, passing lemon wedges separately.

Spring Vegetable Stew

Vignole · *Serves 6*

WHY THIS RECIPE WORKS: Spring vegetables abound in the inland portion of Abruzzo, and *vignole* is a vibrant (and speedy) braise that celebrates them. The fresh favas are traditionally eaten skin on, but their fibrous skins tend to be tough and unpleasant, so we tenderized them by blanching them in a baking soda solution. The drawback? The high pH of the water caused the favas to slowly turn purple during cooking. Counteracting this was simple; all we had to do was rinse them thoroughly after cooking. Sweet peas, savory baby artichokes, and grassy asparagus created layers of springtime flavor. We added the artichokes first to allow them time to cook almost all the way through before adding the more delicate asparagus and peas, and then finally the favas to warm through. We finished the dish with a handful of herbs and some lemon zest. This recipe works best with fresh vegetables; however, if you can't find fresh fava beans and peas, you can substitute 1 cup of frozen, thawed fava beans and 1¼ cups of frozen peas; add the peas to the skillet with the beans in step 4.

1 lemon
4 baby artichokes (3 ounces each)
1 teaspoon baking soda
1 pound fava beans, shelled (1 cup)
1 tablespoon extra-virgin olive oil, plus extra for serving
1 leek, white and light green parts only, halved lengthwise, sliced thin, and washed thoroughly
Salt and pepper
3 garlic cloves, minced
1 cup chicken or vegetable broth
1 pound asparagus, trimmed and cut on bias into 2-inch lengths
1 pound fresh peas, shelled (1¼ cups)
2 tablespoons shredded fresh basil
1 tablespoon chopped fresh mint

❶ Grate 2 teaspoons lemon zest from lemon; set aside. Halve lemon and squeeze lemon halves into container filled with 4 cups water, then add spent halves. Working with 1 artichoke at a time, trim stem to about ¾ inch and cut off top quarter of artichoke. Break off bottom 3 or 4 rows of tough outer leaves by pulling them downward. Using paring knife, trim outer layer of stem and base, removing any dark green parts. Cut artichoke into quarters and submerge in water.

❷ Bring 2 cups water and baking soda to boil in small saucepan. Add beans and cook until edges begin to darken, 1 to 2 minutes. Drain and rinse well with cold water.

❸ Heat oil in 12-inch skillet over medium heat until shimmering. Add leek, 1 tablespoon water, and 1 teaspoon salt and cook until softened, about 3 minutes. Stir in garlic and cook until fragrant, about 30 seconds.

❹ Remove artichokes from lemon water, shaking off excess water, and add to skillet. Stir in broth and bring to simmer. Reduce heat to medium-low, cover, and cook until artichokes are almost tender, 6 to 8 minutes. Stir in asparagus and peas, cover, and cook until crisp-tender, 5 to 7 minutes. Stir in beans and cook until heated through and artichokes are fully tender, about 2 minutes. Off heat, stir in basil, mint, and lemon zest. Season with salt and pepper to taste and drizzle with extra oil. Serve immediately.

Grilled Lamb Skewers

Arrosticini · Serves 6 to 8

. . . .

WHY THIS RECIPE WORKS: The romantic roots of *arrosticini* are steeped in the long shepherding tradition of the region; lore has it that the mountain shepherds of Abruzzo would roast pieces of mutton over the fire as a quick and easy meal while they traveled. Today, arrosticini is a popular street food—the meat is cut into tiny precision cubes by machine, cooked over a specialized grill, and eaten directly off the skewer—though it's also prepared by home cooks. Arrosticini can be made with lamb or mutton, but either way its exterior should be well browned, with the meat basted in its own flavorful fat and cooked until tender. This is generally achieved by cutting the meat very small (we found recipes calling for ⅓-inch cubes) and cooking quickly over a very hot fire. We were able to create a blazing-hot flame on a charcoal grill using our half-grill method: spreading a full chimney of coals over just half the grate to concentrate the heat. With a grill this hot, we found we could cut the meat a bit bigger, into ½-inch pieces, and cook it just as quickly, making prepping meat and threading the skewers less of a chore. Packing the lamb tightly helped keep it from overcooking, and after a quick stint on the grill it was so flavorful that all it required was a dash of salt and pepper for seasoning. You can substitute 2½ pounds lamb shoulder chops (blade or round bone) for the lamb shoulder. You will need twelve 12-inch metal skewers for this recipe.

2 pounds boneless lamb shoulder, trimmed and cut into ½-inch pieces
Kosher salt and pepper
3 tablespoons extra-virgin olive oil

1 Pat lamb dry with paper towels and sprinkle with 1½ teaspoons salt and 1 teaspoon pepper. Tightly thread lamb onto twelve 12-inch metal skewers, leaving top 3 inches of each skewer exposed. Brush skewers with oil.

2A For a charcoal grill: Open bottom vent completely. Light large chimney starter filled with charcoal briquettes (6 quarts). When top coals are partially covered with ash, pour evenly over half of grill. Set cooking grate in place, cover, and open lid vent completely. Heat grill until hot, about 5 minutes.

B For a gas grill: Turn all burners to high, cover, and heat grill until hot, about 15 minutes. Leave all burners on high.

3 Clean and oil cooking grate. Place skewers on hotter side of grill, and cook (covered if using gas), turning frequently, until well browned on all sides, 5 to 7 minutes. Serve.

Under bright blue umbrellas, visitors take in the sun in Atrani, along the vibrant and colorful Amalfi Coast.

PART THREE

Southern Italy
and the Islands

From the ankle to the shin, the heel to the instep to the toe
and the islands—the south sticks to its traditions.

Melting Pot of the Mediterranean

IN SOUTHERN ITALY, the temperature goes up on everything. The air is hotter, the conversation is hotter—and the cooking is hotter. This is the Italy of yesteryear, of children leading donkeys through stone towns, men in suits and dusty shoes assembled in front of faded baroque churches, and women in head scarves cradling vegetables in their aprons. The light is bright and harsh, the hills deforested and dotted with cacti, the valleys golden with wheat, the mountaintops capped with snow. Along

the aquamarine coasts are whitewashed towns with blue doors and shutters, and in the cities, dry squalor and grand architecture are tied together by sagging electric wires and fluttering laundry lines, beneath which tiny cars squeeze along snaking streets. Southern Italian cities are a mass of colorful commerce, where bins of goods spill onto the streets and the air is filled with the yelling of merchants and equally exuberant customers.

Poorer than its northern cousins, the south is composed of farm-based cultures. Its cuisines have always been farm to table, a reflection of its long history as the breadbasket of the Mediterranean. Easily accessible to the greater Mediterranean Basin, Italy's south has both benefited and suffered from waves of dominance by whichever regional player was strongest at the moment. Pride and poverty define the cuisine of the beautiful south. Indeed, there is a saying: "When you come to the south you weep twice; first when you arrive, and then when you leave."

La Cucina Povera

The ancient Greeks introduced the three pillars of southern Italy's diet—oil, wine, and

A common encounter in the interior of Sicily: a herd of sheep on the road

grain—and built a trading network that rivaled any in the Western world. Romans followed the Greeks and established the latifundium system, large farm estates with absentee landlords, typically worked by slaves. Huge amounts of grain and other comestibles were produced in this manner. They fed the legions but starved the locals.

Clementines

Eventually the Romans were displaced by the Vandals and other invaders, including the Arabs in Sicily and Calabria, and the Normans who unified the southern regions under one crown during the medieval era. As sovereignty was passed among various European noble lineages, the latifundium system continued in the form of absentee property owners who harnessed itinerant laborers and local peasantry to work their great estates. Only one step away from slavery, the system reinforced the cycle of poverty in the south. These different cultures also had influence on the food of the region, evident in such traditions as the *agrodolce*—sweet and sour—cooking technique, and the south's love affair with pastries, marzipan, and other confections, both gifts of the Arabs. All regional Italian cooking is based on local ingredients, but because poverty was such a constant companion, the cooking considered traditional in the south today is primarily based on humble staples such as cereals, vegetables, and coastal fish.

The Castello quarter of Cagliari, Sardinia, has a sweeping panorama of the entire city and harbor.

FOOD FESTIVALS OF THE SOUTH

FESTA DELLA PASTA DI GRAGNANO IGP *GRAGNANO (CAMPANIA).* *Maccheroni* festival in the town where the pasta industry began, early September.

GRAN GALÀ DEL PESCE SPADA *BAGNARA CALABRA (CALABRIA).* The swordfish fleet celebrates the catch during mating season (early July), with swordfish *involtini* (rolled and baked fillets) served.

MAGGIO DI ACCETTURA *ACCETTURA (BASILICATA).* Male and female trees are coupled to guarantee a fruitful harvest. Food and folk dancing at this gathering held around Pentecost.

SAGRA DELLE ORECCHIETTE *CARANNA (PUGLIA).* Skilled hands make *orecchiette* in the piazza of this picturesque village nestled among the ancient *trulli,* mid-August.

SAGRA DELLA RICOTTA E DEL FORMAGGIO *VIZZINI (SICILY).* A celebration of all manner of ricotta products, including fresh ricotta and cannoli, late April.

LA SARTIGLIA DI ORISTANO *ORISTANO (SARDINIA).* Prior to Ash Wednesday, a procession of masked riders in traditional costume precedes one of the last ring jousts of Europe. Carnival sweets are the specialty.

Masked rider at Oristano's Sartiglia

Grains and wheat have been the staple of the south since antiquity, in pasta and in loaves. Italian pasta is rooted in the southern regions, whether as *pasta secca* (also called *maccheroni*), dried, packaged pasta made from hard wheat and water, or fresh pasta made at home. The farther south in Italy you go, and the poorer it gets, the fewer eggs find their way into dough. By the time you get to Sicily, there is no egg in the pasta dough at all. Pizza, or flatbread, has been made throughout Italy, but it reaches its zenith of chewy yumminess in Naples. The decorated loaves of Sardinia and Sicily are magnificent examples of folk art.

Primary vegetables are the tomato, introduced from the new world by the Spanish, and the eggplant, from the east. Also prominent are foraged and bitter greens, including the chicories, arugula, and *cime di rapa* (broccoli rabe in American markets). The deep waters of the Tyrrhenian and Ionian Seas yield tuna and swordfish (although stocks have diminished), anchovies and sardines, cuttlefish, octopuses, and bivalves of all sorts. Meat is used sparingly in the south, but when it is—and this is true of all Italy— every part of the animal is eaten. The hill country, however, has lamb and goat, poultry and rabbit, and the perennial provider—the pig—preserved in many ways. While lard is often used in baking, the primary fat in the cuisine of the south is olive oil. Cheese also plays an important part in the diet, especially pecorino, a sheep's-milk cheese, and

Northerners commonly refer to southern Italy as the Mezzogiorno ("twelve o'clock"), in reference to the intense midday sun.

> *A popular digestivo of the south is limoncello, and consequently, it is commonly made at home by Italian Americans.*

caprino from goat's milk. Ricotta, a product of whey, is typically made from sheep's milk. Thick and tangy, it is used in both sweet and savory dishes. Cow's milk makes the superlative *fior di latte* (which Americans tend to call mozzarella). True mozzarella is made from water buffalo milk, the exceptional *mozzarella di bufala*.

Abiding Traditions

Despite this wealth of food in southern Italy, poverty has been persistent. Even after the foundation of the Italian nation, the south was neglected, leading to mass emigrations, one from 1861 to the 1920s, and another from World War II until the 1970s. Between both migrations, about 13 million Italians left the country. These are the people who founded Little Italys all over the United States. Italian-American cuisine thus stems primarily from southern Italian cuisine, though it has long transformed into something very different.

Northern Italians sometimes call the southerners lazy, because they are poor and because life moves slower where it is really hot (and southern Italians disparagingly call the northerners Germans). Indeed, its poverty, conservatism, and clannishness have helped preserve the traditions of the south. At the same time, in southern Italy the good life is not defined by how much money you have, but how you choose to spend what you've got. And nowhere in Italy is the noisy hot stew of Mediterranean life so evident. As the southerners would say, now *that's* Italian.

Above: Backyard harvest in Campania. Opposite: The extraordinary vineyards of Sicily sit below breathtaking mountain ranges.

A 4,000-YEAR-OLD WINEMAKING TRADITION

....

1. Campania: Whites are acidic and delicate, including the Greco di Tufo, made from ancient vines such as Greek Greco. Reds can be herbaceous or fruity and tannic, such as Aglianico del Taburno.

2. Puglia: Most white wine grapes go to vermouth blenders. Verdeca grapes from Locorotondo make a fine tart white that is especially good. Rosé wines go well with the local food, while low-acid and boozy Primitivo is hip with consumers.

3. Basilicata: This modest region produces Aglianico del Vulture, one of the great red wines of southern Italy. The white Moscato and Malvasia grapes, widely grown, are transformed into sparkling and sweet wines.

4. Calabria: The region is well suited to red wines, mainly from the Gaglioppo grape such as the Ciro Classico, awarded to winners of the ancient Olympics.

5. Sicily: Locals drink seafood-friendly whites from grapes such as the flinty Grillo and the mineral Carricante, best from the Mount Etna DOC. The reds include Nerello, the fresh, spicy Frappato used in Cerasuolo di Vittoria, and the versatile Nero d'Avola. Among the sweet wines is the fortified Marsala, key to making zabaglione and tiramisu.

6. Sardinia: The best Sardinian grapes are of Spanish origin, including the herby white Vermentino, the flavorful red Cannonau, and the inky Carignano, which makes the delicious Carignano del Sulcis. Moscato di Sardegna is a sparkling sweet wine similar to Asti.

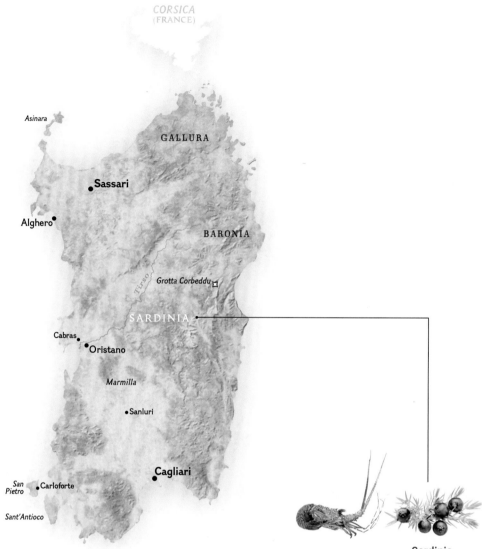

CORSICA
(FRANCE)

Asinara

GALLURA

●**Sassari**

Alghero●

BARONIA

Tirso

Grotta Corbeddu ⌂

SARDINIA

Cabras ●
●**Oristano**

Marmilla

●*Sanluri*

●**Cagliari**

San Pietro
● Carloforte

Sant'Antioco

Campania

Olive oil DOP, wheat, Pasta di Gragnano DOP (*maccheroni*),
Pizza Napoletana STG, San Marzano tomato DOP, buffalo
mozzarella DOP, ricotta DOP, seafood, lemons, anchovies,
hazelnuts, Paestum artichoke IGP, cilantro, fig DOP,
Piennolo tomato DOP, Nocera green onion DOP, chestnuts,
mozzarella STG, rabbit

TYRRHENIAN SEA

Ustica ◦

Sardinia

Lamb IGP, pecorino, breads, *carta da musica*
(bread), suckling pig, *malloreddus, fregula,
curligiones* (stuffed pasta), spiny artichokes
DOP, saffron, myrtle, juniper, jams, honey,
torrone, confections, *bottarga*, seafood, spiny
lobster, wild fennel, tomatoes, tuna, game

M E D I T E R R A N E A N   S E A

Palermo ●
Conca d'Oro

*Egadi
Islands*
Marettimo ◦
Favignana ◦
Marsala ●
Cape Lilibeo

**Mazara
del Vallo** ●

Agrigento —

Geography and Products of Southern Italy and the Islands

Hot weather nurtures the peninsula's premier citrus industry while its ample coastline is
home to some of Italy's most important fisheries. Once the breadbasket of the Roman
Empire, the south is still Italy's most prolific wheat-growing area. The olive and its oil,
the grape, the eggplant, and the tomato reign here.

Strait of Sicily

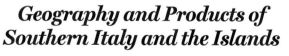

Pantelleria

30 mi
_____
30 km

ADRIATIC SEA

MOLISE

LAZIO

Gargano
Promontory

Foggia

Ofanto

Andria • Bisceglie
• Molfetta
ALTA   • Bitonto
MURGIA   Bari
NATIONAL
PARK

APULIA
(PUGLIA)

• Caranna
• Locorotondo

Puglia

Olive oil DOP, olives DOP, wheat, almonds,
lamb, *burrata* cheese IGP, fava beans, chickpeas, Margherita white onion IGP, red grapes
and white grapes IGP, Altamura bread DOP,
mussels and oysters, *Canestrato* Pugliese DOP

Vesuvius
4,203 ft
1,281 m

CAMPANIA

Naples

Gulf of
Naples

Ischia

Sorrento
Capri   Positano   Amalfi

Sarno
Valley
• Gragnano
Salerno

Potenza

Basento

Accettura

Metaponto

SALENTO

Taranto   • Lecce

Cilento
Coast

Pioppi

BASILICATA

APPENNINI

Gulf of
Taranto

Serra Dolcedorme
7,438 ft
2,267 m

Sybaris

Basilicata

Olive oil, Lucanica sausage, pork, *capocollo,*
Pecorino Filano DOP, goat cheese, Senise
pepper IGP, Matera bread IGP, honey,
manteca, Sarconi beans IGP, Potenza red
eggplant, cauliflower, figs

CALABRIA

Sila

Crotone

Calabria

Olive oil DOP, bergamot DOP, citron, hot peppers, chiles,
eggplant, Caciocavallo Silano cheese DOP, *'ndujia,* figs
DOP, Calabria *capocollo* DOP, tuna and swordfish,
anchovies and sardines, Tropea red onion IGP, red garlic,
butirro cheese, Calabria *soppressata,* licorice IGP

Stromboli
+ Stromboli
3,031 ft
924 m

*Lipari Islands
(Aeolian)*

Filicudi   Salina

Alicudi   Lipari

Vulcano

Lamezia
Terme

Pizzo

Vibo Valentia

Cape Peloro

• Bagnara Calabra
Scilla

IONIAN SEA

Messina

Reggio di Calabria

Nebrodi

Strait of Messina

Etna
10,925 ft
3,330 m

SICILY

Catania

Sicily

Ribera orange DOP, blood orange DOP, Ispica carrots DOP,
Etna cherries DOP, Pantelleria capers, prickly pears, Siracusa
lemons, Messina lemons, Belice olives, Dittaino bread,
Biavone peaches, Bronte pistachios DOP, Pachino tomatoes
IGP, Trapani salt, table grapes, tuna and swordfish, anchovies
and sardines, eggplants, fennel, cannoli

Vizzini

Syracuse

Modica

Cape Passero

SOUTHERN ITALY AND THE ISLANDS • **265**

Campania

Classical Roots, Vesuvio Soil, and Southern Soul

....

IN CAMPANIA THE PEOPLE ARE FRIENDLIER, the sea is bluer, the music is livelier, the tomatoes are redder, and the lemons are yellower than anywhere else in Italy. Here, also, it is noisier, more embracing, and arguably poorer. Every traveler who ventures into this sun-drenched, color-soaked region—sizzling Naples and its enchanted isles, the surrounding countryside with its Greek temples and feral fig and lemon trees—is struck by this exhilarating, unrestrained *napoletanità*, the singular Neopolitan way of living.

Capital of a kingdom that ruled half of Italy for six centuries, Naples today is a bedazzling fusion of baroque magnificence merged with the grit of everyday life. Towering over this scene is smoldering Vesuvius, Vesuvio to the locals, brooding and baleful. Its volcanic fields—the most dangerous in the world—simmer on the other side of the bay, twinkling coquettishly.

The volcano, a mere five miles from the city of Naples (Italy's third largest in population after Rome and Milan), has both tormented and blessed it for millennia. Best known for burying Pompeii and Herculaneum in molten lava and ash in A.D. 79, Vesuvius is still an active volcano, with its last eruption in 1944. Still, the locals cling to their towns and villages, where grapes and tomatoes drape the slopes. Vesuvius's ash, mingled with decomposed seaweed, has made Campania one of Italy's most fertile black-dirt agricultural areas, producing four crop yields every year. A crescent of land straddling Lazio and Calabria along the Tyrrhenian Sea, it shares its inland

An iconic view of the Amalfi Coast from Villa Rufolo, Ravello

The Bay of Naples at night with ever smoldering Vesuvius in the near distance

borders with Molise, Puglia, and Basilicata, regions just as ancient but infinitely more silent.

Provincial Quiddities

In Naples's eponymous province, where over half of the population lives, every scrap of land, every small garden plot, even every balcony is planted. The lava-rich valley is the epicenter of Campania's most emblematic crops—wheat and tomatoes. These are of course the makings of dried pasta, *maccheroni* in Neapolitan lingo, the pillar of the diet, and for the sauce that most frequently anoints it. Caserta, land of the water buffalo and site of a palace built for Bourbon kings that rivaled Versailles, is one vast orchard. Landlocked and rugged Avellino and Benevento provinces are a patchwork of vineyards, olive trees, and famously, hazelnut orchards. The province of Salerno is home to the world's best-known tomato, San Marzano. Salerno has a broad bay of its own, with a soaring peninsula fabled for pastel villages carved into the sheer cliffs. Their names—Amalfi, Positano, and Sorrento—are requisite tourist

Drinking a cappuccino after meals is considered gauche, based on the belief that foamed milk after a meal is bad for proper digestion.

stops along the serpentine Amalfi Coast. Here the steep terraced hills interspersed with orchards are known as much for their thick-skinned lemons and olive oil as for their beauty.

A Classical Greek Pedigree

When they first laid eyes on this region, the ancient Romans dubbed it Campania Felix, "the fortunate country." But they were relative newcomers. The restless Greeks, ever venturing from their cramped, mountainous terrain in search of hospitable land for growing crops, set down roots here first. At a time when Rome was a muddy campsite on the Tiber, the likes of Archimedes and Aeschylus were wandering the Campania coast along with Homer's traveling heroes.

Little besides the joy of living remains of the civilization that took root in Naples and lasted 300 years. The Romans even invented a word for it: *pergraecari,* to act like a Greek, meaning an immoderate enjoyment of food, wine, and fornication. Greek notions about the benefits of a plant-based diet also prevail.

During the centuries following the collapse of Rome, the matter at hand for most was not how to cook, but whether there was anything to eat at all. A feudal system caused near starvation, particularly after a tax was levied on *vruccoli* (turnip tops), a mainstay of the masses. The Greek glow returned during the prosperous Renaissance, if only for the aristocracy. In Naples, the nobles entertained themselves by arranging for mountains of vegetables and livestock to be collected in the public square and set

The Temple of Apollo, the oldest and most important classical temple in Pompeii

Espresso is the child of the industrial revolution, when Italians figured out how to blast ("express") water through ground coffee using steam to extract a syrupy essence.

on fire for the sole purpose of watching flames engulf the starving rabble as they scrambled for free food.

Over six centuries, the French and Spanish-Bourbon courts colonized the south under an increasing expansion, indulging in exotic ingredients of the day. Tomatoes, chiles, potatoes, corn, squashes, beans, and chocolate from the New World as well as coffee and rice from Turkey were adopted. All this eventually transformed how Italy and its gastronomic colonies eat. The legacy of their cooks, *monzù* (a corruption of *monsieur*), endures in such dishes as eggplant *alla parmigiana* and potato *gattò* (from *gâteau*).

If the new gastronomy was the stuff of the upper crust, in the end the traditional cooking was based on the habits of the country people who worked the fields and stirred the royal pots. Today the *cucina napoletana* is an amalgam of Greek and Etruscan traits and baroque sensibilities infused with the common sense and lively spirit of the peasant. Americans know a smattering of dishes that are Neapolitan in origin, *marinara* or *fra diavolo*, for example, created in the imaginations of Campania's emigrants. But this hybrid fare has little in common with the mother cuisine from which they were disinherited.

Gino Sorbillo makes genuine Neapolitan pizza in his celebrated pizzeria in Naples.

Dark and syrupy, espresso is one of the glories of Naples, gulped in one or two swallows from a tiny cup throughout the day. The secret: grinding the beans to a near powder, tamping it down, and blasting boiling local water through it at the highest pressure possible without exploding the machine. In the best bars beans are roasted on-site in small batches. Here is a guide to the options: *espresso:* straight and dense (a lemon twist is heresy!); *ristretto:* very concentrated; *lungo:* an espresso with more water; *macchiato:* espresso "stained" with a dribble of foamed hot milk; *caffè corretto:* ristretto with liqueur, grappa, or cognac; *cappuccino:* espresso with foamed hot milk; *caffè latte:* half hot milk, half espresso.

An afternoon espresso with a side of biscotti

Pasta and Bread: The Stuff of Life

This is wheat country. Bread as well as maccheroni depends on the flavorful high-protein *Triticum durum* that grows near Gragnano, where the dried pasta industry is based. Most common is *pane cafone,* a sourdough loaf virtually identical to a peasant bread described by Hesiod in the first century B.C. And there is the sublime *pizza napoletana,* which has traveled the world, even if the traditional recipe is now codified (STG) under EU protocols to warrant that name. Other members of the doughy tribe include focaccias as well as calzone, pizza folded over a filling.

It was around the Bay of Naples where the climate and wide berth for shipments of Russian wheat to supplement native crops combined to make the region the national maccheroni mecca during the industrial revolution. By the late 1800s 1,500 manufacturers competed for business, ever inventing new shapes to lure customers to their brand. Today there are some 350 variants, including "Vesuvios." Yet every now and then, a pasta maker comes up with another one.

The union of pasta and *pomodoro* took place in Naples around the time of Vincenzo Corrado's experiments with that foreign fruit in 1773. By the next century *pasta al pomodoro* had taken to the streets. Everywhere in the city peddlers sold cooked vermicelli for only two *centesimi* to the half-million *lazzaroni,* homeless, who ate it with their fingers. There was no sauce, only ripe tomatoes simmering lazily in a separate pot—and a tower of grated pecorino near at hand for those who could pay an additional *centesimo.* The masses, once scorned as *mangiafoglie,* leaf eaters, were now dubbed *mangiamaccheroni,* macaroni eaters. The tomato that became an essential accompaniment was eventually transformed into a fast, splendid, and simple topping.

The island of Procida, in the Bay of Naples, hosted settlements as far back as 1600 B.C.

Land of Milky Miracles and Inimitable Flavors

Campania is obsessed with cheese, *cacio,* in all forms. Key table cheeses are bovine *scamorza, caciocavallo*, and provolone; also sheep's-milk pecorinos, and goat cheeses that might be flavored with anise. The most emblematic of these are *latticini,* moist, fresh cheeses that have not ripened or significantly aged. Probably the most irresistible of these is *mozzarella di bufala,* from the milk of the semiaquatic black buffalo that wallow in the wetlands between Caserta and Salerno. By Italian law this milky miracle, sparkling with tang and charm, is the only dairy product that can be termed mozzarella. (The cheesemakers say that it is best eaten the day it is made, ideally within two hours.) Cow's-milk "cheese" made the same way is labeled *fior di latte*—this is what Americans mistakenly call mozzarella. Other latticini include sheep or buffalo ricotta, and its hardened, salted form, *ricotta salata*.

With about half its territory lapped by the sea, the omega-rich *pesce azzurro* of these waters—largely sardines, smelt, and anchovies—are staples. Because the more prized species have become scarce, much of the region's stock is farmed, as elsewhere in Italy. Squid, cuttlefish, crabs, octopuses, and shellfish are abundant. Mussels are put to use in a plethora of dishes. In *impepata di cozze,* the mussels are steamed and once open, treated to good olive oil, chopped parsley, and the squeeze of a lemon. Anchovies have been used for their remarkable natural seasoning properties since ancient times, when salt was a precious commodity. Cetara specializes in both preserving them and making *colatura di alici,* a condiment arrived at by pressing cleaned and salted anchovies to render a potent liquid of sheer umami. Mixed with olive oil and crushed garlic, it gives zest with little effort to sautéed greens, cooked vegetables, or a heap of freshly cooked linguine.

If Life Gives You Lemons, Make *Limoncello*

Limitations on cultivatable space have fostered a reverence for ingredients, but Vesuvius is without a doubt the hot wind in every proverbial sail. For breakfast, there are *sfogliatelle*—coquettish pastries of ruffled *mille foglie* (literally, "a thousand pastry layers"), filled with sweetened ricotta and candied fruit bits. The beloved maccheroni is eaten for lunch, dinner, and even a midnight snack known as *spaghettata di mezzanotte*. Even the bounteous street food is a poem to *bella Napoli:* Think *frittura*, deliciously fried anything, from *arancini* (rice balls) to batter-dipped zucchini flowers stuffed with oozy cheese. On Sundays, there are half-meter-long *ziti,* "bridegrooms" (a phallic symbol, of course), with a sumptuous tomatoey ragù saturated with the juices of tender *bracciole,* cutlets of veal stuffed with garlic, parsley, and cheese. The sweets are legendary, from rum-soaked *babà* to sugary *zeppole.* All is followed by sweet, liquorous *limoncello,* the very symbol of Campania's answer when life presents you lemons.

Limoncello

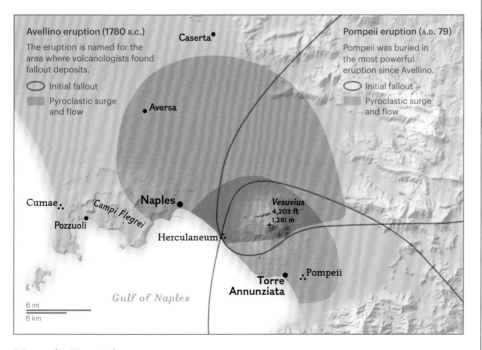

Avellino eruption (1780 B.C.)
The eruption is named for the area where volcanologists found fallout deposits.

◯ Initial fallout
▨ Pyroclastic surge and flow

Pompeii eruption (A.D. 79)
Pompeii was buried in the most powerful eruption since Avellino.

◯ Initial fallout
▨ Pyroclastic surge and flow

Caserta
Aversa
Cumae
Campi Flegrei
Pozzuoli
Naples
Herculaneum
Vesuvius
4,203 ft
1,281 m
Torre Annunziata
Pompeii
Gulf of Naples

6 mi
6 km

Vesuvio Eruptions Erupting many times before and after it buried Pompeii in A.D. 79, Vesuvius has created some of the most bountiful soils in the world.

Fried Mixed Seafood

Fritto misto di mare • *Serves 6*

WHY THIS RECIPE WORKS: *Fritto misto di mare* can be found throughout Italy; however, the most iconic and evocative incarnation hails from Campania. Indeed, it's easy to imagine sitting in a Neapolitan trattoria eating crisp, piping hot tidbits of fried seafood while looking out on the Bay of Naples. Red mullet, squid or cuttlefish, and shrimp are some common choices you might find in classic versions. The seafood is lightly dusted with flour before frying, and it must be eaten right from the pot to be crispy. In a home kitchen, we knew we would need to fry our seafood in batches to prevent the oil temperature from dropping excessively. Adding cornstarch to the mix kept our first batch crispy while we fried the second. (Unlike flour, cornstarch is a pure starch whose molecules lock into place during the frying process to form a dry, brittle coating.) For the fish, easy-to-find, mild-tasting sole or flounder fillets were thin enough to cook through in the time it took the coating to adequately brown. The shrimp are fried and eaten shell and all, as the shell fries up crisp. We found that by cutting through the shells, we could achieve even more delicate results because moisture could quickly escape. To ensure that the shells fry up crisp, avoid using shrimp that are overly large or jumbo. We prefer 31- to 40-count shrimp here, but 26- to 30-count may be substituted. Use a Dutch oven that holds 6 quarts or more. Trim any squid tentacles longer than 3 inches.

12 ounces shell-on medium-large shrimp (31 to 40 per pound)
3 quarts vegetable oil
½ cup all-purpose flour
¼ cup cornstarch
Salt
12 ounces squid, bodies sliced crosswise into ½-inch-thick rings, tentacles left whole

12 ounces skinless sole or flounder fillets, ¼ to ½ inch thick, halved lengthwise, and cut on bias into 1-inch strips
Lemon wedges

❶ Adjust oven rack to middle position and heat oven to 225 degrees. Using kitchen shears or sharp paring knife, cut through shell of shrimp and devein but do not remove shell. Pat shrimp dry with paper towels. Set wire rack in rimmed baking sheet and line with triple layer of paper towels. Add oil to large Dutch oven until it measures about 2 inches deep and heat over medium-high heat to 400 degrees. Whisk flour and cornstarch in large bowl until combined; set aside.

❷ Carefully add shrimp to oil and cook, stirring occasionally, until lightly browned, about 3 minutes. Adjust burner as necessary to maintain oil temperature between 350 and 375 degrees. Using skimmer or slotted spoon, transfer shrimp to prepared rack. Season with salt and transfer to oven.

❸ Return oil to 400 degrees. Pat squid dry with paper towels. Dredge squid in cornstarch mixture, shaking off excess, and carefully add to oil. Cook, stirring as needed to prevent sticking, until squid are crisp and pale golden brown, about 2 minutes. Transfer to rack with shrimp. Season with salt and transfer to oven.

❹ Return oil to 400 degrees. Pat sole dry with paper towels. Dredge sole in cornstarch mixture, shaking off excess, and carefully add to oil. Cook, stirring as needed to prevent sticking, until sole is crisp and pale golden brown, about 3 minutes. Transfer to rack with shrimp and squid. Season with salt and let drain briefly. Serve immediately with lemon wedges.

Spaghetti With Clams

Spaghetti alle vongole · *Serves 6 to 8*

WHY THIS RECIPE WORKS: Ask a Neapolitan, and she might claim that pasta was invented in Campania. While this isn't true—pasta wasn't eaten widely in the region until the 17th century—pasta, and spaghetti specifically, is undoubtedly treasured in Naples. Industrial pasta production began in Naples, and *maccaronari* ("maccheroni-sellers") used to line the streets of the city. One of the most beloved dishes is *spaghetti alle vongole*, which consists of spaghetti lightly tossed with garlic and oil and topped with tiny clams whose liquor contributes a pleasant brininess to the sauce. While spaghetti alle vongole is served in just about every restaurant or trattoria in town, it's also a key dish in the very special Christmas Eve dinner eaten in Naples, *cena della vigilia di Natale*. It can be found served with tomatoes *(e pomodorini)* or without *(in bianco)*. We added just two minced plum tomatoes—barely enough to color the sauce—for sweetness and bright acidity as well as a bit of texture. As for the clams themselves, we needed to find a substitute for the tiny, sweet *vongole veraci* ("true clams"). Large stateside clams like cherrystones and quahogs lacked the distinctive flavor and were tough. Littlenecks (the smaller the better) worked well; they had a fresh brininess and their meat cooked up

tender. Cockles, if you can find them, are also a great choice—the baby clams are almost as small as those you can find in Italy. To ensure the small clams didn't overcook, we steamed them first, stopping when they gave up their juice; we used the juice to build a flavorful sauce and then recombined the clams with the sauce at the last minute, which allowed just enough time for the clams to finish cooking. A half cup of white wine contributed a bright but not overpowering acidity to the sauce and two cloves of garlic, cooked in oil until golden, gave the dish a subtle bite.

4 pounds littleneck clams or
    cockles, scrubbed
½ cup dry white wine
Pinch cayenne pepper
¼ cup extra-virgin olive oil
2 garlic cloves, minced
2 plum tomatoes, peeled, seeded,
    and chopped fine
1 pound spaghetti
Salt and pepper
¾ cup chopped fresh parsley

❶ Bring clams, wine, and cayenne to boil in 12-inch straight-sided sauté pan, cover, and cook, shaking pan occasionally, for 5 minutes. Stir clams thoroughly, cover, and continue to cook until they just

begin to open, 2 to 5 minutes longer. Using slotted spoon, transfer partially opened clams to large bowl. Discard any unopened clams.

❷ Strain clam steaming liquid through fine-mesh strainer lined with coffee filter, avoiding any gritty sediment that has settled on bottom of pan. Set aside 1 cup liquid. (Add water as needed to equal 1 cup.) Wipe out pan with paper towels.

❸ Heat oil and garlic in now-empty pan over medium heat. Cook, stirring often, until garlic turns golden but not brown, about 3 minutes. Stir in tomatoes, increase heat to medium-high, and cook until tomatoes soften, about 2 minutes. Stir in clams, cover, and cook until all clams are completely opened, about 2 minutes.

❹ Meanwhile, bring 4 quarts water to boil in large pot. Add pasta and 1 tablespoon salt and cook, stirring often, until al dente. Drain pasta and return it to pot. Add clam sauce and reserved steaming liquid to pasta and cook over medium heat, tossing to combine, until flavors meld, about 30 seconds. Stir in parsley and season with salt and pepper to taste. Serve immediately.

Fish Poached in Crazy Water

Pesce all'acqua pazza · *Serves 4*

WHY THIS RECIPE WORKS: *Pesce all'acqua pazza,* or "fish in crazy water," is certainly one of the more evocatively named Italian dishes. While romantic, with many proposed stories behind it, the title does little to define the dish. What we do know: *Acqua pazza* refers to the tradition in southern Italy of fishermen cooking a fresh catch in seawater; while the flavorings vary depending on what's on hand, it always includes tomato and oil. Modern recipes have a longer ingredient list—herbs, wine, and garlic are common, and they frequently feature more than one type of fish. We decided to stick with just one kind of fish and chose large red snapper fillets, which held up nicely during simmering and didn't fall apart. Canned diced tomatoes provided bits of texture and bright flavor throughout this dish. We also liked the addition of white wine, which contributed depth to the cooking liquid. Simmering herb sprigs in the broth provided an aromatic backnote. After just a 10-minute simmer, the snapper absorbed the heady flavor of the broth and the broth was enriched by the fish. With garlicky crostini to soak up the broth, dinner is served.

- 1 (6-inch) piece rustic Italian bread, cut into 8 slices
- 3 garlic cloves, peeled (1 whole, 2 sliced thin)
- 6 tablespoons extra-virgin olive oil, plus extra for drizzling
- Salt and pepper
- 1 small red onion, halved and sliced thin
- ¼ teaspoon red pepper flakes
- 2 cups water
- 1 cup dry white wine
- 1 (14.5-ounce) can diced tomatoes, drained
- 2 sprigs fresh oregano
- 1 tablespoon minced fresh parsley, stems reserved
- 4 (4- to 6-ounce) skin-on red snapper fillets, ¾ to 1 inch thick
- Lemon wedges

1 Adjust oven rack to middle position and heat oven to 400 degrees. Arrange bread slices in single layer on rimmed baking sheet and bake until dry and crisp, 8 to 10 minutes, flipping slices halfway through baking. While bread is still hot, rub with garlic clove, drizzle with ¼ cup oil, and season with salt and pepper to taste; set aside for serving.

2 Cook remaining 2 tablespoons oil and sliced garlic in 12-inch skillet over low heat, stirring occasionally, until garlic is pale golden brown, 9 to 12 minutes. Add onion, pepper flakes, and ½ teaspoon salt and cook over medium heat until onion is softened and lightly browned, 5 to 7 minutes.

3 Stir in water, wine, tomatoes, oregano sprigs, and parsley stems. Bring to simmer and cook until flavors meld, about 10 minutes. Season snapper with salt and pepper. Nestle snapper skin side down into broth and spoon some onions and tomatoes on top. Reduce heat to low, cover, and simmer gently until snapper flakes apart when gently prodded with paring knife and registers 140 degrees, about 10 minutes.

4 Discard oregano sprigs and parsley stems. Place one crostini in each individual shallow serving bowl and set snapper fillets on top. Stir parsley into broth and season with salt and pepper to taste. Ladle broth over snapper and drizzle with extra oil. Serve immediately with lemon wedges and remaining crostini.

Eggplant Parmesan

Parmigiana di melanzane • *Serves 8*

WHY THIS RECIPE WORKS: Unlike its Italian American descendant, *parmigiana di melanzane* is a refined, delicate affair: Thin, silky—and unbreaded—eggplant slices are layered with *mozzarella di bufala* and tomato sauce, and topped with Parmigiano Reggiano. In Naples, where eggplant is plentiful all year, they have a saying: *A parmigiana e' mulignane ca se fa a' Napule è semp'a meglio!*, or "The eggplant parmigiana made in Naples is always the best!" Recipes often call for salting the eggplant before frying it in copious amounts of olive oil, making this dish a time-consuming project. We tested numerous methods of salting, frying, and roasting the eggplant and found that we could get creamy, tender eggplant slices simply by roasting them. The dry heat drove off unwanted moisture, making salting unnecessary, and with just a thin brush of olive oil the slices maintained a creamy, delicate interior and a golden, roasted exterior. Be careful when opening the oven in step 3 as the eggplant will release steam. Fresh mozzarella is key to the success of this recipe; do not substitute low-moisture mozzarella. If using fresh mozzarella packed in water, press the slices between layers of paper towels to remove excess moisture before using. If you can't find Italian eggplants, substitute 4 pounds of small globe eggplants.

TOMATO SAUCE

- 1 (28-ounce) can crushed tomatoes
- 1 tablespoon extra-virgin olive oil
- 2 garlic cloves, minced
- ⅛ teaspoon red pepper flakes
- Salt and pepper
- 2 tablespoons chopped fresh basil

EGGPLANT

- ½ cup extra-virgin olive oil
- 8 Italian eggplants (6 to 9 ounces each), sliced lengthwise into ¼-inch-thick planks
- Salt and pepper
- 8 ounces fresh mozzarella, sliced thin
- 7 tablespoons grated Parmigiano Reggiano
- 10 fresh basil leaves, torn into 1-inch pieces

❶ For the tomato sauce: Pulse tomatoes in food processor until smooth, about 10 pulses, scraping down sides of bowl as needed. Cook oil and garlic in large saucepan over medium heat, stirring occasionally, until fragrant, about 2 minutes. Stir in pepper flakes and cook until fragrant, about 30 seconds. Stir in tomatoes and ¼ teaspoon salt, bring to simmer, and cook until thickened slightly, about 10 minutes. Off heat, stir in basil.

❷ For the eggplant: Adjust oven racks to upper-middle and lower-middle positions and heat oven to 450 degrees. Line 2 rimmed baking sheets with aluminum foil and brush each sheet with 1 tablespoon oil. Arrange half of eggplant in single layer on prepared sheets. Brush tops of eggplant planks with 2 tablespoons oil and sprinkle with ½ teaspoon salt.

❸ Roast eggplant until tender and lightly browned, 15 to 20 minutes, switching and rotating sheets halfway through baking. Let eggplant cool slightly on sheets, then transfer, still on foil, to wire racks to cool completely. Line now-empty sheets with additional foil and brush each sheet with 1 tablespoon oil. Repeat brushing, seasoning, and roasting remaining eggplant; transfer to wire racks.

❹ Reduce oven temperature to 375 degrees. Spread ½ cup tomato sauce in bottom of 13 by 9-inch baking dish. Layer one-quarter of eggplant over sauce, overlapping planks as needed to fit. Spread ¼ cup sauce over eggplant, then top with one-third of mozzarella and 1 tablespoon Parmigiano. Repeat layering of eggplant, tomato sauce, mozzarella, and Parmigiano two more times.

❺ Layer remaining eggplant in dish, spread remaining tomato sauce over top, and sprinkle with remaining ¼ cup Parmigiano. Bake until bubbling around edges, about 25 minutes. Let cool for 10 minutes before sprinkling with basil and serving.

Spaghetti With Tomato Sauce

Spaghetti al pomodoro · *Serves 6 to 8*

WHY THIS RECIPE WORKS: The tomato is the most widely used piece of produce in Italian cuisine, and its influence is preponderant in Campania. Not only is Naples home to the celebrated San Marzano tomato, which thrives on the soil at the base of Mount Vesuvius, but the entire industry of tomato canning grew out of the region in the late 19th and early 20th century. And so the nickname *mangiamaccheroni* (macaroni eaters) befits the Neapolitans for their propensity to consume vast quantities of pasta in tomato sauce. Pomodoro sauce should use the best of the sweetest tomatoes available, adorned sparingly.

It is cooked only briefly to ensure that the sweetness and freshness of the tomatoes is preserved. Since climate and seasonality preclude fresh tomatoes' consistency throughout the year, we developed our recipe with canned whole peeled tomatoes (picked at the peak of ripeness) and pulsed them in the food processor to achieve a sauce that coated our noodles well but still had texture. A single clove of garlic was sufficient to add depth of flavor while letting the tomatoes shine. A Neapolitan might balk at adding sugar to tomato sauce, but we found that just a pinch balanced the acidity of the canned tomatoes. We stirred in the requisite fresh basil just at the end of cooking to preserve its aroma. Undercooking the spaghetti in boiling water and allowing it to finish in the sauce infused the pasta with tomato flavor.

> 1 (28-ounce) can whole peeled tomatoes
> 3 tablespoons extra-virgin olive oil, plus extra for serving
> 1 garlic clove, minced
> Salt and pepper
> 2 tablespoons chopped fresh basil, plus extra for serving
> Sugar
> 1 pound spaghetti
> Grated Parmigiano Reggiano cheese

1 Pulse tomatoes and their juice in food processor until mostly smooth, 10 to 12 pulses.

2 Cook oil and garlic in large saucepan over medium heat, stirring occasionally, until fragrant, about 2 minutes. Stir in tomatoes and ½ teaspoon salt, bring to simmer, and cook until thickened slightly, about 10 minutes. Off heat, stir in basil. Season with salt, pepper, and sugar to taste.

3 Meanwhile, bring 4 quarts water to boil in large pot. Add pasta and 1 tablespoon salt and cook, stirring often, until almost al dente. Reserve ½ cup cooking water, then drain pasta and return it to pot. Add sauce and toss to combine. Cook over medium heat, tossing frequently, until pasta is al dente, 1 to 2 minutes. Adjust consistency with reserved cooking water as needed. Sprinkle individual portions with extra basil and drizzle with extra oil. Serve, passing Parmigiano separately.

Lemon Sorbet

Sorbetto al limone · *Makes about 1 quart*

....

WHY THIS RECIPE WORKS: Walk into a *gelateria* in Italy and alongside the gelato you'll also find *sorbetto*; despite being made from just fruit, sugar, and water, it's invariably silky and creamy with a melt-in-the-mouth quality similar to that of gelato. Sorbetto is particularly prolific in Naples. In the late 1600s, steward of the cardinal and culinary writer Antonio Latini—who is credited with creating the first recipe for what we think of as sorbetto today—wrote, "In Naples, it seems everyone is born with the instinctive gift of making sorbetti." Although considered a dessert, sorbetto is also sometimes served during the meal to aid in palate cleansing between courses. In Campania, refreshing lemon sorbet is particularly popular, as the fruit thrives along the Amalfi coast. Making sorbetto is easy if you have an ice cream machine, but many homemade ices are just that: icy. To compensate, some recipes add gelatin (this made the sorbet gummy), whipped egg whites (this created smaller ice crystals but didn't make the sorbet creamy), jam (this was just another way to add more sugar), or corn syrup (this masked fruit flavor). Fortunately, the key to smooth sorbet is actually quite simple: The more sugar you add, the lower the freezing point of the sorbetto. A concentrated sugar syrup won't freeze at the temperature of a home freezer so the sorbetto stays soft and scoopable; the syrup lubricates the ice crystals, making them feel less coarse. Just 1 tablespoon of flavorless vodka also lowered the freezing point of the sorbet, making it easier to scoop. The tartness of lemon zest and plenty of lemon juice balanced the added sugar for the perfect frozen treat.

1¼ cups (8¾ ounces) sugar
2 teaspoons grated lemon zest plus
   ½ cup juice (3 lemons)
Pinch salt
1½ cups water
1 tablespoon vodka (optional)

❶ Pulse sugar, lemon zest, and salt in food processor until combined, about 15 pulses. With processor running, add water, vodka (if using), and lemon juice and process until sugar is completely dissolved, about 1 minute, scraping down sides of bowl as needed. Strain mixture through fine-mesh strainer into large bowl; discard solids. Refrigerate lemon mixture until completely chilled, about 1 hour.

❷ Transfer chilled lemon mixture to ice cream machine and churn until mixture has consistency of thick milkshake, 15 to 30 minutes.

❸ Transfer sorbet to airtight container, pressing firmly to remove any air pockets, and freeze until firm, at least 2 hours. Serve. (Sorbet can be frozen for up to 5 days.)

Puglia

Deep in Greek Italy, With Muslim Flavors

IF PUGLIA, THE HIGH HEEL OF ITALY'S GEOGRAPHICAL BOOT, has lagged behind other parts of the country in terms of modernization, portions of the region have become havens for royals, film stars, and cognoscenti. How could it be otherwise for a peninsula surrounded by 500 miles of dazzling coastline and lapped by the pristine waters of two seas? But its heart beats to an ancient tempo, heedless of the increasing tourist invasions. This is Greek Italy, steeped in the past, as evidenced at the Puglian table.

An Exotic Air, a Punishing Past

Taranto was a powerful and prosperous city, a brilliant jewel in the crown of Magna Graecia. With its wide port and easy access to the motherland, and to Asia, and Egypt, it eventually became the epicenter of their empire. Greece remained the foundational civilization in Puglia for six centuries, until Rome took control in 272 B.C.

"*Ubi panis, ibi patris*—Where there is bread, there is homeland" was the Romans' motto. Wheat, olive oil, and wine were produced in quantity on latifundia, estates worked by slaves, to feed the growing empire. After Rome's collapse in A.D. 476, Ostrogoths and Lombards briefly held the region until the Byzantines took control, reviving the Greek connection for some 500 years. (Saracens and Turks made brutal if brief incursions throughout its history.) The Normans and others that laid waste to the rest of the south followed, subjecting different cities to their rule throughout its history. The latifundia system crept back in the second half of the 19th century on the heels of a

Trulli, the conical houses of Alberobello, were designed to evade taxation.

speculative property boom fueled by unification. Under the new government, the vast northern plateau previously sealed off by the Bourbons was opened up to foreign land speculators, fueling a land scramble that transformed Foggia and Bari into stretches of vast, single-crop plantations run by local managers. So brutal was the 19th-century latifundium, and so fierce the localized insurrections, that by the turn of the century, Puglia became known as "the land of chronic massacres." The wailing folk songs still sung today describe the grueling labor of the farmworkers under the whips of their overseers, as did the spirituals that arose from the American South during slavery. It was from this system that the flight of poor Puglians to America and Argentina began in the last decades of the 19th century.

The hinterlands still retain the feeling of a wild outpost, with many towns and scattered centers separated by vast expanses of land. Today Puglia possesses a solemn, almost otherworldly beauty, strewn with strange, near-windowless *trulli,* centuries-old beehive houses sprouting out of the reddish earth. The region's inwardness took shape in the squat, fortresslike *masserie,* farmsteads that functioned as miniature walled villages. And in the small, sunbaked towns there is often little activity except for a half-starved cat or two sleeping on the street. But pass a stretch of houses, all stone and shutters, and suddenly a heavy door opens to reveal an inner courtyard lush with jasmine and orange trees.

Terroir and Tradition

Puglia is divided into six provinces, but what culinary distinctions exist coincide with the shape given to it in 1222 by Frederick II. As Holy Roman emperor, he carved it up into three distinct political units—northerly Foggia, central Bari, and the Salento peninsula. "It is not really an exaggeration," chef Marcel Boulestin once wrote, "to say that peace and happiness begin, geographically, where garlic is used in cooking." Indeed, the garlic-eaters of Foggia and Bari are considered not only the best cooks on Italy's heel but also inordinately generous people—once you get under their skin. Salento, instead, prefers the charms of onion, proof that garlic is not in every southern Italian's blood type.

This is Italy's granary, growing some 360 types of wheat, but mostly the *Triticum durum* that supplies *semola* (semolina) for the dried pasta industry. *Maccheroni,* in all its myriad shapes, is a pillar of Puglia's diet, as evidenced by a local saying, "Jesus, make it rain *maccarrún* and fill the porticos of [our] balconies with meat sauce." There is an appetite for fresh, handmade pasta, too, working the same sturdy semola used for maccheroni: sunny in color and gritty in texture, and yielding tender, elastic dough in the right hands. Among the *anziani,* or ancients, as elders are called in Italy, those who still remember how, turn out *mignuicchie* (small gnocchi) and numerous other hand-formed wonders. But empress of them all are *orecchiette,* meaning "little ears."

A farmer sells his melons door to door in the town of Montesano Salentino, on Italy's heel.

Bread is likewise important here, with an astounding 90-plus traditional variations made from the region's wheat. The sourdough loaf of Alta Murgia, baked in the oak-fired ovens of the tablelands, has protected status under the auspices of both DOP and Slow Food. *Friselle*, once the mainstay of the peasant, are hardtack purposed to seemingly last forever. Dampened with water and vinegar, crumbled and tossed with tomato, olive oil, and oregano, they form *cialedda*, a divine bread salad. Ring-shaped *taralli*, flavored with fennel or hot pepper or redolent with olive oil alone, are a ubiquitous snack—Puglia's answer to pretzels, but better. Pasta and breads alike are made from various grains, including *grano arso* (literally, "burnt wheat"), *saragolla* (a dark heritage variety), and barley.

Puglia has a fetish for *amaro,* bitter. "Like *maror* at a Passover Seder [it] reminds us about bondage and oppression amidst freedom and affluence," observed Anthony Di Renzo in his book *Bitter Greens.* He was speaking of the south's obsession, *cime di rapa,* turnip tops, here called *rapa.* There is also a passion for *cicoria,* dandelions, once fodder for the dispossessed up and down the Mezzogiorno. Onion-like *lampascioni,* the bitter bulb of a wild hyacinth, are relished, whether pickled or braised. But perhaps nothing evokes Puglia more than *'ncapriata,* fava puree (akin to the Levant's hummus)

Genuine extra-virgin olive oil is a fruit juice loaded with polyphenols and nutrients. Ersatz oils labeled "pure" or "lite" possess neither its powerful anti-oxidants nor its culinary benefits.

Some say the Due Sorelle rock formations mark where two sisters threw themselves into the sea off the Salento peninsula.

and cooked greens served up together. Laced with the region's piercing olive oil, the combination is tantalizingly bracing.

Olive oil is the lifeblood of this region, one that has been cultivating olive trees for more than 5,000 years. Until modern times, much of the product was inedible, destined for lamp oil that lit the streets, homes, and churches of Europe. With the discovery of electricity, Puglia's olive lands went bust. Most of the trees—hundreds, even thousands of years old—were clear-cut to make room for cash crops. However, new olive forests were planted in the 1900s, and today the region is the largest olive oil producer in Italy. With America's increasing acceptance of the unadulterated taste of genuine olive oil, a wider audience now appreciates the bold, herbaceous oils of Bitonto, Molfetta, Andria, and the Salento that are ideal for Puglia's zesty dishes.

Pastoral and Piscatorial Pleasures

The plateaus on the Gargano promontory offer hospitable grazing lands for sheep, leading to Puglia's position in third place after Sardinia and Lazio for lamb- and ewe's-milk cheeses, including Foggia's Canestrato Pugliese. For the initiated are Bari's biting *provolone piccante* or Foggia's *ricotta forte* (strong ricotta), the latter a fermented, spreadable spinoff of its gentle namesake and a doppelgänger of the Greek *kopanisti*. If you can master them, you might consider yourself an honorary Puglian. Other distinctive cheeses and *latticini* have finally gained international celebrity, notably *burrata*, that delectable mozzarella skin wrapped around an oozy filling of curds and thick cream.

Olive trees as old as 3,000 years still grow along the old Roman road from Puglia to Brindisi, where olive oil was shipped to foreign ports.

The long tongue of the Salento peninsula drinks in two seas and a bounty of sea creatures. Fishermen on the Adriatic still use artisan methods, working from ancient timber platforms with nets suspended over the water in the fashion of Abruzzo's *trabocchi,* here called *trabucchi.* The Ionian side has a tradition of oyster and mussel farming that goes back to the Greeks, who harvested them along the peninsula's coast or grew them on wooden rafts set afloat in the sea. The "great sea" and the "little sea," as the waters off the port of Taranto are called, are fed by underground springs, accounting for the biggest mussel harvest in Italy.

Serve It Forth

Unlike in other regions where tourist routes are more deeply rutted, traditions here persist. On the table are *pittule,* little doughy fritters flavored with anchovy, capers, salt cod, or vegetables, eaten hot. *Ciceri e tria,* a mixture of tender and crisp-fried semolina ribbons with chickpeas, is one of countless takes on the union of pasta and beans, Puglia's soul food. A Sunday supper classic is *bombette,* roasted stuffed veal or pork rolls. *Sughi,* called ragù elsewhere, are mahogany-colored with lamb and redolent with wine and rosemary.

It is probably true that people who have been served bitter wine crave sweets. For the Puglian sweet tooth are such treats as a sweet version of taralli painted with a cool glaze of icing sugar. Lecce's cream-filled *pasticciotto* is as succulent as the baroque city itself. In Bisceglie, the *sospiri* (meaning "sighs") come in the form of soft, breast-shaped cookies covered with a pale sugar glaze that might make you do just that—sigh.

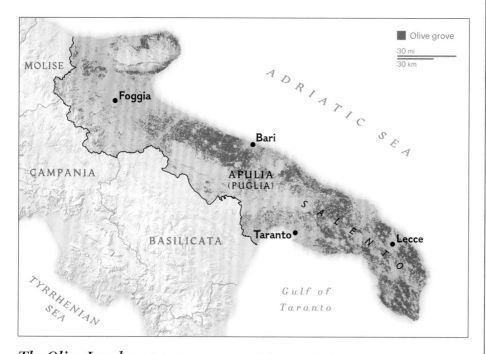

The Olive Lands Puglia's olive groves stretch from northerly Foggia south into the Salento, supplying more than half of Italy's olive oil.

LOCAL FLAVOR
OLIVE OIL SCANDALS

Crime has always been associated with olive oil, a substance so prized in the Mediterranean that its trade has invariably had a dark side. Since ancient times, merchants have been known to cut extra-virgin with cheap oil to increase profits, and swindlers have passed off worthless imitations to the unwary. Whereas once farmers feared bandits waiting in ambush when transporting the precious oil to market, today a different kind of criminal waits on the olive oil trail. These are principally the counterfeiters who have infiltrated much of the industrial olive oil business—a problem that has vexed Puglia's vast olive oil lands especially. While the DOP label guarantees genuine products, plenty of excellent oils are not in the system. Buy from reputable retailers whose buyers are experts; they taste and personally select the oils they sell.

Broccoli Rabe With Garlic and Pepper Flakes

Cime di rapa con aglio e peperoncino · *Serves 4*

WHY THIS RECIPE WORKS: What Americans call broccoli rabe is known by many names in Italy: *cime di rapa* (meaning turnip tops, as it's more closely related to turnips than to regular broccoli), *broccoli di rapa*, *broccoletti di rapa, rape,* or *rapini*. It's a mainstay of Italian cuisine, especially in Puglia where it grows abundantly. It has a bracing, mustardy bite that gives it delicious character—as long as its bitterness is subdued slightly and its leaves and stalks are cooked evenly. Our goal was to find a way to achieve perfectly cooked broccoli rabe every time. As it turns out, broccoli rabe releases its bitter-tasting enzymes when it's cut—a defense mechanism against attack (in this case by a knife). The leaves and florets release more of these enzymes than the stems, so we left them whole, which allowed the flavor to remain relatively mellow. The typical Italian approach to cooking this vegetable is to blanch, shock, drain, and then sauté the broccoli rabe with strong-flavored aromatics. While this technique can subdue pungency, it is a lengthy, multi-pot affair. We found a faster way with an untraditional method: broiling. Five minutes under the broiler turned out lightly charred, crisp leaves and florets and perfectly crisp-tender stalks that remained a verdant green. Plus, the broiler's high heat deactivated the enzyme in the rabe that causes the bitterness. Olive oil, a generous amount of salt, and fiery pepper flakes were all the greens needed, save for a final squeeze of bright lemon. Because the amount of heat generated by a broiler varies from oven to oven, we recommend keeping an eye on the broccoli rabe as it cooks. If the leaves are getting too dark or not browning in the time specified in the recipe, adjust the distance of the oven rack from the broiler element.

3 tablespoons extra-virgin olive oil
1 pound broccoli rabe
1 garlic clove, minced
¾ teaspoon kosher salt
¼ teaspoon red pepper flakes
Lemon wedges

1 Adjust oven rack 4 inches from broiler element and heat broiler. Brush rimmed baking sheet with 1 tablespoon oil.

2 Trim and discard bottom 1 inch of broccoli rabe stems. Cut tops (leaves and florets) from stems, then cut stems into 1-inch pieces (keep tops whole). Transfer broccoli rabe to prepared sheet.

3 Combine remaining 2 tablespoons oil, garlic, salt, and pepper flakes in small bowl. Pour oil mixture over broccoli rabe and toss to combine.

4 Broil until half of leaves are well browned, 2 to 2½ minutes. Using tongs, toss to expose unbrowned leaves. Return sheet to oven and continue to broil until most leaves are lightly charred and stems are crisp-tender, 2 to 2½ minutes. Transfer to serving dish and serve.

Tomato and Burrata Salad With Pangrattato and Basil

Insalata di pomodoro e burrata con pangrattato e basilico · *Serves 4 to 6*

WHY THIS RECIPE WORKS: Puglia has plenty of specialties but the most luxurious might be its *burrata*, the deluxe version of fresh mozzarella in which the supple cheese is bound around a filling of cream and soft, stringy curds. It's quite the delicacy—rich and buttery and made from the flavorful milk of local Podolica cattle, whose diet is rich in fragrant herbs and grasses. Burrata is enjoyed simply, whether on its own, paired with bread and cured meats, or simply drizzled with olive oil. Often it's paired with tomatoes, so we decided to make a flavorful tomato salad featuring this pride of Puglia. We wanted to maximize the flavor of the tomatoes so that the rich, milky cheese wouldn't overwhelm them; to do this we used a combination of standard tomatoes and sweet cherry tomatoes, salted them, and let them sit for 30 minutes to help draw out their watery juices. Blending the olive oil with a little shallot and sweet-tart white balsamic vinegar gave us a simple but flavorful vinaigrette. Finally, we found that a topping of *pangrattato* helped bring the dish together: These garlicky bread crumbs soaked up both the tomato juice and the burrata cream. The success of this dish depends on using ripe, in-season tomatoes and fresh, high-quality burrata.

1½ pounds ripe tomatoes, cored and cut into 1-inch pieces

8 ounces ripe cherry tomatoes, halved

Salt and pepper

3 ounces rustic Italian bread, cut into 1-inch pieces (1 cup)

6 tablespoons extra-virgin olive oil

1 garlic clove, minced

1 shallot, halved and sliced thin

1½ tablespoons white balsamic vinegar

½ cup chopped fresh basil

8 ounces burrata cheese, room temperature

❶ Toss tomatoes with ¼ teaspoon salt and let drain in colander for 30 minutes. Pulse bread in food processor to large crumbs measuring between ⅛ and ¼ inch, about 10 pulses. Combine crumbs, 2 tablespoons oil, pinch salt, and pinch pepper in 12-inch nonstick skillet. Cook over medium heat, stirring often, until crumbs are crisp and golden, about 10 minutes. Push crumbs to sides of skillet. Add garlic to center and cook, mashing it into skillet, until fragrant, about 30 seconds. Stir garlic into crumbs. Transfer to plate and let cool slightly.

❷ Whisk shallot, vinegar, and ¼ teaspoon salt together in large bowl. Whisking constantly, slowly drizzle in remaining ¼ cup oil. Add tomatoes and basil and gently toss to combine. Season with salt and pepper to taste and arrange on serving dish. Cut burrata into 1-inch pieces, collecting creamy liquid. Distribute burrata over tomatoes and drizzle with creamy liquid. Sprinkle with bread crumbs and serve immediately.

Steamed Mussels With Spicy Tomato Sauce

Cozze alla tarantina · *Serves 4 to 6*

WHY THIS RECIPE WORKS: The town of Taranto sits in the crook of Italy's boot, between the heel and sole. Founded as a Spartan colony and nestled between a freshwater lagoon and the gulf of Taranto, its unique geography has endowed it with a long history of excellent mussel and oyster farming. The strong tides of the Mediterranean supply ample food for crustaceans, while the freshwater Mar Picolo regulates both the temperature and salinity of the beds, making for a particularly delicious mussel. The mussels are considered so fine that they need little adornment, other than perhaps a touch of garlic, tomatoes, chiles, and white wine. Traditionally they're steamed in a large pot. But cooking an ample amount can be challenging because the mussels crowd one another and stirring them to facilitate even cooking can be difficult: The mussels closest to the heat source cook faster than the ones on top. We found that oven-steaming in a wide roasting pan prevented overcrowding, and the gentle, enveloping heat promoted even cooking. The flavorful cooking liquor becomes perfect for sopping up with toast or bread. Discard any raw mussels with an unpleasant odor or with a cracked or broken shell or a shell that won't close. Serve with crusty bread.

1 tablespoon extra-virgin olive oil
1 tablespoon tomato paste
3 garlic cloves, minced
¾ teaspoon red pepper flakes
1 cup dry white wine
1 (28-ounce) can crushed tomatoes
¼ teaspoon salt
4 pounds mussels, scrubbed and debearded
2 tablespoons minced fresh parsley

1 Adjust oven rack to lowest position and heat oven to 500 degrees. Heat oil, tomato paste, garlic, and pepper flakes in large roasting pan over medium heat. Cook, stirring constantly, until fragrant and tomato paste has darkened slightly, about 2 minutes. Stir in wine, bring to boil, and cook until slightly reduced, about 1 minute. Stir in tomatoes and salt, increase heat to high, and cook, stirring frequently, until thickened slightly, about 5 minutes.

2 Stir in mussels. Cover pan tightly with aluminum foil and transfer to oven. Cook until most mussels have opened (a few may remain closed), 15 to 18 minutes.

3 Remove pan from oven. Discard any mussels that haven't opened. Sprinkle parsley over mussels and toss to combine. Serve.

Orecchiette With Broccoli Rabe and Sausage

Orecchiette con cime di rapa e salsiccia · *Serves 6 to 8*

WHY THIS RECIPE WORKS: *Orecchiette con le cime di rapa* is a hearty, subtly spicy pasta dish that might be the most signature (and identifiable) dish of Italy's heel. This isn't surprising considering that some dub Puglia "the garden of Italy" for its fertile soil and pleasantly warm climate, which facilitate the growth of vegetables and the wheat used to make the favorite pasta shape of Pugliesi: orecchiette, or "little ears." Like most pasta shapes in Puglia, its name is sweet— telling of the region's affinity for pasta. Orecchiette has a bowl shape that's great for catching a variety of sauces as well as chunky ingredients like the broccoli rabe in this dish. Its shape is particularly well-suited to hand forming from the wheat-and-water-only dough of southern Italy —it's simply pinched off and formed by thumb, so it doesn't require the suppleness of an egg-based dough. Sausage is a common hearty addition, and the pork's richness mingles well with the bitterness of the greens. We prefer the flavor and texture of fresh pasta here, but dried can be used as well. For more information on making your own fresh pasta, see page 366.

- **2 tablespoons extra-virgin olive oil**
- **8 ounces hot or sweet Italian sausage, casings removed**
- **6 garlic cloves, minced**
- **¼ teaspoon red pepper flakes**
- **1 pound broccoli rabe, trimmed and cut into 1½-inch pieces**
- **Salt and pepper**
- **1 pound fresh or dried orecchiette**
- **2 ounces Pecorino Romano, grated (1 cup)**

❶ Heat oil in 12-inch nonstick skillet over medium-high heat until just smoking. Add sausage and cook, breaking up meat into rough ½-inch pieces with wooden spoon, until lightly browned, about 5 minutes. Stir in garlic and pepper flakes and cook until fragrant, about 30 seconds; set aside.

❷ Meanwhile, bring 4 quarts water to boil in large pot. Add broccoli rabe and 1 tablespoon salt and cook, stirring often, until crisp-tender, about 2 minutes. Using slotted spoon, transfer broccoli rabe to skillet with sausage mixture.

❸ Return water to boil, add pasta, and cook, stirring often, until al dente. Reserve 1 cup cooking water, then drain pasta and return it to pot. Add sausage–broccoli rabe mixture, Pecorino, and ⅓ cup reserved cooking water and toss to combine. Adjust consistency with remaining ⅔ cup reserved cooking water as needed. Season with salt and pepper to taste. Serve.

Fava Bean Puree With Sautéed Escarole

Fave e scarola • *Serves 4*

WHY THIS RECIPE WORKS: In wintertime and early spring in Puglia, locals combine their winter stores of dried fava beans with peppery wild chicory into a satisfying, hearty dish. Dried fava beans are typically cooked until they can be mashed into a smooth puree and then topped with sautéed chicory dressed simply with olive oil and salt. Wild chicory isn't commonplace in American markets, but we still embraced the dish's humble roots by using more readily available escarole, which is a member of the chicory family: It's easy to find, quick cooking, and offers a similar pleasant bitterness. To amp up flavor and add brightness to the dish, we added chili flakes and lemon zest to the greens, which balanced out the bitter notes. With the greens settled, we turned our attention to creating a smooth, silky puree from the fava beans. Potato is a traditional addition to this dish, as it lends a smooth, unctuous texture; we found that adding just one potato to the pot with the beans was enough to achieve the consistency we were after. Rather than mash the cooked fava beans and potato with a potato masher, we passed them through a food mill or potato ricer to ensure a silky smooth texture. Finally, we finished the dish with shaved Pecorino for a salty bite that enhanced the complex, earthy flavors of the fava beans.

2½ cups chicken or vegetable broth
2½ cups water, plus extra as needed
8 ounces (1½ cups) dried split fava beans
1 Yukon Gold potato, peeled and cut into 1-inch pieces
3 tablespoons extra-virgin olive oil, plus extra for drizzling
Salt and pepper
3 garlic cloves, minced
¼ teaspoon red pepper flakes
1 head escarole (1 pound), trimmed and cut into 1-inch pieces
1 tablespoon grated lemon zest
1 ounce Pecorino Romano cheese, shaved

1 Bring broth, water, and beans to boil in large saucepan. Reduce to simmer and cook until beans are softened and beginning to break down, about 15 minutes. Stir in potato, return to simmer, and cook until potato is tender and almost all liquid is absorbed, 25 to 30 minutes. Pass bean-potato mixture through food mill or ricer into bowl. Stir in 2 tablespoons oil and season with salt and pepper to taste. Adjust consistency with extra hot water as needed. (Mixture should be consistency of thin mashed potatoes.) Cover to keep warm.

2 Meanwhile, heat remaining 1 tablespoon oil in 12-inch skillet over medium heat until shimmering. Add garlic, pepper flakes, and ¼ teaspoon salt and cook until fragrant, about 30 seconds. Stir in escarole, cover, and cook until wilted, 3 to 5 minutes. Stir in lemon zest and season with salt and pepper to taste.

3 Spread fava bean mixture into even layer on serving dish and arrange escarole on top. Top with Pecorino and drizzle with extra oil. Serve.

Basilicata

From a History of Hunger, a Joy of Eating

BASILICATA, WITHIN THE INSTEP of Italy's boot, has never quite shed its ancient Latin name, Lucania, derived from the Lucani peoples who lived here during the Iron Age. Although nearly bordered on three sides by Puglia, Campania, and Calabria, regions that share Basilicata's history of neglect, its greatest isolating factor has been geography. Basilicata is the most mountainous of Italy's regions, surrounded by some of the steepest heights and highest peaks in Italy that once served to protect the interior from invasions.

Its coast takes in two seas, but a mere 24 miles of narrow shorefront on the Ionian coast—and half that on the Tyrrhenian side—didn't offer much wide-open space for would-be colonists to settle. The first to cultivate its wild hinterlands were Oscan-Samnites who migrated from the Abruzzo Apennines. Versed in hardscrabble skills, they cultivated the valleys and climbed the hills to work the rugged vertical landscape, bringing with them a predilection for pork and hot pepper, the two themes of Lucanian cooking today.

A Wrinkle in Time

Around 700 B.C. the Greeks established a colony on the coastal plains near what is today Metaponto, along the Ionian Sea. The Tavole Palatine (Palatine Tables), a formation of misaligned Doric columns, is all that remains of Magna Graecia Lucana. But these ghostly shafts in the midst of the region's desolation still ignite the imagination. Some locals tell their children the columns are legs of a giant's table where gods, emperors, and magicians

Sunset on the Sassi di Matera, where the poor inhabited caves into the 20th century

The name caciocavallo, meaning "cheese riding a horse," comes from how the spherical cheeses are tied in pairs and slung over a support for air-curing.

once feasted—a fantasy conjured by a hungry people.

The provinces are two. Matera, on the Ionian side, achieved notoriety with the publication of Carlo Levi's 1945 memoir as a political prisoner, *Christ Stopped at Eboli*. This is where the *sassi* are found, primitive cave dwellings in the hollows of limestone canyons, occupied from Paleolithic times well into the 1950s, when the Italian government, shamed by Levi's revelations, finally relocated the 20,000 inhabitants. The second province, Potenza, is on the Tyrrhenian Sea. Its eponymous mountaintop capital is all but vertical, one of the highest (and coolest) of all Italian cities.

Persimmons

Products Precious and Pungent

Neither 2,000 years of malicious raiding nor earthquakes and landslides nor the deep hunger of the populace have been able to erase the timeless, immutable beauty of these mountains. Here the sun-scorched earth is ocher, colored with wild oleander, cactus, persimmon, and fig. The upper reaches are lush with pristine pine forests, but much of the region is barren and steep.

Three agricultural zones correspond to three different altitudes. Vines, olives, fruits, and vegetables grow in the lowlands. Livestock pasture in the Val d'Agri, Basilicata's wild green Apennine heart. On the slopes are scattered many-storied villages, where precipitous terraces are farmed in a system of upright stratification. Mountain farmers raise their own sheep, goats, and Podolica cows, make their own sausages and *salumi*,

Making traditional Pane di Matera IGP

bake their own bread, and make cheese by hand—pecorino, Caciocavallo Podolico, ricotta, and mozzarella. "Today this craftsmanship is rare, even in Italy," said Lou Di Palo, whose grandfather was one of those Lucanian farmers before emigrating to New York City and establishing its most famous cheese shop, Di Palo Fine Foods in Manhattan's Little Italy.

Most rural homes still raise a pig, or even two. "No other animal furnishes more variety to the tongue," wrote Pliny the Elder. "Its meat provides nearly fifty flavors, other animals, only one." Specialties include fiery *soppressata* (literally "compressed" sausage), fresh and air-cured prosciutto, and *capocollo,* a spicy cousin of Emilia–Romagna's *coppa,* as well as *pezzente,* head cheese.

If the old Italian saying "good with good makes good" applies anywhere, it applies in Basilicata, where the iron-rich dirt has not been depleted by modern agricultural practices. This means the fruits of the soil, however hard-won, taste of this place. It is not a landscape well suited to large-scale grain production. Still, Senatore Cappelli, an esteemed heritage durum wheat variety, has made a comeback here, cultivated in a few of the more hospitable southern districts. It is used for handmade fresh pastas and traditional breadstuffs alike, the two staffs of life. Bread, linked to the history of the poor peasant, takes multitudinous forms. *Pane di Matera* is a huge sourdough loaf with a thick russet-hued crust redolent of the wood-fired oven. It cocoons an airy, honeycombed interior that stays soft for days after it bakes. A tradition shared with neighboring Puglia is that of *panella,* leavened bread made from gritty *semola* flour and potato dough formed into a disk the size of a cartwheel. Fresh pasta, shaped from dough using the same flour, has been around since Hellenic times. These include *orecchiette, strascinati* ("dragged" pasta not unlike *cavatelli), lagane,* and *ferretti,* elongated tubelike shapes formed around a knitting needle–like rod. Flours from farro, barley, chickpeas, and beans, starchy staples since before the advent of wheat, are still used for handmade pastas.

La Cucina Poverissima

Remote Basilicata is where you are most likely to find the Italy of the old ways, a place where the fare is prepared with pleasure, pure and unaffected by fashion and international trends. Lucanian cooks make the most of humble ingredients, accomplished in no small part with a boost from peppers, both hot and sweet. The large, hooked, "goat-horn" sweet pepper is first sun-dried, then fried in olive oil and salted, resulting in *cruschi,* crisps relished with fried potatoes or used to spike fresh cheeses and other various sundry dishes. Fiery chiles appear in everything, including *pollo alla potentina,* chicken cooked on the stovetop with white wine, herbs, and tomato, traditionally enhanced with shards of pungent, aged pecorino; and *spezzatino di maiale,* a garlicky, sizzling-hot pork stew. Wild foods are on the table as well, whether truffles or mushrooms. Boar—the perennial scourge of the farmer—often ends up in a sausage casing, or in a winey ragù.

Sweets here are pure and simple. Some are surprising, such as *panzerotti alla crema di ceci:* fried dough half-moons, filled with pureed chickpea, sugar, chocolate, and cinnamon, and dusted with powdered sugar when cool. Notable for the taste of the mountains, or the Mediterranean scrub, upon them, a plethora of honeys sweeten anything from a breakfast of tangy sheep's-milk ricotta to ambrosial ricotta pie. Fir, chestnut, eucalyptus, acacia, and lavender are a mere sampling.

Recently, Matera was chosen as the 2019 European Capital of Culture. The region may no longer be the last, lonely southern outpost of Italy's traditions. Come and visit soon.

Fiery Macaroni

Maccheroni di fuoco • *Serves 6 to 8*

WHY THIS RECIPE WORKS: The heart of this simple dish is a potent chile-garlic oil that dresses bucatini pasta both inside and out, allowing the pasta's hollow strands to absorb the delicious oil. Hot dried chiles are beloved across southern Italy but perhaps nowhere more than in Basilicata, the spiritual home of the *diavolicchio* (little red devil) chile. It's the spiciest pepper used in the region; it boasts a Scoville rating in the five figures and has complex, smoky notes that elevate and punctuate the region's cuisine. *Maccheroni di fuoco* employs these little devils like no other dish, turning a few seemingly modest ingredients into a flavor-packed meal. The essential oils in red chiles are oil-soluble, so blooming chili flakes in hot olive oil produced complex flavor. We gently cooked whole cloves of garlic in the oil as well before mincing them. This allowed their flavor to become sweeter and rounder than if we had minced them before cooking, since cutting raw cloves creates the compound allicin that imparts the harsh flavors generally associated with garlic. Allowing the oil to steep while we toasted bread crumbs (for a little crunch) and cooked our pasta bolstered its intensity. The addition of cheese is contentious, but we appreciated the savory notes that some Parmigiano Reggiano provided. Chiles from Basilicata are not widely available but we found Calabrian peperoncini flakes to be an excellent substitute. Calabrian peperoncini flakes are available at most Italian markets; however, if you can't find them, 1½ teaspoons of ground dried arbol chiles are the next best substitute. This dish is intended to be fiery hot but can be made milder by using the lesser amount of peperoncini flakes.

½ cup plus 1 tablespoon
extra-virgin olive oil
4 garlic cloves, peeled
2 to 4 teaspoons Calabrian
peperoncini flakes
½ cup panko bread crumbs
Salt and pepper
1 pound bucatini
2 tablespoons chopped fresh
parsley
Grated Parmigiano Reggiano
cheese

1 Cook ¼ cup oil and garlic in 8-inch skillet over medium-low heat, turning occasionally, until garlic begins to brown, 5 to 7 minutes. Stir in peperoncini flakes and cook until slightly darkened in color, about 45 seconds. Immediately transfer oil mixture to bowl and let cool for 5 minutes. Transfer garlic to cutting board, mince to paste, then return to oil mixture. Let sit until flavors meld, about 20 minutes.

2 Wipe skillet clean with paper towels. Cook panko, 1 tablespoon oil, and ⅛ teaspoon salt in now-empty skillet over medium heat, stirring often, until lightly toasted, 3 to 5 minutes. Transfer to clean bowl and set aside for serving.

3 Meanwhile, bring 4 quarts water to boil in large pot. Add pasta and 1 tablespoon salt and cook, stirring often, until al dente. Reserve ½ cup cooking water, then drain pasta and return it to pot. Add oil mixture, ¼ cup reserved cooking water, parsley, ½ teaspoon salt, and remaining ¼ cup oil and toss to combine. Adjust consistency with remaining reserved cooking water as needed. Season with salt and pepper to taste. Sprinkle individual portions with bread crumbs and Parmigiano before serving.

Braised Chicken With Tomatoes and Basil

Pollo alla potentina · *Serves 4 to 6*

WHY THIS RECIPE WORKS: Every region of Italy boasts a simple, elemental, comforting braise featuring the flavors of the traditional cuisine—and Basilicata is no exception. Potenza-style chicken is named after the region's capital. This humble dish takes advantage of the area's staples: dried peperoncini (of course), tomatoes, onion, wine, parsley, and plenty of basil. Browned chicken parts are braised in this flavorful mixture, and a thick pan sauce forms that is perfect for spooning over potatoes—a ubiquitous partner to the dish. We started the potatoes in the oven to roast while we cooked our chicken on the stove. Many traditional recipes call for a combination of lard and olive oil to brown the chicken, but we found that we could render plenty of flavorful fat from the chicken skin, so there was no need to add lard. We felt that the nuances of specialty chiles were lost among the other flavors; workaday red pepper flakes were a fine stand-in for the dried peperoncini and provided a similar backnote of heat.

2 pounds Yukon gold potatoes, unpeeled, cut into ¾-inch pieces
¼ cup extra-virgin olive oil
Salt and pepper
4 pounds bone-in chicken pieces (2 split breasts cut in half crosswise, 2 drumsticks, and 2 thighs)
1 onion, halved and sliced thin
¼ teaspoon red pepper flakes
1 cup dry white wine
1 (28-ounce) can whole peeled tomatoes, drained and chopped
½ cup plus 2 tablespoons chopped fresh basil
¼ cup chopped fresh parsley

❶ Adjust oven rack to middle position and heat oven to 425 degrees. Toss potatoes with 3 tablespoons oil in bowl and season with salt and pepper. Arrange potatoes in single layer on rimmed baking sheet and cover tightly with aluminum foil.

❷ Roast potatoes for 20 minutes, then remove foil and continue to roast until sides of potatoes touching sheet are crusty and golden, about 15 minutes. Flip potatoes using metal spatula and continue to roast until crusty and golden on second side, about 8 minutes. Season with salt and pepper to taste.

❸ Meanwhile, pat chicken dry with paper towels and season with salt and pepper. Heat remaining 1 tablespoon oil in 12-inch skillet over medium-high heat until just smoking. Brown half of chicken on all sides, 8 to 10 minutes; transfer to plate. Repeat with remaining chicken; transfer to plate.

❹ Add onion and ½ teaspoon salt to fat left in skillet and cook over medium heat until softened and lightly browned, 6 to 8 minutes. Stir in pepper flakes and cook until fragrant, about 30 seconds. Stir in wine, scraping up any browned bits, and cook until reduced by about half, about 5 minutes. Stir in tomatoes, ½ cup basil, and parsley. Return chicken to skillet along with any accumulated juices and bring to simmer. Reduce heat to medium-low, cover, and cook until breasts register 160 degrees and drumsticks/thighs register 175 degrees, 10 to 12 minutes, rotating chicken halfway through cooking.

❺ Transfer chicken to serving dish, tent with aluminum foil, and let rest while finishing sauce. Return sauce to simmer and cook until thickened slightly, about 3 minutes. Season with salt and pepper to taste. Spoon sauce over chicken, sprinkle with remaining 2 tablespoons basil, and serve with potatoes.

Potato and Tomato Gratin

Patate alla lucana · *Serves 6 to 8*

WHY THIS RECIPE WORKS: Lucania, the area of Italy settled by the Lucani in ancient times, encompassed much of the area that is now Basilicata and, even today, residents will still refer to themselves as Lucani. In keeping with much of the local cuisine, this rustic dish is simple and intended to showcase the humble fruits of the region's rich soil as well as to provide field workers with a hearty, economical, and nutrient-dense lunch. A common incarnation involves baking layered rings of tomatoes, onions, and potatoes until tender along with some oregano for seasoning, a sprinkling of Pecorino for richness, and crumbled stale bread for texture. When we made the dish with field tomatoes, onions, and waxy potatoes (which are typical of the region), we found that the vegetables exuded an unappealing amount of moisture. Switching to plum tomatoes cut down on liquid and slowly sautéing our onions until golden brown not only drove away more water but added a layer of complexity. Using starchy russet potatoes improved matters further, as the cooked starch granules helped soak up the remaining juices. It is important not to slice the potatoes any earlier than the beginning of step 3 or they will begin to brown (do not store them in water; this will make the gratin bland and watery). Slicing the potatoes ⅛ inch thick ensures they cook evenly and relatively quickly, so the tomatoes don't break down too much in that time; use a mandoline, a V-slicer, or a food processor fitted with an ⅛-inch-thick slicing blade.

¼ cup extra-virgin olive oil
2 onions, halved and sliced thin
1 tablespoon minced fresh oregano
Salt and pepper
2 pounds russet potatoes
3 pounds plum tomatoes, cored and sliced ¼ inch thick
3 ounces Pecorino Romano cheese, grated (1½ cups)
¼ cup panko bread crumbs

❶ Heat 2 tablespoons oil in 12-inch skillet over medium heat until shimmering. Add onions, 1 teaspoon oregano, ½ teaspoon salt, and ¼ teaspoon pepper and cook, stirring frequently, until soft and golden brown, 15 to 20 minutes.

❷ Adjust oven rack to upper-middle position and heat oven to 400 degrees. Grease 13 by 9-inch baking dish. Combine remaining 2 teaspoons oregano, ½ teaspoon salt, and ½ teaspoon pepper in bowl.

❸ Peel and slice potatoes ⅛ inch thick. Shingle half of tomatoes evenly in prepared dish, then sprinkle with ½ cup Pecorino. Shingle half of potatoes on top, then sprinkle with half of oregano mixture. Spread onions over potatoes, then shingle remaining potatoes over top, followed by remaining tomatoes. Sprinkle with remaining oregano mixture and drizzle with remaining 2 tablespoons oil.

❹ Bake, uncovered, for 1 hour. Sprinkle with remaining 1 cup Pecorino, then panko, and bake until top is well browned and potatoes are tender (paring knife can be slipped in and out of potatoes with little resistance), about 20 minutes. Let cool for 30 minutes before serving.

Calabria

In the Battered Toe of Italy, Greek Bones and a Penchant for Pepper

ONCE, THERE WAS A SHINING Greek colony on the Calabrian coast called Sybaris. Rich from the fruits of its slaves' labors in the silver mines, fertile plains, and rich forests, it became infamous for its hedonism, inspiring a new word, *sybaritism*. Today Calabria is Italy's poorest region. After decades of the postwar "economic miracle" that promised to bring relief to the south, its GDP is less than a quarter of any given northern region. By the end of the 20th century entire villages emptied out in the exodus to America and other places that offered a better life or, at the least, a full stomach.

Like Basilicata, Calabria finds respite in the joys of food. Raw ingredients, the fruit of so much hard labor in the face of nature's whims, are held in reverence. These are transformed into simple but highly flavored and colorful dishes following traditions that have evolved during its rich if painful history.

A Mountain People

The rugged toe of Italy's boot is poised at the Strait of Messina at Sicily's pointed cape, as though to kick a stone across the sea. The Apennines—beginning at the toe's Aspromonte, or "harsh mountain"—continue their march north, descending into valleys with clustered villages and soaring back into bleached towns spiraling up precariously lofty hilltops. The savage peaks rise to 7,438 feet at the Serra Dolcedorme, "sweet sleeping mountain," leaving little arable land in their path. The two mountains' names are in

Scilla, named after a sea monster of Greek myth, is crowned by the Ruffo Castle.

> *Calabria is one of the only places in the world where bergamots grow, a citrus fruit that tastes like a cross of lime and blood orange.*

curious contrast, an apt metaphor for this region that is alternatingly savage and serene. Earthquakes have razed entire villages, and its hardscrabble land is thirsty. Yet 485 miles of breathtaking shoreline, all fluorescent azure with alternating white beaches and quiet coves, frame its slopes.

The Sila, Calabria's broad mountain plateau, is blanketed with pine forests and dense chestnut woods where forest beds sprout wild mushrooms well into December. Fruit and citrus orchards—citron, lemon, and bergamot—fringe the Tyrrhenian Riviera. Here grow some of the most delicious figs in the world. If they aren't eaten fresh, or dried in the sun and strung in wreaths, they are wrapped in their own sweet leaves and slow-roasted in wood ovens before being stuffed with almonds or candied orange peel and dipped into dark chocolate. Clementine, peach, and olive trees blanket the broad Gulf of Taranto, making a detour around the mournful remains of Sybaris.

Purple and red are Calabria's colors, the first for eggplant and the second for peppers (sweet and hot, but mostly hot). All the south loves *melanzana*, but Calabria adores it. Hot pepper tints and ignites the region's superb *salumi—capocollo, soppressata,* and *'nduja, a* spicy, spreadable sausage peculiar to this region.

The abandoned village of Roghudi in the Aspromonte, one of many that emptied out following emigration or natural disasters

the truth about: LIFE IS BETTER WITH BITTER GREENS

Brassica rapa, variously *cime di rapa, broccoletti di rapa, rapini, rappini, rapi, vrucculi, vruccoli, friarielli,* and a gaggle of other aliases depending on what part of Italy you are in—descends from the wild mustard that has carpeted Italy's boot since primeval times. In America, it is dubbed "broccoli rabe" by the produce industry, a nickname that makes native Italians itch. Despite its vague resemblance to broccoli, *rapa* belongs to the turnip tribe. Rich in fiber, it is loaded with vitamins and compounds that deactivate carcinogens. Its tantalizing bitterness gives you a surprising jab in the mouth that gets your juices flowing, making your taste buds plead for pork sausages, a combination Calabria adores.

Southern Italy's beloved *Brassica rapa* has many names.

Bread has been the antidote to hunger for millennia. Rituals for abundant harvests and fruitful baking hark back to pagan times. The Levant's vapors can be seen in the array of flatbreads and *pitta* (pizza). These might be topped with tomato and chile *(chicculiata),* or folded and baked with a filling of livers or other offal, oregano, tomato, and the requisite chiles (a dish called *murseddu*).

Calabria has a metaphor for lovers: *Cascano come il formaggio sui maccheroni*—"They fall like cheese onto macaroni." Pasta—as well as cheese—holds high status. This is the land of Pecorino Crotonese, small rounds of tangy ewe's-milk cheese with a citrusy zing and lovely crosshatched rind (its pattern formed by the baskets in which it ages). There are also sparkling ricottas from both ewe's and goat's milk. For extended storage, these are salted and aged, resulting in *ricotta salata* and its smoked variant. Others include *provola,* a sharp yet sweet cow's-milk cheese ranging from soft and fresh *(provola dolce)* to firm and piquant (provolone). Aged versions are formidable grating cheeses suitable for the boldest of Calabria's pasta dishes. *Caciocavallo,* common to other southern regions, is similar but milder. *Butirro* resembles it with its characteristic topknot, but its porcelain white skin hides a surprise inside, a generous filling of butter. And *fileja* is shaped to pair with heavy or spicy sauces.

The region's handmade *semola* and water pastas include *lagane,* identical to the broad fresh noodles of classical times with precisely the same name (indeed, the precursor of our lasagna), and even prepared in the same way that Horace described in one of his satires: "Often in the Forum I stop at a fortune teller's, then take myself home to a bowl of leeks, laganum, and lasagna." Even if times are changing at a fast pace elsewhere, homemakers still make *pasta ru ferretto,* sturdy noodles formed by wrapping dough around knitting needles to form long, thin, hollow tubes designed for goat or pork ragù.

EGGPLANT, HOW DO I LOVE THEE?

Let me count the fiery ways . . .

- *Melanzane ripiene:* Stuffed with pork, chile, and mint, or with bread crumbs, pecorino, egg, garlic, chile, and basil
- *Polpette di melanzane:* Spicy eggplant "meatballs"
- *Parmigiana di melanzane:* Eggplant parmigiana, little meatballs tucked between the spicy sauced layers
- *Portafogli di melanzane:* Spicy eggplant sandwiches in a golden crust
- *Melanzane all'agrodolce:* Sweet and sour eggplant with raisins, chocolate, chile, cinnamon, walnuts, pine nuts, all simmered in sugar and vinegar—the most ardent of all.

In a region where every hospitable surface is precious, a whopping quarter of Calabria's arable land is planted with olives, making it the second largest producer of olive oil after Puglia. Numerous labels are distinguished with DOP certification, with Lamezia Terme's regarded by knowledgeable chefs as the best of them all.

A Sea People

Calabria's catch—principally *pesce azzurro,* or oily fish—includes tuna and amberjack (*ricciola),* both prized as game fish and for their culinary attributes. At Scilla and Bagnara Calabra in the province of Reggio Calabria, fishing fleets harpoon for swordfish, much as they have done for ages. Vibo Valentia, on the Tyrrhenian, has an important tuna catch centered on the seaport of Pizzo, resulting in its canned tuna and *bottarga* industries. The old port's restaurants offer up such specialties as spaghetti with the local bottarga and *tonno alla ghiotta*—fresh tuna baked with bread crumbs, tomato, capers, olives, and hot pepper. Just leave enough room for Pizzo's *tartufo,* a layered mound of ice cream filled with molten chocolate around a glacé cherry in the center. (The best ones are artisan-made, not the frozen, commercial versions.)

Potent Flavors in Every Kitchen

Calabria's overall approach to cooking is the same as the rest of Greek Italy—a foundation of ingredients left in as natural a state as possible with flourishes that can be traced to the Byzantines, Aragonese, Muslims, and others in between. The region's food forms a tapestry as much as its ancestry does. You can taste it in Reggio's sweet-and-sour swordfish and in *sarde a scapece,* fried crumb-coated sardines soused in hot vinegar, garlic, and mint.

The pungent greens of the south, whether cultivated or foraged, are close to the Calabrian heart as well, especially *vruccoli,* turnip tops. They are usually cooked *affogato,* "drowned" in olive oil with hot pepper, and maybe served up with hot sausages—with extra-hot pepper applied at the end. Rib-sticking soups, so typical of mountain regions, are a frequent one-pot meal. Among them are *pasta e fagioli* variations joining anything from fava to chickpeas to white beans, with various pastas.

The *pasticcerie* are bedecked with baked goods and confections, but some are still made at home. As elsewhere in Italy, *dolci* are imbued with religious significance, such as *cuddhuraci,* wreaths of sweet dough embedded with hard-boiled eggs, an Easter specialty. *Cedro candito* is the glass-green candied peel of the citron fruit that grows here, used to flavor fillings for any number of pastries. Also popular, *chinulille* are fried ravioli stuffed with chocolate, chestnuts, candied fruit, and nougat. All sweet proof that the great god Pan is not dead in Italy, not even in the harshest hills of its poorest region.

A tuna butcher in Roccella wields a very sharp knife to fillet fish.

Vegetable Stew

Ciambotta · *Serves 6 to 8*

WHY THIS RECIPE WORKS: Eggplant might as well be the official vegetable of Calabria. Unlike populations in northern and central Italy who have viewed the vegetable with great suspicion throughout history (myth had it that the eggplant caused mental disorders), Calabrians have long loved the vegetable that was introduced to Italy by the Arabs. The unique soil in Calabria allows the growth of eggplant that's less bitter and more concentrated in its flavor than other varieties. We particularly love eggplant's role in the traditional dish *ciambotta*. The word refers to "a mess" or a "mix-up," which makes sense: A medley of vegetables—zucchini, tomatoes, peppers, potatoes and, of course, eggplant—is stewed until thick and almost creamy from the broken-down eggplant. To keep the zucchini and peppers from diluting the stew, we used a skillet to cook off their juices before adding them to the pot. To thicken the tomato-enriched sauce, we embraced the eggplant's natural tendency to fall apart, simmering it until completely broken down (microwaving it first banished excess moisture). To deepen the stew's flavor, we browned the eggplant along with the onion and potatoes, and then sautéed tomato paste to develop plenty of flavorful fond before adding the liquid to the pot. Finally, we found that stirring a quick basil and oregano *pestata*—basically a pesto without cheese or nuts—into the vegetables gave the stew a bold, bright herbal flavor. If coffee filters are not available, food-safe, undyed paper towels can be substituted when microwaving the eggplant. Be sure to remove the eggplant from the microwave immediately so that the steam can escape.

PESTATA

⅓ cup chopped fresh basil
⅓ cup fresh oregano leaves
6 garlic cloves, minced
2 tablespoons extra-virgin olive oil
¼ teaspoon red pepper flakes

STEW

12 ounces eggplant, peeled and cut into ½-inch pieces
Salt
¼ cup extra-virgin olive oil
1 large onion, chopped
1 pound russet potatoes, peeled and cut into ½-inch pieces
2 tablespoons tomato paste
2¼ cups water
1 (28-ounce) can whole peeled tomatoes, drained with juice reserved, chopped coarse
2 zucchini, halved lengthwise, seeded, and cut into ½-inch pieces
2 red or yellow bell peppers, stemmed, seeded, and cut into ½-inch pieces
1 cup shredded fresh basil

❶ For the pestata: Process all ingredients in food processor until finely ground, about 1 minute, scraping down sides of bowl as needed; set aside.

❷ For the stew: Toss eggplant with 1½ teaspoons salt in bowl. Line entire surface of plate with double layer of coffee filters and lightly spray with vegetable oil spray. Spread eggplant in even layer on coffee filters. Microwave until eggplant is dry and shriveled to one-third of its original size, 8 to 15 minutes (eggplant should not brown). Transfer eggplant immediately to paper towel–lined plate.

❸ Heat 2 tablespoons oil in Dutch oven over high heat until shimmering. Add eggplant, onion, and potatoes and cook, stirring frequently, until eggplant browns and surface of potatoes becomes translucent, about 2 minutes. Push vegetables to sides of pot. Add 1 tablespoon oil and tomato paste to center and cook, stirring frequently, until brown fond develops on bottom of pot, about 2 minutes. Stir in 2 cups water and tomatoes and juice, scraping up any browned bits, and bring to boil. Reduce heat to medium, cover, and simmer gently until eggplant is completely broken down and potatoes are tender, 20 to 25 minutes; remove from heat.

❹ Meanwhile, heat remaining 1 tablespoon oil in 12-inch skillet over high heat until just smoking. Add zucchini, bell peppers, and ½ teaspoon salt and cook, stirring occasionally, until vegetables are browned and tender, 10 to 12 minutes. Push vegetables to sides of skillet. Add pestata to center and cook until fragrant, about 1 minute. Stir pestata into vegetables; transfer to bowl. Off heat, add remaining ¼ cup water to now-empty skillet, scraping up browned bits.

❺ Stir zucchini mixture and water from skillet into Dutch oven. Cover and let sit for 20 minutes. Stir in basil and season with salt to taste. Serve.

Pasta With Spicy Tomato Sauce

Pasta all'arrabbiata · *Serves 6 to 8*

WHY THIS RECIPE WORKS: Calabrian chiles come in different varieties, but all chiles from the region are prized for their fiery yet balanced, flavorful heat. Known far and wide, *pasta all'arrabbiata* (arrabbiata means "angry" in Italian) is pasta in a spicy tomato sauce. Although this dish is often associated with Roman cuisine, the version made in Calabria makes use of the local fresh chiles instead of common pepper flakes, making the dish uniquely piquant. The simplest versions blend tomatoes, garlic, olive oil, and, of course, chiles, though we found these bare-bones sauces to be one-dimensional and mouth-searing in their heat. We wanted a dish more characteristic of the round, nuanced flavors of fresh Calabrian chiles. First, we focused on ingredients that would enhance savory depth: Stirring ¼ cup of Pecorino into the sauce improved both its body and flavor. Another winning addition was tomato paste, which, like the cheese, is rich in glutamates—a couple of tablespoons gave

the sauce savory, umami notes. Anchovies were a less obvious candidate; while often found in Italian cooking, they are rarely seen in arrabbiata. Still, we welcomed the umami boost of a few minced fillets. For the chiles, we knew we'd be hard-pressed to get our hands on fresh ones from Calabria, so we turned to the next best thing: dried Calabrian peperoncini flakes. And to add more complexity to the dish's spice without making it overwhelmingly hot, we bolstered our pepper flakes with some sweet paprika, which offered pepper flavor without upping the heat quotient. Some jarred pickled peperoncini contributed fresh bite and a vinegary punch that the dish was missing. We were able to remain true to this dish's "angry" roots using easier-to-source ingredients while adding a layer of richness and complexity that offered more to love than just heat. Calabrian peperoncini flakes are available at most Italian markets; however, if you can't find them, substitute red pepper flakes.

1 (28-ounce) can whole peeled tomatoes
¼ cup extra-virgin olive oil
¼ cup stemmed, patted dry, and minced jarred peperoncini
2 tablespoons tomato paste
1 garlic clove, minced
1 teaspoon Calabrian peperoncini flakes
4 anchovy fillets, rinsed, patted dry, and minced to a paste
½ teaspoon paprika
Salt and pepper
¼ cup grated Pecorino Romano cheese, plus extra for serving
1 pound fresh or dried penne

❶ Pulse tomatoes and their juice in food processor until mostly smooth, 10 to 12 pulses.

❷ Cook oil, peperoncini, tomato paste, garlic, pepper flakes, anchovies, paprika, ½ teaspoon salt, and ½ teaspoon pepper in large saucepan over medium-low heat, stirring occasionally, until deep red in color, 7 to 8 minutes. Stir in tomatoes and Pecorino, bring to simmer, and cook, stirring occasionally, until thickened, about 20 minutes. Season with salt and pepper to taste.

❸ Meanwhile, bring 4 quarts water to boil in large pot. Add pasta and 1 tablespoon salt and cook, stirring often, until al dente. Reserve ½ cup cooking water, then drain pasta and return it to pot. Add sauce and toss to combine. Adjust consistency with reserved cooking water as needed. Serve, passing extra Pecorino separately.

Grilled Swordfish With Salmoriglio Sauce

Pesce spada al salmoriglio · *Serves 4*

WHY THIS RECIPE WORKS: The waters surrounding the Calabrian peninsula are a treasure trove of seafood to be enjoyed. Among the riches, fishermen have long had a favorite. The local swordfish are enormous, as long as 12 to 13 feet, and celebrated with an elaborate festival featuring a procession of boats surely carrying fishermen whose greatest joy is harpooning one. A favorite pairing in Calabria is grilled swordfish and a citrusy, herbal sauce called *salmoriglio*, which provides a tangy foil to the smoky, meaty fish. When grilling thick swordfish steaks, we found it was important to leave the fish in place long enough that it developed good grill marks before moving it. A two-level fire was necessary so the fish could sear over the hot fire and then cook through on the cooler part of the grill. Making the sauce was as easy as whisking together garlic, lemon juice, minced oregano, and olive oil. If swordfish isn't available, you can substitute halibut.

SALMORIGLIO SAUCE

¼ cup extra-virgin olive oil
1½ tablespoons minced fresh oregano
1 tablespoon lemon juice
1 garlic clove, minced
⅛ teaspoon salt
⅛ teaspoon pepper

FISH

4 (4- to 6-ounce) skin-on swordfish steaks, 1 to 1½ inches thick
2 tablespoons extra-virgin olive oil
Salt and pepper

❶ For the salmoriglio sauce: Whisk all ingredients in bowl until combined; set aside for serving.

❷ For the fish: Pat swordfish dry with paper towels, rub with oil, and season with salt and pepper.

❸ **A** For a charcoal grill: Open bottom vent completely. Light large chimney starter filled with charcoal briquettes (6 quarts). When top coals are partially covered with ash, pour two-thirds evenly over half of grill, then pour remaining coals over other half of grill. Set cooking grate in place, cover, and open lid vent completely. Heat grill until hot, about 5 minutes.

B For a gas grill: Turn all burners to high, cover, and heat grill until hot, about 15 minutes. Leave primary burner on high and turn other burner(s) to medium-high.

❹ Clean cooking grate, then repeatedly brush grate with well-oiled paper towels until black and glossy, 5 to 10 times. Place swordfish on hotter side of grill and cook, uncovered, until streaked with dark grill marks, 6 to 9 minutes, gently flipping steaks using 2 spatulas halfway through cooking.

❺ Gently move swordfish to cooler side of grill and continue to cook, uncovered, until fish flakes apart when gently prodded with paring knife and registers 140 degrees, 1 to 3 minutes per side. Serve with sauce.

Fileja With 'Nduja Tomato Sauce

Fileja alla 'nduja · *Serves 6 to 8*

WHY THIS RECIPE WORKS: So soft it's spreadable, *'nduja*—a kind of *salumi* that traces to the small town of Spilinga—may be thrifty in its composition but represents an indulgence of the highest order. Named for its resemblance to French andouille, it's often made from a mix of pork shoulder, belly, and fatback as well as various less valuable cuts; liberally spiced to a fiery brick red; and slow-fermented so it takes on a notable tangy funk. What brings 'nduja's heat? Hot Calabrian peppers, of course. Traditionally served at room temperature and spread on slices of bread or served with cheese, 'nduja is also added to tomato sauce; the salami effectively melts into the sauce, making it piquant and super-savory. We paired the sauce with another Calabrian treasure, *fileja,* an eggless pasta named for its screw shape. We wanted the 'nduja's flavor to shine in our pasta, so after trying several amounts we settled on a full 6 ounces, which we stirred into our simple tomato sauce before tossing it with al dente fileja. Garnishes of grated Pecorino and chopped basil provided welcome bright, fresh, and salty counterpoints to the supersavory sauce. You can find 'nduja in most Italian markets. We prefer the flavor and texture of fresh pasta here, but dried can be used as well. For more information on making your own fresh pasta, see page 366.

1 (15-ounce) can whole peeled tomatoes
2 tablespoons extra-virgin olive oil
½ onion, chopped fine
Salt and pepper
1 garlic clove, minced
6 ounces 'njuda sausage, casings removed
1 pound fresh or dried fileja
2 tablespoons chopped fresh basil
Grated Pecorino Romano cheese

1 Pulse tomatoes and their juice in food processor until mostly smooth, 10 to 12 pulses.

2 Heat oil in large saucepan over medium heat until shimmering. Add onion and ½ teaspoon salt and cook until softened and lightly browned, about 4 minutes. Stir in garlic and cook until fragrant, about 30 seconds. Stir in tomatoes, bring to simmer, and cook, stirring occasionally, until thickened slightly, about 10 minutes. Add 'nduja, breaking up meat with wooden spoon, until fully incorporated. Season with salt and pepper to taste.

3 Meanwhile, bring 4 quarts water to boil in large pot. Add pasta and 1 table-spoon salt and cook, stirring often, until al dente. Reserve ½ cup cooking water, then drain pasta and return it to pot. Add sauce and toss to combine. Adjust consistency with reserved cooking water as needed. Sprinkle with basil and serve, passing Pecorino separately.

Sicily

An Island Cuisine That Embodies Mediterranean Foodways

....

THE GREEK TEMPLES of Agrigento march along a bluff above the Mediterranean Sea, magnificent and white against a bright blue sky. Between the Temple of Castor and Pollux and the Temple of Vulcan nestles the ancient garden of Kolymbetra, a place of palms, gnarled olive groves, aromatic myrtle, bay, and rosemary, and of citrus trees so loaded with fruit the branches bend to the grassy floor. No wonder it has been compared to Eden. • It almost seems like Sicily could be paradise. It is a deeply ancient place, farmed

since the dawn of history, and home to sophisticated cities that attracted the likes of Archimedes, Plato, and Aeschylus. But it is also a modern place rife with contradictions: monumental traffic jams might include donkeys, disco-themed restaurants serve peasant foods, and ladies wear modest dress, glittering with sparkling bugles. Sicily is a place where antiquity collides with modernity, the cultures of the East meet those of the West, and the rich must face the poor.

Erupting With Riches

Sicily, the largest region in Italy, is in the center of the Mediterranean Basin. The island is surrounded by three seas—the Tyrrhenian, the Ionian, and the Mediterranean—and separated from the Italian mainland by the narrow Strait of Messina. It is also girded by smaller islands, including the UNESCO-designated volcanic Aeolians. Sicily itself is mostly deforested mountains, with near-constant seismic activity. Mount Etna in

Anna Tasca Lanza Cooking School at Tenuta Regaleali farm and estates

Catania province burps ash and smoke so often waiters keep paper lids on hand to cover their patrons' drinks in the outdoor cafés. This mineral-rich ash is a source of agricultural nutrients that, in the wide plain of Catania, shape the deeply flavorful character of the local wine and food. Sicily's climate is subtropical and Mediterranean, with mild wet winters and hot dry summers intensified by the sirocco winds originating over the Sahara. The mean temperature is such that by the time the winter vegetables have passed, the early spring vegetables are coming in. For northern Europeans, Sicilian peas in their marketplace are a welcome harbinger of warmer days.

On the Sicilian flag is the Trinacria, three bent running legs that recall the triangular shape of the island and represent the three capes: Peloro, Passero, and Lilibeo. In the center stares Medusa's head, a Gorgon symbolizing the island's fertility. For Sicily is indeed agriculturally rich. Very rich. Every edible variety of citrus is grown here, most famously, blood oranges—Sicily is Europe's leading provider—and the island supplies more than 86 percent of Italy's lemons. Other significant agricultural products are olives, olive oil, and grapes. Almonds, which have been grown in Sicily since at least 1000 B.C., make up 90 percent of Italian production. Distinctive cultivars of cherries, tomatoes, capers, prickly pears, peaches, pistachios, sweet onions, carrots, and tiny lentils are grown here as well. And there are also popular crops of purple cauliflower, thorny artichoke, eggplant, peas, fennel, and long *cucuzza* squash, large as baseball bats.

In this mountainous terrain, goat and lamb predominate. The island's black pigs—present since the Greek era but a forbidden food during the island's Muslim domination—are the source of prosciutto, *lardo*, *guanciale*, and *salame*. Sheep's milk makes

Prickly pears in Palermo, a DOP food

The silent hill towns of Sicily, beautiful in their isolation

feather-light ricotta and *ricotta salata,* as well as pecorino cheese, which the Roman naturalist Pliny described as the best in Italy. The coastal areas are dotted with fishing ports (about 25 percent of the national fishing fleet is registered in Sicily), and grain, particularly wheat, is farmed inland. Grain has been a mainstay of Sicilian agriculture for almost 3,000 years and the island was always a surplus producer. It is still Italy's primary exporter of durum wheat.

A Mediterranean Melting Pot

Sicily's strategic location in the center of the Mediterranean world attracted settlement and occupation by different cultures for thousands of years. A modern Sicilian's DNA is likely composed of them all. The first wave of historical inhabitants was made up of the Elymians in the west, the Sicanians in the center, and the Sicels in the east, who gave the island its name. Seafaring Phoenicians from Carthage set up a salt trade on the western coast that is still active today. Greek immigration to the eastern coast began in the eighth century B.C. Their capital, Syracuse, became one of the grandest city-states of the ancient world. Sicily was significant enough to play a role in classical mythology as the center of the cult of Demeter, Greek goddess of grain and mother of spring.

Sicily's five largest open-air markets are the Ballaro, Capo, and Vucciria in Palermo, and the Piazza Carlo Alberto and Pescheria markets in Catania.

A Sicilian named Francesco Procopio dei Coltelli (Procope for short) opened the first ice-cream parlor, in Paris in 1686. It still exists as Procope on the Rue de l'Ancienne Comédie.

Dried pasta cooked until al dente is the norm in Sicily.

Greeks established the foundational foods upon which Sicilian—and Mediterranean—cuisine rests: grapes and winemaking (Mamertino was Julius Caesar's favorite wine and the fortified Marsala is world famous), olives and oil extraction, and grain and refined flour. All three products were imported throughout the ancient world. When the Romans took over Sicily in the third century B.C., they converted the island into the granary of the empire and Sicily has produced grain ever since, although the island's overlords would change, and change again.

After the fall of the Roman Empire, Vandals and Byzantine governors from Constantinople controlled the island, but their cultural impact was minor compared to the Arabs that arrived from North Africa in the ninth century. These settlers brought advances in agriculture, such as terracing and siphon irrigation, and have been credited with introducing apricots, eggplant, spinach, rice, and saffron—used to make the divine *arancine*, fried rice balls stuffed with beef ragù and peas—nutmeg, cloves, pepper, melons, cinnamon, pistachios, citrus, and couscous. They also brought sugarcane, setting the stage for Sicily's love affair with sweets, including *sorbetti* and *granite*, fruit ices made with snow from Mount Etna. With them, too, came a taste for *agrodolce*, sweet and sour flavor combinations, most famously captured in caponata, a tomatoey eggplant stew studded with capers, olives, raisins, and pine nuts, and even the founding of a pasta industry near Palermo, their capital.

But quarrels between the emirs left the island vulnerable, and in the 11th century

Tasting of Franchetti's *vino rosso* at Passopisciaro on the slopes of Mount Etna

The Perfume of Citrus

It hangs over everything: the fragrance of citrus. Lemons, limes, grapefruit, citron, and all sorts of oranges—these are the scents of Sicily.

Prior to the arrival of the Arabs, Sicilians farmed from autumn until spring, when the rains ceased. Arab farmers, however, had experience with dry weather farming. They repaired and extended the crumbling Roman aqueducts and integrated them with systems to trap, store, and distribute water, creating a year-round water supply. Palermo, their ancient capital on the island's northern coast, is well suited to citrus cultivation, sheltered by mountains and warmed by almost constant sunshine. Combined with the elaborate irrigation systems, this area known as the Conca d'Oro—"golden bowl"—provided the perfect environment to produce orange and lemon trees in profusion.

The ancestors of Sicily's citrus fruits are the citron—similar to a huge knobby lemon—the mandarins of China, and the pomelo, a grapefruit-like citrus from Malaysia. These fruits have been crossbred to produce all the different citrus we know today. As early as A.D. 70 Jews emigrating to Calabria brought citron with them. But the first citrus to really take off in Italy were sour oranges and lemons, a hybrid of sour oranges and citron brought by the Arabs.

Sour orange, called *arangias*, is inedible raw, but used in cooking, it lends what writer Helena Attlee called an "almost incense-like, incredibly distinctive bitterness." During the Middle Ages, sour orange was a status food for the elite, used to flavor meats in conjunction with rare spices from the east. Their popularity was eventually displaced by other citrus fruits cultivated in Sicily, most famously blood oranges, so named for their ruby red flesh. Blood oranges continue to be cultivated extensively in the eastern part of the island, where they are used to flavor fish dishes and fruit ices, and in salads along with cured black olives and raw fennel.

But it was lemons that made Sicily rich. The island supplied them to the British Navy in the 1700s to counter scurvy, a vitamin C deficiency, and sent citric acid to the United States. But those markets eventually changed, and by the end of World War I, Sicily's dominance of the citrus industry was over, though the perfumed orchards remain.

Opposite: Lemons grow all along the coast: These were gathered in Syracuse. Right: Blood oranges are a Sicilian specialty.

Citrus, Sicily, and the Mob

In the 1860s citrus in Sicily earned more money than any other agricultural category. The promise of profits, centuries of absent landlords in the Conca d'Oro, and post-unification political chaos in Palermo created the circumstances that birthed the Mafia. When legislation broke up the big estates, smaller farms filled the void. But lemon groves were expensive to own, water, and protect from thieves. The Mafia offered to help, for a fee—those who didn't pay might find their grove cut down. By the end of the 1960s cheap fruit from elsewhere cut into profit margins, and the Mafia moved on to other cons, including real estate, developing the Conca d'Oro beyond recognition.

The fourth-century Greek poet Archestratus wrote Gastronomia, *about the pleasures of the Sicilian table.*

the Normans—Christian Vikings from France—invaded Sicily with the blessings of the pope. The Sicilian passion for *baccalà* (preserved codfish) is of Norman origin. The Normans unified Sicily with Apulia and Calabria under a single crown called the Kingdom of Two Sicilies. During the medieval era, that crown was swapped among the various noble houses of Europe and they, like the Romans before them, were mostly absent landlords. The era of foreign kings did introduce an appreciation for culinary opulence, however, still evident in elaborate foods including *timballo di maccheroni* and *cassata,* a dense sponge cake festooned with glacé fruits.

By the 15th century Spain ruled Sicily. They introduced New World crops like corn, hot peppers, tomatoes, and chocolate (still made in Modica according to Aztec formulas), but the island suffered from incessant tax demands, refusal of the nobility to pay their share, devastating earthquakes, disease, and chronic food shortages. Sicilians had to subsist on pasta and bread. Bread crumbs were sprinkled in sauces and on roasted meats

Isola Bella, near Taormina, is one of Sicily's many beautiful surrounding islands and islets.

Cannoli, a Sicilian invention, feature a filling of sweetened, whipped ricotta.

to add calories (a practice now firmly in the culinary vernacular), and pasta such as *maccheroni, cavatelli,* and ziti were made without eggs and often served with vegetables.

The Sicilians hated the Spanish. They hated the French, too, and the Austrians, all of whom held the island's crown at one time or another. But it was not until Garibaldi and his dream of a unified Italy did the Sicilians rise up. Post-unification, however, the island was ignored yet again and subsequently descended into a period of corruption and lawlessness. This was the climate that allowed for the emergence of organized crime specializing in agricultural extortion, the predecessors of today's infamous Sicilian Mafia.

A Foot in Many Cultures

Sicilians are a passionate if suspicious people. Waves of invaders have left their imprint on the culture and food, but the victuals most common among the *paisani* remain the foods upon which life on the island was built: cereals, vegetables, and fish.

Wheat is still the primary cereal, used in pasta and bread. The small round loaves called *muffuletta* are ubiquitous and used to make the sandwiches that fuel a vibrant street food scene, especially in Palermo. Hot greasy innards; vegetables such as tomato, escarole, and fennel; fried potato croquettes; even ice cream may be stuffed in a brioche or roll, or spread on focaccia.

LOCAL FLAVOR
PIG OF THE SEA

From time immemorial, the North Atlantic bluefin tuna has migrated into the Mediterranean Sea in May and June to spawn. Sicilian fishermen traditionally captured schools of these huge fish in a maze of nets; then they funneled the tuna into an interior chamber, where they were slaughtered with harpoons. Called the *mattanza*, the hunt has all but disappeared, as have the tuna themselves.

The Italians call tuna "pig of the sea" because of its relative size and because all parts are eaten. Heads and tails are slow-cooked in tomato sauce, the scraps made into a *salame* called *ficazza di tonno,* the loin cured like a beef *bresaola,* and the roe salted, dried, and pressed. The latter, called *bottarga,* is shaved onto grilled bread, fennel salad, and pasta. Tuna is also preserved in oil, the best being the tuna belly, sweet with fat.

Vegetables are a common main course here, often fortified with bread crumb stuffing. Most ubiquitous are eggplant, the "meat of the earth," and tomato, both used most famously in the classic *pasta alla Norma*. But the tang of Sicilian cooking comes from anchovy. Fresh and preserved, they flavor everything from pizza to pasta. With such a bounty of pristinely fresh seafood, the Sicilians have developed a *crudo* cuisine: swordfish, tuna, and the exceptional red shrimp of Mazara are often served raw, drizzled with oil and a squirt of citrus. The humble creatures of the sea are cooked to marvelous effect in Sicily. Sardines are, with wild fennel, key to the classic *pasta con le sarde,* and tender snails, clams, eels, and squid find their way into aromatic couscous or pasta or are pan-cooked with sweet and sour sauces.

Of all the regions in Italy, nowhere are sweets more important. Marzipan candies are an art form, molded and colored to represent everything from corncobs to olives. Cannoli, popular all over the world, is at its silky, crispy best in Sicily. Zabaglione, a divine frothy custard served warm or chilled, is not to be missed, and the gelato is so achingly good the Sicilians actually take a daily break to eat some, just like they do an espresso. Cakes, pastries, cookies of all sorts, puffs, and fritters—all soften the blows of life.

Sicily is the pot into which the different cuisines of the Mediterranean Basin have been stirred. Its cookery is a homogenization of the region's food history, trade opportunities, and cultural inclinations. Indeed, Sicilians, and the pleasures of their table, are quintessentially Mediterranean.

The ancient Mercato del Capo in Palermo is as much street theater as food market.

Sicily's Citrus Groves Citrus plays a significant role in the local economy, where many varieties, including lemon, grapefruit, and blood orange, are grown.

Fennel, Orange, and Olive Salad

Insalata di finocchi, arance e olive • *Serves 4 to 6*

WHY THIS RECIPE WORKS: This light, bright salad celebrates ingredients that are abundant in Sicily. Citrus fruits, in particular, flourish and come in many varieties. *Taroccos*, or blood oranges, are the most popular and prized variety, so it seemed only fitting that we use them for this salad. We liked the fennel best when it was sliced as thin as possible; this ensured its texture was delicate and crisp rather than tough and chewy, making it an ideal pairing with the sweet, juicy oranges. To ensure that they were evenly distributed in the salad, we cut the oranges into bite-size pieces and tossed the salad gently to keep the segments from falling apart. To finish our salad, we added some oil-cured black olives, which added briny contrast, plus fresh mint, lemon juice, olive oil, salt, and pepper.

2 blood oranges
1 fennel bulb, stalks discarded, bulb halved, cored, and sliced thin
¼ cup pitted brine-cured black olives, sliced thin
3 tablespoons extra-virgin olive oil
2 tablespoons coarsely chopped fresh mint
2 teaspoons lemon juice
Salt and pepper

Cut away peel and pith from oranges. Quarter oranges, then slice crosswise into ½-inch-thick pieces. Combine oranges and any accumulated juices, fennel, olives, oil, mint, and lemon juice in bowl. Season with salt and pepper to taste. Serve.

Fried Risotto Balls

Arancini · *Makes 14*

WHY THIS RECIPE WORKS: Rice used to be a staple crop in Sicily, and while it's no longer farmed in the region, it's still enjoyed, especially in one of the island's most iconic foods. Meaning "little oranges," arancini consist of rich saffron risotto formed into large balls around a stuffing of cheese or meat and peas and deep fried until a crispy crust develops, which provides an appealing contrast to the creamy rice. It is generally believed the dish dates back to the Muslim era as the Arabs introduced both citrus fruits and saffron to Sicily. The frying stage was added later, in the 13th century, to make arancini portable and therefore one of Sicily's first take-out foods—and now one of the most commonplace bar or street foods. Since it's deep-fried, the dish might sound best left to vendors, but it's a popular dish to make at home, too; home cooks make arancini to avoid pitching leftover risotto. Arancini are actually quite simple to put together using our foolproof *Risotto alla milanese* (page 85) for the base. We found that ½ cup of risotto wrapped around a filling of mozzarella (we liked the molten center this simple filling created) heated through in the time it took to brown the outside while turning the cheese gooey. A coating of finely ground panko bread crumbs turned supercrisp after frying and resisted absorbing oil and becoming greasy.

1½ cup panko bread crumbs
1 tablespoon minced fresh parsley
Salt and pepper
⅛ teaspoon cayenne pepper
2 large eggs
1 recipe Saffron Risotto
  (page 85), chilled
4 ounces mozzarella, fontina,
  or provolone cheese, cut into
  ½-inch pieces
3 quarts vegetable oil
Lemon wedges

❶ Process bread crumbs in food processor to fine crumbs, 20 to 30 seconds; transfer to shallow dish. Stir in parsley, ½ teaspoon salt, ¼ teaspoon pepper, and cayenne until combined. Beat eggs in second shallow dish. Using your moistened hands, shape ½ cup risotto into disk roughly 3 inches wide and 1 inch thick. Make shallow indentation in center of disk and pack it with 3 pieces mozzarella. Carefully fold edges of risotto over mozzarella to enclose. Gently roll risotto between your hands to form sealed ball; transfer to parchment paper–lined rimmed baking sheet. Repeat with remaining risotto and mozzarella. (You should have 14 rice balls; rice balls can be refrigerated for up to 24 hours.)

❷ Working with 1 rice ball at a time, coat in egg, allowing excess to drip off, then coat with bread crumbs, pressing gently to adhere; return to sheet.

❸ Line second rimmed baking sheet with triple layer of paper towels. Add oil to large Dutch oven until it measures about 2 inches deep and heat over medium-high heat to 375 degrees. Carefully add 5 rice balls to oil and cook until well browned, about 5 minutes, rotating rice balls halfway through cooking. Adjust burner as necessary to maintain oil temperature between 350 and 375 degrees. Using skimmer, transfer arancini to prepared sheet; let drain. Serve immediately with lemon wedges.

Caponata

Caponata · Makes about 3 cups

WHY THIS RECIPE WORKS: Prepared in Calabria and Sicily, caponata, a sweet-and-sour eggplant relish, is a bit different in every village. The dish has been revered for centuries, and it's easy to see why: Bolstered by the bold Mediterranean flavors of capers, olives, raisins, and pine nuts, with celery providing crunch, the vegetable mélange is good enough to eat straight out of the bowl, though it's traditionally served on bruschetta or with grilled meat or fish. (Funnily enough, caponata got its name from *caupone,* the taverns around Sicily's ports where it was originally a seafood dish—a mix of squid, celery, and eggplant.) Eggplant tends to absorb oil like a sponge, so we started by microwaving it on a bed of coffee filters, an effective technique we've used for many eggplant dishes; it works surprisingly well to collapse the eggplant's cells, enabling it to absorb the flavors of the other ingredients rather than the cooking oil. We added concentrated tomato flavor in the form of V8 juice—an unlikely twist, but it avoided the pulpy texture of canned tomatoes. Brown sugar, raisins, and red wine vinegar created the traditional sweet-and-sour profile, while minced anchovies provided an umami boost and briny black olives offered balance. Although we prefer the flavor of V8 juice, tomato juice can be substituted. If coffee filters are not available, food-safe, undyed paper towels can be substituted. Be sure to remove the eggplant from the microwave immediately so that the steam can escape.

1½ pounds eggplant, cut into ½-inch pieces
½ teaspoon salt
¾ cup V8 juice
¼ cup red wine vinegar, plus extra for seasoning
2 tablespoons packed brown sugar
¼ cup chopped fresh parsley
3 anchovy fillets, rinsed and minced
1 large tomato, cored, seeded, and chopped
¼ cup raisins
2 tablespoons minced black olives
2 tablespoons extra-virgin olive oil, plus extra as needed
1 celery rib, chopped fine
1 red bell pepper, stemmed, seeded, and chopped fine
1 small onion, chopped fine
¼ cup pine nuts, toasted

1 Toss eggplant with salt in bowl. Line entire surface of plate with double layer of coffee filters and lightly spray with vegetable oil spray. Spread eggplant in even layer on coffee filters. Microwave until eggplant is dry and shriveled to one-third of its original size, 8 to 15 minutes (eggplant should not brown). Transfer eggplant immediately to paper towel–lined plate.

2 Whisk V8 juice, vinegar, sugar, parsley, and anchovies together in bowl. Stir in tomato, raisins, and olives.

3 Heat 1 tablespoon oil in 12-inch nonstick skillet over medium-high heat until shimmering. Add eggplant and cook, stirring occasionally, until edges are browned, 4 to 8 minutes, adding 1 teaspoon more oil if skillet appears dry; transfer to bowl.

4 Add remaining 1 tablespoon oil to now-empty skillet and heat over medium-high heat until shimmering. Add celery, bell pepper, and onion and cook, stirring occasionally, until softened and edges are spotty brown, 6 to 8 minutes.

5 Reduce heat to medium-low and stir in eggplant and V8 juice mixture. Bring to simmer and cook until V8 juice is thickened and coats vegetables, 4 to 7 minutes. Transfer to serving bowl and let cool completely. (Caponata can be refrigerated for up to 1 week; bring to room temperature before serving.) Season with extra vinegar to taste and sprinkle with pine nuts before serving.

Pasta With Tomato and Almond Pesto

Pasta con pesto alla trapanese · *Serves 6 to 8*

WHY THIS RECIPE WORKS: While the basil pesto of Genoa (see page 73) gets most of the attention, other regions "pound" together local ingredients to create different pastes. The pesto that originated in the port town of Trapani isn't all about the herbs; rather, basil plays a mere supporting role to fresh tomatoes, which tint the sauce and lend fruity, vibrant sweetness. Ground almonds, which replace pine nuts, thicken the sauce and offer richness. The sauce is often made by the families of fishermen, tossed with pasta, and served under left-over pieces of the fishermen's tiny, unwanted catches to stretch the small amount of fish. For a sauce we could make year-round, we turned to cherry or grape tomatoes rather than seasonal farmers' market varieties. One-half cup of basil allowed just enough of its flavor to work in tandem with the tomatoes. Sometimes this pesto features a bit of heat, which we liked, so we added just a scant ½ teaspoon of minced jarred peperoncini and an optional pinch of red pepper flakes, which gave the pesto a welcome zing.

12 ounces cherry or grape tomatoes
½ cup fresh basil leaves
¼ cup slivered almonds, toasted
1 tablespoon stemmed, patted dry, and minced jarred peperoncini
1 garlic clove, minced
Salt and pepper
Pinch red pepper flakes (optional)
⅓ cup extra-virgin olive oil
1 pound linguine or spaghetti
1 ounce Pecorino Romano cheese, grated (½ cup), plus extra for serving

❶ Process tomatoes, basil, almonds, peperoncini, garlic, 1 teaspoon salt, and pepper flakes, if using, in food processor until smooth, about 1 minute, scraping down sides of bowl as needed. With processor running, slowly add oil until incorporated. (Pesto can be refrigerated for up to 3 days. To prevent browning, press plastic wrap flush to surface or top with thin layer of olive oil. Bring to room temperature before using.)

❷ Meanwhile, bring 4 quarts water to boil in large pot. Add pasta and 1 tablespoon salt and cook, stirring often, until al dente. Reserve ½ cup cooking water, then drain pasta and return it to pot. Add pesto and Pecorino and toss to combine. Adjust consistency with reserved cooking water as needed. Season with salt and pepper to taste. Serve, passing extra Pecorino separately.

Pasta With Eggplant and Tomatoes

Pasta alla Norma · *Serves 6 to 8*

WHY THIS RECIPE WORKS: *Pasta alla Norma* is Sicily's most iconic pasta dish. It consists of a lively combination of tender eggplant and robust tomato sauce which is seasoned with herbs, mixed with al dente pasta, and finished with shreds of salty, milky ricotta salata. The dish gets its name from the epic opera *Norma,* which was composed by Vincenzo Bellini, a native of Catania; just as the opera is associated with perfection, so too is the hearty pasta. As we did for our Caponata (page 333), we salted and microwaved the eggplant to quickly draw out its moisture so that it wouldn't absorb too much oil. We found that it was best to wait until the last minute to combine the eggplant and sauce; this prevented the eggplant from soaking up too much tomato and becoming soggy. If coffee filters are not available, food-safe, undyed paper towels can be substituted when microwaving the eggplant. Be sure to remove the eggplant from the microwave immediately so that the steam can escape. For a spicier fish, use the larger amount of pepper flakes.

1½ pounds eggplant, cut into ½-inch pieces
Salt
¼ cup extra-virgin olive oil
4 garlic cloves, minced
2 anchovy fillets, minced
¼ to ½ teaspoon red pepper flakes
1 (28-ounce) can crushed tomatoes
6 tablespoons chopped fresh basil
1 pound ziti, rigatoni, or penne
3 ounces ricotta salata, shredded (1 cup)

1 Toss eggplant with ½ teaspoon salt in bowl. Line entire surface of plate with double layer of coffee filters and lightly spray with vegetable oil spray. Spread eggplant in even layer on coffee filters; wipe out and reserve bowl. Microwave until eggplant is dry and shriveled to one-third of its original size, 8 to 15 minutes (eggplant should not brown). Transfer eggplant immediately to paper towel–lined plate. Let cool slightly.

2 Transfer eggplant to now-empty bowl, drizzle with 1 tablespoon oil, and toss gently to coat; discard coffee filters and reserve plate. Heat 1 tablespoon oil in 12-inch nonstick skillet over medium-high heat until shimmering. Add eggplant and cook, stirring occasionally, until well browned and fully tender, about 10 minutes. Remove skillet from heat and transfer eggplant to now-empty plate.

3 Add 1 tablespoon oil, garlic, anchovies, and pepper flakes to now-empty skillet and cook using residual heat, stirring constantly, until fragrant and garlic becomes pale golden, about 1 minute (if skillet is too cool to cook mixture, set it over medium heat). Add tomatoes and bring to simmer over medium-high heat. Cook, stirring occasionally, until slightly thickened, 8 to 10 minutes.

4 Gently stir in eggplant and cook until heated through and flavors meld, 3 to 5 minutes. Stir in basil and remaining 1 tablespoon oil. Season with salt to taste.

5 Meanwhile, bring 4 quarts water to boil in large pot. Add pasta and 1 tablespoon salt and cook, stirring often, until al dente. Reserve ½ cup cooking water, then drain pasta and return it to pot. Add sauce and toss to combine. Adjust consistency with reserved cooking water as needed. Serve, passing ricotta salata separately.

Tuna With Sweet-and-Sour Onions

Tonno all'agrodolce · *Serves 4*

WHY THIS RECIPE WORKS: Tuna with sweet-and-sour onions, or *tonno all'agrodolce,* was born of the blending of Sicily's natural resources and the regional cuisine's prevalent Arab influence. The waters of Sicily are famed for their tuna and swordfishing industries, while early Arab rule brought North African ingredients and flavors to the island, including *agrodolce*—the sour-sweet profile. A great tonno all'agrodolce is all about achieving a sauce that has the perfect balance of vinegar and sugar and is bulked up with plenty of sautéed onions. We started with the onions, drawing out their moisture by adding water and cooking them covered; this allowed us to get good browning quickly once we lifted the lid. Adding the sugar for our sauce to the onions during the last few minutes of cooking encouraged extra caramelization. After much tinkering and tasting, we found the right amount of red wine vinegar (½ cup), added it to our caramelized onions, and reduced it to intensify its flavor but mellow its bite. We tossed in mint, a classic addition, off the heat to keep it fresh and bright. Traditional recipes call for cooking the tuna to varying degrees, from rare to well done throughout. We typically like our tuna rare, but in this application we preferred it cooked to medium-rare so there was some contrast between the flesh and the soft texture of our onions. If you like your tuna rare, however, cook the tuna just 1 to 2 minutes per side until it's translucent red at center and registers 110 degrees. Only purchase tuna steaks that are deep purplish red, firm to the touch, and devoid of any "fishy" odor.

1½ pounds red onions, halved and sliced thin
⅓ cup water
¼ cup extra-virgin olive oil, plus extra for drizzling
¼ teaspoon red pepper flakes
Salt and pepper
7 teaspoons sugar
½ cup red wine vinegar
½ cup minced fresh mint
4 (4- to 6-ounce) tuna steaks, about 1 inch thick

❶ Bring onions, water, 1 tablespoon oil, pepper flakes, and ½ teaspoon salt to boil in 12-inch nonstick skillet over high heat. Cover and cook until water has evaporated and onions start to sizzle, 5 to 7 minutes. Uncover, reduce heat to medium-high, and continue to cook until onions begin to brown, 7 to 10 minutes.

❷ Sprinkle onions with sugar and cook, stirring occasionally, until well browned, about 3 minutes. Stir in vinegar and cook until mostly evaporated, about 1 minute. Off heat, stir in 2 tablespoons oil and ⅓ cup mint. Transfer to bowl and cover to keep warm. Wipe skillet clean with paper towels.

❸ Pat tuna steaks dry with paper towels and season with salt and pepper. Heat remaining 1 tablespoon oil in now-empty skillet over medium-high heat until just smoking. Place tuna in skillet and cook until well browned and reddish pink at center when checked with tip of paring knife and registers 125 degrees (for medium-rare), 2 to 3 minutes per side.

❹ Transfer onion sauce to serving dish and nestle tuna steaks on top. Drizzle with oil and sprinkle with remaining mint. Serve.

Sicilian Pizza

Sfincione · *Serves 6 to 8*

WHY THIS RECIPE WORKS: Walk among the street vendors in Palermo, and you'll see pizza that probably looks more like focaccia than pizza as you know it. But its thick, soft crust and restrained, perfectly balanced amount of big-flavor toppings will have you craving it just as avidly. Sold in bakeries, purchased on the street, and made at home, *sfincione* is famous for being prepared most often for New Year's celebrations. That's great, because it's probably the easiest pizza variety to pull off at home—no dough tossing talent or 900-degree oven required for stellar results. The rectangular pizza's thick base has a tight, even, cakelike crumb (*sfincione* loosely translates to "thick sponge") and crisp bottom. The crust is pale yellow and has an almost creamy texture thanks to the semolina flour used in the dough. Semolina flour is made from durum wheat and is the same type used to make many Italian pastas, couscous, and a variety of Sicilian breads. Spread over the top of this crust is a concentrated, complex tomato sauce bolstered by plenty of onion; a modest layer of Sicilian cacio-cavallo cheese; anchovies; and a sprinkling of bread crumbs. To get a crust with the crumb we were looking for, we used a three-pronged approach: We incorporated a generous amount of olive oil into the dough to tenderize it; we let the dough slowly rise in the refrigerator overnight to let flavors develop without large bubbles forming; and then we rolled it out and weighed it down with another baking sheet during the second rise to keep the crumb even and tight. To approximate the flavor of caciocavallo, which can be at once sweet and sharp and spicy, we used a mixture of creamy provolone and sharp, nutty Parmigiano, which we stirred into the bread-crumb mixture we sprinkled on top. This recipe requires refrigerating the dough for 24 to 48 hours before shaping it. King Arthur all-purpose flour and Bob's Red Mill semolina flour work best in this recipe. It is important to use ice water in the dough to prevent overheating during mixing.

DOUGH

- 2¼ cups (11¼ ounces) all-purpose flour
- 2 cups (12 ounces) semolina flour
- 1 teaspoon instant or rapid-rise yeast
- 1⅔ cups ice water
- 3 tablespoons extra-virgin olive oil
- 1 teaspoon sugar
- 2¼ teaspoons salt

SAUCE

- 2 onions, grated
- ½ cup water
- 1 (14.5-ounce) can whole peeled tomatoes, drained
- 2 tablespoons extra-virgin olive oil
- 3 anchovy fillets, rinsed, patted dry, and minced
- ½ teaspoon dried oregano
- ¼ teaspoon red pepper flakes
- ¼ teaspoon salt

PIZZA

- 7 tablespoons extra-virgin olive oil
- 1 cup panko bread crumbs
- 1 ounce Parmigiano Reggiano cheese, grated (½ cup)
- Pinch salt
- 8 ounces provolone, sliced
- 8 anchovy fillets, rinsed, patted dry, and sliced in half lengthwise (optional)
- ¼ teaspoon dried oregano

1 For the dough: Whisk all-purpose flour, semolina flour, and yeast together in bowl of stand mixer. Whisk water, oil, and sugar in 4-cup liquid measuring cup until sugar has dissolved. Using dough hook on low speed, slowly add water mixture to flour mixture and mix until cohesive dough starts to form and no dry flour remains, 1 to 2 minutes. Cover bowl tightly with plastic wrap and let dough rest for 10 minutes.

2 Add salt to dough and knead on medium-low speed until dough is smooth and elastic and clears sides of bowl, about 8 minutes. Transfer dough to lightly floured counter and knead by hand to form smooth, round ball, about 30 seconds. Place dough seam side down in lightly greased large bowl or container, cover tightly with plastic, and refrigerate for at least 24 hours or up to 2 days.

3 For the sauce: Place onions and water in medium saucepan and bring to boil over medium heat. Reduce heat to low, cover, and simmer gently for 1 hour. Meanwhile, process tomatoes, oil, anchovies, oregano, pepper flakes, and salt in food processor until smooth, about 30 seconds. Add tomato puree to onion mixture and continue to cook, stirring occasionally, until reduced to 2 cups, 15 to 20 minutes. Transfer to bowl and let cool completely before using.

4 For the pizza: One hour before baking, adjust oven rack to middle position, set baking stone on rack, and heat oven to 500 degrees. Spray rimmed baking sheet (including rim) with vegetable oil spray, then coat bottom of sheet with ¼ cup oil. Press down on dough to deflate. Transfer dough to lightly floured counter and dust with flour. Press and roll dough into 18 by 13-inch rectangle. Loosely roll dough around rolling pin and gently unroll it onto prepared sheet, fitting dough into corners. Cover loosely with greased plastic, then place second rimmed baking sheet on top and let dough rise for 1 hour.

❺ Remove top sheet and plastic. Using your fingertips, gently press dough into corners of sheet. Stir panko, Parmigiano, salt, and remaining 3 tablespoons oil together in bowl. Spread provolone slices over dough in even layer. Using back of spoon or ladle, spread tomato sauce in thin layer on surface of dough, leaving ½-inch border. Sprinkle panko mixture evenly over sauce and dough. Lay anchovy slices, if using, evenly over panko mixture and sprinkle with oregano.

❻ Place pizza in oven and reduce oven temperature to 450 degrees. Bake until bottom crust is evenly browned and cheese is bubbly and partially browned, 20 to 25 minutes, rotating sheet halfway through baking. Let pizza cool in sheet on wire rack for 5 minutes, then transfer to cutting board with metal spatula. Cut into squares and serve.

Pistachio Gelato

Gelato al pistacchio · *Makes about 1 quart*

WHY THIS RECIPE WORKS: Highly prized Bronte pistachios are grown on the hillsides of eastern Sicily, and they're used in a wide variety of Sicilian dishes. They're especially celebrated in sweets, the arguable king of which is gelato. Theories as to the origins of gelato abound in Italy, with many believing it evolved from the sorbetto that the Arabs introduced. But its birthplace was most certainly Sicily. And while gelato is a close cousin to ice cream, there are key differences: Gelato typically has less cream and more milk and is served at a warmer temperature than American-style ice cream. The lower fat percentage and higher serving temperature allow its concentrated, pure flavors to taste more intense than those of ice cream; these same factors also keep gelato soft and creamy. To make pistachio gelato at home, we first tested ratios of milk and heavy cream for our base. We found that using mostly whole milk with just a bit of cream gave us the ideal dense, rich texture we were looking for. For pistachio flavor, some recipes we researched called for pistachio paste, a challenging-to-find specialty Sicilian product made from sweetened ground pistachios and oil. While pistachio paste is generally delicious and intensely flavored, we found that the percentages of sugar and fat varied from brand to brand, which would affect the texture of the gelato. Instead, we turned to raw pistachios. Grinding the nuts and steeping them in the warmed milk and cream released their volatile oils and deeply flavored the base, and straining the solids through cheesecloth ensured a velvety smooth texture. From there, we thickened our base with cornstarch, which is traditional, and egg yolks. Not all Sicilian recipes include yolks, but we liked the rich creaminess they contributed to our version since homemade gelato doesn't benefit from commercial

equipment. But we also added a surprise ingredient: corn syrup. Like the cornstarch, corn syrup helped absorb excess water and slow the formation of ice crystals, keeping the custard smooth. Gelato will stay within the ideal temperature range for up to 6 hours of freezing time, but after that we needed to temper the frozen gelato in the refrigerator until it warmed to the ideal serving temperature of 10 to 15 degrees for a creamy, intensely pistachio-flavored treat, perfect for bringing sunny Sicilian afternoons home. If using a canister-style ice cream maker, be sure to freeze the empty canister for at least 24 hours and preferably for 48 hours before churning. For self-refrigerating ice cream makers, pre-chill the canister by running the machine for 5 to 10 minutes before pouring in the custard.

> 2½ cups (11¼ ounces) shelled pistachios
> 3¾ cups whole milk
> ¾ cup (5¼ ounces) sugar
> ⅓ cup heavy cream
> ⅓ cup light corn syrup
> ⅓ cup plus ¼ teaspoon salt
> 5 teaspoons cornstarch
> 5 large egg yolks

❶ Process pistachios in food processor until finely ground, about 20 seconds. Combine 3½ cups milk, sugar, cream, corn syrup, and ¼ teaspoon salt together in large saucepan. Cook, stirring frequently, over medium-high heat until tiny bubbles form around edge of saucepan, 5 to 7 minutes. Off heat, stir in pistachios, cover, and let steep for 1 hour.

❷ Line fine-mesh strainer with triple layer of cheesecloth that overhangs edges and set over large bowl. Transfer pistachio mixture to prepared strainer and press to extract as much liquid as

possible. Gather sides of cheesecloth around pistachio pulp and gently squeeze remaining liquid into bowl; discard spent pulp.

❸ Whisk cornstarch and remaining ¼ cup milk together in small bowl; set aside. Return pistachio-milk mixture to clean saucepan. Whisk in egg yolks until combined. Bring custard to gentle simmer over medium heat and cook, stirring occasionally and scraping bottom of saucepan with rubber spatula, until custard registers 190 degrees, 4 to 6 minutes.

❹ Whisk cornstarch mixture to recombine, then whisk into custard. Cook, stirring constantly, until custard thickens, about 30 seconds. Immediately pour custard into bowl and let cool until no longer steaming, about 20 minutes.

❺ Fill large bowl with 6 cups ice, ½ cup water, and remaining ⅓ cup salt. Set bowl with custard over ice bath and let chill, stirring frequently, until custard registers 40 degrees, about 1½ hours. (Alternatively, custard can be covered and refrigerated for at least 6 hours or up to 24 hours.)

❻ Whisk custard to recombine, then transfer to ice cream maker and churn until mixture resembles thick soft-serve ice cream and registers 21 degrees, 15 to 30 minutes. Transfer gelato to airtight container, pressing firmly to remove any air pockets, and freeze until firm, about 6 hours. Serve. (Gelato can be stored for up to 5 days; if frozen for longer than 6 hours, let gelato sit in refrigerator for 1 to 2 hours until it registers 10 to 15 degrees before serving.)

Sardinia

On a Remote Pastoral Island, Food That Is Out of This World

··

MODERN PEOPLE SOMETIMES WONDER what food tasted like when the planet was purer. One just might find out in Sardinia, a far-flung island of granite and schist that emerged during the separation of continents from Pangaea, 65 million years ago. Birthed in the bisection of Europe and Africa, it was formed long before the Alps and the Apennines were forced to the surface. The Greeks called it Ichnusa, "footprint," a stepping-stone to Africa. The Romans renamed it Sardinia, presumably after the prehistoric Sárdara whose

ancestors appear to have been here as early as 13,500 B.C., a fact established after human remains were discovered in Grotta Corbeddu. (Traces of Neanderthal inhabitation go back as far as 150,000 B.C.)

Due south of Corsica, 120 miles equidistant from mainland Italy and the Tunisian rim, Sardinia is suspended in place and time, its glassy sea of concentric cobalt and turquoise surrounding more than 1,200 miles of uninterrupted coastline. Thousands of rare animals and plants inhabit the region: Tiny feral horses gambol about on its prairie. Miniature white donkeys, foals at their flanks, roam an island off the northwest coast, seemingly their private domain. On Cagliari's pristine beachfront you can see flamingos nest in the grasses or fly overhead in a moving cloud of pink. Its desert landscapes might well be the moon but for the mingled sight and smells of prickly pear, pomegranate, myrtle, and juniper, grounding you back to earth and the enticing vapors of Sardinia's kitchens.

The old port in La Maddelena, province of Sassari, founded in prehistoric times

> *Gallura is the site of a 4,000-year-old olive tree, the oldest in Italy.*

"All That Is Bad Comes From the Sea"

The Sardinian sea is insanely gorgeous and bountiful, even in a time of depleted oceans. Yet native people have historically detested it. From the island's early history, incessant piracy and invasions forced them into the interior. This became the cradle of Nuragic civilization, named for the *nuraghi*, Bronze Age stone towers enthroned upon the rocky highlands. Cicero called the inhospitable territory with its swiftly rising heights and savage landscape Barbagia, "land of the barbarian." Today it's the region's central province, its name an epithet proudly accepted by the indomitable inhabitants.

The Romans who sailed into Cagliari's harbor planted wheat in the fertile lowlands to feed their armies, only to leave behind 1,000 years of malaria. Vandals, Goths, Byzantines, and Saracens all raped and pillaged coastal towns. In the Middle Ages, Genoese galleons unloaded their mercenaries. The Spanish occupied the littoral for 400 years. The Piedmontese House of Savoy, Sardinia's 18th-century masters, stripped shepherds and farmers of their right to collective land ownership (a custom since Nuragic times). The last invasion was a quiet one: In the 1950s Prince Karim Aga Khan IV bought

Antico Caffè in Cagliari's historic center, founded in 1855 and a hub for artists and locals, is listed with the Ministry of Cultural Assets.

Colorful Cagliari, washed in golden light at dusk. Founded in the eighth century, it is one of Europe's most ancient cities.

12,000 acres on the ravishing Emerald Coast from the local shepherds. Some of the most pristine and stunning shoreline in all the Mediterranean, promoted as an "economic miracle," was transformed into an exclusive enclave for the international plutocracy. Few locals can afford to live there.

Fruits of Earth and Sea

Since the last century, reclamation of the malarial shorefront has made the markets of Cagliari a paradise for those seeking Mediterranean fish and sea creatures. Sant'Antioco and Alghero are famous for spiny lobster. Italy's best *bottarga,* mullet or tuna roe, is pressed and salted around the immense saltwater lake at Cabras. And in Carloforte, on San Pietro Island, the controversial Girotonno festival to capture the endangered bluefin tuna continues. The 600-year-old method used to attract the tuna into a "death chamber," where they are slaughtered by fishermen, is as brutal and bloody a spectacle—and as honored locally—as a Spanish bullfight.

But above all, this sparsely populated island hosts an uninterrupted continuation of 5,000 years of pastoral customs. Shepherds continue making cheese from the milk of both ewes and goats. Locals attribute the phenomenon of Sardinia's famous "blue zone"—mountain areas where it is not uncommon for people to live well past 100—to

Nespole and peaches sit ready for purchase at San Benedetto market

TERROIR TO TABLE
CAGLIARI'S FISH MARKET

At the San Benedetto market, Europe's biggest, you'll find real *Cagliaritani* in all their color: farmers, artichoke whittlers, shepherds' wives. Of all the stalls, those of the fish sellers with all the sea creatures of the Mediterranean on display are the most remarkable. If you don't know how to cook them, the customers will tell you how. "Eels make good *panadas*, but lamprey, even better!" "See the octopuses with two rows of suckers? They taste best!" What to do with those wicked looking scorpionfish? "Make *cassola!*" You'll leave with new recipes and new friends.

their consumption of the local red wine, and of *gioddu,* a yogurt rich in probiotics based on a starter with origins in antiquity.

Sardinia is the largest producer of pecorino, sheep's-milk cheese following essentially the same methods shepherds of the Barbagia used thousands of years ago. After Pecorino Romano, the less salty and more delicate Fiore Sardo is the island's most well known cheese.

Sardinia's lambs and kids roam freely in the hills feeding on aromatic herbs and shrubs. The pig, the formidable reserve of meat and cooking fat, is as ubiquitous here as elsewhere in Italy. Traditionally, rural families fattened a hog every year for an annual supply of *salumi,* prosciutto, and fresh sausage.

Heritage Grain and Indigenous Plants

Today, as in Roman antiquity, much of the island's arable land is devoted to growing durum wheat, the backbone of the Sardinian diet. This is used for making such pasta quiddities as *malloreddus,* small, slender versions of gnocchi tapered at the ends. Or try *curligionis,* beautiful pasta pillows with a tangy ewe ricotta and pecorino filling tinged with saffron, sealed closed with a handsome twisted seam that recalls Sardinia's exquisite embroidery. The tendency toward skilled handiwork—whether in stuffed pasta artistry, tapestries, basketry, or doughy specialties—breaks forth in *loringhitas,* intricately hand-braided infinity pasta loops that apparently require a lifetime of practice to master. There are only a few women living who still know how

Nuns on an afternoon *passeggiata* near their convent in Cagliari's old town

Pecorino Romano: Roman Name, Sardinian Cheese

Sardinia's hilly landscapes offer ideal terroir for sheep. These great reserves of wool and milk like nothing more than to graze on fragrant Mediterranean maquis, and their charms emerge in every wheel of ewe's-milk cheese. The island is the biggest producer of Pecorino Romano, the oldest known Italian cheese, a direct descendant of the one that the Roman populace sprinkled on their porridge and that the empire's soldiers carried in their backpacks. If its name denotes a sheep (*pecora* in Italian) cheese of Roman origin, why does most of it come from Sardinia? Tuscany's Grosseto province makes it as well. But here, in a region that's twice the size and one fraction of the population, where there may be three times as many sheep as people, it only made sense for Lazio's cheesemakers to expand their production. They made the move at the turn of the 20th century, at the same time that Italian immigrants popularized the cheese in America, increasing the demand by 60 percent. You can tell the regional origin of each cheese from the markings on the rind, which indicate the origin, dairy, and date of production. If you pay attention, you will note the subtle differences in flavor. While

---

Opposite: Shepherds collect ewe's milk in Spumonte, a timeless Sardinian scene. Right: The finished pecorino.

only the eight-month cheese is exported, purposed for grating, a mellower five-month version is aged for the table.

There is nothing subtle about the salty punch of aged Pecorino Romano. The originators of the formula for making the cheese, Roman shepherds, liked it that way, using it to flavor their food in place of costly salt. Unfortunately, because of poor handling, too many specimens of this cheese outside of its homeland lack the charms of the original. The common practice of breaking up whole wheels to be displayed precut and wrapped, or grated into tubs, leaves it dry and excessively salty. While saltiness is characteristic, this cheese should be rich and moist. Buy from a knowledgeable cheesemonger, and bring home only as big a wedge as needed for immediate use. Once unwrapped, use it as soon as possible, rewrapping any left over well and chilling at once. Because pre-grated cheese loses its flavor and dries out quickly, grate it just before using.

Pass the Cheese, Please!

Grated Pecorino Romano enhances bold, southern-style pasta dishes, most notably, *spaghetti con acciughe e cipolle* (spaghetti with anchovy and onions). With its salty virility, it is just what is needed to encourage the salty anchovy and the sweet onion in the sauce to talk to each other. A little sprinkle and in a flash, the modest meeting can become a love affair on the palate.

With other dishes where the ingredients cannot bear the domineering presence of another, hold the Romano and instead pass the Parmigiano Reggiano (or some other such nuanced wedge). So, *attenzione*, before you say, "Pass the cheese, please."

to make them, and locals say the pasta loops will become extinct when these *anziani*, ancients, die.

Above all, bread is Sardinia's most important food, as much sacrament as sustenance, as evidenced in the religious significance assigned to various forms it can take and the sheer quantities eaten. We are told that the typical household in rural Marmilla—Sardinia's ancient granary where bread is still made at home—requires at least 45 pounds of flour to make a week's supply for a family of six. There are over 200 traditional kinds of bread, including *pane carasau,* once a portable staple for the shepherd who might be away from home for months at a time. Also called *carta da musica*—music paper, relating to its incredible thinness and crunch—the unleavened sheets of dried bread today comes in stacks of 20, shrink-wrapped to preserve their freshness. Traces of the same bread were unearthed in excavations of nuraghi dating to 1000 B.C. *Civraxiu*, another favorite, is quite different: a large, fragrant sourdough loaf shaped like a turban, with a dense crust enclosing a moist and chewy center that lasts for days.

If Sardinia belongs to nowhere and no one except itself, so do some of its fruits and vegetables. Some Sardinian produce may seem exotic because it does not often

Vigne Surrau, Sassari. Roses planted at the end of vine trellises, like canaries and coal mines, flag problems early when the flowers show stress.

Sardinia is scattered with more than 7,000 enigmatic monuments known as nuraghi, megalithic structures that were the centers of the indigenous Nuragic culture from circa 1800 B.C. until the Roman conquest in 238 B.C. Their origins can be traced back to human settlements some 10,000 years earlier. Skilled metalworkers, the Nuragic people traded the island's bronze and iron with other Mediterranean civilizations, making Sardinia an important center of the western sea during the times of the Mycenaeans, the Hittites, the Sumerians, and the Egyptians. There are more nuraghi remaining in Sardinia than all the ruins of the Roman Empire combined.

Nuraghe Mereu, in the Supramonte

leave the island. *Pompia,* a citrus fruit that looks like a bumpy grapefruit, is one such plant. It grows only on the maquis of Baronia, on the Nuoro coast, hanging on a tree that looks like orange wood. The rind flavors local spirits, and its pith is candied in honey for use in traditional desserts. Bright orange *cachi,* persimmons, and *fichi d'India* (cactus pear), all harvested in the wild, are also relished here. Many varieties are indigenous, including s*pinoso sardo,* a chokeless spiny artichoke considered exceptional for its depth of flavor. This armored species is an apt metaphor for Sardinia's people: They are not like the extroverts of the mainland south, but their heart is full.

Ancient Cuisine of the Earth, a Modern Taste for the Sea

Some guidebooks say that Sardinian cuisine is an amalgam of Spanish, Genoese, and Sicilian flavors. You can taste Spain in such dishes as *cassola,* a tomatoey fish soup brimming with garlic and heat; *panadas,* a take on empanadas; and in the penchant for saffron. You can hear it in the name fastened to fried pies stuffed with fresh, tangy ewe's-milk cheese and drenched in honey—*sebadas*. Cagliari's *fainè* is a close relative of Liguria's *farinata* (flat chickpea flour pancake). *Burrida,* a poached whole fish steeped in extra-virgin olive oil, hazelnuts, garlic, and vinegar is indubitably Genoese. Sicily shows up in the predilection for *frugula,* Sardinia's answer to couscous.

But many islanders will tell you something else. "Sardinia is not in the cities," shared Giuseppe De Martini, a sommelier and proprietor of one of Cagliari's wine and food shops. "You have to go to the center to understand the culture." It is here that cooking traditions remain unaffected by foreign invaders or mainland Italy. Here is a cuisine of utter simplicity and bold flavors, its staples being bread, meat, game,

In addition to Italian, numerous native languages are spoken throughout Sardinia's five provinces.

and cheese. Favored aromatics are myrtle, juniper, rosemary, wild fennel, and mint. Lamb and game are roasted on the spit. Every household grows olives for oil and for the table, and raises a pig or two for their anticipated feast of *porceddu,* suckling pig impaled on a branch of aromatic wood and roasted over juniper, myrtle, and grape vine. In a more complicated method of cooking, whole animals or meat is placed in a pit lined with heated stones layered with myrtle, a technique said to have originated with the interior's fabled bandits (now extinct) to hide their whereabouts. Hot embers are set on top and the meat slow-roasted until it is moist and buttery, the skin crackling. After roasting, the meat is wrapped in more myrtle for added flavor.

Speaking Sardinian

Even with best efforts, the various native languages can make it a challenge to order from a menu in Sardinia. Words here can be as strange to the modern ear as the foods can be exotic, based primarily on Paleo-Sardinian languages intertwined with a smattering of Punic. Phoenician, Etruscan, Middle Eastern tongues, Byzantine Greek, Catalan, and Spanish elements were added along the way. Such dishes as *puddighinos* (roasted small chickens with sun-dried tomato-studded bread stuffing), or *arazada* (candied orange peel and almond sweets) evoke the island's mystery, while dishes like *zikki* (a flatbread) have the pure ring of prehistoric man. You may ask for one thing, and be brought something completely different instead. All part of the adventure.

Cala Cipolla, a wild cove where flamingos, herons, and Great Cormorants mingle with sunbathers

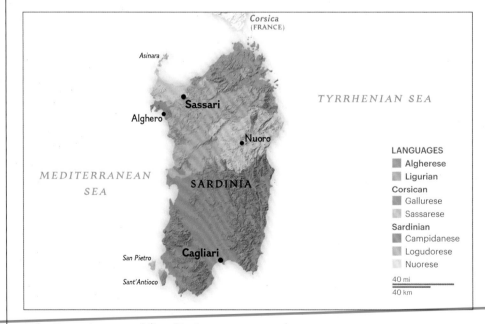

The Languages of Sardinia Although Italian is the official language, there are at least five native tongues still spoken throughout the region.

In Sardinia important festivities, sacraments, and life passages are observed with special breads and sweets. *Coccois pintaus* is a decorative bread wreath of considerable artistry reflecting different themes. Intricate designs and insignia festoon these edible masterpieces, including flora, fish, fruit, animals, human figures, or keys—symbols of spiritual significance. A number of decorative confections perform the same function. Among the most beautiful are *pastissus*, a specialty of Sanlurli. These cookies with folkloric motifs are formed into various shapes enclosing an almond filling. *Gattò*, made for saints days, are crisp cakes with edible gold and colored sugar embellishments under a snowy veil of icing—the same idea as gingerbread houses, but replicating a church or other significant building.

Sardinian Gnocchi With Fava Beans and Mint

Malloreddus con fave e menta • *Serves 6 to 8*

WHY THIS RECIPE WORKS: *Malloreddus,* also known as *gnocchetti sardi,* are tiny Sardinian gnocchi made by hand from an eggless semolina pasta dough. Often perfumed and painted with saffron—Sardinia's "red gold"—malloreddus (which means "fat little bulls" in the local dialect) are a most beloved pasta shape. They're often prepared for holidays, festivals, and weddings where, traditionally, a Sardinian bride prepares a batch of malloreddus on her wedding night to share with her new husband. Their ribbed shape comes from rolling them against the round reeds of a small basket used for making and carrying them. To make our own malloreddus, we infused our 100 percent semolina pasta dough with saffron and rolled individual pieces down the tines of a fork to create petite ridged dumplings in the characteristic shape. Malloreddus are served with a wide range of sauces and other complements, from hearty meat ragùs and sausages, to briny clams and other seafood, to simple tomato sauces and vegetables. To let the texture, flavor, and color of our malloreddus shine, we paired them with a classic spring combination of tender fava beans (prized in Sardinia for their meaty flavor and nutrition), tangy Pecorino (sheep's-milk cheese is a pride of Sardinia), and fresh mint (a favorite herb of the region). If you can't find fresh fava beans, you can substitute 2 cups of frozen, thawed fava beans. We prefer the flavor and texture of fresh pasta here, but dried can be used as well. For more information on making your own fresh pasta, see page 366.

2 pounds fava beans, shelled (2 cups)
1 pound fresh or dried malloreddus
Salt and pepper
3 tablespoons extra-virgin olive oil
½ onion, chopped fine
2 garlic cloves, minced
Pinch red pepper flakes
1 ounce Pecorino Romano cheese, grated (½ cup), plus extra for serving
½ cup chopped fresh mint

❶ Bring 4 quarts water to boil in large pot. Fill large bowl halfway with ice and water. Add beans to boiling water and cook for 1 minute. Using slotted spoon, transfer beans to ice water and let sit until chilled, about 2 minutes; drain well. Using paring knife, make small cut along edge of each bean through waxy sheath, then gently squeeze sheath to release bean; discard sheath.

❷ Return water to boil, add pasta and 1 tablespoon salt, and cook, stirring often, until al dente. Reserve 1½ cups cooking water, then drain pasta in colander. Toss pasta with 1 tablespoon oil in colander and set aside.

❸ Heat remaining 2 tablespoons oil in 12-inch skillet over medium heat until shimmering. Add onion and cook until softened and lightly browned, 5 to 7 minutes. Stir in garlic and pepper flakes and cook until fragrant, about 30 seconds. Stir in beans and ½ cup reserved cooking water and cook until beans are tender and liquid has mostly evaporated, 3 to 4 minutes.

❹ Stir in pasta, ½ cup reserved cooking water, and Pecorino and cook, stirring often, until cheese has melted and sauce has thickened slightly, 1 to 2 minutes. Adjust consistency with remaining ½ cup reserved cooking water as needed. Sprinkle with mint and serve, passing extra Pecorino separately.

Fried Zucchini

Zucchini fritti alla sarda · *Serves 4 to 6*

WHY THIS RECIPE WORKS: The use of semolina flour is a hallmark of Sardinian cuisine; it appears in everything from flatbreads to pasta to sweets. It's no surprise then that Sardinian cooks also turn to semolina to create a crispy coating for fried foods, especially vegetables such as fennel, eggplant, and zucchini. We were intrigued by *zucchini fritti*—frying would be a great way to enjoy this abundant summer vegetable—but we knew it would be a challenge; zucchini is notoriously watery, so we'd have to find a way to keep it crispy after frying. Removing the watery inner seed pulp was key, and slicing the zucchini into thin half-moons rather than thicker spears helped the pieces keep their shape without becoming limp or soggy. Plain zucchini is quite mild in flavor, so many recipes call for salting or brining the squash before coating and frying it. We found that brining the slices offered the most even seasoning, and just 30 minutes in the brine gave the zucchini balanced flavor. We then dredged the drained slices in a coating of semolina flour and fried them in hot oil for just a minute or two to create golden-brown pieces of zucchini with crispy exteriors and creamy, nicely seasoned interiors—a perfect Sardinian snack. You can find fine semolina (sometimes labeled *semola rimacinata*) in most Italian markets or in the international aisle of some well-stocked supermarkets. Avoid conventional semolina, which is too coarse for this recipe and will not work.

Kosher salt
2 zucchini (8 ounces each), halved lengthwise, seeded, and sliced very thin crosswise
1 cup fine semolina flour
2 quarts vegetable oil
Flake sea salt
Lemon wedges

1 Dissolve ¼ cup kosher salt in 4 cups water in large container. Submerge zucchini in brine and let sit at room temperature for 30 minutes.

2 Place semolina in shallow dish. Set wire rack in rimmed baking sheet and line with triple layer of paper towels. Add oil to large Dutch oven until it measures about 1½ inches deep and heat over medium-high heat to 400 degrees.

3 Drain zucchini and pat dry with paper towels. Dredge half of zucchini in semolina, shaking off excess, and carefully add to oil. Cook, stirring as needed to prevent sticking, until golden, 1 to 2 minutes. Adjust burner as necessary to maintain oil temperature between 375 and 400 degrees. Using wire skimmer or slotted spoon, transfer zucchini to prepared rack and season with sea salt to taste. Return oil to 400 degrees and repeat with remaining zucchini. Serve with lemon wedges.

Chickpea and Fennel Soup

Zuppa di ceci e finocchi · *Serves 4 to 6*

WHY THIS RECIPE WORKS: Wild fennel grows abundantly throughout Sardinia, where it's prized for its health and digestive benefits in addition to its exquisite flavor. Fennel's fronds, flowers, and seeds add an anise aroma to everything from salads, fish, and meat dishes to sausages, soups, and stews. One such dish is a satisfying chickpea and fennel soup in which the unique, delicate flavor of the fennel balances the ultrasavory presence of cooked chickpeas and pancetta. Since we would need to rely on milder cultivated fennel for our version of this Sardinian soup, we used the bulbs in addition to the fronds and added some dried fennel seeds to achieve ample fennel flavor. Hearty chickpeas—or *ceci*—form the backbone of this soup. To ensure our chickpeas were soft and creamy with tender skins, we soaked them overnight in salted water. Traditionally, some kind of pork fat is added to give this soup a mild meaty flavor and a touch of richness; in our version, a bit of pancetta does the job. For a well-rounded finish, we topped individual portions with extra-virgin olive oil and tangy, salty sheep's-milk Pecorino, another Sardinian staple. If you're pressed for time you can quick-soak your beans. In step 1, combine the salt, water, and beans in a Dutch oven and bring to a boil over high heat. Remove the pot from the heat, cover, and let stand for 1 hour. Drain and rinse the beans and proceed with the recipe. Look for bright white fennel bulbs with firm stalks and fresh fronds.

Salt and pepper
1 pound (2¾ cups) dried chickpeas, picked over and rinsed
1 tablespoon extra-virgin olive oil, plus extra for serving
2 ounces pancetta, chopped fine
2 fennel bulbs, 2 tablespoons fronds minced, stalks discarded, bulbs quartered, cored, and sliced thin crosswise
1 onion, chopped fine
4 garlic cloves, minced
1 tablespoon tomato paste
1 teaspoon fennel seeds
¼ teaspoon red pepper flakes
5 cups chicken or vegetable broth
2 bay leaves
Grated Pecorino Romano cheese

❶ Dissolve 3 tablespoons salt in 4 quarts cold water in large container. Add chickpeas and soak at room temperature for at least 8 hours or up to 24 hours. Drain and rinse well.

❷ Cook oil and pancetta in Dutch oven over medium heat until fat begins to render, about 2 minutes. Stir in sliced fennel, onion, and ½ teaspoon salt and cook until softened and lightly browned, 8 to 10 minutes. Stir in garlic, tomato paste, fennel seeds, and pepper flakes and cook until fragrant, about 30 seconds.

❸ Stir in 7 cups water, chickpeas, broth, and bay leaves and bring to boil, skimming off any foam that rises to surface. Reduce to gentle simmer and cook until chickpeas are tender, 1¼ to 1¾ hours.

❹ Discard bay leaves. Stir in fennel fronds and season with salt and pepper to taste. Serve, drizzling individual portions with extra oil and passing Pecorino separately.

Fregula With Clams and Saffron Broth

Sa fregula con vongole • *Serves 4 to 6*

WHY THIS RECIPE WORKS: This soup of pasta and clams is a Sardinian classic that's all about simplicity. It relies chiefly on the flavor inherent in the soup's two main ingredients: chewy, toasty spherical *fregula,* and *arselle,* the small, briny, succulent hard-shell clams found along the coast. Broth enriched with tomatoes (in various forms depending on the recipe), parsley, garlic, a touch of fragrant saffron, pepper flakes, and olive oil traditionally constitute the soup base. We cooked the pasta using the absorption method, right in our soup's base of chicken broth and water; this way, the fregula soaked up the flavorful broth during cooking. As a substitute for the Sardinian arselle, which aren't widely available in the United States, we landed on diminutive cockles, which are sweet and readily accessible. To cook the clams perfectly, we used our standard test kitchen method of steaming them in a shallow covered skillet and removing the clams as they opened. We chose sun-dried tomatoes, which are found in some traditional versions of this recipe, for our tomato product; given the soup's quick cooking time, their deep, concentrated flavor was a bonus. A sprinkle of parsley and lemon zest contributed a bright finish to a dish that was simply satisfying. Cockles are traditional here and our preferred choice, but if unavailable, you can substitute small littleneck clams.

2 tablespoons extra-virgin olive oil, plus extra for serving
2 garlic cloves, minced
⅛ teaspoon red pepper flakes
⅛ teaspoon saffron threads, crumbled
2 cups chicken broth
2 cups water
⅓ cup oil-packed sun-dried tomatoes, patted dry and chopped coarse
¼ cup minced fresh parsley
1½ cups fregula
2 pounds cockles, scrubbed
1 cup dry white wine
¼ teaspoon grated lemon zest
Salt and pepper

1 Heat oil in Dutch oven over medium heat until shimmering. Add garlic, pepper flakes, and saffron and cook until fragrant, about 30 seconds. Stir in broth, water, tomatoes, and 2 tablespoons parsley and bring to boil. Stir in fregula and cook, stirring often, until al dente.

2 Meanwhile, bring cockles and wine to boil in covered 12-inch skillet over high heat. Cook, shaking skillet occasionally, until cockles have just opened, 6 to 8 minutes. Using slotted spoon, transfer cockles to large bowl. Discard any unopened cockles. Cover to keep warm.

3 Strain cockle cooking liquid through fine-mesh strainer lined with coffee filter into pot, avoiding any gritty sediment that has settled on bottom of pan.

4 Stir in lemon zest and remaining 2 tablespoons parsley and season with salt and pepper to taste. Top individual portions with cockles and drizzle with extra oil before serving.

Fresh Egg Pasta

Makes 1 pound

WHY THIS RECIPE WORKS: The pasta of northern and central Italy is made rich and supple from the addition of eggs to the dough. (The amount of egg varies from region to region; the fresh pasta of Emilia-Romagna has a reputation for being the most luxurious, with a vibrant golden hue from so many yolks.) We wanted a rich, versatile egg pasta dough, one that would work for both strand pasta and filled pastas, and for recipes from all over northern and central Italy. It needed to be easy to roll and should cook up delicate and springy. Six egg yolks, in addition to two whole eggs and a couple tablespoons of olive oil (an ingredient whose merit as an addition to pasta dough is debated in Italy but which assists workability here), made the dough a dream to roll and gave it good flavor. Resting the dough for at least 30 minutes allowed the gluten—the protein network that forms when flour and liquid interact and which makes doughs chewy—time to relax so the dough didn't contract after rolling out in a pasta machine. If using a high-protein all-purpose flour, such as King Arthur brand, increase the number of egg yolks to seven. Steps to cutting pasta strands from Fresh Egg Pasta follow; see specific recipes for instructions on making filled pastas with this dough. Our favorite pasta machine is the Marcato Atlas 150 Wellness Pasta Machine. The pasta will be very thin and semi-transparent when rolled to setting 7 on this machine; settings may vary with other machines.

2 cups (10 ounces) all-purpose flour, plus extra as needed
2 large eggs plus 6 large yolks
2 tablespoons extra-virgin olive oil

❶ Process flour, eggs and yolks, and oil in food processor until mixture forms cohesive dough that feels soft and is barely tacky to touch, about 45 seconds. (If dough sticks to fingers, add up to ¼ cup flour, 1 tablespoon at a time, until barely tacky. If dough doesn't become cohesive, add up to 1 tablespoon water, 1 teaspoon at a time, until it just comes together; process 30 seconds longer.)

❷ Transfer dough to clean counter and knead by hand to form uniform ball. Wrap tightly in plastic wrap and let rest for 30 minutes or up to 4 hours.

1

2

CUTTING STRAND PASTA

1 Transfer dough to clean counter, divide into 5 pieces, and cover with plastic. Flatten 1 piece of dough into ½-inch-thick disk. Using pasta machine with rollers set to widest position, feed dough through rollers twice.

2 Bring tapered ends of dough toward middle; press to seal. Feed dough seam side first through rollers again. Repeat feeding dough tapered ends first through rollers set at widest position, without folding, until dough is smooth and barely tacky. (If dough sticks, lightly dust with flour and roll again.)

3 Narrow rollers to next setting; feed dough through twice. Progressively narrow rollers, feeding dough through each setting twice, until dough is very thin and semi-transparent. (If dough becomes too long to manage, halve crosswise.) Transfer sheet of pasta to kitchen towel and let air-dry for about 15 minutes; meanwhile, roll out remaining dough. Line 2 rimmed baking sheets with parchment paper and liberally dust with flour. Liberally dust pasta sheets with flour and cut into approximately 12-inch lengths.

4 A If cutting with a machine: Fit pasta machine with noodle attachment and feed 1 pasta sheet through rollers to cut into strands.

B If cutting by hand: Starting with 1 short end, gently fold pasta sheet at 2-inch intervals until it's been folded into flat, rectangular roll. With sharp chef's knife, slice pasta crosswise to desired width (¼ inch for fettuccine, ⅜ inch for tagliatelle, or ¾ inch to 1 inch for pappardelle).

5 Use fingers to unfurl pasta, liberally dust strands with flour, and arrange in small bundles on prepared sheet. Repeat with remaining pasta sheets. (Strands can be held at room temperature for up to 30 minutes, refrigerated for up to 4 hours, or chilled in freezer until firm, then transferred to zipper-lock bag and frozen for up to 1 month. If frozen, do not thaw before cooking.)

1

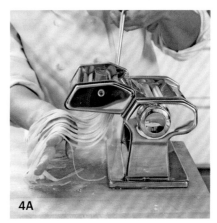

2

3

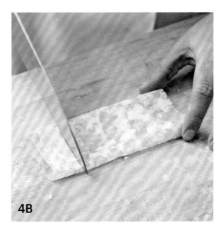

4A

4B

5

Fresh Semolina Pasta

Makes 1 pound

WHY THIS RECIPE WORKS: In southern Italy, pasta is usually made from nothing more than water and hard durum wheat, making this variety more rugged than its eggy counterpart. The logic: Eggless doughs made with rougher semolina flour hold on to and absorb sauces better so the pasta becomes infused with the sauce's flavor rather than the sauce remaining a separate entity. By contrast, a dough made from all-purpose flour and water was gummy and the resulting pasta tasted like boiled dough. For the perfect chew, we used warm water rather than cold, which jump-started gluten development, and we gave the dough a generous knead in a stand mixer. You can find fine semolina (sometimes labeled *semola rimacinata*) in most Italian markets and in some well-stocked supermarkets. Conventional semolina is too coarse. This recipe was developed using a 4.5-quart stand mixer. If using a 7-quart stand mixer, you will need to double the recipe so the dough is properly kneaded. Steps to creating the different pasta shapes we make with semolina pasta dough follow.

2 cups (11½ ounces) fine semolina flour
1 teaspoon salt
⅔ cup warm water, plus extra as needed

❶ Whisk flour and salt together in bowl of stand mixer, then stir in warm water. Using your hands, knead dough in bowl until shaggy, dry ball forms and no dry flour remains, about 3 minutes. If dry flour remains, add up to 2 teaspoons extra water, 1 teaspoon at a time, until flour is absorbed. (Dough will still be very dry and barely hold its shape.)

❷ Using dough hook, knead dough on medium speed until smooth and elastic, 10 to 12 minutes. (Dough may break into smaller pieces while kneading.) Transfer dough to clean counter and knead by hand to form uniform ball. Wrap tightly in plastic wrap and let rest for 30 minutes or up to 4 hours.

FRESH SAFFRON SEMOLINA PASTA DOUGH
Saffron adds aroma and golden color and is a traditional addition.

Combine warm water and ½ teaspoon saffron in bowl and let steep for 15 minutes before adding to flour mixture in step 1.

1

2

SHAPING ORECCHIETTE

1 Liberally dust 2 rimmed baking sheets with fine semolina flour. Transfer dough to clean counter, divide into 8 pieces, and cover with plastic wrap. Stretch and roll 1 piece of dough into ½-inch-thick rope, then cut rope into ½-inch nuggets.

2 Working with 1 dough nugget at a time, arrange cut side down on counter and press into ⅛-inch-thick disk using tip of butter knife. Holding top of disk in place with your thumb, position knife serrated side down on dough and drag toward you to form 1-inch-long oval with jagged surface.

3 Lightly dust smooth side of dough oval with flour. Using your lightly floured fingers, place floured side of oval over tip of thumb and gently pull on sides to form even cup shape. Remove pasta from your thumb and transfer to prepared sheets. Repeat rolling, cutting, and shaping remaining dough pieces. (Orecchiette can be kept at room temperature for up to 30 minutes, refrigerated for up to 4 hours, or chilled in freezer on baking sheet until firm, then transferred to zipper-lock bag and frozen for up to 1 month. If frozen, do not thaw before cooking.)

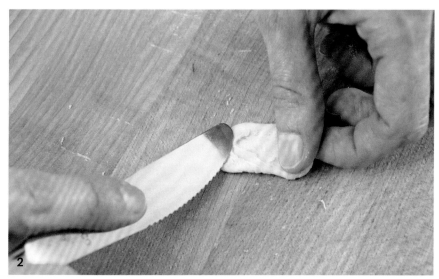

SHAPING FILEJA

1 Liberally dust 2 rimmed baking sheets with fine semolina flour. Transfer dough to clean counter, divide into 16 pieces, and cover with plastic wrap. Stretch and roll 1 piece of dough into ¼-inch-thick rope, then cut rope into 3-inch lengths.

2 Working with 1 dough length at a time, position at 45-degree angle to counter edge. Place thin wooden skewer at top edge of dough, parallel to counter. Arrange palms of your hands at ends of skewer, apply even pressure against dough, and roll toward you in fluid motion. (Dough will coil around skewer.)

3 Slide fileja off skewer onto prepared sheets. Dust skewer with flour as needed if dough begins to stick. Repeat rolling, cutting, and shaping with remaining dough pieces. (Fileja can be kept at room temperature for up to 30 minutes, refrigerated for up to 4 hours, or chilled in freezer on baking sheet until firm, then transferred to zipper-lock bag and frozen for up to 1 month. If freezing, do not thaw before cooking.)

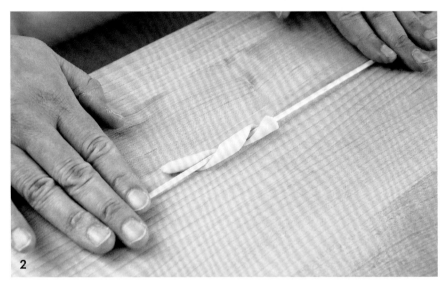

SHAPING MALLOREDDUS

1 Liberally dust 2 rimmed baking sheets with fine semolina flour. Transfer dough (we use Fresh Saffron Semolina Pasta Dough) to clean counter, divide into 8 pieces, and cover with plastic wrap. Stretch and roll 1 piece of dough into ½-inch-thick rope, then cut rope into ½-inch nuggets and lightly dust with extra flour.

2 Working with 1 dough nugget at a time, place cut side down on inverted tines of dinner fork. Press and stretch dough along tines into ⅛-inch-thick strip.

3 Using your thumb, gently roll dough strip down tines to form curled pasta shape with ridged exterior. Transfer malloreddus to prepared sheets. Repeat rolling, cutting, and shaping remaining dough pieces. (Malloreddus can be kept at room temperature for up to 30 minutes, refrigerated for up to 4 hours, or chilled in freezer on baking sheet until firm, then transferred to zipper-lock bag and frozen for up to 1 month. If frozen, do not thaw before cooking.)

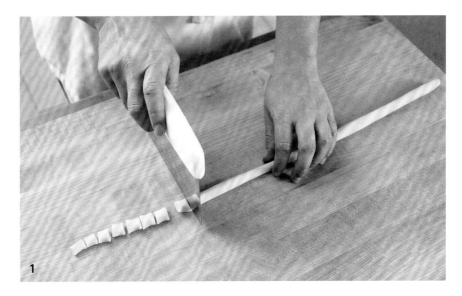

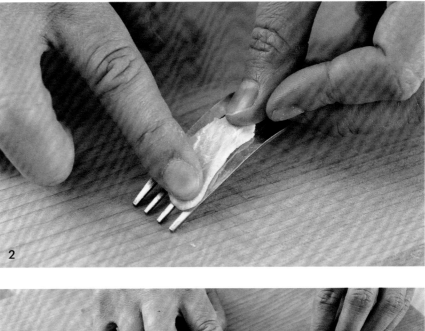

Glossary

al dente: Tender but resistant to the bite

antipasto/antipasti: Literally, "before the meal," starter/starters of any kind

aperitivo: Light alcoholic drink offered before dinner

baccalà: Skinned, boned, air-dried salt cod

bar: Informal café serving coffee, pastries, alcoholic drinks, snacks, and gelato

battuto: Chopped foundation vegetables and herbs used for some dishes. Once sautéed, it's called a soffritto.

béchamel/balsamella/besciamella: Classic base sauce made from butter, flour, and milk

bottarga: Pressed, salted mullet or tuna roe

burrata: Mozzarella skin wrapped around an oozy filling of curds and thick cream

caffè: Casual eatery serving coffee, drinks, and food

carpaccio: Thinly sliced raw filet of beef invented by Harry's Bar in Venice

contorni: Side dishes, typically vegetables

coperto: Cover charge for table service

cucina casalinga: Home cooking

digestivo: Drink taken before or after the meal to aid digestion

DOC (Denominazione di Origine Controllata): Legal regulations that strictly govern a wine's geographic territory, grape varieties permitted, composition, quality, authenticity, and stylistic attributes

DOCG (Denominazione di Origine Controllata e Garantita): A higher category than DOC, this is the most prestigious designation with the strictest regulations possible.

dolce/dolci: Sweet/sweets

DOP (Denominazione di Origine Protetta): This designation assures the product's geographic origin, specific ingredients used, methods of production, and traditions of craftsmanship. DOP foods typically support an entire local economy.

enoteca: Specialty wine bar or high-end wine shop

fare la scarpetta: To mop up juices on a plate with bread

farinata: Thin bread of chickpea flour, water, and olive oil

fatto in casa: Homemade

grana: Family of hard and granular cheeses, including Parmigiano Reggiano and Grana Padano

IGP (Indicazione Geografica Protetta): A more lax version of DOP/PDO; it applies to genuine food products made at least in part in a particular geographical area and following certain strict production guidelines.

IGT (Indicazione Geografica Tipica): This designation encompasses wines from specific regions that don't meet DOC or DOCG requirements but are considered superior to ordinary table wines.

latticini: Unfermented dairy products such as mozzarella and ricotta

maccheroni: See pasta secca

merenda/merende: Snack/snacks

minestra: Medium-weight soup; same term denotes any type of first course (primo), whether soup, rice, or pasta of some kind

minestrone: Thick soup of many different vegetables

norcino: A masterly pork butcher

odori: Fresh aromatics

olio di oliva: Extra-virgin olive oil as defined by EU and Italian law mandating the presence of no more than 0.8 percent oleic acid and pressing methods by mechanical means (no chemical processing) only

osteria/osterie: Restaurant/restaurants specializing in local wines

panino/panini: Filled roll/rolls, sometimes grilled

pasta all'uovo: Fresh or dried pasta that includes egg in the dough

pasta fatta a mano: Handmade pasta

pasta fresca: Fresh pasta

pasta secca: Industrial dried pasta made from hard wheat flour; alias maccheroni

pasticceria: Pastry shop

pesce azzurro: Oily fleshed fish such as sardines or mackerel

pecorino: Sheep's-milk cheese

piatto unico: Dish served as a single course

polenta: A porridge of some kind

pranzo: Lunch

primo: First course in an Italian meal

prosciutto cotto: Cooked ham

prosciutto crudo: Raw, air-cured ham

ragù: Meat sauce, with or without tomato

risotto: Fluid rice dish based on specific types of Italian short-grain rices, and broth

ristorante: Restaurant

salame/salami: Salt-cured dried sausage

salsa: Sauce

salsa di pomodoro: Tomato sauce

salume/salumi: Cured meats/meats, including salami

secondo: Second of several courses in an Italian meal

sfoglia: Fresh pasta from refined white flour and egg alone

Slow Food: An important movement founded by Carlo Petrini in reaction to fast food, this group works to preserve traditional cuisine and advocates for sustainable local agricultural practices in the face of destructive industrial farming methods.

STG (Specialità Tradizionale Garantita): This latest addition to the system serves to codify recipes with a cultural heritage.

spuntino/spuntini: Snack/snacks

sugo/sughi: Liquid extracted from fruit or meat during cooking; sauce

taralli: Small, savory or sweet baked "knots" made throughout southern Italy

terroir: Natural environment in which wine grapes or other foods grow, including soil, climate, and topography

tramezzino/tramezzini: Small triangular bar sandwich/sandwiches made with sliced bread

trattoria/trattorias: Informal restaurant/restaurants

zuppa: Dense soup

Metric Conversions

The recipes in this book were developed using standard U.S. measures following U.S. government guidelines.
The charts below offer equivalents for U.S. and metric measures.
All conversions are approximate and have been rounded up or down to the nearest whole number.

WEIGHT CONVERSIONS

ounces	grams
½	14
¾	21
1	28
1½	43
2	57
2½	71
3	85
3½	99
4	113
4½	128
5	142
6	170
7	198
8	227
9	255
10	283
12	340
16 (1 pound)	454

VOLUME CONVERSIONS

U.S.	metric
1 teaspoon	5 milliliters
2 teaspoons	10 milliliters
1 tablespoon	15 milliliters
2 tablespoons	30 milliliters
¼ cup	59 milliliters
⅓ cup	79 milliliters
½ cup	118 milliliters
¾ cup	177 milliliters
1 cup	237 milliliters
1¼ cups	296 milliliters
1½ cups	355 milliliters
2 cups (1 pint)	473 milliliters
2½ cups	591 milliliters
3 cups	710 milliliters
4 cups (1 quart)	0.946 liter
1.06 quarts	1 liter
4 quarts (1 gallon)	3.8 liters

OVEN TEMPERATURES

fahrenheit	celsius	gas mark
225	105	¼
250	120	½
275	135	1
300	150	2
325	165	3
350	180	4
375	190	5
400	200	6
425	220	7
450	230	8
475	245	9

Converting Temperatures
From an Instant-Read Thermometer
We include doneness temperatures in many of the recipes in this book. We recommend an instant-read thermometer for the job. Refer to the above table to convert Fahrenheit degrees to Celsius. Or, for temperatures not represented in the chart, use this simple formula: Subtract 32 degrees from the Fahrenheit reading, then divide the result by 1.8 to find the Celsius reading.

Selected Bibliography

The authors drew from the selected books and citations listed here, which they encourage for further reading.

For current Italian agricultural statistics, readers can check the following websites: Eurostat (ec.europa.eu), Italian National Institute of Statistics (istat.it), and the FAO (fao.org).

Information about Italian tourism can be found at Italian Tourism (italia.it/en). For general information about Italy and Italian food, we recommend the Italian Government Tourist Board (italiantourism.com), Italian Touring Club publications, Gambero Rosso (gamberorosso.it/en), plus the following: Slow Food (fondazioneslowfood.com), identitagolose.com, academiabarilla.com, iitaly.org, made-in-italy.com, deliciousitaly.com, italyheritage.com, and everfest.com.

GENERAL

- Alberini, Massimo, and Giorgio Mistretta. *Guida all'Italia gastronomica*. Milano: Touring Club Italiano, 1984.
- Anderson, Burton. *The Foods of Italy: An Endless Adventure in Taste*. 4th ed. Italian Trade Commission, 2007.
- ———. *Treasures of the Italian Table: Italy's Celebrated Foods and the Artisans Who Make Them*. New York: William Morrow and Co., 1994.
- Angeli, Franco. *DOC Cheeses of Italy: A Great Heritage*. Milano: Franco Angeli, 1992.
- Attlee, Helena. *The Land Where Lemons Grow: The Story of Italy and Its Citrus Fruit*. New York: Particular Books, 2014.
- Barzini, Luigi. *The Italians: A Full-Length Portrait Featuring Their Manners and Morals*. New York: Atheneum, 1964.
- Bastianich, Joseph, and David Lynch. *Vino Italiano: The Regional Wines of Italy*. New York: Clarkson Potter, 2002.
- Capatti, Alberto, and Massimo Montanari. *Italian Cuisine: A Cultural History*. New York: Columbia University Press, 2003.
- Cùnsolo, Felice. *Gli Italiani a tavola*. Milano: Mursia, 1965.
- Del Conte, Anna. *Gastronomy of Italy*. Rev. ed. London: Pavilion Books, 2013.
- Del Giudice, Luisa, ed. *Oral History, Oral Culture, and Italian Americans*. New York: Palgrave MacMillan, 2009.
- della Croce, Julia. *The Classic Italian Cookbook*. London: Dorling Kindersley Publishing, 1996.
- ———. *Pasta Classica: The Art of Italian Pasta Cooking*. San Francisco: Chronicle Books, 1987.
- ———. *The Vegetarian Table: Italy*. San Francisco: Chronicle Books, 1994.
- De Vita, Oretta Zanini. *Encyclopedia of Pasta*. Translated by Maureen Fant. Berkeley: University of California Press, 2009.
- DeWitt, Dave. *Da Vinci's Kitchen: The Birth of Italian Cuisine*. Albuquerque: Foodways Editions, 2015.
- Di Palo, Lou. *Di Palo's Guide to the Essential Foods of Italy: 100 Years of Wisdom and Stories From Behind the Counter*. New York: Ballantine Books, 2014.
- Di Renzo, Anthony. *Bitter Greens: Essays on Food, Politics, and Ethnicity From the Imperial Kitchen*. Albany: State University of New York Press, 2010.
- Fernandez, Dominique. *The Mother Sea: Travels in South Italy, Sardinia, and Sicily*. New York: Hill and Wang, 1967.
- Field, Carol. *Celebrating Italy*. New York: William Morrow and Co., 1990.
- Flandrin, Jean-Louis, and Massimo Montanari, eds. *Storia dell'alimentazione*. Roma-Bari: Laterza, 1997.
- Grandazzi, Alexandre. *The Foundation of Rome: Myth and History*. Translated by Jane Marie Todd. Ithaca: Cornell University Press, 1997.
- Hauser, Ernest O. *Italy: A Cultural Guide*. New Jersey: Stratford Press, 1982.
- Hazan, Marcella. *Essentials of Classic Italian Cooking*. New York: Knopf, 1992.
- Hazan, Marcella, and Victor Hazan. *Ingredienti: Marcella's Guide to the Market*. New York: Scribner, 2016.
- Kostioukovitch, Elena. *Why Italians Love to Talk About Food: A Journey Through Italy's Great Regional Cuisines, From the Alps to Sicily*. Translated by Anne Milano Appel. New York: Farrar, Straus and Giroux, 2006.
- Mueller, Tom. *Extra Virginity: The Sublime and Scandalous World of Olive Oil*. New York: W. W. Norton and Co., 2012.
- Parasecoli, Fabio. *Food Culture in Italy*. Westport: Greenwood Press, 2004.
- Pelli, Maurizio. *Fettuccine Alfredo, Spaghetti Bolognaise & Caesar Salad: The Triumph of the World's False Italian Cuisine*. Self-published, 2015. Kindle edition.
- Piras, Claudia, and Eugenio Medagliani, eds. *Specialità d'Italia: Le regioni in cucina*. Italian edition. Köln: Culinaria Könemann, 2000.
- Revel, Jean-François. *Culture and Cuisine: A Journey Through the History of Food*. New York: Doubleday and Co., 1982.
- Rizzoli, Irene. *Alice or Acciuga? History, Anecdotes, Fascinating Facts and Recipes of the World's Most Delicious Canned Fish*. Self-published, 2015.
- Root, Waverly. *The Cooking of Italy*. New York: Time-Life Books, 1968.
- ———. *Food: An Authoritative and Visual History and Dictionary of the Foods of the World*. New York: Simon and Schuster, 1980.
- ———. *The Food of Italy*. 1971. Reprint. New York: Vintage, 1977.
- Tannahill, Reay. *Food in History*. New York: Stein and Day, 1973.

Piedmont

- Bone, Eugenia. *Mycophilia: Revelations From the Weird World of Mushrooms*. Emmaus: Rodale, 2011.
- Canavese, Antonio. *Cucina piemontese*. Florence: Demetra, 2007.
- italiannotes.com/rice-fields-in-italy
- langhe.net/sight/international-alba-white-truffle-fair
- piemonteforyou.it/

Liguria

- "Artistic Handicrafts on the Italian Riviera di Levante." Accessed August 2, 2017. portofinocoast.it/en/artigianato-corzetti.aspx.
- "Consorzio del Pesto Genovese." Accessed August 3, 2017. mangiareinliguria.it/consorziopestogenovese.
- "Liguria, Presidi Slow Food." Accessed August 2, 2017. slowfood.it/liguria/presidi-slow-food.

Lombardy

- Bricchetti, Edo. "Lombardy's Key Role in World Canal History." *IWI Campaigns* (blog). May 29, 2012. blog.inlandwaterwaysinternational.org/?p=163.
- Regione Lombardia. *Journey Amongst the Flavours of Lombardy*. Milan: Regione Lombardia, 2015.
- Regione Lombardia Direzione Generale Agircolo della Lombardia. *Sights and Flavours of Lombardy*. Milan: Regione Lombardia, 2001.
- Smith, R. Baird. *Italian Irrigation: Being a Report on the Agricultural Canals of Piedmont and Lombardy*. Edinburgh: William Blackwood and Sons, 1855.
- Steiner, Carlo. *Il ghiottone lombardo*. Milan: Bramante Editrice, 1964.

Trentino–Alto Adige

- Trafoier, Sonya and Jörg. *I segreti della val Venosta, Alto Adige*. Bolzano: Arkadia Editore, 2003.
- altoadige.it
- browsingitaly.com/trentino-altoadige-sudtirol/speck-south-tyrol/2089/
- hotelelephant.com
- speck.it
- suedtirolerspezialitaeten.com
- visitdolomites.com

Veneto

- Coltro, Dino. *La cucina tradizionale veneta*. Roma: Newton and Compton, 2003.
- della Croce, Julia. *Veneto: Authentic Recipes From Venice and the Italian Northeast*. Photography by Paolo Destefanis. San Francisco: Chronicle Books, 2003.
- Divari, Luigi. Belpesse: *Pesci pesca e cucina ittica nelle lagune venete*. 2nd ed. Chioggia: Il Leggio, 2015.
- Lorenzetti, Giulio. *Venice and Its Lagoon: Historical Artistic Guide*. Trieste: Edizioni Lint, 1004.
- McCarthy, Mary. *Venice Observed*. New York: Harcourt Brace Jovanovich, 1963.
- Morris, Jan. *Venice*. London: Faber and Faber, 1993.

- Rorato, Giampiero. *La pedemontana trevi-giana: Dai colli asolani alle pendici del Cansiglio.* Treviso: De Bastiani, 2004.
- Touring Club Italiano, eds. *Venezia.* Original ed. Milano: Touring Editore, 1997.

Friuli–Venezia Giulia
- Bone, Eugenia. "Italian Farmhouse Feasts." *Saveur* (July 2001).
- Cremona, Luigi. *Un amore chiamato Friuli.* Camera di Commercio Industria Artigianato e Agricoltura di Udine, 1999.
- Del Fabro, Ariano. *Le ricette della tradizione friulana.* Colognola ai Colli: Demetra, 1994.
- Plotkin, Fred. *La Terra Fortunata: The Splendid Food and Wine of Friuli–Venezia Giulia.* New York: Broadway Books, 2001.
- Mucignat, Rosa, ed. *The Friulian Language: Identity, Migration, Culture.* Newcastle-upon-Tyne: Cambridge Scholars Publishing, 2014.

Valle d'Aosta
- aledo.it/mediasoft/italy/valle_aosta/valle_aosta_en.htm#agriculture
- enchantingitaly.com/regions/valledaosta/
- jewelsofthealps.com/datapage.asp?id=70&l=3
- ultimate-ski.com/ski-resorts/italy/aosta-valley.aspx

Emilia–Romagna
- Contoli, Corrado. *Guida alla veritiera cucina romagnola.* Bologna: Edizioni Calderini, 1972.
- Ingrasciotta, Frank. "Blood Type: Ragù." One-man show. 2009. New York: fingrasciotta.com/home.
- Kasper, Lynne Rossetto. *The Splendid Table: Recipes From Emilia-Romagna, the Heartland of Northern Italian Food.* New York: William Morrow and Co., 1992.

Tuscany
- Harris, Valentina. *The Food and Cooking of Tuscany.* London: Aquamarine, 2009.
- Mayes, Frances. *Under the Tuscan Sun: At Home in Italy.* New York: Broadway Books, 1997.
- Moffat, Alistair. *Tuscany: A History.* Edinburgh: Birlinn, 2011.
- Vossen, Paul. "Olive Oil: History, Production, and Characteristics of the World's Classic Oils." *HortScience* (August 2007), 1093–1100.

Umbria
- Boini, Rita. *La cucina umbra: Sapori di un tempo.* Perugia: Calzetti Mariucci, 1995.
- Buitoni, Silvia, and Marcella Cecconi. *Quello che le cuoche non dicono.* Perugia: Alieno, 2015.
- della Croce, Julia. *Umbria: Regional Recipes From the Heartland of Italy.* Photography by John Rizzo. San Francisco: Chronicle Books, 2002.
- Della Croce, Maria Laura, and Giulio Veggi. *Umbria: Lungo i sentieri dell'arte e dello spirito.* Vercelli: White Star, 1995.

Le Marche
- Pradelli, Alessandro Molinari. *La cucina delle Marche.* Rome: Newton and Compton, 2001.
- Sheraton, Mimi. "One Fish, Two Fish." *New Yorker* (November 24, 2008).
- le-marche.com/

Lazio
- Angell, Roger. "Sprezzatura." *New Yorker* (March 3, 2013).
- della Croce, Julia. *Roma: Authentic Recipes From In and Around the Eternal City.* Photography by Paolo Destefanis. San Francisco: Chronicle Books, 2004.
- De Vita, Oretta Zanini. *Popes, Peasants, and Shepherds: Recipes and Lore From Rome and Lazio.* Translated by Maureen Fant. Berkeley: University of California Press, 2013.
- Grescoe, Taras. "More Than Meets the Eye." *New York Times,* September 13, 2015.
- Jannattoni, Livio. *La cucina romana e del Lazio.* Roma: Newton and Compton, 1998.
- Malizia, Giuliano. *La cucina romana e ebraico romanesca.* Roma: Newton and Compton, 2001.
- Parla, Katie, and Kristina Gill. *Tasting Rome: Fresh Flavors and Forgotten Recipes From an Ancient City.* New York: Clarkson Potter, 2016.

Abruzzo and Molise
- Di Gregorio, Luciano. *Italy: Abruzzo.* 3rd ed. Guilford: Globe Pequot Press, 2017.
- Giobbi, Edward. *Italian Family Cooking.* New York: Random House, 1971.
- Pesaresi, Cristiano. *The "Numbers" of Molise Mountain Municipalities (Italy): New Data, Old Problems, Development Opportunities.* Rome: Nuova Cultura, 2014.
- italia.it/en/discover-italy/molise/poi/the-tratturi-in-molise.html
- lettera43.it/it/articoli/viaggi/2015/04/28/weekend-in-abruzzo-per-la-festa-dei-serpari/195256/
- lifeinabruzzo.com

Campania
- Consiglio, Alberto. *I maccheroni.* Roma: Newton Compton, 1973.
- Schwartz, Arthur. *Naples at Table: Cooking in Campania.* New York: HarperCollins, 1998.
- Spieler, Marlena. *A Taste of Naples: Neapolitan Culture, Cuisine, and Cooking.* New York: Rowman and Littlefield, 2018.

Puglia
- Jenkins, Nancy Harmon. *Flavors of Puglia: Traditional Recipes From the Heel of Italy's Boot.* New York: Broadway Books, 1997.
- Sada, Luigi. *La cucina pugliese.* Roma: Newton Compton, 1994.
- Snowden, Frank M. *Violence and Great Estates in the South of Italy: Apulia, 1900–1922.* Cambridge: Cambridge University Press, 1986.

Basilicata
- Stapinski, Helene. "Discovering the Ruins of Italy's Ionian Coast" *New York Times,*

March 6, 2015. nytimes.com/2015/03/08/travel/discovering-the-ruins-of-italys-ionian-coast.html.

Calabria
- Costantino, Rosetta, and Janet Fletcher. *My Calabria: Rustic Family Cooking From Italy's Undiscovered South.* New York: W. W. Norton and Co., 2010.
- Furfari, Grazia. *La cucina calabrese.* Catanzaro: Rubbettino, 2011.

Sicily
- Basile, Gaetano. "Sicilian Cuisine Through History and Legend." Translated by Gaetano Cipolla. Supplement VI, *Arba Sicula,* 1998.
- Brussat, Nancy. "Sicily I: 'A Salvador Dali Weekend.' " *My Italian Journeys* (blog), August 14, 2016. nancybrussat.wordpress.com/2016/08/14/sicily-i-a-salvador-dali-weekend/.
- Di Camillo, Kevin. "The Tradition of the Saint Joseph's Day Table." *National Catholic Register* (blog), March 20, 2016. ncregister.com/blog/dicamillo/the-tradition-of-the-saint-josephs-day-table.
- Di Lampedusa, Giuseppe. *The Leopard.* Translated by Guido Waldman. New York: Pantheon, 2007. Kindle edition.
- Giudice, Agata, and others. "Environmental Assessment of the Citrus Fruit Production in Sicily Using LCA." *Italian Journal of Food Science* 25 (2013): 202–12.
- Lanza, Anna Tasca. *The Heart of Sicily: Recipes and Reminiscences of Regaleali, a Country Estate.* New York: Clarkson Potter, 1993.
- Muller, Melissa. *Sicily: The Cookbook; Recipes Rooted in Traditions.* New York: Rizzoli, 2017.
- Norwich, John Julius. *Sicily: An Island at the Crossroads of History.* New York: Random House, 2015.
- Simeti, Mary Taylor. *On Persephone's Island: A Sicilian Journal.* New York: Vintage, 1986.

Sardinia (Sardegna)
- Da Re, M. Gabriella, and Iose Meloni. *Pani e Dolci in Marmilla.* Cagliari: Parco e Museo Archeologico Menna Maria Villanovaforru and Istituto di Discipline Socio-Antropologiche dell'università di Cagliari, 1987.
- Lakeman, Sandra Davis. *Sardegna, the Spirit of an Ancient Island: The Art and Architecture of Pre-Nuraghic and Nuraghic Culture.* Bologna: Grafiche dell'Artiere, 2014.
- Melis, Paolo. *The Nuraghic Civilization.* Sassari: Carlo Delfino, 2003.
- Pilia, Fernando, and Nino Solinas. *Sapori di Sardegna.* Cagliari: Editoriale L'Unione Sarda, 1988.
- Regione Sardegna Assessorato Agricoltura. "In Sardegna C'È."
- Ruiu, Franco Stefano. *Maschere e carnevale in Sardegna.* Nuoro: Imago Edizioni, 2013.
- Sassu, Antonio. *La vera cucina in Sardegna.* Roma: Casa Editrice Anthropos, 1986.

About the Contributors

Jack Bishop, America's Test Kitchen Chief Creative Director, was part of the original team that launched *Cook's Illustrated* in 1993. He directed the launch of *Cook's Country* magazine in 2005 and the building of the company's book publishing division. Bishop is the tasting lab expert on the company's television shows, and he leads the creative teams working on the company's TV shows, magazines, books, websites, and online cooking school. An expert in Italian cooking, he is the author of several cookbooks, including *Pasta e Verdura* and *The Complete Italian Vegetarian Cookbook*. He lives in Boston.

Eugenia Bone, whose paternal family hails from Le Marche, is a nationally known food and nature journalist and author. Her work has appeared in many magazines and newspapers, including *Saveur, Food & Wine, Gourmet, Fine Dining, Wine Enthusiast, Sunset, Martha Stewart Living,* the *New York Times,* the *Wall Street Journal,* and the *Denver Post.* She is the author of six books and has been nominated for a variety of awards, including a Colorado Book Award and a James Beard Award. Her most recent book is *Microbia: A Journey Into the Unseen World Around You.* Her writing and recipes have been anthologized in a number of publications, including *Best Food Writing*, among others. Contact her at eugeniabone.com.

Julia della Croce comes from Apulian and Sardinian stock and has traveled widely in Italy since she was a child. An authority on Italian food, she is the author of more than a dozen books, many translated and distributed worldwide. Della Croce has been nominated for James Beard and IACP awards and received the Diplôme d'honneur of France for her *Classic Italian Cookbook.* Her book *Veneto* won first place in the Italian cuisine category at the World Cookbook Awards. She has broadcast extensively on national radio and television and written for many prominent publications. Della Croce conducts acclaimed culinary sailing tours of the Venetian lagoon on board a historic sailboat, and advocates for the preservation of traditional cuisine through her blog, Forktales. Learn more at juliadellacroce.com.

The recipes in this book have been tested, written, and edited by the test cooks, editors, and cookware specialists at America's Test Kitchen, a 15,000-square-foot kitchen located in Boston's Seaport District. It is the home of *Cook's Illustrated* magazine and *Cook's Country* magazine, the public television shows *America's Test Kitchen* and *Cook's Country from America's Test Kitchen,* and the online America's Test Kitchen Cooking School. For more information, visit americastestkitchen.com and follow along on Facebook (AmericasTestKitchen), Twitter (@TestKitchen), and Instagram (@TestKitchen).

Acknowledgments

Eugenia and Julia would like to acknowledge the kind assistance of the following people who have helped in our research: Salvatore Biancardi, Kevin Bone, Bob Bruno, Silvia Buitoni (Perugia), Viola Buitoni, Massimo Cannas of MAXCO International, John Carafoli, Flavia Destefanis, Paolo Destefanis (Catania, Sicily), Amy Beth Dorkin, Paul Greenberg, Edward Giobbi, Nathan Charles Hoyt, Nancy Harmon Jenkins, Gail Whitney Karn, Augusto Marchini, Maurizio Pelli (Dubai), Italian Trade Agency (New York), Oldways Preservation Trust, Greg Patent, Cynthia Scaravilli, Rosario Scarpato and the Italian Cuisine Forum, Marlena Spieler, Helene Stapinski, Guido Zuliani (Friuli–Venezia Giulia), and Beatrice Ughi of Gustiamo.

The following Italians have enriched our knowledge of their regions: Eva Agnesi (Liguria); Mauro Stoppa of Cruising Venice; Luigi Divari, Luca Fraccaro, and Paolo Pietrobon of Pasticceria Fraccaro 1932 (Veneto); Margherita Falqui, Giuseppe Nonne, Alessandra Viana, and Giuseppe De Martini (Horeca Enoteca) of Cagliari (Sardegna); Donatella Platoni (Umbria); Fabio Trabocchi (Le Marche); Fabbri 1905 (Bologna) and Giovanni Tamburini (Bologna); Identità Golose, Gioia Gibelli (Milan); Marina Saponari and Mara Battista of Dire, Fare Gustare Cooking School (Conversano), Giuseppe Sportelli, Giuseppe Montanaro at Amastuola winery, Massafra (Taranto), Catherine Faris (Pascarossa Olive Oil, Martina Franca), Anna Gennari of Museo della Civiltà del Vino Primitivo (Manduria) of Puglia; Cecilia Baratta (Agriturismo Seliano, Paestum) of Campania; Pamela Sheldon Johns (Agriturismo Poggio Etrusco, Montepulciano, Tuscany); Nicoletta Polo ("Cooking with the Duchess," Palermo, Sicily), Luisella Reali (Bettona, Umbria), Margherita Sciattella (Bettona, Umbria), Chef Maria Luisa Scolastra (Villa Roncali, Foligno, Umbria). Thanks to the following artisans and purveyors who shared their exquisite products and knowledge about making them: Carpigiani Gelato University (Bologna); Consiglia Lisi of Olio Merico Salento (Miggiano, Puglia); Benedetto Cavalieri Pasta (Maglie, Puglia); Chefs Gianni Tarabini and Franco Aliberti at Agriturismo La Fiorida & la Présef (Sondrio, Lombardy); Elisabetta Serraiotto and Consorzio Tutela Grana Padano (Veneto); Sandra and Ulisse Braendl of Podere il Casale (Pienza, Tuscany); Consorzio Parmigiano Reggiano (Parma); Consorzio Chianti Classico (Florence, Tuscany); La Mola Olive Oil (Castelnuovo di Farfa, Lazio); Igor and Ivan Lupatelli (Morello Austera, Cantiano, Le Marche); Rolando Beramendi and Rustichella Pasta (Penne, Abruzzo); and Rosario Safina (daRosario Truffles).

This book would not have been possible without the hard work and dedication of those at National Geographic and America's Test Kitchen. At National Geographic, thank you to Publisher Lisa Thomas, Deputy Editor Hilary Black, Editorial Project Manager Allyson Johnson, Art Director Elisa Gibson, Photo Editor Moira Haney, Creative Director Melissa Farris, Director of Photography Susan Blair, and Production Editor Judith Klein. For her careful editing of Italian language throughout, thank you to Flavia Destefanis. For their extensive research and detailed maps, thanks to Senior Production Cartographer Jerome N. Cookson, Map Researchers Shelley Sperry and Theodore A. Sickley, and Map Editors Irene Berman-Vaporis and Rosemary P. Wardley.

A large team of editors and cooks, photography, and production experts at America's Test Kitchen collaborated with National Geographic to explore Italy in and out of the kitchen. Special thanks to Chief Creative Officer Jack Bishop; Editorial Director, Books, Elizabeth Carduff; Executive Editors Julia Collin Davison and Adam Kowit; Executive Food Editors Suzannah McFerran and Dan Zuccarello; Senior Editors Andrew Janjigian, Sara Mayer, Stephanie Pixley, and Anne Wolf; Associate Editors Leah Colins, Lawman Johnson, Nicole Konstantinakos, Sacha Madadian, and Russell Selander; Test Cooks Kathryn Callahan, Afton Cyrus, Joseph Gitter, and Katherine Perry; Editorial Assistant Alyssa Langer; Design Director, Books, Carole Goodman; Deputy Art Directors Allison Boales and Jen Kanavos Hoffman; Graphic Designer Katie Barranger; Photography Director Julie Bozzo Cote; Senior Staff Photographer Daniel J. Van Ackere; Staff Photographers Steve Klise and Kevin White; Additional Photographers Keller + Keller and Carl Tremblay; Food Stylists Catrine Kelty, Chantal Lambeth, Kendra McKnight, Marie Piraino, Elle Simone Scott, and Sally Staub; Photoshoot Kitchen Manager Timothy McQuinn; Photoshoot Test Cook Daniel Cellucci; Photoshoot Assistant Test Cooks Mady Nichas and Jessica Rudolph; Imaging Manager Lauren Robbins; Production and Imaging Specialists Heather Dube, Dennis Noble, and Jessica Voas; Copy Editor Elizabeth Emery; and Proofreader Pat Jalbert-Levine.

Illustration Credits

All recipe photographs by America's Test Kitchen: photography, Joe Keller, Steve Klise, Carl Tremblay, Daniel J. van Ackere; food styling, Catrine Kelty, Chantal Lambeth, Kendra McKnight, Sally Staub.

Front cover, Andrea Di Lorenzo; 1, Gallery Stock; 2-3, Francesco Iacobelli/Getty Images; 4-5, Cedric Angeles/Intersection Photos; 11, Florian Jaenicke/laif/Redux; 14 (UP), Caroline Cortizo/Alamy Stock Photo; 14 (LO), Francesco Vignali/LUZphoto/Redux; 18-19, Andrea Comi/Getty Images; 20, Cedric Angeles/Intersection Photos; 22 (UP), Shutterstock/Anastasiia Malinich; 22 (LO), Markus Kirchgessner/Laif/Redux Pictures; 23, Rupert Sagar-Musgrave/Alamy Stock Photo; 24, Andrea Wyner; 25 (UP), SIME/eStock Photo; 25 (LE), Courtesy of Le Terre Di Stefano Massone; 25 (RT), Courtesy of Tommasi; 26, Shutterstock/Elena Abramova (asparagus), Shutterstock/Igor Normann (gorgonzola), Shutterstock/PixMarket (pears), Alexlukin/Alamy Stock Photo (bread), Shutterstock/Jiang Hongyan (chestnuts), Walter Pfisterer/StockFood (Bra cheese), Shutterstock/O.Bellini (meat), Shutterstock/Nattika (basil), Shutterstock/bonchan (farinita); 27, Shutterstock/topseller (apples), Dorling Kindersley Ltd/Alamy Stock Photo (Asiago), Shutterstock/Igor Klimov (prosecco), MARKA/Alamy Stock Photo (Montasio), Shutterstock/Wealthylady (radicchio), Shutterstock/Vadym Zaitsev (fish), Shutterstock/Nattika (cherries), Shutterstock/Voronin76 (mushrooms), Shutterstock/Only Fabrizio (ham); 28, Francesco Bergamaschi/Robert Harding; 30, Juan Carlos Jones/Contrasto/Redux; 31, Thomas Linkel/laif/Redux; 32, SIME/eStock Photo; 33 (UP), Thomas Linkel/laif/Redux; 33 (LO), Gualtiero Boffi/Alamy Stock Photo; 40, Dagmar Schwelle/laif/Redux; 42 (LE), Shutterstock/MaskaRad; 42 (RT), Clay McLachlan/National Geographic Creative; 43, SIME/eStock Photo; 44, Mark Weinberg/Offset; 45, Roberto Moiola/Robert Harding; 46, Giuseppe Cacace/AFP/Getty Images; 47, Andrea Astes/iStock/Getty Images; 48, fbxx/iStock/Getty Images; 49 (UP), Clay McLachlan/National Geographic Creative; 49 (LO), Julie Woodhouse f/Alamy Stock Photo; 50, Shutterstock/Nataly Studio; 51, Yadid Levy/Robert Harding; 62, Gallery Stock; 64 (UP), victoriya89/iStock/Getty Images; 64 (LO), Jean-Pierre Lescourret/Getty Images; 74, Andrea Wyner; 76, mauritius images GmbH/Alamy Stock Photo; 77, Joel Micah Miller/Gallery Stock; 78, Stefano G. Pavesi/Contrasto/Redux; 79, Alfredo Cosentino/Alamy Stock Photo; 80, Realy Easy Star/Toni Spagone/Alamy Stock Photo; 81, Loren Irving/age fotostock/Robert Harding; 90, Florian Jaenicke/laif/Redux Pictures; 92, Heiner Heine/Robert Harding; 93, SIME/eStock Photo; 102, Guy Vanderelst/Getty Images; 104, Lisa J. Goodman/Getty Images; 105, Sebastian Wasek/Robert Harding; 106 (LE), Shutterstock/islavicek; 106 (RT), Fulvio Zanettini/laif/Redux Pictures; 107, Cedric Angeles/Intersection Photos; 108, Shutterstock/Elena Masiutkina; 109, Nedim_B/iStock/Getty Images; 110, LOOK Die Bildagentur der Fotografen GmbH/Alamy Stock Photo; 111, SIME/eStock Photo; 112, Johner Images/Getty Images; 113, Ethel Davies/Robert Harding; 124, Berthold Steinhilber/laif/Redux; 126, Charles Bowman/Robert Harding; 127, Shutterstock/Angel Simon; 129, Frieder Blickle/laif/Redux; 136, Ellen Rooney/Robert Harding; 138, 139, Andrea Wyner; 140, The Picture Pantry/StockFood; 141, 142, Franco Cogoli/SIME/eStock Photo; 143, angorius/iStock/Getty Images; 144, Max Cavalarri/Robert Harding; 145, Christine Webb/Getty Images; 146, Franco Cogoli/SIME/eStock Photo; 147, Fracesco Riccardo Iacomino/Getty Images; 162-63, Aneesh Kothari/Robert Harding; 164, Cedric Angeles/Intersection Photos; 166 (UP), Shutterstock/Jiang Hongyan; 166 (LO), Angelo Cavalli/Robert Harding; 167, Peter Cook/Alamy Stock Photo; 168, Toni Anzenberger/Anzenberger/Redux; 169 (UP), Michele Borzoni/TerraProject/contrasto/Redux; 169 (LE), Courtesy of Costanti; 169 (RT), Courtesy of Santa Cristina Winery (Tusany); 170, Shutterstock/Only Fabrizio (Pecorino); Shutterstock/Volosina (chestnuts), Shutterstock/bonchan (farro); Shutterstock/Christos Theologou (gelato); Shutterstock/Alis Photo (fish); 171, Shutterstock/Christos Theologou (oil), Shutterstock/Scisetti Alfio (marjoram); Gizelka/iStock/Getty Images (chocolates), Shutterstock/baibaz (meats), erierika/iStock/Getty Images (potatoes), Shutterstock/Marco Speranza (saffron), kgfoto/Getty Images (carrots); 172, GOZOOMA/Gallery Stock; 174 (LE), Quanthem/iStock/Getty Images; 174 (RT), Luigi Morbidelli/iStock/Getty; 175, Pedro Diaz Cosme/Getty Images; 176, karayuschij/iStock/Getty Images; 177, Andrea Wyner; 178, Simona Romani; 179, Ricardo de Vica de Oumptich/StockFood; 180, Susan Wright/The New York Times/Redux Pictures; 181, Nathan Hoyt/Forktales; 182, Cedric Angeles/Intersection Photos; 183, Dagmar Schwelle/laif/Redux; 196, Dorothea Schmid/laif/Redux; 198, Christiana Stawski/Getty Images; 199, funkyfood London–Paul Williams/Alamy Stock Photo; 200 (LE), Sabrina Rothe/Jalag/Seasons; 200 (RT), Nathan Hoyt/Forktales; 210, Giorgio Filippini/SIME/eStock Photo; 212 (UP), Shutterstock/Tim Ur; 212 (LO), Dagmar Schwelle/laif/Redux; 213, Toni Anzenberger/Anzenberger/Redux; 220, Andrea Wyner; 222, Nathan Hoyt/Forktales; 223, Nico Tondini/Robert Harding; 224, Reynold Mainse/Design Pics/National Geographic Creative; 225, Andrea Wyner; 226, SIME/eStock Photo; 227, Teamarbeit/iStock/Getty Images; 228, Shutterstock/ChiccoDodiFC; 229, Nathan Hoyt/Forktales; 231, Neale Clark/Robert Harding; 242, Ken Gillham/Robert Harding; 244, Salvatore Leanza/SIME/eStock Photo; 245, Shutterstock/Sergiy Kuzmin; 246 (UP), Paolo Spigariol; 246 (LO), Karisssa/iStock/Getty Images; 247, Guido Baviera/SIME/eStock Photo; 248, Antonio Violi/Alamy Stock Photo; 256-257, Chris M. Rogers/Gallery Stock; 258, Andrea Wyner; 260 (UP), Shutterstock/Oleksandr Muslimov; 260 (LO), Christina Anzenberger-Fink & Toni Anzenberger/Redux; 261, Andreas Solaro/AFP/Getty Images; 262, Massimo Bassano/National Geographic Creative; 263 (UP), Andrea Wyner; 263 (LE), Courtesy of Donnachiara; 263 (RT), Alko/Alamy Stock Photo; 264, Shutterstock/Nuttapong (green onion), Shutterstock/zcw (clams), unpict/iStock/Getty Images (torrone), valentinarr/iStock/Getty Images (juniper), Shutterstock/Valery Eviakhov (lobster); 265, chengyuzheng/iStock/Getty Images (grapes), Shutterstock/Yuri Samsonov (almonds), jirkaejc/iStock/Getty Images (honey), cynoclub/iStock/Getty Images (sausage), anna1311/iStock/Getty Images (cauliflower), Shutterstock/Kovaleva_Ka (peppers), kaewphoto/iStock/Getty Images (bergamot), Dmytro/iStock/Getty Images (bread), Shutterstock/Mr. Suttipon Yakham (salt), repinanatoly/iStock/Getty Images (capers); 266, Ben Pipe Photography; 268, Jason Joyce/Gallery Stock; 269, Jeremy Villasis/Getty Images; 270, Giovanni Cipriano/The New York Times/Redux; 271, Nathan Hoyt/Forktales; 272 (UP), Ben Pipe Photography; 272 (LO), maxsol7/iStock/Getty Images; 273, Patrizio Martorana/Alamy Stock Photo; 284, Markus Lange/Robert Harding; 287, Nathan Hoyt/Forktales; 288, Markus Lange/Robert Harding; 296, Roberto Moiola/Robert Harding; 298 (UP), Shutterstock/jiangdi; 298 (LO), Franco Cogoli/SIME/eStock Photo; 306, Toni Anzenberger/Anzenberger/Redux; 308, Dorothea Schmid/laif/Redux; 309, DonatellaTandelli/iStock/Getty Images; 310, Shutterstock/Sergey Fatin; 311, 318, Andrea Wyner; 320, Mel Longhurst/Camera Press/Redux; 321, Dorothea Schmid/laif/Redux; 322, Nicolò Minerbi/LUZ/Redux; 323, Andrea Wyner; 324, Nicolò Minerbi/LUZphoto/Redux; 325, Shutterstock/Yellow Cat; 326, 327, 329, Andrea Wyner; 344, Malte Jaeger/laif/Redux; 346, Nathan Hoyt/Forktales; 347, Blend Images LLC/Gallery Stock; 348 (UP&LO), 349, Nathan Hoyt/Forktales; 350, Dorothea Schmid/laif/Redux; 351, Davies & Starr/Getty Images; 352, Nathan Hoyt/Forktales; 353, Luca Picciau/REDA&CO/Getty Images; 355, Andrea Wyner; 368, from top: Susan Hornyak, Nathan Hoyt/Forktales, Eve Bishop, Steve Klise; back cover, Patrick Dieudonne/Robert Harding; back cover picture strip, from left, America's Test Kitchen, Francesco Bergamaschi/Robert Harding, America's Test Kitchen, fbxx/iStock/Getty Images.

MAPS

13, socialexplorer.com; 15, Julia della Crocce; 16, Guido Zuliani, The Cooper Union for Advancement of Science and Art; 50, Gian Bartolomeo Siletto, Piedmont Region Territorial and Environmental Information System; 80, Claudio Repossi, Navigli Lombardi Project; 112, Julia della Crocce; 128, Eugenia Bone; 146, Qualigeo.eu; 182, Anthony Tuck, University of Massachusetts Amherst; 201, Quattrocalici.it; Kathy Bechtel, Italia Outdoors Food and Wine; 230, European Association of the Vie Francigene; 249, motoitinerari.com; 273, Giuseppe Mastrolorenzo and Lucia Pappalardo, Osservatorio Vesuviano, Naples; Pier Paolo Petrone, University of Naples; Michael Sheridan, University of Buffalo, New York; 289, InnovaPuglia Spa – Servizio Territorio e Ambiente; 328, Regione Siciliana, Assessorato del Territorio e dell'Ambiente; 354, Anna Oppo et al., "The Languages of Sardinia," Sardinia Department of Education, Cultural Heritage, Information, and Sport.

Map Data: Mapdata © Openstreetman Contributors, Available Under Open Database License:openstreetmap.org/Copyright; European Union, Copernicus Land Monitoring Service 2012, European Environment Agency; Global Land Cover Facility; NASA Goddard Space Flight Center

Index

Since 1888, the National Geographic Society has funded more than 13,000 research, exploration, and preservation projects around the world. National Geographic Partners distributes a portion of the funds it receives from your purchase to National Geographic Society to support programs including the conservation of animals and their habitats.

National Geographic Partners
1145 17th Street NW
Washington, DC 20036-4688 USA

Get closer to National Geographic explorers and photographers, and connect with our global community. Join us today at nationalgeographic.com/join

For information about special discounts for bulk purchases, please contact National Geographic Books Special Sales: specialsales@natgeo.com

For rights or permissions inquiries, please contact National Geographic Books Subsidiary Rights: bookrights@natgeo.com

Library of Congress Cataloging-in-Publication Data
Names: America's Test Kitchen (Firm)
Title: Tasting Italy : a culinary journey / foreword by Jack Bishop ; Italian
   Culinary Essays by Julia della Croce and Eugenia Bone ; recipes by
   America's Test Kitchen.
Description: Washington, D.C. : National Geographic, [2018] | Includes index.
Identifiers: LCCN 2018003169 | ISBN 9781426219740 (trade hardcover)
Subjects: LCSH: Cooking, Italian. | LCGFT: Cookbooks.
Classification: LCC TX723 .T38 2018 | DDC 641.5945--dc23
LC record available at https:// lccn.loc.gov_2018003169

Printed in China

18/RRDS/1

TRAVEL THE WORLD
WITH NATIONAL GEOGRAPHIC BOOKS

NATIONAL GEOGRAPHIC

VISUAL ATLAS OF THE WORLD

SECOND EDITION

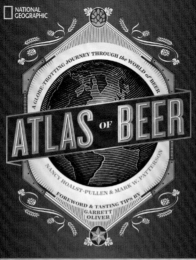

NATIONAL GEOGRAPHIC

A GLOBE-TROTTING JOURNEY THROUGH *the* WORLD *of* BEER

ATLAS *of* BEER

NANCY HOALST-PULLEN & MARK W. PATTERSON

FOREWORD & TASTING TIPS BY
GARRETT OLIVER

NATIONAL GEOGRAPHIC

TIMELESS JOURNEYS

TRAVELS TO THE WORLD'S LEGENDARY PLACES